Electronically Monitored Punishment

Electronic monitoring (EM) is a way of supervising offenders in the community while they are on bail, serving a community sentence or after release from prison. Various technologies can be used, including voice verification, GPS satellite tracking and – most commonly – the use of radio frequency to monitor house arrest. EM originated in the USA in the 1980s and has spread to over 30 countries since then. This book explores the development of EM in a number of countries to give some indication of the diverse ways it has been utilized and of the complex politics which surround its use.

A techno-utopian impulse underpins the origins of EM and has remained latent in its subsequent development elsewhere in the world, despite recognition that it is less capable of effecting penal transformations than its champions have hoped. This book devotes substantive chapters to the issues of privatization, evaluation, offender perspectives and ethics. While normatively more committed to the Swedish model, the book acknowledges that this may not represent the future of EM, whose untrammelled, commercially-driven development could have very alarming consequences for criminal justice.

Both utopian and dystopian hopes have been invested in EM, but research on its impact is ambivalent and fragmented, and EM remains undertheorized, empirically and ethically. This book seeks to redress this by providing academics, policy audiences and practitioners with the intellectual resources to understand and address the challenges which EM poses.

Mike Nellis is Emeritus Professor of Criminal and Community Justice in the School of Law, University of Strathclyde, UK. He was formerly a social worker with young offenders, has a PhD from the Institute of Criminology in Cambridge, and was involved in the training of probation officers at the University of Birmingham. He has written widely on the fortunes of the probation service, alternatives to imprisonment and particularly the electronic monitoring of offenders.

Kristel Beyens is Professor of Penology and Criminology at the Criminology Department of the Vrije Universiteit Brussel, Belgium. She has published on prison overcrowding, sentencing and the implementation of prison sentences and sentences in the community, such as electronic monitoring and community service. She is a member of the editorial board of the *European Journal of Probation* and of the *European Working Group on Community Sanctions*.

Dan Kaminski is Professor at the UCLouvain (University of Louvain-la-Neuve), Belgium, and President of the CRID&P (Interdisciplinary Research Centre on Deviance and Penality). He holds a PhD in Criminology and has published on managerialism, penal treatment of drug use, prisoners' rights, alternatives to prison and electronic monitoring.

Electronically Monitored Punishment

International and critical perspectives

Edited by Mike Nellis, Kristel Beyens and Dan Kaminski

Routledge
Taylor & Francis Group

LONDON AND NEW YORK

First published 2013
by Routledge
2 Park Square, Milton Park, Abingdon, Oxon OX14 4RN

Simultaneously published in the USA and Canada
by Routledge
711 Third Avenue, New York, NY 10017

Routledge is an imprint of the Taylor & Francis Group

British Library Cataloguing in Publication Data
A catalogue record for this book is available from the British Library

Library of Congress Cataloging in Publication Data
Nellis, Mike.
Electronically monitored punishment : international and critical
perspectives / Mike Nellis, Kristel Beyens, Dan Kaminski. – 1st ed.
    p. cm.
    Includes index.
    1. Electronic monitoring of parolees and probationers. I. Beyens,
Kristel. II. Kaminski, Dan. III. Title.
    HV9275.N45 2012
    364.6'8–dc23   2012011261

ISBN: 978-1-84392-273-5 (hbk)
ISBN: 978-0-203-10302-9 (ebk)

Typeset in Times New Roman
by Wearset Ltd, Boldon, Tyne and Wear

Contents

Illustrations

Figures

Tables

Contributors

Jolande uit Beijerse is an Associate Professor of Criminal Law and Law of Criminal Procedure at the Erasmus University Rotterdam (EUR), the Netherlands, and a Judge at the Court of Rotterdam, where she mostly deals with juvenile criminal law cases. She is also a member of the supervising committee of one of the main youth institutions in the Netherlands. Most of her publications are in the field of pre-trial detention, penal sanctions (especially alternatives to custody), juvenile justice and youth institutions. Her research focuses on the tension between legal principles and social needs.

Kristel Beyens is Professor of Penology and Criminology at the Criminology Department of the Vrije Universiteit Brussel, Belgium. She has published on prison overcrowding, sentencing and the implementation of prison and community sentences, such as electronic monitoring and community service. She is a member of the editorial board of the *European Journal of Probation* and chair of the *European Working Group on Community Sanctions*.

Younoh Cho is a Professor at Dongguk University, Seoul, Korea. She joined the Dongguk University in 2008 after nearly three years on the doctoral programme at John Jay College of Criminal Justice in the City University of New York (Graduate Center). She received her PhD after she wrote a dissertation on 'An analysis of the automated voiceprint recognition program for juvenile probationers in South Korea'.

Anita Gibbs worked as a probation officer in the UK before undertaking her doctorate at Bristol University. She then worked at the Centre for Criminology in Oxford, before joining the Department of Social Work and Community Development at Otago University, New Zealand. Since then she has completed a variety of projects on Home Detention, Compulsory Community Treatment Orders and, more recently, Intercountry Adoption.

Anthea Hucklesby is Professor of Criminal Justice and Deputy Director of the Centre for Criminal Justice Studies at the University of Leeds, UK. Her research focuses upon the treatment of suspects, defendants and offenders in the criminal justice process. She has particular interests in bail and pre-trial detention, electronic monitoring and community sentences, prisoner resettlement, prisons, drugs and voluntary and private sector involvement in criminal justice.

Dan Kaminski is Professor at the UCLouvain (University of Louvain-la-Neuve), Belgium, and President of the CRID&P (Interdisciplinary Research Centre on Deviance and Penality). He holds a PhD in Criminology and has published on managerialism, penal treatment of drug use, prisoner's rights, alternatives to prison and electronic monitoring.

Byung Bae Kim is EM Programme Manager of the Division of Probation and Parole at the Ministry of Justice, Republic of Korea.

René Lévy is Director of Research at the Centre National de la Recherche Scientifique, France, and currently Director of the Groupe Européen de Recherches sur les Normativités, Guyancourt, France. He is a researcher at the Centre de Recherches Sociologiques sur le Droit et les Institutions Pénales (CESDIP, a joint centre of CNRS/Université de Versailles/Ministry of Justice). He is also the Director of the journal *Crime, Histoire & Sociétés* (*Crime, History & Societies*).

J. Robert Lilly is Professor of Sociology/Criminology and Adjunct Professor of Law at Northern Kentucky University, USA. Along with Richard Ball and Ronald Huff he was one of the pioneering writers on electronic monitoring in the United States and became influential in early debates about it in Britain and mainland Europe. He is co-author of *Criminological Theory: Context and Consequences*, now in its fifth edition, and is a co-editor of the *Howard Journal of Criminal Justice*. As well as a range of interests in mainstream criminal justice, he has also published widely on rape and military justice in the Second World War, in French and Italian translations as well as English.

George Mair is Professor of Criminal Justice and Head of Research in the Law School at the Liverpool John Moores University, UK. He was co-founder of the journal *Criminology and Criminal Justice* and jointly edited it from 2001 to 2006. He is a member of the editorial board of the *Liverpool Law Review*, the *Probation Journal* and the *European Journal of Probation*. He has been writing about and researching aspects of criminal justice since 1980. He spent 16 years in the Home Office Research and Planning Unit. During that time he carried out, among other topics, the first evaluation of electronic monitoring.

Mike Nellis is Professor of Criminal and Community Justice at the University of Strathclyde, UK. He is a former social worker with young offenders. He holds a PhD in Criminology and has published on many aspects of penal change, especially the toughening of community penalties, probation values, the training of probation officers, the role of voluntary organizations in criminal justice, the significance of prison movies and prisoner autobiographies and electronic monitoring.

Craig Paterson worked for Group 4 Securicor for three years on the UK electronic offender monitoring programme, before leaving in 2001 to undertake his PhD on the role of surveillance technologies in criminal justice. He joined Sheffield Hallam University in January 2007 as a Senior Lecturer in Criminology, having previously worked at the John Grieve Centre for Policing and Community Safety at Buckinghamshire New University. In 2009 he published *Understanding The Electronic Monitoring of Offenders in England and Wales* (Saarbrucken: VDM Verlag).

Marc Renzema has been a Professor of Criminal Justice at Kutztown University in Pennsylvania since 1982. In 1987 he founded the *Journal of Offender Monitoring*. He has written dozens of articles on electronic monitoring and the post-release adjustment process and presented at both academic and practitioner conferences both in the United States and Europe. He has a bachelor's degree from Johns Hopkins University and a master's degree from Temple University, both in psychology. He earned his PhD in Criminal Justice at the University at Albany. Since 2001 he has been working on a meta-analysis of the electronic monitoring literature for the Campbell Collaboration.

Julian Roberts is a Professor of Criminology in the Faculty of Law, University of Oxford, UK. He was Editor-in-Chief of the *European Journal of Criminology* and is Associate Editor of the *Canadian Journal of Criminology and Criminal Justice*. He is currently a member of the Sentencing Council of England and Wales. Recent books include *Principled Sentencing* (Hart Publishing, 2009, edited with A. Ashworth and A. von Hirsch) and *The Role of Previous Convictions at Sentencing: Applied and Theoretical Perspectives* (Hart Publishing, 2009).

Russell G. Smith has qualifications in Law, Psychology and Criminology from the University of Melbourne and a PhD from King's College London. He practised as a lawyer in Melbourne in the 1980s and then lectured in criminology at the University of Melbourne, before taking up a position at the Australian Institute of Criminology, where he is now Principal Criminologist and Head of the Global Economic and Electronic Crime Program. He has published extensively on aspects of computer crime, fraud control and professional regulation. He is President of the Australian and New Zealand Society of Criminology Inc.

René van Swaaningen is Professor of International and Comparative Criminology at the Erasmus University Rotterdam (EUR), the Netherlands, and Scientific Director of the inter-university PhD Research School on Safety and Justice (OMV). His inaugural lecture of 2007 was entitled 'Towards a Cosmopolitan Criminology'. His present research is oriented on international comparisons, notably on the relation between social developments and policies on crime and insecurity in European (port) cities and on global criminology. He is the author of *Critical Criminology: Visions from Europe* (Sage,

1997), a social epistemological study into the development of critical criminology in Europe.

Suzanne Wallace-Capretta received her MA in Psychology at Carleton University, Ottawa. She has worked as a researcher with the Solicitor General Canada and the Department of Justice Canada for more than 15 years. She has conducted research, co-authored publications and led research teams in a variety of criminal justice and community corrections areas, including risk prediction, alternatives to imprisonment, female offenders, family violence and cyber crime. She frequently guest lectures in these areas. Recently she has joined Public Safety Canada as a Senior Policy Specialist in the Community Safety and Partnerships Branch.

Inka Wennerberg has a master's degree in Psychology and works at the National Police Board in Sweden on policy development of victim issues. She has been in the steering group for a project concerning the use of electronic monitoring in relation to restraining orders. She has also been involved in the planning of the last two European conferences on electronic monitoring, including a survey of the use of electronic monitoring in Europe. Previously she has, as a research analyst, been responsible for the evaluation of the use of electronic monitoring within the prison and probation service and has written several research reports in that area.

Acknowledgements

It took us too long to finish this book and we take full responsibility for that. First of all we thank Brian Willan and the authors of the different chapters for their endless patience in the 'birth' of this book. We also thank Ralf Bas for initiating this project and Sofie De Bus and Steven De Ridder, assistants at the Criminology Department of the Vrije Universiteit Brussel, for their help with editing the references.

Introduction

Making sense of electronic monitoring

Mike Nellis, Kristel Beyens and Dan Kaminski

Introduction

Since the 1980s, the electronic monitoring (EM) of offenders has been successfully introduced in over 30 countries worldwide, having originated in the United States. As both a means of enforcing compliance with curfews and home confinement, and (less so) of monitoring the general whereabouts of offenders in the community, it has become established in Western Europe, and in some countries it has already moved beyond experimental status and has become a mainstream, if not a dominant, penal measure. The practical application of EM has not only been extended on a considerable scale, the measure itself has already been transformed, technologically and penally, in a number of different ways. A wide range of decision-makers have become involved in its administration, e.g. prosecutors, judges, administrative bodies, prison governors, parole boards or sentence implementation courts. In most countries, commercial organizations are involved as technology suppliers or as full-service supervisors, and in some countries private sector employees are even involved in 'breach' decisions. Finally, EM has created a new category of penal subject, offenders who have experienced supervision in the community in ways that are distinctively different from probation and community service. While it is indeed important to recognize that EM has not been as penally transformative as some of its champions hoped and some of its opponents feared when it first arose, it is by no means insignificant, and this book is premised on the idea that – for policy-makers, practitioners and academics – there is much more to be said about it than has been said before. Neither 'the sociology of punishment' nor 'surveillance studies' – the two intellectual fields which can contribute most to understanding EM – have had much to say so far. The resources of both could be used to much better effect to appraise the meaning and significance of this penal innovation.

Apart from Mayer *et al.*'s (2003) publication of the proceedings of a European Workshop on EM, and the publications for the CEP conferences (of which, more below), no international comparative study has been published to date to describe and analyse the contours and various applications of EM. Some of the pioneering scholars that participated at this workshop at that time are also involved in this book project, e.g. René Lévy, Mike Nellis and Robert Lilly. The starting question of this book almost ten years ago was: *Will electronic monitoring have a future in Europe?* Well, today we can start this book by answering that question in an affirmative way: EM has had a future in Europe, both West and East, and seems likely to continue to have one. The empirical literature on EM is richer now than then, and the theoretical sources for studying it far greater, but one still needs to begin with some basic data about its use and incidence.

What of EM's scale? Systematic and sound international comparative quantitative data on the scale of the development of EM are non-existent, or at least incomplete. The SPACE II statistics, for example, give the number of persons serving an EM on 31 December 2009 in the member states of the Council of Europe. The following 14 countries had at that time introduced EM: Belgium ($N=1,548$); Denmark ($N=123$); Estonia ($N=41$); France ($N=4,489$); Luxembourg ($N=9$); the Netherlands ($N=468$); Norway ($N=41$); Poland ($N=33$); Portugal ($N=524$); Spain ($N=1,912$); Catalonia ($N=48$); Sweden ($N=493$); Switzerland ($N=37$) and England and Wales ($N=15,244$) (Aebi *et al.* 2011: 11–12). However, these data are incomplete, because Hessen (Germany) introduced EM in 2000 and this jurisdiction does not appear in the list. CEP, the European Organisation for Probation, conducts a survey on EM on a regular basis. Their 2011 survey, which does not have complete coverage either, shows that the number of countries that has introduced or is introducing EM has increased worldwide and is still expanding. EM is spreading from the United States to Canada and Western Europe, with England and Wales being the first jurisdiction in Europe to introduce EM, which was in 1989. Also, Eastern European (Poland, Bulgaria, Estonia) and Latin American (Argentina, Brazil, Columbia) countries have adopted it. Once EM has been adopted, its use in each country tends to increase. England and Wales are the majority users of EM in Europe, with an EM ratio of 40/100,000 inhabitants. Other jurisdiction rates in the CEP survey vary between 3 and 14 per 100,000 inhabitants.

Unlike probation and community service, EM has been implemented in diverse phases in the criminal justice system, at the pre-trial as well as the sentencing stage, as a modality to execute a prison sentence or as an early release measure (separately or as part of a parole licence). It has even been used, on a very small scale, as a means of monitoring inmate movements within prisons, or as an electronic perimeter around open prisons (Halberstadt and La Vigne 2011). Among both European and US policy-makers the terms 'front door' and 'back door' have been used to denote the use of EM as a pre-prison or after-prison measure, but these are crude terms of limited analytic value in understanding its function or gauging its trajectory. An important policy debate has taken place about its use as a stand-alone punishment (commonplace in England and Wales, but less so elsewhere in Europe) versus its use as a component in intensive supervision and treatment programmes, although even in regard to the latter there have been arguments as to whether it is included simply as a punitive element in the package, or whether it serves to support other, more rehabilitative components. It has been targeted at a wide range of offenders, of variable risk, for a wide range of crimes – from motoring offences to drug offences, from car thieves to murderers on parole – depending on what other measures it may or may not be combined with. Women make up a smaller proportion of offenders on EM than men, as they do on all community penalties, and home confinement may well have gendered consequences. Some countries use EM on juvenile offenders (United States, Britain, France and the Netherlands). Some types of offender are excluded from some types of programme, although this can have as much to do with presumed perceptions of what would be publicly acceptable than the precise levels of control being imposed. Sex offenders are excluded from some early release and home confinement programmes, although they can be specifically targeted by tracking programmes.

Looking across the different jurisdictions, EM has almost always been introduced in a context of rising prison populations and prison overcrowding (including at the remand stage) for which governments seek to find quick and cheap – but at the same time publicly credible – solutions. EM has certainly been regarded as a near-panacea for overburdened prison systems (slowing rates of admission, offsetting the need to build new prisons, enabling release earlier than would otherwise have been feasible). At the same time – although this is a slightly different point – EM can meet the perceived need for more controlling community penalties and for greater diversity in the range of intermediate sanctions between prison and probation, which can be a policy development in its own right, independent of its effect on prison numbers. In the United States, EM became caught up in the 1990s debates about 'intermediate sanctions', mid-way (in terms of penal intrusiveness) between probation and prison, without ever making much difference to local prison populations (Morris and Tonry 1990). Both aspects of EM – its potential as a means of reducing prison use and as a means of making community supervision tougher – usually require the discursive construction of EM as a more demanding intervention than has been used hitherto.

'Demanding', however, blurs important differences between *punishment* and *control*. We have called our book 'electronically monitored *punishment*' because it is indeed as *punishment* that EM has largely been used and discussed, although there have been exceptions where it is portrayed – more neutrally and more accurately, in fact – as a form of control, a merely regulatory mechanism. This is how 'surveillance studies' has viewed it, mindful that surveillance can have both benign and destructive expressions. As regulation and control, EM can potentially be used either in support of retributive punishment (as in stand-alone, end-in-itself house-arrest) or as a component of rehabilitation (stabilizing offenders with chaotic lifestyles – a means to an end – while they undergo treatment programmes). Such differences of emphasis can have different implications for the selection of offenders for programmes, the impact of the measure and even the critical direction that analyses of EM might take.

EM has rightly been seen by a number of analysts as an expression of managerialist tendencies in criminal justice (Jones 2000; Bottoms 1995; Raine and

Willson 1997). Its rise was indeed coterminous with the emergence of the penal strategies that Feely and Simon (1994) dubbed 'actuarial justice', strategies that were often presented to the public as merely pragmatic and depoliticized, concerned primarily with efficient risk management and cost-effectiveness, and detached from traditional penological aims. While the prospect of cost reduction may have given EM some public appeal, it was more difficult in some countries than others to present it as 'painless dentistry', as Corbett and Marx (1992: 92) called it. In both the United States and Britain it was invariably distanced a little from merely actuarial approaches by politicians who doubted that it would be seen as a credible substitute for imprisonment if it were not discursively characterized as a 'tough and demanding' punishment. In both countries this backfired. The public, aided and abetted by a sceptical media, were disinclined to see EM – being sentenced to stay at home – as a severe punishment, and more inclined to see it as a mild and easily evaded form of control (tags could be cut off with scissors), worth trying with low-risk, low-seriousness offenders but manifestly not a serious substitute for imprisonment. The sociology of punishment needs to take account of the very variable cultural perceptions of EM's actual punitivity, and not take at face value the political and commercial discourse that has had a vested interest in portraying it as the onerous simulation of 'jailspace' in the home or community (Martinovic 2010). It must, as Tom Daems (2008) has put it, 'respect the integrity of the subject' – accurately depict its character – rather than aligning itself, at least in the first instance, with pre-determined political views of it. It is preferable, therefore, to conceptualize EM neutrally, as a 'surveillant control' technology that could be used in a number of different and perhaps contradictory ways, and with different results, rather than presume that it serves either a punitive purpose, empirically or symbolically, or that it actually enhances rehabilitative and reintegrative approaches in the way Bonta *et al.*'s (2000a, 2000b) research suggested, and as some of its founders still claim (Gable and Gable 2007).

'Surveillant control', of course, while not intrinsically punitive, is not an ethically or politically neutral capacity. The ever-more meticulous forms of regulation associated with managerialism (and the technologies through which it is actualized) can lead in extremis to regimented and centralized forms of social order that are every bit as repressive as those associated with 'punitive excess', more so, perhaps, in that they encompass all citizens, not just the specific category of offender. Nils Christie (1978) warned long ago that reductions in the use of imprisonment must not be pursued at the expense of turning society itself into a prison, and some have seen in EM a panoptic potential that would do exactly this.

What is electronic monitoring?

Taking their cues from surveillance studies, Nellis and Rossell (2011) define EM as follows: 'EM technology must be understood as nothing more or less than a form of remote surveillant control, a means of flexibly regulating the spatial and temporal schedules of an offender's life.' This is a very generic definition which shows (from a traditional probation perspective, at least) the 'emptiness' of EM as a stand-alone measure. Yet its 'emptiness' is also its strength (from the standpoint of politicians and criminal justice managers): it can be used in so many different ways, it can be ascribed many different aims and it can easily be adapted to different situations. It has the 'chameleon' character of a multi-usable device, and can be presented as a solution to several different types of penal problem, e.g. prison overcrowding, the need for toughness in community penalties. The intended effect of monitoring is to remind the offender that he is being watched (continuously or haphazardly and regularly), and that his compliance or otherwise with the spatial and temporal regulations that the court or prison has imposed on him will be relayed to a judicial or penal authority, with the possibility that he may be 'breached' and subject to a more severe penalty (or recalled to prison) if a 'violation' has been deemed to occur.

EM is not one single thing, technologically speaking. Different types of technologies are being used and innovation continues. The first and still most dominant type uses radio frequency (RF) to ensure an offender – fitted with a signalling device on his ankle (or more rarely wrist) – remains within proximity of a transceiver in his home, which relays his presence (or absence) via landline or mobile phone telephony to a monitoring centre which may be hundreds of miles away. By such means, and with a number of anti-tamper mechanisms built into the device, curfews or house arrest can be affected. Colloquially, in Britain, this was called 'tagging' and the term has been used elsewhere, although not in the United States, where it had the somewhat uncommercial connotation of electronically tracking cattle on the open range. Voice verification technology was developed soon after RF tagging as a potentially cheaper – and less stigmatizing – means of fixed-location monitoring. No wearable (and potentially visible) device was needed. Offenders were identified by their unique biometric voice-print, recorded and computerized at the point of sentence, and matched with the offender each time he or she phones (or is phoned by) the monitoring centre. Unlike RF tagging, voice verification can more easily be used to monitor presence in a sequence of locations (e.g. home, job centre, community service placement) but it has not been widely used. The United States has made use of remote alcohol monitoring (RAM), which combines RF tagging with a breathalyser to randomly monitor violations of bans on drinking at home, to which some offenders can be subject for the duration of their sentence. The subject breathes into the transceiver/breathalyser, and his or her alcohol level is relayed directly to the monitoring centre. The identity of the subject (who may be tempted to ask a sober surrogate to breathe on his behalf) can be guaranteed by voice verification, manually recognized photo-ID or (in later machines) computerized facial recognition technology. RAM has been trialled in both Sweden and the Netherlands, neither of whom were convinced of the reliability of the technology, but in the United States the correctional desirability of banning offenders' alcohol use has encouraged the development of devices which can measure alcohol intake transdermally (via anklets). The pursuit of a device which transdermally monitors other sorts of substance abuse remains the holy grail of the EM industry, but so far none has become commercially available.

The Global Positioning System (GPS) created by the US Department of Defense in the late 1970s for military and (free) civilian navigation purposes comprises a network of 24 geostationary satellites 11,000 miles above the earth. Any three of these (four if altitude is also needed) can be used to pinpoint a person's outdoor location, in real time, on the earth's surface to within (nowadays) under ten metres. Vast and complex civilian uses of GPS have developed. Offender tracking, although it had been imagined two decades beforehand and in some senses represented an ideal of what EM might accomplish, was a relatively late application, beginning in the United States in 1997 and focusing particularly on sex offenders after 2005. The basic GPS system requires some augmentation to work reliably as a means of supervising offenders and is usually combined with the mobile phone system to guarantee coverage of people indoors as well as outdoors. It can be used to create inclusion zones (the equivalent of house arrest), exclusion zones (around victims' homes or areas of previous offending) or to specify particular routes (e.g. home to work) that the offender must take. It can be done in real time (a very immediate form of monitoring) or retrospectively, which can still act as a deterrent. It can be combined with crime-scene software to tally an offender's movements with known crime scenes, exonerating or incriminating them, and some believe that an offender's complex movement patterns could be analysed over time to discern criminal intentions. Technical problems have arisen with GPS – it creates false alerts and heavy workloads for supervisors – but the tradeoff in terms of public protection (despite some serious crimes being committed by tracked offenders in the United States) is still thought to be considerable. Such is the obvious versatility of GPS tracking that, particularly as it has grown much cheaper, the question 'Is there a future for RF in a GPS world?' has inevitably been asked. This is a valid question, and as other countries develop their own geolocation satellite systems – Galileo in Europe, GLONASS in Russia and Compass in China – its potential will increase immensely. At the same time, more localized terrestrial tracking systems are also in development which may yet have a future. Periodically, and usually couched in dystopian terms, the question of using electronic implants on offenders arises, but this underestimates both the health risks associated with implanted RFID chips and the continuing versatility of wearable devices (Nellis 2012). The usual pattern has been for countries to use RF EM first, then develop GPS – although after a pilot in 2004–2006, England and Wales (2007) decided against GPS – but some newcomer countries have adopted GPS without ever having used RF tagging (Ireland and South Korea) and some have piloted them simultaneously, e.g. Saudi Arabia. This probably constitutes a new phase in EM development.

The various forms of EM arguably constitute a form of 'virtual' supervision, perhaps reflecting, in a penal context, widespread movements in 'the network society' towards 'telematic' practices that affect behaviour at a distance in more or less real time through an array of communication channels. EM does not visualize offenders directly (in the manner of CCTV), but via on-screen signifiers it does make them – specifically, their location, presence (or absence) – 'telepresent' to supervisors who may be many miles from them. It creates the potential for what William Mitchell has called (in a commercial context) 'economies of presence' in penal supervision: cost (or risk)-based judgements about the balance needed between personal face-to-face contact and impersonal, remote (maybe one-way only) communication (or just discrete monitoring) necessary to achieve particular aims (akin to the decisions a businessman might make to close a deal with a customer on the other side of the world). In the case of an offender, non-compliance with virtual means can still have material consequences, and as with any controlling measure, 'the virtual' should not be over-emphasized. EM remains what Foucault (1979) would call 'biopower' and at its crudest it is as much (if not more) a technique for regulating the spatio-temporal location of bodies as it is a means of affecting offenders' minds. Whether all this is a good or bad penal development – what its meaning and significance is – is something that neither the 'sociology of punishment' nor 'surveillance studies' have yet addressed, but it is hardly new now, and long overdue for study. Ultimately, however, EM must not be considered as a technology alone, virtual or otherwise. It is not simply a device. It is best understood as an 'automated socio-technical system' (Lianos and Douglas 2000). EM is automated in the sense that the continuous signalling and computerized storage of data on which 24/7 monitoring depends do not, once harnessed and programmed, require constant human oversight, but it is also 'socio-technical' in that it requires human input to fit tags, install equipment in people's homes, monitor screens to check on compliance or otherwise, take breached cases to court using locational data as evidence and to respond (if only by telephone) to violation alerts or requests for help from tagged offenders and their families. The boundaries of the 'socio-technical system' arguably extend into, and blur with, the legal and correctional institutions who decide who should be tagged and for how long, and into the policy networks that formulate aims and strategies for EM and allocate resources to it. This takes us back to the sociology of punishment.

Why study electronic monitoring?

In their book *Alternatives to Prison: Options for an Insecure Society*, Bottoms *et al.* (2004: 5–10) describe 'successive eras' in the development of non-custodial options. The 1990s are defined as the era of the 'new generation' of community penalties. Here, the emphasis lay on punishment in the community and the enforcement of orders to ensure that offenders actually experience the intended restrictions on their liberty. The authors point out that this era was characterized by a growing reliance on the use of technology to enforce the requirements of community orders, combined with a 'managerial revolution' in the probation service where the imposition of New Public Management principles were seen to require the contracting-out of some of its services to the private sector (as it had in the prison service). Another important feature of this new generation of community penalties has been the 'creative mixing' of different kinds of interventions, aiming for more controlling and/or more individualized sentences. Ten years on, it can be seen that the developments of EM perfectly fits their picture of this new generation of community penalties, in the sense that England and Wales have used it extensively (but not exclusively) as a stand-alone measure, and other European countries have thought it worth adopting. Important and accurate as this analysis is, it arguably does not capture what is distinctive about EM, and tends to treat it as just another new community sanction, akin to all the others. This underplays its significance at both macro and micro levels. A whole contractual/commercial infrastructure has grown up around EM that does not impinge on other alternatives, except in the sense that some of the same service-providing countries would also like privatized versions of probation, community service and bail hostels (and with respect of the latter, England and Wales already do). The new category of penal subjects – remotely surveilled subjects – are required to comply with regulations in ways that have had no real precedent in community supervision, especially in respect of GPS tracking.

EM undoubtedly has the potential to have a transformative impact on the nature of offender supervision, although whether it does, and in what ways – for better or for worse – remains to be seen. The reduction of the prison population is not always a result, which suggests that there are deeper social, technological and political reasons why different varieties of this technology are introduced and sustained. In many countries the attractiveness of EM to policy-makers is indeed obvious: EM is seen as a product which might simultaneously reduce the prison population and re-offending rates. This seems at first sight to satisfy many political intentions in the penal field, from the most liberal ones – e.g. imagining crime as a problematic interaction to be restored with respect to human rights, avoiding incarceration wherever possible – to the most repressive or conservative ones – e.g. being tough on crime via retribution, deterrence and incapacitation or neutralization.

To a greater or lesser degree – the impact is different in different countries – the emergence of this technology is challenging the traditional approaches to offender supervision, if only by diverting resources that might otherwise have been spent on them, creating a new space alongside them. The full nature of this challenge, and its likely outcomes, is not well understood yet, but it has both theoretical and practical dimensions on which academics in 'critical criminology' (which encompasses the sociology of punishment) might not agree, although we think it would be best if they tried to. Many European penal reformers and probation practitioners were hostile towards EM in the 1980s, and hoped the 'American example' would not be followed. Although the initial scepticism and hostility towards EM by critical observers is slowly fading away today – and much supportive literature has been produced by in-house research and evaluation – the more critical questions still need to be asked and are articulated in a number of the contributions to this book. It is not hard to find a critical intellectual starting point. Looking back at Stanley Cohen's (1985) seminal work *Visions of Social Control*, the dangers he anticipated in the development of alternative sanctions all seem very pertinent to EM. Following his work, it can first be stated that the development of EM entails a *widening of the penal net* (not necessarily beyond the existing array of alternatives, but in the sense that it only rarely makes a difference to prisoner numbers). In many of the countries described it leads to a net increase of penal control (substituting for notionally softer measures like probation and fines) and it changes the 'quality' and 'nature' of penality, or at least some aspects of it. Second, in this ostensibly more intensive and controlling community sanction we see thinning of the mesh (of prison) exemplified, albeit in ways that entail *thickening the mesh* from a traditional probation standpoint. Third, the *boundaries* between institutionalized and non-institutionalized forms of control get *blurred* by infusing penal control into the 'privacy' of the home (and, in the case of GPS, into the hitherto anonymous public spaces of the community – see also Aungles 1994; Kaluszynski and Froment 2003). Fourth, penal control shifts from the state to civil society – what Cohen called *penetration* – in the case of EM into the private sector, who in some countries, under contract to governments, have significant operational responsibilities in respect of this new punishment. With the advent of EM, all the so-called 'old' dangers of net-widening, intrusion into civil society, a soft version of technological determinism and commercially driven corrections justifiably remain current areas of vigilance. This book was put together to take into account broader factors in EM's development and to look for probable and possible consequences beyond the alleged 'reduced prison use' and 'reduced offending rates' in which policy-makers have hitherto been mostly interested. We do not doubt the dilemmas and difficulties that 'liberal' penal policy-makers, penal reformers and probation managers have had to face in the past three decades – in Europe, as in the United States, EM has had its liberal supporters (Whitfield 1997, 2001) alongside 'conservative' ones – but without a deep understanding of the socio-technological and commercial momentum behind EM (which makes it so different from other community sanctions) it is difficult to know if it can actually have 'liberal', progressive consequences in practice.

We wished to go further in understanding the form of penal change that EM represents than *Visions of Social Control* permits us to do. Nonetheless, it is good to recall Stanley Cohen in this context because he recognized the importance of the critical criminology of praxis, accepting that practitioners faced genuinely hard choices in work with offenders, and were always brokers in lesser evils. Similarly, he never ceased searching for strategies that could realistically challenge the immense symbolic and political harms of imprisonment, and accepted that such struggles were forever 'unfinished' (Cohen 1992).

How to study EM?

We deliberately chose an international and – on a chapter-by-chapter basis – a comparative approach. EM is worldwide and could probably not be understood in terms of the penal dynamics of one country alone. Increasingly it has been recognized that deeper and richer understandings of penal cultures and practices are required to make sense of differences in approaches to punishment and control. There are different ways to do comparative research and it has a lot of pitfalls (Nelken 2010). In order to understand the full complexities of the dynamics of EM, selected scholars from the pioneering countries have been invited to explain the establishment and developments of EM in their countries. We opt for an embedded and situated description and critical analysis of the implementation of EM in the different jurisdictions, written by academics who are familiar with a particular penal, organizational, political and social context of the use of EM. Not all would count themselves 'critical criminologists', but all have reflected on the significance of EM in their respective countries, and the different registers in which their chapters are written reflect the range of ways in which discourse on EM has been constructed.

EM is so widespread, and the types of scheme in which it is used so diverse, that obviously not all of its manifestations around the world (or even just in the United States) could be considered in this book. First of all, this comparative project incorporates only a selection of jurisdictions. Largely for pragmatic reasons we included countries with an established pattern of use of EM on the one hand, but also countries that have undertaken some kind of evaluation research, so that at least something can be said about outcomes. To take only a few examples of geographical exclusion: Columbia, the Eastern European countries and those of the Far East (except South Korea) were not considered because of their rather recent experiences with EM or their lack of local research, but it is clearly not without significance that EM has expanded in these regions. This book is mostly focused on the use of EM with offenders in the criminal justice system, and it recognizes only in passing that it has uses in victim protection (forms of restraining orders), as a civil measure (for parents who refuse to pay child support), as a regulatory measure with terrorist suspects and asylum seekers, and even, in the United States, as a means of preventing truancy from school.

Nine jurisdictions that can be considered to be 'pioneering' countries are selected. Outside Europe these are the United States, Canada, Australia, New Zealand and South Korea. Within Europe we chose as exemplars England and Wales and France, and for smaller but also pioneering countries we chose Sweden, Belgium and the Netherlands. The focus is thus on those countries where EM is most deeply established (or, paradoxically, where EM has only recently emerged, like South Korea, moving straight to GPS without ever using RF EM, one of the first countries to do this), and where there have been distinctively different implementation strategies, presented in a way that permits us to see both contrasts and similarities. This selection of countries was determined some years ago and as time has passed other countries with interesting experiences have emerged, such as Portugal and Spain. Unfortunately, they are not included in this book. However, we are convinced that, with the countries we selected, the most important arguments and insights about contemporary EM are covered in this book

The book starts with a chapter on the United States because EM originated there and is widely used there, though not in fact as extensively or as transformatively as its pioneers anticipated. The United States – and Florida in particular – retains a key role as a technological innovator (e.g. with satellite tracking) and can be regarded as a breeding ground of the principal controversies about EM. Many European countries have been very sensitive to the transfer of American penal innovations, and while they perhaps had no choice to begin with but to learn from them, as time has gone by, and as EM has expanded, they have been more able to learn from each other. Canada, Australia, New Zealand and many Western European countries may yet experience more penological and social innovations in their use and development of EM, possibly even liberal ones. Complex cultural and political dynamics in the receptor country contribute to the legal and practical outcomes when a policy (or form of practice) is transferred from one country to another – rarely does it prove to be an exact copy. Except probably in the case of England and Wales, the international developments are no longer simply a consequence – as they were at the outset – of 'policy transfer' from America (Nellis 2000; Jones and Newburn 2002, 2007). Nonetheless, the software and the equipment used in EM looks remarkably similar around the world, partly because there are only a limited number of companies (many of which have a global reach) developing it, and some abiding similarities of practice and purpose cannot be denied. It seems unlikely that simple technological determinism is occurring simultaneously at the specific, local level of penal practice, but it does make sense to see EM as an affordance of a worldwide information and communication technology infrastructure – it would not exist in its present forms without computerization, the internet, the global mobile phone network and GPS satellites – which all governments might choose to make use of as they modernize their public services or emulate Western approaches to development. This infrastructure and its social ramifications – what Manuel Castells (1996) calls 'the network society' – may be contributing to an element of 'global convergence' in penal practice – diverse countries shaping similar responses to similarly defined problems because they see through a similar technological lens – without much recourse to country-by-country 'policy transfer'.

Nonetheless, cross-national transfer will still occur. In Europe, the CEP has played a significant role in the development of EM in Europe, devoting more time to this topic than any other, precisely because it was seen to be potentially threatening to the interests of probation and potentially illiberal in its consequences. In 2011 they organized their seventh EM conference and, although, as always, it had a primarily European focus, it also attracted visitors from farther afield because this event has become a key 'networking hub' for people who wish to learn about EM and integrate their understanding of its political, practical, financial and technological aspects. Commercial companies (both commercial and technology providers) sponsor the conference, present and put their latest generation of monitoring equipment on the market, entertain established customers and seek new ones. Their display stands and salespeople seek to convince policy-makers and practitioners of the effectiveness and importance of the use of monitoring devices in their criminal justice systems. Policy-makers and practitioners pool their experiences of establishing and running EM schemes, and engage the commercial organizations in dialogue. Arguably, the event does play a pivotal role in the process of policy transfer – assisting global convergence – all over the world. The dominant discourse at the CEP conferences is premised on the understanding that EM will expand. They were established on the basis that EM would develop regardless and that it would be better for probation to try to shape it, even incorporate it, than allow free rein to politicians and commercial bodies to develop it as they saw fit, without reference to existing professional expertise in offender supervision. The CEP has sought to be liberal in respect of EM, to promote it as a 'useful tool' for probation (a form of control that probation could not otherwise provide) which could, if used wisely, genuinely assist in the reduction of prison populations and improve public safety. It has taken a mundane, practical view of EM, neither utopian nor dystopian. Whether the moderate, liberal view of EM is itself utopian, or whether EM is bound to displace probation and help to corrode the humanistic values which have hitherto informed its traditions and practice, remains to be seen. What the CEP has not done is underestimate EM's significance – it was prescient in that respect – and many people, including those in commercial organizations, are better informed as a result of its conferences. Academics have not been excluded from them, but these have not been fora where 'critical criminology' can be aired, and in truth 'critical criminology', unlike CEP, was slow to see that this penal innovation warranted serious and informed investigation.

With the exception of the United States chapter, each chapter starts from a number of clearly formulated research questions aiming to stimulate, in respect of each country, a comparable account of different and similar developments in EM. They focus on the history, structure, scale and administrative location of EM projects; the philosophy, the contours of the professional and public debate about EM, the anticipated future of EM and – in the author's view – how EM fits with and contributes to prevailing penal developments in each country. Not all of these questions could be dealt with equally in the different jurisdictions, because the authors could not always access the necessary information. By and large, however, the following questions supply the penological axes of each chapter.

Thematic debates in EM

As well as covering national developments in nine countries, this book also includes a series of chapters on controversial themes in EM. They too are international in orientation, although we are aware that they reflect the standpoint of particular authors and that they may seem to some countries to have overstated some issues and underplayed others. Nonetheless, we hope that these chapters on ethics, evaluation, privatization and offender perspectives take the debate further forward.

While strident for-and-against judgements on EM have been commonplace, surprisingly little has been written about the ethics of EM, or indeed the ethics of offender surveillance more generally. Some of the early US literature addressed privacy concerns relating to EM house arrest, as if this was the key, or indeed only, issue. (The role of the private sector has been addressed as an ethical issue, which we deal with separately below.) Liberal champions of EM tended to take for granted that while EM might be controlling, it was ethically acceptable simply because it is 'better than' (that is, less painful than) the destructive experience of prison. This is an important consideration, but it is not an ethically sufficient defence in itself. Each type of so-called 'alternative to prison' and each argument for 'toughening' supervision needs its own specific ethical justification. Drawing on moral and social philosophy, Mike Nellis explores the ethics of EM as a form of remote surveillance, and seeks to establish credible limits on the use of technology to affect offender behaviour. He utilizes offenders' own experiences of being monitored to illuminate ethical dilemmas, and addresses the way in which human rights might inform the creation of minimum standards for the use of EM.

Marc Renzema, an American academic who has followed the development of EM from the beginning, and the founder of the *Journal of Electronic Monitoring*, would be the first to say that there is only a limited amount of acceptable evaluative research on EM, much of it produced by official government researchers rather than by independent academic evaluators, with a strong focus on cost-effectiveness and a primary concern with reducing offending. Summing up the available research in 2005, Renzema and Mayo (2005) concluded that the few reliable studies did not suggest that RF EM house arrest had, or could have, by its very nature, a crime-reductive effect. This played a part in shifting American corrections agencies to consider GPS tracking in the hope that the surveillance of offenders' whereabouts in general, as opposed to the monitoring of a single designated location, would remedy the manifest 'control-deficits' of mere RF EM house arrest. Evaluations have been undertaken in Europe, and although consistent evaluative studies are missing, Marc Renzema summarizes the world-wide state of knowledge on EM's effects. As we will suggest below, this is not the only kind of research that needs to be done on EM, but it is important to know, in policy-makers' own terms, what the consequences of their programmes have been, and whether research does in fact influence policy, or whether other factors are in play.

The private sector is involved in the contracted provision of EM to governments in two ways – technology manufacture and service provision (the provision of monitoring officers separate from existing probation services). Some organizations combine both functions. England, Wales and Scotland have fully fledged private sector providers, contracted for five-year periods. Even in the United States, state agencies have tended to buy or loan equipment, and do the monitoring themselves. Other mainland European countries have considered Britain's private sector model, or are considering it, but there is no clear evidence that it is the cheaper or more effective way. Drawing on Lilly and Knepper's concept of 'the commercial corrections complex', Craig Paterson's chapter explores the development of EM in the context of international developments in private security and penal provision, reflecting on their operation role and their potential for influencing penal policy

With the introduction of EM, new monitoring agents have entered the field of crime control. The question of whether the daily monitoring of the offenders should be contracted out to the private sector was and still is a highly political and sensitive debate. More research is needed to understand the meaning and burden of EM for the offenders and the family members of the offenders being put under EM. How does this sentence interfere in family life and daily relationships and what role do family members play in the process of compliance? Anthea Hucklesby's chapter focuses on the perspectives of those on the receiving end of EM and of the private sector monitoring staff involved in supervising them, drawing on the findings of an exploratory study undertaken in the north of England in the mid-2000s. Specific attention is given to the issues of compliance and desistance. The possible positive impact of EM on desistance is, however, anything but straightforward and being under EM can be counterproductive for organizing one's daily life. Nonetheless, Hucklesby finds that curfew orders can play an important role in breaking habits or dissolving the connections that curfewees had with anti-social associates and environments. Hucklesby's research also shows the importance of the nature of the contact with the monitoring staff and of the characteristics of this staff in the process of desistance.

Conclusion

It is not difficult to conjure a dystopian penal vision out of EM. Both house arrest and the tracking and tracing of one's every move by the state have long been potent totalitarian tropes, and although the precise contours of the world that Orwell (1949) envisaged in *Nineteen Eighty-Four* never materialized, there have been many subsequent iterations of the view that in Weber's 'iron cage' lie all our futures. Certain abstract characterizations of Foucault's 'disciplinary society' (1979), Deleuze's 'societies of control' (1992) and Bogard's 'telematic society' (1996) all point ineluctably towards the increased use of surveillance technologies as a form of domination. Deleuze even cites 'electronic tracking' as an example of the kind of control he means. Such accounts – directly or by implication – sometimes cast EM in an unnecessarily difficult 'thin end of the wedge' position, denying all its manoeuvrability on the political spectrum. It has thus come to be opposed less for what it actually is (or could be) in the here and now, and more in terms of the imagined greater danger – the more fearsome forms of surveillance and control – into which it is assumed it will inexorably mutate in the future. The simplistic argument has then been made 'don't do this now, because of what it will lead to in the years ahead'. We are not unmindful of this argument, despite its very simplistic assumption that EM won't flourish if only 'we' (probation, liberal penal reformers and critical criminologists) don't give credence and legitimacy to it now. We absolutely accept that there are things to fear about EM as a form of penal control, that it may well presage totalitarian political forms, as one among several components of 'a maximum surveillance society'. Where we differ from this dystopian position – and its implicit technological determinism – is in the role we give to culture and politics in shaping the way technology is used, and indeed in shaping and sustaining justice, democracy and decency in society itself.

For this reason we do recognize the importance of the shaping role that the CEP, through its conferences, has tried to play in respect of EM in Europe. We acknowledge also the difficult choices that liberal penal administrators have had in the face of 'populist punitiveness' and demands for increased public safety and straitened financial circumstances, to find progressive ways forward, or simply to hold existing ground. EM may well appeal to modernizing penal con-servatives who want nothing more than new permutations of punishment, but in some contexts it has genuinely looked like a viable liberal contribution to the enduring problems of incarceration, which could simultaneously reduce prison use, save money and increase legitimate degrees of control over offenders in the community. There is certainly evidence to suggest that despite experiencing it as onerous, many offenders and their families prefer it to more protracted periods in custody, and this ought not to surprise anyone. To say to any of these people – hard-pressed administrators and incarcerated offenders – that this liberal option of, say, several months on EM should not be pursued because, despite tangible gains now, institutionalizing it will make things worse in the future, is not an ethically tenable position, even though the worse-in-the-future argument, all things being equal, may well be plausible. Critical criminology, we recognize, as Stanley Cohen recognized, needs a praxis which sees relevant tactical differ-ences between the alleviation of unnecessary penal severity in the short term and the prevention of injustice and oppression in the long term, without ever entirely separating the two. Critical criminology cannot – and should not – just stand on the intellectual sidelines and condemn. While sophisticated social analyses, ethnographies and studies of penal subjects are crucial to understanding the complexities and effects of EM, it cannot entirely walk away from the pressing practical question of 'what works?' (even if it rejects the narrowly managerial and technocratic way in which that term is usually understood).

So, ethically and politically, there is something to be said for practice-oriented research that looks at the part EM might play in desistance and the ways in which it can affect compliance with community supervision, as Anthea Huck-lesby has done, for helping practitioners to find constructive uses of various types of EM technology in different criminal justice contexts. It is equally im-portant to equip policy-makers with normative arguments and empirical evid-ence against the naïve and destructive uses of EM (24-hour lockdowns and rigid, punitive responses to merely technical violations), but they have to be the kind of arguments that have some purchase in the arena of real political debate, not the kind that only make lofty sense in the convivial intellectual spaces of academia. None of this is to say that critical criminologists should not also paint compelling pictures of how the worst may well come to the worst, of what severe penal regression and oppressive 'surveillance societies' might look like, to help us 'see them coming'. This is an important intellectual task, but as

Zedner (2002) observed in a telling critique of Garland, unduly abstract dystopias can often be irrelevant to hard-pressed practitioners, and at worst immobilizing and self-fulfilling if, by instilling a sense of futility, they stifle the very struggle that might have countered them.

Critical criminologists need also to envision, if not fully fledged penal utopias, then at least what penal progress might look like in the twenty-first-century 'network society', and to assess what leeway there may be in the here-and-now to take halting steps towards it. The egalitarian and humanistic values that have informed penal reform in the past – commitment to social justice, respect for personal dignity, care and understanding of the vulnerable, censure of violence and confidence that people can be helped to change for the better – can never be dispensed with; there can never be purely technocratic solutions to engrained structural and cultural problems. It is true that the endless, amnesiac search for more and better alternatives to prison, built to run alongside prison in the hope that by attrition this will steadily reduce its use, is forlorn: research has proved time and again that this strategy does not work on a large scale over an extended period. And yet, whatever social, political and legal strategies may one day be devised to minimize prison use in democratic societies – we hope for that – many offenders who would otherwise do harm will still require support and supervision in the community. In the twenty-first century it would seem absurd (and counter-intuitive in the light of all we know about processes of penal change, which always reflect and express aspects of their cultural milieu) to rule out the possibility that the affordances of 'the network society' could have a legitimate place in such supervision. A progressive penal imaginary in our time would not have a large place for EM and all its forms, but it would be sociologically surprising if it had no place for it at all.

Not all our contributors may agree with this – or with other things that we have said here – but the parameters of 'responsible speech' on a subject like EM are wider than Daems (2008) believes. We wish to thank them all for their chapters. There is as yet no settled view as to EM's nature or significance, its constructive potential or its dangers. We do not take a definitive view here, but we hope our book steers readers towards a more informed understanding.

References

Aebi, M., Delgrande, N. and Marguet, Y. (2011) *Council of Europe Annual Statistics SPACE II: Non-custodial sanctions and measures served in 2009 – Survey 2009* (PC-CP (2011) 4) (Strasbourg: Council of Europe).

Aungles, A. (1994) 'Three bedroomed prisons in the Asia Pacific region: home imprisonment and electronic surveillance in Australia, Hawaii, and Singapore', *Just Policy*, 2, pp. 32–37.

Bogard, W. (1996) *The Simulation of Surveillance: Hypercontrol in telematic societies* (Cambridge: Cambridge University Press).

Bonta, J., Wallace-Capretta, S. and Rooney, J. (2000a) 'Can electronic monitoring make a difference? An evaluation of three Canadian programs', *Crime & Delinquency*, 46, pp. 61–75.

Bonta, J., Wallace-Capretta, S. and Rooney, J. (2000b) 'A quasi-experimental evaluation of an intensive rehabilitation supervision program', *Criminal Justice and Behavior*, 27, pp. 312–329.

Bottoms, A. (1995). 'The philosophy and politics of punishment and sentencing', in C.M.V. Clarkson and R. Morgan (eds) *The Politics of Sentencing Reform* (Oxford: Clarendon Press), pp. 17–49.

Bottoms, A., Rex, S. and Robinson, G. (eds). (2004) *Alternatives to Prison: Options for an insecure society* (Collumpton: Willan).

Castells, M. (1996) *The Rise of the Network Society* (Oxford: Blackwell).

Christie, V. (1978) 'Prison in society, or society as a prison: a conceptual analysis', in J. Freeman (ed.) *Prisons Past and Future* (London: Heinemann), pp. 179–188.

Cohen, S. (1985) *Visions of Social Control: Crime, punishment and classification* (Cambridge: Polity Press).

Cohen, S. (1992) 'It's all right for you to talk: political and sociological manifestos for social work action', in Cohen, S. (ed.) *Against Criminology* (London: Transaction Publishers), pp. 95–113.

Corbett, R.P. and Marx, G.T. (1992) 'Emerging technofallacies in the electronic monitoring movement', in J.M. Byrne, A.J. Lurigio and J. Petersilia (eds) *Smart Sentencing: The emergence of intermediate sanctions* (London: Sage), pp. 85–100.

Daems, T. (2008) *Making Sense of Penal Change* (Oxford: Oxford University Press).

Deleuze, G. (1992) 'Postscript on the societies of control', *October*, 59, pp. 3–7.

Foucault, M. (1979) *Discipline and Punish: The birth of the prison* (New York: Vintage Books).

Feeley, M. and Simon, J. (1994) 'Actuarial justice: the emerging new criminal law', in D. Nelken (ed.) *The Futures of Criminology* (London: Sage), pp. 173–201.

Gable, R.K. and Gable, R.S. (2007) 'Increasing the effectiveness of electronic monitoring: perspectives', *Journal of the American Probation and Parole Association*, 31:1, pp. 24–29.

Halberstadt, R.L. and La Vigne, N.G. (2011) 'Evaluating the use of radio frequency identification device (RFID) technology to prevent and investigate sexual assaults in a correctional setting', *The Prison Journal*, 91:2, pp. 237–249.

Jones, R. (2000) 'Digital rule: punishment, control and technology', *Punishment and Society*, 2:1, pp. 5–22.

Jones, T. and Newburn, T. (2002) 'Policy convergence and crime control in the USA and the UK', *Criminology and Criminal Justice*, 2:2, pp. 173–203.

Jones, T. and Newburn, T. (2007) *Policy Transfer and Criminal Justice: Exploring US influence over British crime control policy* (Berkshire: Open University Press).

Kaluszynski, M. and Froment, J.-C. (2003) *Sécurité et Nouvelles Technologies. Évaluation comparée dans cinq pays européens (Belgique, Espagne, France, Grande-Bretagne, Suisse) des processus de recours au placement sous surveillance électronique* (Grenoble: CERAT-IEP).

Lianos, M. and Douglas, M. (2000) 'Dangerisation and the end of deviance: the institutional environment', in D. Garland and R. Sparks (eds) *Criminology and Social Theory* (Oxford: Oxford University Press), pp. 98–117.

Martinovic, M. (2010) *The Complexity of Punitiveness of Electronically Monitored Sanctions: The western world's analysis* (Saarbrucken: Lambert Academic Publishing).

Mayer, M., Haverkamp, R. and Lévy, R. (2003) *Will Electronic Monitoring Have a Future in Europe?* (Freiburg: Max-Planck-Institut).

Morris, N. and Tonry, M. (1990) *Between Prison and Probation: Intermediate punishments in a rational sentencing system* (New York: Oxford University Press).

Nelken, D. (2010) *Comparative Criminal Justice: Making sense of difference* (Los Angeles, CA: Sage).

Nellis, M. (2000) 'Law and order: the electronic monitoring of offenders', in D. Dolowicz (ed.) *Policy Transfer and British Social Policy: Learning from the US?* (Buckingham: Open University Press), pp. 103–126.

Nellis, M. (2012) 'Implant technology and the electronic monitoring of offenders: old and new questions about compliance, control and legitimacy', in A. Crawford and A. Hucklesby (eds) *Legitimacy and Compliance in Criminal Justice* (London: Routledge) (forthcoming).

Nellis, M. and Rossell, N.T. (2011) *Electronic Monitoring and Probation: Offender rehabilitation and the reduction of prison populations – Report on 7th European Electronic Monitoring Conference, 5–7 May, Évora, Portugal* (Utrecht: CEP).

Orwell, G. (1949). *Nineteen Eighty-Four: A novel* (London: Secker & Warburg).

Raine, J.W. and Willson, M.J. (1997) 'Beyond Managerialism in Criminal Justice', *The Howard Journal of Criminal Justice*, 36:1, pp. 80–95.

Renzema, M. and Mayo-Wilson, E. (2005) 'Can electronic monitoring reduce crime for moderate to high-risk offenders?', *Journal of Experimental Criminology*, 1:2, pp. 215–237.

Whitfield, D. (1997) *Tackling the Tag* (Winchester: Waterside Press).

Whitfield, D. (2001) *The Magic Bracelet* (Winchester: Waterside Press).

Zedner, L. (2002) 'Dangers of dystopias in penal theory', *Oxford Journal of Legal Studies*, 22:2, pp. 341–366.

Part I

National experiences

1   The limits of techno-utopianism

Electronic monitoring in the United States of America

J. Robert Lilly and Mike Nellis

Introduction

It is well known that electronic monitoring (EM) originated in the United States, but a definitive account of its emergence and developmental trajectory there has yet to be written, and there is no clear consensus as to what the theoretical and empirical parameters of such a narrative would be. There is a vast US literature on EM, either policy-based (published by or on behalf of the National Institute for Justice) or practice-based (published predominantly in *Federal Probation* and the *Journal of Offender Monitoring*). Such evaluative literature as there is leaves a lot to be desired, methodologically and substantively (see Renzema, this volume) and few academic commentators believe that EM's growth has been informed by significant evidence of its effectiveness. Only a rather small amount of critical literature has sought to understand the social and political context in which EM appeared, and even someone as attuned to the nuances of penal innovation as David Garland (2000) pays it little heed. Ball *et al.* (1988) did the foundation work on EM's criminological significance in the United States, but even they played down the technological changes which made EM possible, concentrating more on the way it had revived the 'ancient' penalty of house arrest. No single work has yet synthesized and expanded on this early critical literature, or embedded it in an adequate and up-to-date understanding of socio-technical developments. Corbett and Marx's (1992) much-cited article on 'emerging technofallacies in the electronic monitoring movement' signposted the way, but even Marx's (2007) own recent observations on 'the engineering of social control' have little specific to say on EM.

Corbett and Marx set the development of EM in the 1980s in the context of what Marx (1988) had already called 'the new surveillance' – in essence, technologically augmented forms of policing, the growth of drug testing and computerized databases – but this post-dated the era in which the proto-forms of EM actually originated (see also Le Mond and Fry 1975; Albanese 1984). Their 'ten technofallacies of electronic salvation' are important but they tend to give them each equal weighting, not to see that some are more central (and more fallacious) than others in explaining the seductive appeal of EM, and not to see the bigger cultural picture of which they are a part. In an effort to develop a more cultural understanding of

EM, we will argue that the discourse of those who have championed it has been infused with 'technological utopianism', a term used by historian Howard Segal (2005) to denote a distinctively US outlook on social progress, in which technology is considered indispensable to the creation of a convivial life and to the solution of pressing social and political problems. Although it has periodically been condensed into specific programmes for the advancement of 'technocracy', the mentality has deep roots in the creation of America itself, in the conviction of early settlers that technological ingenuity and prowess would be essential to turn a wilderness into a civilized nation. In the twentieth century that conviction grew to encompass the taming/transforming of human nature itself – the ability to modify man himself through education or conditioning – and became pervasive (Brooks 2005). A certain 'future mindedness' – an expectation of perpetual improvement in the American condition – is manifested in concentrated visible form in US science fiction and futurology, but to a greater or lesser degree it is also layered into everyday consciousness, and supported (not countered) by another pervasive American tradition, that of pragmatism, which supplies the 'can-do' attitude. This is not to deny that in a pluralistic society 'techno-utopian' projects are often contested, that they fare better in some cultural and institutional contexts than others, that the selfsame visions are easily (and often rightly) re-cast by opponents as dystopias, and that some visions have either made little headway or been stillborn – but, nonetheless, the allure of technological innovation has tended to inspire and energize initiatives in the United States which may never even have been experimented with elsewhere, at least until processes of 'policy transfer' carried them farther afield (Nellis 2000; Jones and Newburn 2007).

Explicit reference to 'technological utopianism' has been rare in accounts of penal change, although the reformative hopes invested in penitentiary architecture in the eighteenth and nineteenth centuries – note Bentham's (1787 [1995]) apt reference to 'a machine for grinding rogues honest' – and the more recent accounts of the development of the electric chair give inchoate expression to it (Moran 2002). Understanding the emergence of 'techno-corrections' in the late modern world, including EM, requires greater recognition of utopian impulses. The now somewhat distant era in which the prototypes of EM first rose and fell was infused by vigorous and confident public debate about the potential of science and technology to transform American society (Harrington 1965; Toffler 1970; Crowe 1972; Corn and Horrigan 1984), the space programme being its most public manifestation. In essence, we will argue, the forerunners of what came to be called EM were born in a moment when techno-utopian tropes were particularly powerful, and gained initial credence because of them.

The origins of EM for offenders

The origins of what we call 'electronic monitoring' are nowadays routinely mentioned in the literature, but in a strangely truncated way. Harvard behavioural psychologist Ralph K. Schwitzgebel (aided by his brother, Robert) tested portable but unwieldy (and short-range) tracking devices (which permitted bi-directional communication) on students, psychiatric patents and offenders in Cambridge and Boston between 1964 and 1970. The devices contained equipment adapted from a guided missile system which enabled 'the experimenter unobtrusively to record the location of the [delinquent]' and ascertain where he 'spends his time' (Schwitzgebel 1963:13). The technology was patented and the results published in authoritative legal and scientific journals (Schwitzgebel *et al.* 1964; Schwitzgebel 1964, 1966, 1968, 1969, 1970, 1971; Schwitzgebel and Bird 1970; Schwitzgebel and Schwitzgebel 1973). What is less often remarked upon is the milieu in which this work took place, and the fact that there were other researchers involved in the same area of work, whose ideas have largely been written out of the narrative by critics and champions alike. The 1960s research milieu in which the Schwitzgebels operated was dominated by the behavioural psychology of B.F. Skinner and a widespread sense among many academic social scientists that his elaboration of 'operant conditioning' could have a transformative impact in education and crime control, perhaps approximating the utopia that Skinner (1948) had envisioned in a novel before his career as a psychologist began. Skinner was a great inventor of gadgets to aid 'operant conditioning' and the Schwitzgebels described their area of work as 'psychotechnology', an intellectual niche which brought together behavioural psychologists and early pioneers of neuroscience, including Jose Delgado (1969), whose experiments with 'electrical stimulation of the brain' (ESB) sought to reduce men's violent impulses. Both 'psychotechnology' and Delgado's dream of a 'psychocivilised society' were strikingly techno-utopian projects, although had it been known at the time how much of it was funded by the US military it may have been seen in more sinister terms (Schrag 1978; Moran 1978).

Mathematician and computer scientist Joseph Meyer (1971) was not formally connected to the psychotechnology movement, but was attuned to the zeitgeist. Depressed by the scale of America's crime problem, and by the apparent failings of all existing responses, Meyer proposed a 'transponder surveillance system' using a nation-wide network of computer-linked transceivers, high on the walls of buildings (inside and outside) in every neighbourhood in the land. These would pick up in real time a unique radio-frequency (RF) identifier signal from unremovable 'transponders' attached to the wrists of some 25 million convicted criminals (usually released from prison) in the United States. Curfew and territorial restrictions could be programmed into the system, tailored to individual offenders, and some transceivers would cause any nearby transponder to sound an alarm, warning the wearer to keep away and (probably) alert the authorities regarding them. Criminologists Ingraham and Smith (1972) did have connections with psychotechnology, and went further. They proposed the remote monitoring of both an offender's location and physiology – heart, pulse and brainwaves – and a capacity (possibly automated) to remotely zap their brains (via implanted 'stimoceivers') if the signals received back at the monitoring centre 'suggested' they were contemplating or committing an offence. More so than Meyer's, and in the context of a growing backlash against behaviourism, this proposal helped to create the sense that psychotechnology was finally going too far.

The Schwitzgebels had themselves once entertained the idea of subjecting substance-using offenders to 'a small portable shock apparatus with electrodes attached to the wrist' (Schwitzgebel, undated, quoted in Mitford 1974: 226) but still formally conceived of their work in rehabilitative terms. They hoped that by monitoring the movements of offenders and praising them for sticking to agreed zones and schedules they would be able to supply the 'positive reinforcement' that Skinnerians considered essential to – and superior to punishment in – effecting individual behavioural change. They wanted their particular technology to have a practical application but were less convinced that ESB could be taken out of the laboratory and applied in the real world.

Despite their different perspectives, Schwitzgebel, Meyer and Ingraham and Smith were all toying with forms of *tracking* – the monitoring of mobile subjects – rather than ways of restricting offenders to a single location. Augmenting house arrest was not what they had in mind. The possibility of being able to pinpoint an individual in a crowded city or a small town seemed at the time like a particularly spectacular and commanding application of science and technology, a significant advance in crime control. But none of the technologies were adopted by criminal justice agencies, or subject to further research and development, nor did they find commercial sponsors. What happened? Stephen Mainprize's (1996) contention in respect of the Schwitzgebels' technology is that their emphasis on it as a form of rehabilitation clashed with a shift in penal sensibility towards punishment and control, although the President's Commission on Law Enforcement and the Administration of Justice (1967) had in fact given a considerable boost to 'community corrections'. What brought the proto-forms of EM, and the edifice of 'psychotechnology' to a somewhat abrupt end was the burgeoning backlash against the illiberal implications of behaviourism (as expressed by Skinner (1971)), the ascendancy of the personalist and libertarian values of the counterculture and the exposure and critique of military funding of university research. The Schwitzgebels' own work may have been relatively innocuous in comparison to some of what was going on, but their ideas were undoubtedly tainted by events. Most rehabilitation and community corrections professionals could not reconcile surveillance with humanistic social work practices, and were increasingly confident that probation and parole services could be improved, and imprisonment reduced, without recourse to technology (Morris 1974).

There was no governmental or professional attempt to revive interest in the work of the Schwitzgebels, Meyer or Ingraham and Smith, and EM as we came to know it arrived almost surreptitiously. In 1977, Judge Jack Love, a district judge in Albuquerque, became interested in ways of facilitating temporary release for young adult offenders from the local penitentiary. Love realized that public confidence required knowing where people were outside the prison. To this end, he randomly collected information on location monitoring: swipe-card systems used in supermarkets, animal and cargo tracking technologies and – famously – a copy of a Spiderman comic strip syndicated in a local newspaper, in which a villain fits a (potentially explosive) tracking device to Spiderman's wrist, enabling him to offend with impunity because he could now stay one step ahead of the superhero. Love sought unsuccessfully to interest the New Mexico Department of Corrections in the idea of location monitoring released prisoners. He pursued the idea independently after a riot in the penitentiary in 1980 revealed how brutal conditions were. He asked a computer salesman, Michael Goss, if such a device were possible. Goss checked the Schwitzgebel patents and realized that with the smaller electronic components now available, something approximating it could be built – not, as yet, a tracking device, but a device which monitored a person's proximity to a base station, relaying any violations via telephone to a control centre. Love liked the 'Gosslink', and in March 1983 used his discretion within his own local court to subject a probation violator to it – the first of five, before his judicial superiors forbade further use of it (Timko 1986; Renzema 1992; Love 2005).

Love deserves credit for originating the modern form of EM in the United States (and therefore the world): he stimulated the development of an operational version of it, and made the first practical use of it. Nonetheless, by the early 1980s, other states – and small commercial organizations – developed and implemented variants of the technology. Florida had established a state-wide 'community control programme' (using house arrest in a punitive manner, initially without EM) in early 1983; the West Palm Beach jurisdiction adopted EM shortly afterwards; and in December 1983 Judge Allison deFoor sentenced a repeat unlicensed driver to it (Renzema 1992). A small project in Kenton County, Kentucky became the first Department of Corrections-funded, probation-run EM scheme in the United States in 1984. Because both of these schemes (unlike Judge Love's) were subject to a preliminary evaluation (Lilly *et al.* 1987, 1993; Lilly and Ball 1990, 1992) and widely publicized in professional literature they became the starting points for the expansion of EM house arrest. Florida – a traditionally conservative, law-and-order state – in particular became and has remained a major user and innovator of EM technology: the cultural, commercial and political reasons for this warrant study in their own right.

Probation, home confinement and EM

Organizationally, EM developed largely in the context of probation services, although sometimes they were administered by sheriff's or police departments, using equipment bought or loaned from private vendors. Probation in the United States is mostly administered at the state level, with the rest split between state and county, or run by counties. From the 1970s onwards, under the rubric of 'community corrections', its primary emphasis on rehabilitation became entwined with reducing prison use and offering greater public protection. House arrest (also called home confinement, home detention or home incarceration) was an early 'community corrections' innovation – the first scheme was in St. Louis in 1971 – and was initially envisaged as a means of sparing juveniles the pains and stigma of imprisonment. Rising numbers of adult prisoners, the consequent rise in overcrowding and the sheer cost of incarceration soon prompted its extension to adults (Ball and Lilly 1986; Renzema 1992). Local volunteers were initially used to check up on home-confined offenders (by home visits or by phone), partly to take pressure off of overstretched probation and parole officers, partly because of their relative cheapness, but also, crucially, to act on behalf of the local community and thereby ease the social reintegration of the offender (Ball and Lilly 1988). In practice, volunteer use never became extensive, and within a decade house arrest was being perceived as an impractical, unenforceable sanction. The somewhat fortuitous advent of EM, however, offered a novel, alternative means of checking on offenders and, in essence, supplied 'the missing component that makes [house arrest] effective' (Goss 1989: 106).

EM did not, however, develop *merely* as a technical means of making house arrest viable; it became a key part of the burgeoning intensive probation (and parole) movement (Morris and Tonry 1990). This was eventually to be characterized as a shift from 'community corrections' to 'intermediate sanctions', which aimed simultaneously at reducing offending, reducing prison overcrowding and reducing prison costs. It required probation services to become part of control systems which openly supported surveillance and punishment (retribution, deterrence and incapacitation), and in doing so to transform themselves. Discursively, at least, it was possible for interested politicians to present EM as a surveillant and confining measure – turning the home into 'jailspace' – that was significantly more controlling than therapeutic forms of probation. Although EM appealed to some fiscal conservatives among Republicans as a money-saving measure, it arguably appealed more to Democrats for whom its very ambiguity as a simultaneously 'inclusive' (leave in the community) and 'exclusive' (confine to home) penalty was a pragmatic way of remaining liberal – reducing imprisonment, but still 'getting tough' and exerting control. To that end all politicians were prone to rhetorically exaggerating EM's punitive characteristics. The difficulty for conservatives was that even when EM appealed on fiscal grounds it was never sufficiently incapacitative to replicate the total exclusion that imprisonment always promised.

There was never a standard model of EM use in 'community corrections' or in 'intermediate sanctions'. EM home confinement was in principle a 24-hour restriction, but from the start offenders were typically given permission 'to leave for work, school, religious, medical or treatment-related reasons' or to shop (Meyer 2004: 103–104) Some spent 50 hours per week undertaking community service or doing treatment (Renzema 1992). Different programmes used slightly different technologies to remotely monitor presence at home, including biometric voice verification, which required a 'client to verbally repeat a random sentence that is compared to a voice sample stored in the central computer or to perform some task in front of a camera such as holding up a certain number of fingers' (Meyer 2004: 105). The Dallas County Adult Probation Department installed Luna Video Phone Systems in designated offenders' homes and in the course of random phone calls asked 'the probationer to send a photo through the Luna System to verify his/her presence' (Enos *et al.* 1992: 90). Some programmes forbade or limited visitors to the offender's home (Rackmill 1994).

Some banned the consumption of alcohol, using monitoring devices (breathalysers with cameras) to enforce this. Some used drive-by monitoring to supplement the monitoring centre by using hand-held devices pointed at the offender's home (or workplace, or at bars from which he had been forbidden to enter). Some deliberately heightened punitive elements, tending 'to use bulkier devices that are harder to conceal and [to] make calls to offenders, sometimes at annoying times' (Meyer 2004: 116).

The intermediate sanctions movement created a milieu which, largely for the first time in community corrections, gave commercial organizations an incentive to enter territory traditionally occupied by statutory and voluntary (not-for-profit) organizations:

> Electronic monitoring equipment has been developed by private entrepreneurs and aggressively marketed as a solution to prison and jail overcrowding. Vendors extolling the virtues of this equipment present a case that is very attractive; the systems are foolproof, safe, punitive, cheap and can reduce institutional crowding. Such a sales pitch presented to potential clients desperate for viable alternatives is almost certain to generate sales.
>
> (Maxfield and Baumer 1990: 522)

The role of commercial organizations – and the profit motive – was important in the advancement of EM in the United States and it is in their brochures, adverts and sales talk that an incipient techno-utopianism is most often to be found. With varying degrees of visual and verbal imaginativeness, they encourage traditional correctional agencies to become 'modern', the hallmark of modernity being use of smart technology. 'Leap into the Future' invites Shadowtrack, for example, extolling the virtues of a voice verification system (advertisement, *Journal of Offender Monitoring*, 19:1, 2006: 10). Initially, as if this would appeal to correctional personnel in its own right, more emphasis was placed on the impressive technical specifications of the equipment than on the ways it could actually help with the supervision of offenders. As time passed, the companies became more adept at articulating the latter. Many small, local companies were involved in EM to begin with; as the technology took off they came to be absorbed in what Lilly and Knepper (1992, 1993) and Lilly and Deflem (1996) subsequently called 'the commercial corrections complex', an amorphous, endlessly recomposing ensemble of profit-driven organizations contracted to provide services (initially private prisons) at various levels of state administration. Early evaluators of EM were painfully aware that it had often been oversold, that many pilot schemes were poorly thought-out and that the monitoring devices and systems were of poor quality. One dubbed EM 'equipment in search of a programme' (Schmidt 1991: 52), a phrase that resonates still. Papy and Nimer (1991) warned against overselling EM lest it create unrealistic expectations of efficient crime control and public protection – although Nimer subsequently went to work for an EM company.

Even with commercial impetus, EM never had a transformative impact on the practice of community corrections. It grew slowly and haphazardly, largely at the discretion of particular local agencies, despite the clear signal of federal government support in 1986, when the Bureau of Prisons, the Probation Service of the US Courts and the Parole Commission initiated an early release from prison scheme using EM. In the same period, 'the National Institute of Justice [also] provided publicity for this new technology [and] increased its funding of home incarceration and electronic monitoring projects' (Lilly and Ball 1990: 78). This never resulted in large numbers, or proportions, of offenders being placed on EM. In the period 1980–1990 the number of offenders under community supervision in the United States increased by 126 per cent, to have 2.5 million people under EM at any one time (Durham 1994: 180). Nationally, there were 17 offenders per day on EM house arrest in 1985, 95 in 1986 and 826 in 1987, a 900 per cent increase, in 21 states, largely the result of the federal government's early release initiative. Daily numbers increased to 2,277 in 1988 (in 33 states) and 6,400 in 1989, remaining at this level until 1996 when it rose again to 7,480, then to 10,827 in 1998 (Meyer 2004: 99). As Harris and Byrne (2007) point out, this is less than 1 per cent of all offenders on probation in the United States at the time, and only 1.4 per cent of those on parole. They decry the absence of more recent data on the national extent of EM use. At the end of its first decade, if one extrapolates from a daily to an annual figure – on the (admittedly arbitrary) assumption that an average period of EM supervision was two months – there were still under 100,000 offenders per year on EM in the United States. The majority, unsurprisingly, were men: in 1988, the year EM took off, only 13 per cent of those being monitored were women.

Expansion was accompanied by a shift in the target populations for EM, and the waning of hopes that intermediate sanctions would enable a significant reduction in the prison population. The initial EM target group of probationers gave way to a greater focus on parolees and pre-trial defendants. As the political climate became more punitive, it became marginally easier to argue for the slightly earlier-than-otherwise release of those already imprisoned than it was to argue against the use of a prison sentence in the first place (and also that the technically innocent should as far as possible not be confined before trial) (Renzema 1989). Expansion also entailed a shift from less serious offences (shoplifting, minor assaults) – which in many jurisdictions would never have attracted a custodial sentence – to more serious ones, including sexual and violent offences (including domestic violence), whose risk level had been deemed sufficiently low to warrant early release from prison. Despite the growing crisis of incarceration, neither local probation services nor their national professional associations were clamouring to use EM (although there were individuals who were intrigued from the start). Harris *et al.* (1989) acknowledged a shift towards more controlling attitudes among probation and parole officers, but only a small proportion of them actively bought into EM. It did not figure in McAnany *et al.*'s (1984) ruminations on the future of probation, and John Conrad (1984) specifically argued against loading surveillance functions (of this kind) into probation. In the Wisconsin Community Structured Supervision Programme (CSSP) run by the Milwaukee Probation Service, Walter Dickey (1990) found EM to be onerous and counterproductive:

> Though the original concept of the [CSSP] was for heavy reliance on electronic monitoring, this seemed to be not only unnecessary, but also destructive when used. It was 'too much' for the clients, when less was desired. Its use resulted in many minor violations that could not go unnoticed but which deflected attention from more important matters and brought 'failure' when 'success' was what clients needed. The unit did not use electronic monitoring except in unusual situations after the [probation staff] realised its effects.
>
> (Dickey 1990: 61–62)

Local politicians, however, were often easily drawn to a 'technical fix' which could so easily be presented to electorates as more punitive than mere probation, and in the long run probation services had to accommodate it. As even Dickey acknowledged, 'sheer pressure of numbers' on probation caseloads 'create[d] enormous pressure to have a repressive system. Human engagement, understanding and compassion [became] less valued and receive[d] less attention' (Dickey 1990: 6). Throughout the 1990s, more probation and parole officers began to concede that EM was indeed a potentially useful tool if it was used in conjunction with other forms of supervision. Some genuinely felt this, others were merely being pragmatic, fearing either that EM would be more of a threat if it developed apart from a probation ethos, or that commercial EM organizations would supplant probation services as providers of community supervision. Some academics began to defend it in similar terms, and to conjure dystopian penal visions *if EM was not embedded in humanistic forms of rehabilitation* (which had an analogue in American prison-of-the-future movies – Nellis 2006). Enos *et al.* (1992: 151), for example, feared that EM on its own could be the precursor of measures whose 'ultimate extreme [would be] the implanting of various electronic devices in the offender's body or brain', a notion which, as we have seen, had indeed figured in the pre-history of EM but had thus far never surfaced in practice. In the context of rising prison numbers, Enos and colleagues argued that probation had an obligation to become more controlling and to risk incorporating EM into its practice:

> The destructive capacity of incarceration and institutionalization *far outweigh the dangers and risks of electronic monitoring.* . . . [By enabling more and more serious offenders to receive treatment in the community] electronic monitoring may provide an opportunity to break the dangerous and destructive psychopathological socialisation patterns fostered within prison systems. In short, there is every possibility that an Orwellian world may be embodied in electronic monitoring, but there is a darker world of the jail and the prison system that may far outweigh that contingency.
>
> (Enos *et al.* 1992: 163; emphasis added)

By discursively representing EM as a 'more tightly controlled version of *traditional forms*' of probation, rather than as something extraneous and alien to probation, Enos and colleagues sought to facilitate its assimilate into probation. The obvious danger was that 'the time and equipment costs of EM are likely to mean the sacrifice of other possible [probation] programmes' (Enos *et al.* 1992: 55). Nonetheless, they welcomed the opportunity that EM afforded to re-appraise best practice in the supervision of offenders, and in the spirit of intermediate sanctions, argued that EM might genuinely enhance the quality of supervision. They saw the traditional polarization of counselling and surveillance as a 'false dichotomy' and that the automated aspects of EM actually 'free[d] the probation officer to concentrate his or her efforts in a counselling framework' (Enos *et al.* 1992: 159). For some dissenting probation academics this was still a compromise too far. To Todd Clear (1994: 109), for example, EM exemplified a move towards punishment and control, to which, in his view, probation should never reconcile itself. He claimed that

> the attractiveness of electronic monitoring and other new community programmes is tied up in imagery of nastiness, to the point that several programmes promote themselves on their records that some prisoners would rather be in prison than in the community alternative programme.

EM was still not widespread at the end of the 1990s, and Enos *et al.* (1999: iii) were perhaps exaggerating when they stated that it had 'become a standard tool in the probation and parole officer's arsenal of supervision technology'.

Ironically, the 'substantial public opposition to the use of home confinement' (Durham 1994: 185) that did arise came from the opposite end of the political spectrum to Clear. To the right, EM was simply not a very punitive measure. Nationally and locally, the influential pressure group Mothers Against Drink Drivers (MADD) never accepted EM house arrest as a penalty for driving under the influence (DUI), claiming that it was both inadequate as censure and that, compared to the fully segregative penalty of imprisonment, it still left neighbourhoods vulnerable to re-offending. Many politicians also accepted that EM was a lenient sentence: in 1992 in New Jersey, state senator Louis Kosko sought to restrict EM use after two incidents in which monitored offenders were involved in violent crime, one with lethal results (Durham 1994: 195). Nonetheless, as the 1990s progressed, and the escalating costs of mass incarceration began to affect state budgets, politicians and professionals alike were forced to become more positive about EM, whether they liked it or not. It could be made to sound onerous and it appealed to America's latent sense of technological possibility. In the foreword to the second edition of Enos' book, Congressman James Traficant said:

> Electronic monitoring could and should be a method that could make alternative sentencing programs feasible.... While [it] does not represent a magical solution to America's crime problems, it should and must be

actively examined as an integral part of this nation's long term strategy to deal with problems of crime and prison overcrowding.

(Quoted in Enos *et al.* 1999: ii)

Traficant's tone almost implied taking an experimental approach to EM, which was somewhat ironic given that it had already existed for 17 years and that it had always held out the promise of making 'alternative sentencing programs feasible'. Notwithstanding local evaluations which were helpful to the programmes which undertook them, no large-scale, comprehensive evaluative research had been done on EM to assess its effect on recidivism or the forms of its use which actually did reduce imprisonment. The very diversity of EM-based programmes, stand-alone and in conjunction with other combinations of elements, for variable periods of time, has made it impossible to isolate a single 'EM effect', implying that among policy-makers it has been the image and symbolic association of the technology – alongside notionally reduced savings on imprisonment – rather than hard evidence which has underpinned its persistence. Randy Gainey and Brian Payne (2000) undertook a considerable amount of qualitative research into offender experiences of EM, finding in the main that they did consider it onerous but preferred it to prison, although some preferred prison because, like other community penalties, it made fewer demands on them.

Despite the small proportion of offenders subject to EM home confinement, once the technology was introduced it was always expected to expand, and was frequently commented on as if it represented the inexorable future of community corrections. Such is the American way: technology always evolves. Writing at the start of the 1990s, Sullivan warned that 'we are seeing only the beginning of the use of new technologies for total surveillance and punishment', and that 'the dominant trend is certainly toward a stricter punitive control apparatus that heavily emphasises incarceration or technological surveillance over the more traditional Progressive methods of fines, probation and parole' (1990: 136). Lilly and Ball (1990: 86) agreed, fearing that EM foreshadowed 'deep and very insidious trends toward *total social discipline* and the complete suppression of individuality under the guise of humanitarianism and progress'. The tendency among critical penal reformers has always been to see Marx's 'new surveillance' and 'America's prison binge' as going hand in hand, as different but complementary expressions of the same political/punitive impulse, rather than approaches which – in practice – were possibly contradictory, or at least in tension with each other – or that each might impose checks and constraints on the other. Surveillant penalties never in fact became dominant or hegemonic, but the tendency to speak of them as if they *still might become so* has endured. A decade after Sullivan and Ball and Lilly had written, Blomberg and Lucken (2000: 224) continued to anticipate that 'the major difference in penology today and in the future will be the increasing role of technology in offender supervision and control'. The constant upgrading that had taken place by then in respect of RF EM, and the advent of GPS tracking, lent greater credence to their prediction, but still begged the question of why EM had not expanded more than it had.

The advent of GPS tracking

As noted earlier, EM was imagined as a form of monitoring mobility *before* it was conceived of as a means of enforcing house arrest. The prospect of this step change in the very nature of community supervision may have been a part of its initial utopian appeal. The fact that the first generation of technology turned out to be somewhat more mundane than 'tracking' – locating offenders in one place rather than monitoring their movements – came to be glossed in terms of the 'technical incapacity' that prevailed at the time, although, as we showed, there had also been a strongly ethical reaction against the perceived excesses of surveillance and behaviour modification. This tends to be written out of the histories of EM. It is true that in the 1980s there was no national communication infrastructure available to make terrestrial tracking viable, but whether this was the sole reason requires further investigation. In the event, it was America's military-owned GPS satellites that became the basis of offender tracking systems, in conjunction with the terrestrial (mobile phone) systems that had once been envisaged as their mainstay. GPS satellites had been available for non-military use since the late 1970s, but interestingly no-one seems to have imagined using them in a correctional context. Even the futurological article by Colorado probation officer Max Winkler (1991), who proposed the idea of electronic 'walking prisons', which does appear to have played a part in the actual advent of tracking, was not premised on the use of GPS. Like Joseph Meyer in the 1970s, Winkler thought in terms of terrestrial tracking systems – a nationwide mobile phone system was finally coming on stream – but more worryingly he also echoed Ingraham and Smith by seriously proposing that a remote 'zapping' capacity be incorporated into the tracking technology.

Several US electronics companies were in fact pursuing the basic idea of personalized tracking at the same time as Winkler's article appeared, and when Winkler was taken up by Dr Joseph Hoshen of Lucent Technologies (publishing in a sister journal to the one used by Meyer a quarter-century before) the 'zapping' idea was dropped (Hoshen *et al.* 1995; Hoshen and Drake 2001). Hoshen was awarded the first patent for tracking technology in 1995, but commercial competition was coming from Westinghouse (funded by the National Institute for Justice in 1994) and Motorola, plus the Canadian company Strategic Technologies Inc. (Blakeway 1995). In addition, the New Mexico Corrections Department (which had once been very sceptical of Jack Love's initiative) had asked Sandia National Laboratories in California to explore real-time tracking technologies, and Sandia and Spectrum Industries came close to marketing a device. It was, however, a Florida company, ProTech, which decisively tilted offender tracking technologies towards GPS-based systems and quickly became the leader in the field (Drake n.d.).

By the time satellite tracking was introduced for offenders, GPS-based geolocation was already in widespread civilian use for car rental, bus and taxi fleet management, journey planning, mobile phone location and wildlife management, and by dint of being commonplace if unobtrusive it may have shed some of the fearful Orwellian resonances that personalized location monitoring might once have had. Tracking's obvious advantage over EM house arrest was its ability to monitor movement in general and to monitor the perimeters of designated exclusion zones (around former victim's homes, or areas where the subject had routinely offended), but it too could restrict offenders to a single place (inclusion zones) or combine with traditional forms of EM to accomplish this. In both its active (real time), passive (retrospective) and hybrid (mixture of both) forms it was presented – and seen – as a more total form of control, and higher-risk sex offenders were seen as core targets from the outset, usually after a period of imprisonment. Tracking was never fully restricted to high-risk offenders any more than conventional EM had been, although cost considerations – it was initially four times more the daily cost of conventional EM – usually suggested more parsimonious use of it. By 2001 it was being used in a number of states on small batches of offenders (often fewer than 30), and the professionals were still testing the quality of the equipment (Johnson 2002). Florida began using it in conjunction with 'CrimeTrax' software, which enabled corrections and law enforcement computer systems to coordinate offender movements to each day's new crime scenes, either to incriminate or exonerate them. Florida has generated some of the larger evaluative studies of EM (Sipes 2009; Padgett *et al.* 2006; Bales *et al.* 2010). The Padgett *et al.* study of 'community control' was and remains the largest cohort study of EM in the United States, and while it blurred differences between EM house arrest and tracking, and ignored the possible influence of probation on the offenders being studied, it showed fairly convincingly that there was a crime suppression effect on offenders while they were actually on EM, if not necessarily afterwards. They then inappropriately extrapolated this to support the idea of lifetime GPS tracking for released sex offenders, for which a number of states had legislated. It does not actually follow that a measure which offenders find bearable for 6–12 months remains bearable – or ethically defensible – for life. Despite the commonsense assumption that it is always advantageous to know where high-risk sex offenders are, Button *et al.* (2009) recently questioned the blanket (as opposed to individualized) use of GPS tracking on them because is fails to take account of sex offenders' known patterns of recidivism.

Pertinently – and in a confidently techno-utopian spirit – Dennis Doffing (2009: 12) (a senior manager in Satellite Tracking of People (STOP)) has asked 'Is there a future for RF in a GPS world?' Despite a clear sense that in technical terms RF systems have been stagnating in recent years, reaching the limits of efficiency, and despite the putative advantages of GPS, his answer is complicated and takes account of institutional realities which are often overlooked in accounts of penal innovation. Probation services remain heavily invested in RF systems, which they purchased, which their staff are familiar with and which can still be maintained and renewed by service companies. GPS tracking systems – which are usually leased to correctional agencies, rather than sold – remain more expensive, and although the price is falling, that alone is an obstacle to adoption. Only as old RF systems decay and as a new younger generation of correctional officials emerges, in no way in thrall to the technologies of the past, will GPS increase its market share. Whether it will come to dominate the EM scene remains moot. Doffing thinks it will. Marc Renzema (2009: 11), on the other hand, has voiced the possibility of a different future, one in which individuated EM packages of the kind which exist now become obsolete, 'an item of only historic interest, as we morph into an "on camera 24/7" society, with visual monitoring, GPS location and communication recording integrated with massive databases that track offenders and non-offenders'. Notwithstanding the still low numbers of people on GPS (and, relatively speaking, on EM generally), this decisively returns us, as debates on the future of EM invariably do, to the pervasive techno-utopian/dystopian discourses which invariably frame them. In the post-9/11 age, and all that that has entailed in terms of surveillance, however, there are good reasons for doing so.

EM and the expansion of surveillance in post-9/11 America

Gary Marx (2007) has rightly encouraged examination of EM in the context of a broad swathe of techno-corrections, as well as in relation to the widespread surveillance practices that affect law-abiding citizens as much if not more than offenders. Useful lines of research could indeed be pursued here, which connect to the tropes of techno-utopianism explored in this chapter, and require a sophisticated understanding of recent US politics. The ascendancy of the neoconservatives in the United States undoubtedly boosted the principle and practice of surveillance as a general strategy for securing social and political order. In the view of historian Richard Drayton (2005: 3), the Project for the New American Century 'was a monster borne upon the high tide of techno-euphoria of the 1990s'. New developments in both weapons *and* surveillance technology were to be harnessed to give the United States 'full spectrum dominance' in military and political conflicts around the globe. Mastery was, in significant part, to be achieved from space, using satellites whose data would feed into a 'global information grid' and give what one American general unabashedly called a 'God's Eye' view of the earth, and of the electronic chatter-channels which traverse it. More recently this same impulse has generated the development of surveillance drones the size of tiny bugs which have local policing as well as worldwide military implications (Bumiller and Shanker 2011).

The events of 9/11 provided a pretext for implementing the Project for the New American Century that the neoconservatives might not otherwise have had, but the foundations of it preceded the terrorist attack. In respect of the perceived terrorist threat to the security of American interests worldwide, the Pentagon's Information Awareness Office (IAO) promised 'total information awareness', a hitherto unprecedented expression of techno-utopianism, and a development which, like B.F. Skinner's aspirations for behaviourism 30 years previously, triggered a backlash against itself. But although the IAO was closed as a result of Congressional pressure, the ethos lived on in other agencies. Workplace surveillance increased. Public CCTV schemes multiplied. The retrospective discovery (in Autumn 2005) that in 2002 President Bush had covertly ordered the National Security Agency to conduct email and telephone surveillance of selected US citizens (ostensible allies as well as potential enemies) without court warrant was indicative of how important surveillance-in-practice was from the very outset of the 'war on terror'. Neoconservative developments affected the use of EM in three ways. First, it created a 'cultural mood' in which the concept of surveillance in general became (even more) intellectually and emotionally appealing as a means of dealing with threats to social order; the corollary of this, even in a local criminal justice context, was that anyone arguing against surveillance practices did so 'against the grain', from a weakened position. Second, and related to the above, neoconservative discourse blurred (to a degree) the distinction between 'terrorist' and 'ordinary criminal' as threats to social order, and weakened still further the already precarious claims of humanistic (constructive and supportive) interventions with ordinary criminals, implicitly displacing or subordinating them in favour of ostensibly more controlling ones like EM. Third, politico-military demand for increased surveillance capacity boosted technological innovation in this area, which inevitably – given the pre-existing linkages between military and criminal justice institutions, and the commercial technology vendors who service both sectors – created new surveillance options for correctional and law enforcement agencies. 'Bilateral EM' was piloted in respect of domestic violence, to keep victims and offenders apart (Erez *et al.* 2004). GPS tracking of offenders had some momentum of its own before 9/11: after, it had more. The possibility of implanting RFID chips to facilitate personal identification of offenders was canvassed in the immediate aftermath of 9/11 in a classically techno-utopian manner which both ignored the potential health risks of implants, mobilized resistance to 'biotech' innovations that would otherwise have remained dormant and underestimated the continuing versatility of wearable monitoring technology (Nellis 2012). RF-based inmate tracking systems began to be used inside prisons, which, while never widespread, might conceivably be said to symbolize the co-option of EM by an institution to which, despite the best of intentions, it has never really managed to become an alternative (Halberstadt and La Vigne 2011).

Conclusions

For all that it was born in the United States, EM has not wrought major changes in US penal policies. Its growth and development cannot be understood without reference to distinctively American techno-utopian impulses which stimulate continuous innovation in many areas of the nation's life, although in this specifically penal context these impulses have been held in check by a deeper and more pervasive commitment to mass incarceration. Far from being the transformative technology that its early champions claimed it would be, it came over time, and with experience, to be perceived as just another intermediate sanction, neither more nor less useful than any of the others. In their comprehensive account of 'hyperincarceration' in the United States, Cavadino and Dignan (2006) do not even mention EM, not even the fragile new hope that it once seemed to represent, and in retrospect, its potential for slowing or reversing the momentum of incarceration there was never great (although it may have had more traction in this respect elsewhere). In a recent US textbook, *Rethinking Corrections*, there is a single 12-line entry on EM which concludes dismissively with the comment: 'As was found with ISP [intensive supervision], EM was not effective in reducing later criminal activities of probationers' (Mackenzie 2011: 114). This statement – so narrowly technical in its judgement of EM – begs many questions about the ways and context in which EM was actually used, and the better alternatives that might possibly have been constructed with it in a different penal climate, with different political dynamics (Roberts 2004: Gable and Gable 2005, 2007). There was never, in fact, any reason to think that EM by itself might have affected offenders' *longer-term* (post-EM) behaviour, but there was a slender hope of a crime suppressive effect over the duration of an order, and anticipation that this could have been harnessed in intensive probation programmes which might then, incrementally, have made a difference to incarceration or recidivism rates, or even both.

None of this is to say that EM has been without significance over the past 30 years, or to rule out it having vastly greater significance in a high-tech penal future, although the signs of the US penal system becoming predominantly 'panoptic' or 'telematic' are not auspicious (Bogard 1996). EM undoubtedly does represent a new penal modality, customized from the all-pervasive networks of information and communication technology, which is different in kind both from imprisonment and from other intermediate sanctions. In both its RF and GPS forms it constitutes a surveillance-based intervention unlike other forms of community supervision, which requires offenders to orient their routines and schedules to the (court or prison ordered) demands of remote, unseen officials. Without wishing to exaggerate the relational elements in traditional forms of community supervision – large probation caseloads inhibit the formation of relationships – it can safely be said that EM is intrinsically less relational than them, and that it introduces a novel element of 'the virtual' into supervision, while by no means dispensing with material constraints and consequences. Numerous pieces of research have shown that it is a qualitatively different experience of punishment from community service or probation, and the experiences of the many thousands of offenders who have now experienced it cannot be discounted or minimized. EM may have been harnessed to some dismally traditional purposes – retribution and deterrence – but it is simultaneously a distinctive penal innovation which only became possible because of the affordances of a new global communication architecture, in whose creation the United States had itself been at the fore.

And yet, even in a country with an engrained susceptibility to technical fixes, EM has made far less headway than its champions expected, and while a general explanation of why it failed to develop on a larger scale is easily sketched, it would still be useful to ascertain why and how it grew in some US states and counties more than others. The perception of it as an inherently punitive measure is misleading. EM is, in fact, best characterized as a managerial form of control, whose affinities lie far more with 'actuarial justice' than with populist punitivism, and whose fortunes have reflected the tensions between those two penal movements (Feeley and Simon 1994). Ball and Lilly (1988: 162) had presciently sensed this: 'We suspect that the electronic devices evoke an almost totemic imagery of considerable symbolic force', they wrote, 'with elemental connotations of order, efficiency and control.' The pursuit of managed order and efficiency is common to both techno-utopianism and actuarialism, and while having both popular and political appeal (often on fiscal grounds) it never manages to match or challenge the more visceral and reassuring appeal of punishment and sequestration, or to symbolize the even more potent tendency to 'degrade' that Whitman (2003) discerns in US penal practice. Arguably, the failure of EM to become more influential has reflected the larger failure of 'actuarial justice' to fully resist the recalcitrant populist punitivism which has underpinned mass incarceration, and even, in both cases, to be drawn into its service. EM was repeatedly claimed by its champions to mimic harsh forms of punishment: it was sometimes discursively likened to incapacitation, or deliberately rendered stigmatizing by unnecessarily large ankle bracelets. But, quite simply, it never really registered as properly punitive with public opinion, and in popular culture – movies, TV and cartoons in particular – its pretensions in this respect were usually mocked (Nellis 2003).

In the interests of better understanding how technical change impacts on penal practice, the manifest patchiness – state by state variation in its use – of EM's development in the United States could be turned to analytical advantage. What is needed are several historical ethnographies of techno-correctional innovation which trace the impact (or not) of EM on existing local configurations of policing, probation and imprisonment. What changes and why? What technological infrastructure needed to be in place to make monitoring possible? Who championed and who opposed it? Whose interests were served by its introduction, and whose sidelined? What – and how complex – was the matrix of decision-making? What sustained EM over time? Such an analysis would likely require specific attention to the role and influence of the private sector organizations who promote EM, and also to the susceptibility or otherwise of correctional agencies to techno-utopian pitches. The possibility that the adoption of EM in a particular place may have more to do with the internal dynamics of the commercial–corrections complex operating at a local level than to any research-based response to crime would have to be considered; penal developments are never necessarily rational in this respect. Existing case studies of prison privatization provide a model of what could be done in respect of EM (Shichor and Gilbert 2001); it is actually surprising that none have yet appeared in the literature. But until we know more about the ways in which the prevailing forms and patterns of EM use came into being in the United States, our capacity to estimate its future penal trajectory will remain unnecessarily restricted.

Whether the contemporary forms of EM survive or not, the geolocation of offenders is unlikely to be a 'fad' if there are cheap and accessible means of accomplishing it (although to the extent that EM corrodes humanistic values, it may also presage and facilitate a 'new brutalism' towards offenders). Notwithstanding the muting of 'war on terror' rhetoric, nothing substantial has changed in respect of surveillance culture with the coming of the Obama administration. The GPS tracking of offenders found a military analogue in the growing use of Predator drones controlled from the United States to search-and-destroy terrorist targets in Afghanistan (Singer 2009; Wall and Monahan 2011). Similarly, immense intelligence efforts were put into tracing and tracking Osama bin Laden, and the fact that in May 2011 the president and his staff in Washington were able to watch the assassination in Pakistan of America's most wanted man live and in real time (via a soldier's helmet-mounted camera) legitimated – and almost sanctified – the potency of global 'optoelectronics' (Virilio 2005), specifically of pinpointing and scanning technologies, in contemporary securitization strategies. Yet whatever sustenance military strategy and high-profile 'tracking events' might obliquely give to EM, none of it means that mass incarceration in the United States is imminently threatened by superior telematic means of social control. 'The future is already here', the American science fiction writer William Gibson (1999) has said, 'it's just not very evenly distributed'. It may never be otherwise. Techno-utopianism can demonstrably mobilize new penal developments but without ever becoming a dominant, transcendent force – it can be countered and checked by competing narratives and restrained by the inertia of existing practices, and as a result its expression can be compromised and its impact made patchy. Such has been the story of EM in the United States. There are clear structural and cultural factors underpinning its uneven influence and impact (which are not likely to be ironed out any time soon), the force of which, and the tension between which, may even intensify. Imprisonment in the United States has a function, momentum and implacability that sets definite limits on the impact that any non-custodial measure is likely to have, including those based on intrusive surveillance, despite the culturally sanctioned allure of technological innovation and the commercial forces which sustain and exploit it.

References

Albanese, J.S. (1984) *Justice, Privacy and Crime Control* (New York: University Press of America).

Bales, W., Mann, K., Blomberg, T., McManus, B. and Dhungana, K. (2010) 'Electronic monitoring in Florida', *Journal of Offender Monitoring*, 22:2, pp. 5–12.

Ball, R.A. and Lilly, J.R. (1986) 'A theoretical examination of home incarceration', *Federal Probation*, 70:1, pp. 17–24.

Ball, R.A. and Lilly, J.R. (1988) 'Home incarceration with electronic monitoring' in J.E. Scott and T. Hirschi (eds) *Controversial Issues in Crime and Justice* (London: Sage), pp. 147–165.

Ball, R.A., Huff, R. and Lilly, J.R. (1988) *House Arrest and Correctional Policy: Doing Time at Home* (Newbury Park, CA: Sage).

Bentham, J. (1787 [1995]) *The Panopticon Papers* (London: Verso).

Blakeway, D.H. (1995) 'Electronic supervision systems: innovations in technology'. in K. Schulz (ed.) *Electronic Monitoring and Corrections: the policy, the operation, the research* (Vancouver: Simon Fraser University), pp. 213–230.

Blomberg, T.G. and Lucken, K. (2000) *American Penology: A history of control* (Hawthorne, NY: Aldine de Gruyter).

Bogard, W. (1996) *The Simulation of Surveillance: Hypercontrol in telematic societies* (Cambridge: Cambridge University Press).

Brooks, D. (2005) *On Paradise Drive* (New York: Simon and Schuster).

Bumiller, E. and Shanker, T. (2011) 'War evolves with drones, some tiny as bugs', *New York Times*, 19 June.

Button, D.M., DeMichele, M. and Payne, B.K. (2009) 'Using electronic monitoring to supervise sex offenders: legislative patterns and implications for community corrections officers', *Criminal Justice Policy Review*, 20:4, pp. 414–436.

Cavadino, M. and Dignan, J. (2006) *Penal Systems: A comparative approach* (London: Sage).

Clear, T. (1994) *Harm in American Penology: Offenders, victims and their communities* (Albany, NY: State University of New York).

Conrad, J.C. (1984) 'The redefinition of probation: drastic solutions to solve an urgent problem', in P.D. McAnany, D. Thomson and D. Fogel (1984) *Probation and Justice: Reconsideration of a mission* (Cambridge, MA: Oelgeschlagler, Gunn and Hain Publishers Inc.), pp. 251–273.

Corbett, R.P. and Marx, G.T. (1992) 'Emerging technofallacies in the electronic monitoring movement', in J.M. Byrne, A.J. Lurigio and J. Petersilia (eds) *Smart Sentencing: The emergence of intermediate sanctions* (London: Sage), pp. 85–100.

Corn, J.J. and Horrigan, B. (1984) *Yesterday's Tomorrows: Past visions of the American future* (Baltimore, MD: John Hopkins University Press).

Crowe, M.J. (1972) 'A new age in science and technology?', in R. Weber (ed.) *America in Change: Reflections on the sixties and seventies* (Notre Dame, IN: University of Notre Dame), pp. 141–153.

Delgado, J.M.R. (1969) *Physical Control of the Mind: Towards a psychocivilised society* (New York: Harper and Row).

Dickey, W. (1990) *From the Bottom Up: Probation and parole supervision in Milwaukee* (Madison, WI: University of Wisconsin Law School).

Doffing, D. (2009) 'Is there a future for RF in a GPS world?', *Journal of Offender Monitoring*, 22:1, pp. 12–15.

Drake, G.B. (n.d.) 'Developing a successful gps offender tracking program'. Online. Available at www.correcttechllc.com (accessed 22 July 2011).

Drayton, R. (2005) 'Shock, awe and Hobbes have backfired on America's neocons', *Guardian*, 28 December.

Durham, A.M. (1994) *Crisis and Reform: Current issues in American punishment* (Boston: Little, Brown and Company).

Enos, R., Black, C.A., Quinn, J.F. and Holman, J.E. (1992) *Alternative Sentencing: Electronically monitored correctional supervision* (Bristol, IN: Wyndham Hall Press).

Enos, R., Holman J.E. and Carroll, M.E. (1999) *Alternative Sentencing: Electronically monitored correctional supervision*, 2nd edn (Bristol, IN: Wyndham Hall Press).

Erez, E., Ibarra, P.R. and Lurie, N.A. (2004) 'Electronic monitoring of domestic violence cases: a study of two bilateral programmes', *Federal Probation*, 68:1, pp. 15–20.

Feeley, M. and Simon, J. (1994) 'Actuarial justice: the emerging new criminal law', in D. Nelken (ed.) *The Futures of Criminology* (London: Sage), pp. 173–201.

Gable, R.K. and Gable, R.S. (2005) 'Electronic monitoring: positive intervention strategies', *Federal Probation*, 69:1. Online. Available at: www.uscourts.gov/fedprob.

Gable, R.K. and Gable, R.S. (2007) 'Increasing the effectiveness of electronic monitoring: perspectives', *Journal of the American Probation and Parole Association*, 31:1, pp. 24–29.

Gainey, R.R. and Payne, B.K. (2000) 'Understanding the experience of house arrest with electronic monitoring: an analysis of quantitative and qualitative data', *International Journal of Offender Therapy and Comparative Criminology*, 44:1, pp. 84–96.

Garland, D. (2000) *The Culture of Control: Crime and social order in contemporary society* (Oxford: Oxford University Press).

Gibson, W. (1999) 'The science in science fiction'. On *Talk of the Nation*, NPR, 30 November.

Goss, M. (1989) 'Electronic monitoring: the missing link for successful house arrest', *Corrections Today*, 51:4, pp. 106–108.

Halberstadt, R.L. and La Vigne, N.G. (2011) 'Evaluating the use of radio frequency (RFID) technology to prevent and investigate sexual assaults in a correctional setting', *The Prison Journal*, 91:2, pp. 227–249.

Harrington, M. (1965) *The Accidental Century* (Harmondsworth: Penguin).

Harris, P.M. and Byrne, J.M. (2007) 'Community corrections and hard technology', in J.M. Byrne and D.J. Rebovitch (eds) *The New Technology of Crime, Law and Social Control* (Monsey, NY: Criminal Justice Press), pp. 287–326.

Harris, P.M., Clear, T.R. and Baird, S.C. (1989) 'Have community service officers changed their attitudes towards their work?', *Justice Quarterly*, 6:2, pp. 233–246.

Hoshen, J. and Drake, G.B. (2001) *Offender Wide Area Continuous Electronic Monitoring Systems: Final Report to the US Department of Justice*. National Criminal Justice Reference System No. 187101 (Washington, DC: Department of Justice).

Hoshen, J., Sennott, J. and Winkler, M. (1995) 'Keeping tabs on criminals', in *Spectrum IEEE*, 32:2, pp. 26–32. Republished in the *Journal of Offender Monitoring*, 8:3, 1995, pp. 1–7.

Ingraham, B.L. and Smith, G.S. (1972) 'The use of electronics in the observation and control of human behaviour and its possible use in rehabilitation and parole', *Issues in Criminology*, 7:2, pp. 35–53.

Johnson, K. (2002), 'State's use of offender tracking systems', *Journal of Offender Monitoring*, 15:2, pp. 15–23.

Jones, T. and Newburn, T. (2007) *Policy Transfer and Criminal Justice: Exploring the US influence over British crime control policy* (Maidenhead: Open University Press).

Le Mond, A. and Fry, R. (1975) *No Place to Hide: A guide to bugs, wire taps, surveillance and privacy invasions* (New York: St. Martin's Press).

Lilly, J.R. and Ball, R.A. (1990) 'The development of home confinement and electronic monitoring in the United States', in D.F. Duffee and F. McGarrel (eds) *Community Corrections: A community field approach* (Cincinnati, OH: Anderson Publishing Ltd), pp. 73–92.

Lilly, J.R. and Ball, R.A. (1992) 'The Pride Inc Programme: an evaluation of 5 years of electronic monitoring', *Federal Probation*, 56:4, pp. 42–47.

Lilly, J.R. and Deflem, M. (1996) 'Profit and penality', *Crime and Delinquency*, 42, pp. 3–20.

Lilly, J.R. and Knepper, P. (1992) 'An international perspective on corrections', *Howard Journal of Criminal Justice*, 31, pp. 174–191.

Lilly, J.R. and Knepper, P. (1993) 'The commercial–corrections complex', *Crime and Delinquency*, 39:2, pp. 150–166.

Lilly, J.R., Ball, R.A and Wright, J. (1987) 'Home incarceration with electronic monitoring in Kenton County, Kentucky', in B.R. McCarthy (ed.) *Intermediate Punishment: Intensive supervision, home confinement and electronic surveillance* (Monsey, NY: Willow Tree), pp. 189–203.

Lilly, J.R., Ball, R.A, Curran, G.D. and McMullen, J. (1993) 'Electronic monitoring of the drunk driver: a seven year study of the home confinement alternative', *Crime and Delinquency*, 39:4, pp. 462–484.

Love, J. (2005) 'Electronic monitoring'. Paper presented at the ElmoTech 10th Anniversary in Europe Conference, Nerola, Italy, October 2004. Available on CD-Rom.

McAnany, P.D., Thomson, D. and Fogel, D. (1984) *Probation and Justice: Reconsideration of a mission* (Cambridge, MA: Oelgeschlager, Gunn and Hain Publishers Inc.).

Mackenzie, D. (2011) 'Probation: an untappped resource in US corrections', in L. Gideon and H. Sung (eds) *Rethinking Corrections: Rehabilitation, re-entry and reintegration* (New York: Sage), pp. 97–127.

Mainprize, S. (1996) 'Elective affinities in the engineering of social control: the evolution of electronic monitoring', *Electronic Journal of Sociology*. Online. Available at: www.sociology.org/content/vol002.002/mainprize.html

Marx, G. (1988) *Undercover: Police surveillance in America* (Berkeley, CA: University of California Press).

Marx, G. (2007) 'The engineering of social control: intended and unintended consequences', in D. Rebovitz and J.M. Byrne (eds) *The New Technology of Crime, Law and Social Control* (Monsey, NY: Criminal Justice Press), pp. 347–371.

Maxfield, M.G. and Baumer, T.L. (1990) 'Home detention with electronic monitoring: comparing pretrial with postconviction programmes', *Crime and Delinquency*, 36:4, pp. 521–536.

Meyer, J.A. (1971) 'Crime deterrent transponder system', *Transactions on Aerospace and Electronic Systems*, 7:1, pp. 1–22.

Meyer, J.F. (2004) 'Home confinement with electronic monitoring', in G.A. Caputo (ed.) *Intermediate Sanctions in Corrections.* (Denton, TX: University of North Texas Press), pp. 97–123.

Mitford, N. (1974) *The American Prison Business* (London: George Allen and Unwin).

Moran, R. (1978) 'Biomedical research and the politics of crime control: a historical perspective', *Contemporary Crises*, 2, pp. 335–357.

Moran, R. (2002) *Executioner's Current: Thomas Edison, George Westinghouse and the invention of the electric chair* (New York: Knopf).

Morris, N. (1974) *The Future of Imprisonment* (Chicago, IL: University of Chicago Press).

Morris, N. and Tonry, M. (1990) *Between Prison and Probation: intermediate punishments in a rational sentencing system* (Oxford: Oxford University Press).

Nellis, M. (2000) 'Law and order: the electronic monitoring of offenders', in D. Dolowicz (ed.) *Policy Transfer and British Social Policy: Learning from the US?* (Buckingham: Open University Press), pp. 103–126.

Nellis, M. (2003) 'News media, popular culture and the electronic monitoring of offenders in England and Wales', *Howard Journal*, 42:1, pp. 1–31.

Nellis, M. (2006) 'Future punishment in American science fiction movies', in P. Mason (ed.) *Captured by the Media: Prison discourse and popular culture* (Cullompton: Willan), pp. 210–228.

Nellis, M. (2012) 'Implant technology and the electronic monitoring of offenders: old and new questions about compliance, control and legitimacy', in A. Crawford and A. Hucklesby (eds) *Legitimacy and Compliance in Criminal Justice* (Cullompton: Willan) (forthcoming).

Padgett, K., Bales, W. and Blomberg, T. (2006) 'Under surveillance: an empirical test of the effectiveness and implications of electronic monitoring', *Criminology and Public Policy*, 5:1, pp. 61–92.

Papy, J.E. and Nimer, R. (1991) 'Electronic monitoring in Florida', *Federal Probation*, 55, pp. 31–33.

President's Commission on Law Enforcement and the Administration of Justice (1967) *Crime in a Changing Society* (Washington: Department of Justice. U.S. Government Printing Office).

Rackmill, S.J. (1994) 'An analysis of home confinement as a sanction', *Federal Probation*, 58:1, pp. 45–52.

Renzema, M. (1989) 'Annual monitoring census: progress report', *Journal of Offender Monitoring*, 2, pp. 20–21.

Renzema, M. (1992) 'Home confinement programmes: development, implementation and impact', in J.M. Byrne, A.L. Lurigio and J.R. Petersilia (eds) *Smart Sentencing: The emergence of intermediate sanctions* (New York: Sage), pp. 41–53.

Renzema, M. (2009) 'Rationalizing the use of electronic monitoring', *Journal of Offender Monitoring*, 22:1, pp. 1–11.

Roberts, J.V. (2004) *The Virtual Prison* (Cambridge: Cambridge University Press).

Schmidt, A.K. (1991) 'Electronic monitors: realistically, what can be expected?', *Federal Probation*, 55:2, pp. 47–53.

Schrag, P. (1978) *Mind Control* (New York: Dell Publishing).

Schwitzgebel, R.K. (1963) 'Delinquents with tape recorders', *New Society*, 31 January.

Schwitzgebel, R.K. (1964) *Streetcorner Research: An experimental approach to the juvenile delinquent* (Cambridge, MA: Harvard University Press).

Schwitzgebel, R.K. (1966) 'Electronic innovation in the behavioural sciences: A call to responsibility', *American Psychologist*, 22:5, pp. 364–370.

Schwitzgebel, R.K. (1968) 'Electronic alternatives to imprisonment' *Lex et Scientia*, 5, pp. 99–104.

Schwitzgebel, R.K. (1970) 'Behavioural electronics could empty the world's prisons', *The Futurist*, April, pp. 59–60.

Schwitzgebel, R.K. (1971) *Development and Legal Regulation of Coercive Behavior Modification Techniques with Offenders* (Rockville, MD: National Institute of Mental Health).

Schwitzgebel, R.K., Schwitzgebel, R.L., Panke, W.N. and Hurd, W.S. (1964) 'A programme of research in behavioural electronics', *Behavioral Science*, 9, pp. 233–238.

Schwitzgebel, R.L. (1969) 'A remote instrumentation system for behavior modification', in C. Franks and R.D. Rubin (eds) *Advances in Behaviour Therapy* (New York: Academic Books), pp. 181–203.

Schwitzgebel, R.L. and Bird, R.M. (1970) 'Sociotechnical design factors in remote instrumentation with humans in natural environments', *Behaviour Research Methods and Instrumentation*, 2, pp. 212–231.

Schwitzgebel, R.L. and Schwitzgebel R.K. (eds) (1973) *Psychotechnology: Electronic control of mind and behaviour* (New York: Holt, Rheinhart and Wilson).

Segal, H.P. (2005) *Technological Utopianism in American Culture* (Syracuse, NY: Syracuse University Press).

Shichor, D. and Gilbert, M.J. (2001) *Privatisation in Criminal Justice: Past, present and future* (Cincinnati, OH: Anderson Publishing).

Singer, P. (2009) *Wired for War: The robotics revolution and conflict in the 21st Century* (New York: Penguin Books).

Sipes, L.A. (2009) 'Use of GPS in law enforcement and community corrections', *Journal of Offender Monitoring*, 21:2, pp. 5–7.

Skinner, B.F. (1948) *Walden Two* (New York: Macmillan).

Skinner, B.F. (1971) *Beyond Freedom and Dignity* (London: Jonathan Cape).

Sullivan, L.E. (1990) *The Prison Reform Movement: Forlorn hope* (Boston, MA: Twayne Publishers).

Timko, F.K. (1986) 'Electronic monitoring: how it all began – conversations with Love and Goss', *Journal of Probation and Parole*, 17, pp. 15–16.

Virilio, P. (2005) *The Information Bomb* (London: Verso).

Wall, T. and Monahan, T. (2011) 'Surveillance and violence from afar: the politics of drones and liminal security-scapes', *Theoretical Criminology*, 15, pp. 239–254.

Whitman, J.Q. (2003) *Harsh Justice: Criminal punishment and the widening divide between America and Europe* (Oxford: Oxford University Press).

Winkler, M. (1991) 'Walking prisons: the developing technology of electronic controls', *The Futurist*, July–August, pp. 34–36.

2 The evolution of electronic monitoring in Canada

From corrections to sentencing and beyond

Suzanne Wallace-Capretta and Julian Roberts

Introduction

As this volume documents, electronic monitoring (EM) has evolved in different ways around the world. In Canada, the evolution of this form of offender monitoring has been relatively gradual. The technology has moved from the correctional sphere to the domain of sentencing without attracting controversy among criminal justice professionals or the general public. In this respect, Canada has yet to experience some of the heated debates about the utility of this form of technological monitoring. As well, the federal nature of the country has meant that EM is currently employed very differently across the country.

This chapter has three objectives: first, to describe the evolving role of EM in the Canadian criminal justice system; second, to summarize findings from research conducted in this country upon the impact of EM on the system (as well as the individuals subject to this form of monitoring); third, to discuss the current use of EM and its relationship with one specific sanction, known in Canada as a conditional sentence of imprisonment. The chapter explores issues such as the success rates of EM programmes to date and offenders' experiences with, and perceptions of daily life while being subject to, an electronic monitor. Rather than describing the gradual and partial implementation of EM across the whole country we concentrate in this chapter on the provinces in Canada that have embraced surveillance technology to the greatest extent. It is not possible, at present, to provide a detailed and comprehensive statistical profile of the offenders subject to EM across the country. Canada lags far behind many other jurisdictions such as England and Wales or Belgium in this regard; such statistics are not annually released by the principal statistical agency (Statistics Canada). We begin, however, with a brief historical overview of the evolution of EM in this jurisdiction.

Origins and evolution of EM in Canada

EM emerged in Canada as a new technological element of the correctional environment, and only latterly became associated with sentencing. No single triggering event was responsible for the introduction of this form of monitoring

– it simply emerged as a result of correctional policy transfer from the United States. Unsurprisingly, in light of its proximity to the United States, Canada has adopted a number of penal reforms that originated south of the border. The introduction of EM was a natural consequence of the close links between Canadian and American correctional authorities. As will be seen in this chapter, the evolution of EM in Canada has been slow and sporadic. This may explain why it has not become a high-profile criminal justice issue. Rather, the Canadian public has become gradually aware that prisoners in several parts of the country were being subject to monitoring as part of their release programme from prison. Most Canadians will have become familiar with the concept of individual electronic surveillance from their widespread exposure to US news media.

Until recently, EM could therefore be described as a 'sleeper issue' in the field of criminal justice in this country as a consequence of (1) its sporadic and limited application; (2) its familiarity from coverage in the US media; and (3) the absence of any high-profile case in which EM played a role. Although a great deal of research has been conducted into Canadian attitudes to criminal justice, it is surprising that to date no survey has explored public knowledge of, or reaction to EM. This fact alone attests to the low profile that this penal innovation has assumed in the Canadian context. Coverage of the issue in the Canadian news media has been subdued. While a 'spike' in the frequency of stories occurred at the time EM was introduced in British Columbia (see below), there has been no dramatic 'story' around the use of EM. When correctional issues appear in the media, newspaper headlines have focused on high-risk offenders, prison conditions, the right of prisoners to vote and the future of parole, rather than the EM of offenders in the community.

Canada's experience with EM has been shaped by the fact that responsibility for criminal justice is shared among the federal and ten provincial and three territorial governments. The federal level of government is responsible for the creation of criminal law, while the administration of justice, including police and court administration, falls within the jurisdiction of the provinces and territories under Sections 91 and 92 of the Constitution Act (1867). One consequence of this divided jurisdiction is that EM has not received a nation-wide 'roll-out' as has been the case in other countries. Instead, a number of provinces have adopted the technology in response to institutional overcrowding while others continue to rely on human verification to ensure compliance with the conditions of parole or temporary absence from prison.

In large measure, the introduction of EM can be attributed to concern about rising prison populations across the country. Provincial and territorial admissions to custody increased by 22 per cent in the decade between 1980 and 1990 (Foran 1992). In 1996, a federal report on the corrections population growth reported that the provincial prison population had risen on average 12 per cent from 1989/1990 to 1994/1995 (Canada 1996). The increasing prison population was problematic from both an offender management and fiscal perspective and provoked a search for solutions. These remedies included the use of EM as an alternative to incarceration in order to reduce the number of prisoners through early release mechanisms such as parole. The application of EM in Canada has thus proceeded from corrections to sentencing – from a tool to permit closer supervision of prisoners released early, to a means of surveillance for offenders who may well serve their entire sentence in the community.

One other feature of the Canadian correctional environment is worth noting. Sentences of imprisonment are served either in provincial prisons or federal penitentiaries. Terms of custody of up to two years less one day fall within the provincial jurisdiction; longer sentences are served in federal penitentiaries, as set out in Section 743.1 of the Canadian Criminal Code. EM has to date primarily been used with offenders sentenced to 'provincial' terms, namely the less serious cases.

EM and early release correctional programmes

British Columbia

The first use of EM in Canada (and indeed outside the United States) can be traced to the Corrections Branch of British Columbia, which in August 1987 instituted this form of offender supervision as an alternative to incarceration for low-risk offenders. The pending closure of one of the correctional centres in a provincial plan to update facilities was expected to displace a growing intermittent custody population, thereby causing prison overcrowding. Intermittent sentences of imprisonment are served at specified times, usually weekends, and carry a statutory maximum length of 90 days. EM was considered an economical and viable solution to monitoring an offender population serving a sentence composed of short prison stays and periods on probation. In this way, EM was seen as a solution to institutional overcrowding and a way of avoiding the costs of constructing a new correctional facility.

As part of the pilot project, a Citizen Advisory Group was formed with membership from several non-governmental organizations to provide feedback in relation to the project, its policy development and implementation strategy. The EM pilot project began in the lower mainland of British Columbia. Following a successful evaluation of the year-long pilot in which high success rates were reported (Neville 1989), the programme was expanded to apply to other low-risk offenders throughout the province. The number of EM offenders in British Columbia continued to rise, and by the late 1990s the EM programme was managing 15 per cent of the daily count of provincially sentenced offenders, ranging from 250–350 individuals, thus making it the largest EM programme in the country.

The goal of the BC EM programme was to provide a humane and cost-effective alternative to incarceration that also provided the necessary safeguards to maintain public safety. The criteria for participation in the programme stipulated that an offender should not represent a danger to the public and the offender's participation must not cause public alarm, undermine the intent of the sentence or bring the administration of justice into disrepute. To be eligible for

EM early release the offender had to have a full-time residence with telephone, employment and/or educational commitments or the prospect thereof. It was also necessary that the offender's presence not constitute an undue hardship for their families or other co-residents (Government of British Columbia 1987). In order to qualify for EM, low-risk, non-violent offenders had to have received either an intermittent sentence of imprisonment or a sentence of more than seven days but fewer than four months in jail (or had the equivalent remaining to serve). If an offender was deemed to have met all of these criteria – and consented to abide by the conditions of the EM programme – then temporary release from custody was granted by way of Section 7(1) of the Federal statute, entitled the Prison and Reformatories Act and Sections 15 and 16 of British Columbia's Corrections Act (British Columbia Corrections Branch 1995).

Ontario

Unlike British Columbia, an Ontario EM programme piloted in 1989/1990 failed to result in the establishment of a permanent programme. The proposed EM programme was intended to be a community release strategy for offenders who would not have qualified for other temporary absence programmes but were considered to be at sufficiently low risk of re-offending. The programme was quite restrictive and access to it was restricted by a number of exclusionary criteria. For example, if the offender had previous convictions for a crime of 'extreme' violence, domestic violence, sexual aggression (or other sexual offence) or impaired driving, they were not eligible. In addition, adverse probation reports or unfavourable submissions from family or employers would also disentitle candidates from consideration for the programme (Government of Ontario 1991).

An evaluation of the 18-month pilot project concluded that although the use of EM promoted rehabilitation (by allowing participants to continue to work and maintain family contact), the offenders accepted for community release with EM (i.e. 29 per cent of 552 applications) would have been eligible for existing release programmes (Government of Ontario 1991). In this regard, the benefits of EM in terms of diverting offenders from prison were understandably modest. The outcomes, however, were positive. Offenders placed on the programme achieved a high success rate: 88 per cent completed their sentence on EM without violation, while a further 5 per cent completed their terms with only a 'minor violation'. Less than 1 per cent of the offenders were returned to the institution as a result of an allegation of fresh offending (Government of Ontario 1991).

The results of a cost–benefit analysis of the pilot project reported that although the per day costs of EM were significantly lower than those of incarceration, the cost of the EM pilot project was $275,000, while the estimated expense of keeping the EM participants in custody was only $59,000. It was recognized that a programme designed as an alternative to incarceration would not achieve cost savings unless the number of offenders diverted was large enough to either close sections of, or entire, correctional facilities (Government of

Ontario 1991). As a result, Ontario discontinued its use of EM following the initial pilot period. It was not until 1996, following the closure of all Ontario halfway houses the previous year, that EM was re-introduced for low-risk prisoners released on temporary absence permits (Borgida 2001). The halfway houses had been part of Ontario's community reintegration strategy and their closures meant that an estimated 400 offenders were returned to custody (John Howard Society of Ontario 1996).

By 1998 EM had become a permanent feature of Ontario's temporary absence programme. Non-violent offenders assessed as low to medium risk that had been sentenced to fewer than 365 days in prison (or had 365 or fewer days remaining in their prison sentence) were eligible for release subject to EM. Once again, certain categories of offenders were excluded, including those convicted of spousal assault, a sexual offence, drug trafficking or who had previous violent convictions. As a result of the strictness with which the offence criteria were applied, the EM programme averaged a daily count of only 52 offenders in 1999, with approximately 2,000 EM participants since the programme began. The result was that the programme never fully reached its capacity or fulfilled its potential (Borgida 2001).

The Ontario EM programme's objectives were two-fold: to promote the reintegration of offenders and to demonstrate the provincial government's commitment to a tougher, more effective correctional system that imposed tighter controls on offenders serving part of their sentence in the community. This duality explains much of the appeal of EM in Canada. EM is supported by correctional authorities since it assists in managing offender populations, and by prisoner advocates because it permits prisoners who otherwise would have been incarcerated to return to their homes and communities. At the same time, by increasing the perceived punitiveness of a community sentence EM makes a term of community supervision more acceptable to the public (see discussion in Roberts 2004).

Newfoundland & Labrador

Newfoundland & Labrador also developed a voluntary conditional release programme with EM and brought together a community advisory committee during its implementation. Between 1991 and 1994 Newfoundland & Labrador experienced chronic prison overcrowding as a result of a 30 per cent increase in admissions over a two-year period and the doubling of the average sentence length. The introduction of EM was intended to address this problem.

The EM programme targeted non-violent offenders who had served at least one-sixth of their sentence in custody, but excluded sexual offences and domestic assaults. However, unlike the EM programmes in British Columbia and Ontario, the Newfoundland & Labrador programme included a compulsory treatment condition aimed at reducing recidivism by addressing the criminogenic needs (e.g. alcohol/substance abuse, anger management and cognitive life skills training) of medium-risk offenders (Scoville 2001). The Learning Resources

Program was an intensive cognitive and behavioural treatment programme provided by the local chapter of the John Howard Society, a non-governmental agency devoted to helping ex-offenders. In an independent evaluation that measured how closely a correctional treatment programme adheres to known principles of effective offender rehabilitation, the Learning Resources Program scored in the top 10 per cent of 230 programme assessments. As with EM programmes in other provinces, successful completion rates were high. By early 2000, over 550 prisoners had participated in the EM programme. Of these, approximately 95 per cent had successfully completed their sentences under electronic surveillance.

From corrections to sentencing: EM in Saskatchewan

All the programmes discussed thus far employed EM within the jurisdiction of correctional authorities. In 1990 the first court-ordered (judicial) programme of EM was piloted in Saskatchewan; full-scale implementation followed six months later. This programme was thus a 'front end' alternative to incarceration rather than an early release programme within the correctional sphere (Lang 1996). Courts were empowered to impose a sentence of probation with a condition of EM instead of a term of custody. The intensive probation supervision with EM targeted two categories of offender: (1) offenders who met the criteria for a custodial term but who posed a manageable risk to the community; and (2) low-risk offenders convicted of serious non-violent offences (e.g. large-scale fraud; see Clements 2001). Special consideration was given to aboriginal offenders – who have been over-represented in the Canadian penal population for decades (see Roberts and Melchers (2003) for trends) – and female offenders with dependents.

Evaluating EM programmes in Canada

Assessing programme success requires a consideration of programme objectives. In the case of EM programmes in Canada, most were created to constrain rising prison populations by diverting offenders from prison to the community (either before or after committal to custody). They constituted an alternative to incarceration or a way in which part of a custodial sentence could be discharged in the community. A programme designed as a community alternative to imprisonment may include multiple goals. Thus Gomme identified

> four fundamental and interconnected goals of EM: 1) to reduce the population in custody; 2) to reduce the costs of corrections that are generated by custodial sentences; 3) to provide humane punishment while promoting rehabilitation and reintegration; and 4) to maintain the security and the safety of the public.
>
> (Gomme 1995: 505)

We shall now examine some of these goals in light of the experience in Canada.

Reductions in prison populations and costs

Despite the fact that EM programmes have been part of the penal landscape for almost a generation, few evaluations of EM have been conducted in Canada. Those that have studied EM did so prior to the introduction of a new (for Canada) form of community imprisonment that will be discussed later in this chapter. Evaluating EM as an alternative to incarceration with the goal of constraining the prison populations inevitably leads to a discussion of cost effectiveness and 'net widening'. In order for EM to constitute a cost-effective alternative to incarceration it would need to be restricted to offenders who would otherwise have been incarcerated (to prevent net widening) and it would need to divert enough offenders from prison to justify the closure of correctional facilities or prevent new capital expenditures (Hill 2001).

It is difficult to be accurate about the costs of alternatives to incarceration since estimates are often based on projections of future trends – for example, programme expansion, prison reductions, offender–staff ratios, as well as the social benefits of offenders remaining in the community. Cost–benefit analyses often neglect to take into account all of these considerations. For example, the initial pilot project in Ontario was discontinued even though the daily costs of EM were less than incarceration – the programme itself was considered too costly. Similarly, the original long-term estimates in British Columbia grossly under-estimated the cost of introducing an EM programme. It was predicted that there would be a 70 per cent reduction in the number of intermittent offenders, resulting in cost savings by 1992. In the end, a reduction of only 42 per cent was achieved.

Along with the goals of reducing prison populations and correctional costs, preventing crime through reduced re-offending has been cited as a goal of EM. Only one study, carried out by the federal government in the late 1990s, compared the success rates of offenders both within and across jurisdictions to assess the effectiveness of EM offenders on post-programme recidivism. This empirical evaluation included the EM programmes in British Columbia, Saskatchewan and Newfoundland & Labrador using data collected between 1995 and 1997.[1] Variations in the administration of these programmes allowed researchers to examine a number of additional issues of interest, such as client selection, programme processes, offender and staff perceptions and post-programme recidivism rates. Efforts were made to compare findings between provinces as well as between matched samples of offenders serving sentences of incarceration and probation, wherever possible (Bonta *et al.* 1999, 2000a).

The most important findings from that evaluation may be summarized in the following way:

1   Despite considerable differences between admission criteria for the various programmes, no significant differences emerged in terms of completion rates. Successful completion rates were uniformly high, ranging from 86 per cent to 89 per cent of cases.

2   The use of EM did not reduce subsequent recidivism rates. The researchers compared the outcomes of offenders subject to EM with others, having controlled for a priori risk of re-offending, and found no statistically significant differences between groups.

3   A significant proportion of the offenders who had been placed on EM had low-risk scores, and may well have been managed equally successfully in the community by conventional surveillance techniques. This raises the possibility of 'net-widening'.

4   Several factors were associated with programme failure, including: the number of current offences, having been arrested as a youth, being unemployed and having a current drug-use problem.

5   Knowledge of the offender's risk needs score was the most important factor in terms of predicting programme outcome as well as post-programme recidivism rates.

The researchers did find that reductions in recidivism were achieved when higher-risk EM offenders participated in an intensive, rehabilitative, community supervision programme which provided a cognitive behavioural approach to treatment in order to address offenders' criminogenic needs (Bonta *et al.* 2000b). Lower-risk offenders provided with the same intensive treatment showed increases in recidivism when compared to offenders who did not receive any treatment. These findings support a body of research indicating that in order to achieve reductions in recidivism, offender risk levels should be matched with the intensity of intervention (Andrews and Bonta 2003).

Reactions of offenders, family members and supervisory personnel

A number of studies in Canada have explored the perceptions and experiences of offenders serving time in the community while being subject to EM. Early research in British Columbia involving interviews with male EM participants reported positive effects in terms of EM as a rehabilitative tool. Individuals subject to EM reported that the programme facilitated attendance at work or school, alcohol abstinence and reduced the social stigma of incarceration (Mainprize 1995). Subsequent research on the effects of EM home confinement (again with male participants) found that offenders identified maintaining contact with family as the single most important benefit of being electronically monitored (Bonta *et al.* 1999). This advantage was cited by four out of five EM offenders surveyed. Somewhat surprisingly, maintaining the freedom to seek or maintain employment was identified by far fewer respondents – slightly more than half the sample identified this as an important benefit of being placed in an EM programme. Other aspects of serving a sentence in the community that were perceived as beneficial by EM offenders to varying degrees across programmes included the ability to attend treatment (Bonta *et al.* 1999). Most crucially, however, approximately nine out of ten offenders placed on EM in the three provinces studied agreed with the statement that 'electronic monitoring was a fair programme'. Consistent with research on offenders in other jurisdictions, then, male offenders subject to EM reacted positively to the experience.

This said, gender appears to play an important role in mediating responses to EM. Findings from research involving female offenders serving sentences in the community with electronic surveillance provide a rather different picture. Maidment (2002) investigated the reactions of women in Newfoundland & Labrador who had been subject to EM house arrest. She found that a number of the women reported that serving their time at home had been more difficult than a term of imprisonment, principally as a result of the increased stress associated with the monitoring device. Prison was easier, the offenders reported, because they had less to do; they did not have to worry about the day-to-day challenges of raising children and running a household – tasks that become more complicated due to the restrictions of home confinement. However, isolating the impact of EM from the effects of home confinement remains a challenge in this area.

Some of the reactions to EM home confinement may arise from the experience of being confined to one's residence – independent of whether a monitor is worn or present in the offender's home. The reactions of offenders in Maidment's (2002) research are similar to those of offenders interviewed by Roberts (2004), who found that some interviewees reported that home confinement had worsened their domestic relationships, and that in these cases prison may have been a preferable sanction. In other research, family members, mostly female spouses, reported some positive effects of having their spouses at home on EM but also reported experiencing additional stresses as a result of the offender's home confinement (e.g. fewer social contacts and an assumption of more household responsibilities outside of the home – see Doherty (1995)).

Offender perceptions of supervising officers

Surveys of offenders who had just completed an EM programme revealed significant variations in their perceptions of supervising officers across different programmes. For example, less than half of the participants in British Columbia, but eight out of ten in Newfoundland and Saskatchewan agreed that they 'could talk about personal problems [with supervising officers]' (Bonta *et al.* 1999). Similarly, only 46 per cent of British Columbia respondents but 75 per cent of participants in Newfoundland and 91 per cent in Saskatchewan agreed that their supervising officer had 'given me real help'. Clearly, the nature of the client–supervisor relationship has an important impact on the success of the programme. These findings underscore the importance of appropriate implementation and this obviously includes ensuring the support of supervisors. In general, outcomes were most positive in locations where probation officers conducted the supervision.

EM and community custody (home confinement)

The evolution of EM in Canada was affected by the creation, in 1996, of a new (for Canada) form of custody served in the community.[2] The conditional sentence of imprisonment (hereafter CSI) is a sentence of custody that the offender serves at home, subject to a number of conditions. Offenders found to have breached one or more of these conditions without lawful excuse may be sentenced to a period in custody, up to the maximum amount of time remaining on the order. The CSI was introduced as part of a wider sentencing reform initiative, one goal of which was to reduce the use of imprisonment in a safe and principled way (Roberts and Cole 1999; Roberts 2004). Unlike comparable community custody sanctions around the world, the CSI has a very broad ambit of application. The statutory framework permits a court to make any sentence up to two years less a day conditional in nature (served at home). Two years less one day is, statistically speaking, a very high threshold; 96 per cent of all custodial terms imposed in Canada are under two years in length (Marth 2008). The consequence is that as long as the other statutory prerequisites have been met,[3] a court may sentence all these offenders to serve their sentences of imprisonment at home under prescribed conditions.

One of the weaknesses of the statutory framework of the new community custody sanction was that it bore too close a resemblance to a term of probation. A community-based sentence of imprisonment should carry more onerous conditions than probation, and unjustified violation of those conditions should provoke an expeditious and firm response from the justice system.[4] However, the statutory conditions of the conditional sentence are little different from those that must be imposed upon offenders sentenced to a term of probation. The principal distinction between the two sanctions is that a court may order an offender serving a conditional sentence to attend an officially sanctioned treatment programme, while treatment as part of a probation order may only be imposed with the offender's consent. In practice, however, courts in Canada rarely impose treatment without the agreement of the offender, regardless of the sanction imposed. Also, with respect to unjustified breach of conditions, it can be argued that breach of probation is regarded more seriously. Breaching a conditional sentence order results in a breach hearing at which the court may choose from among a range of responses, including the option of doing nothing other than warning the offender. Breach of a probation order, however, constitutes a criminal offence.

In this context the Supreme Court handed down a guideline judgement[5] in 2000 regarding the use of the new sanction. One of the important lessons in that judgement was that since the conditional sentence was a form of custody, it should carry some prison-like conditions. In the absence of a statutory mechanism to accomplish this (see above), the Court directed judges to consider a strict curfew or house arrest as the norm, not the exception. Since EM represents an effective way of ensuring compliance with a curfew, this direction from the highest court was expected to increase the use of EM as a condition of the CSI. The addition of EM also makes a community sentence more punitive (Martin 2001; Roberts 2004).

Conflicts between judiciary and correctional authorities

An interesting element of the Canadian experience has been the tension or conflicts that have arisen between the sentencing authority and the agencies responsible for administering sentences in the community. In an ideal world, the two authorities would work together in an integrated and coordinated manner. Judges would be aware of the correctional resources available, and when administering the sentence correctional authorities would be mindful of the sentencer's intentions. However, this has not been the experience in Canada. The conflicts between sentencing and corrections have emerged in a number of ways.

First, as noted, trial courts have been directed to toughen the home confinement sanction by imposing strict curfews, or absolute house arrest. However, being practical people, judges have become aware that probation officers who supervise offenders serving sentences in the community do not have adequate resources to ensure that conditions imposed by the courts are respected. For example, in the province of Ontario probation officers have high case loads, approaching an average of 100 cases per officer (Roberts et al. 2005). Moreover, probation officers in the province do not work in the evenings, on weekends or statutory holidays. The consequence is that ensuring compliance with court-ordered conditions is far from easy. One solution to this state of affairs is to allow courts to impose EM, but until recently the decision to place an offender on EM was made by correctional authorities, not the judiciary in Ontario.

The situation is further complicated by the federal–provincial jurisdictional split to which reference was made at the outset of this chapter. The conditional sentence of imprisonment was created by the federal government and as such is available as a sanction in every province and territory. However, the creation of an EM programme falls within the jurisdiction of the provincial correctional authorities, with the result that EM is available in some but by no means all provinces. Judges in some parts of the country may therefore impose specific conditions such as house arrest with electronic supervision, safe in the knowledge that the requisite monitoring will ensure offender compliance, while judges elsewhere have no such assurances. In hindsight, the federal government should have created a sanction (or release programme) with a statutory foundation that included the possibility of EM and simultaneously transferred the necessary funds to each province and territory to launch such a programme. The difficult and occasionally fractious state of federal–provincial–territorial relationships has precluded adoption of such a comprehensive solution.

Some courts have taken the view that sentencing authority is being usurped by correctional authorities. In a ruling handed down from the Provincial Court of Newfoundland & Labrador in May 1996, immediately prior to the CSI becoming available, the trial judge in R. v. Oliver[6] expressed concern that the intent of sentencing was being undermined by the decisions of correctional authorities to release offenders into the community under EM despite the fact that a court had sentenced them to prison. Believing that the offender in this case would serve the sentence in the community even if the court determined a fit sentence to be a period of custody, the offender was given a suspended sentence with probation and restitution. On appeal, the provincial Supreme Court found that the post-sentencing decisions of correctional authorities should not have been considered in the determination of the sentence and varied the sentence. In the time that lapsed between the original trial and the appeal (May 1996 to September 1997), the CSI had become available. For reasons associated with the passage of time and partial sentence already served, the Provincial Court of Appeal varied the offender's sentence to a seven-month CSI, admittedly less restrictive then would have otherwise been imposed.

Current use of EM in Canada

Since the Supreme Court decision in *R.* v. *Proulx* (2000) there has been an increase in the use of curfews or house arrest and this in turn has increased the use of EM in some parts of the country. In fact, the primary use of EM in Canada today is as an optional sentence administration tool to ensure offender compliance with court-imposed conditions such as house arrest or curfew. The latest statistics (from 2004–2005) reveal that across the country approximately four-fifths of EM cases involve an offender serving a sentence of imprisonment in the community. The remaining cases accounted for high-risk individuals released on parole or some other form of release programme. The number of offenders or defendants subject to EM remains relatively small, however. For example, in Saskatchewan, one of the provinces that has employed EM for a number of years, only 173 individuals were admitted to the EM programme in 2008. The average daily count of individuals (sentenced offenders or remand prisoners) in that year was 88 (Government of Saskatchewan 2010).

While the authority to assign offenders to EM has changed, the impact on the number of offenders being electronically supervised has varied by province. In British Columbia, for example, in 2004/2005 there were 3,333 conditional sentence admissions. Of these, 2,634 – almost 80 per cent – contained a condition of curfew and/or house arrest. Despite this high use of a curfew, only 5 per cent of the cases were subject to EM. In other provinces the situation is rather different. Almost one-third (30 per cent) of cases with house arrest in Saskatchewan in the same year were subject to EM. In Ontario the inception of the new Electronic Supervision Program has been justified in part by the 'judiciary's desire for more vigilant supervision of offenders sentenced to conditional sentences [of imprisonment served at home]' (Government of Ontario 2005: 3).

Contemporary prospects of EM in Canada

To summarize, across Canada EM is currently used in the following ways: (1) as a condition of judicial interim release (bail); (2) to monitor offenders serving intermittent sentences of custody; (3) to monitor offenders serving a conditional sentence of imprisonment at home; (4) as a condition of probation in high-risk cases; (5) to monitor adult prisoners leaving a correctional institution on a Temporary Absence Program; and (6) to assist in the supervision of offenders released on parole. In terms of the relative frequency of application, the vast majority of electronically monitored cases involve offenders serving a conditional sentence of imprisonment in the community.

At present, six provinces (British Columbia, Saskatchewan, Ontario, New-foundland & Labrador, Nova Scotia (Nova Scotia Department of Justice 2005) and Alberta (Government of Alberta 2005, 2008/2009) employ EM pro-grammes. Nova Scotia, unlike the other four, employs GPS technology to supervise adults and has begun a pilot examining its use with youth. Another, Manitoba (Government of Manitoba 2008), has launched a GPS pilot project with high-risk young vehicle thieves, which is also likely to result in perma-nent programmes. One province (Quebec) has taken the decision not to imple-ment EM. Correctional authorities in this province have decided against adopting EM for several reasons that include: (1) no convincing evidence demonstrating that EM is any more effective than traditional means of offender supervision in preventing recidivism and maintaining public safety; (2) there is a clear potential for net widening; and (3) the alleged benefits cannot justify the costs of establishing a monitoring programme (Gou-vernement du Québec 2000). EM is therefore not available to monitor offend-ers in the country's second most populous province (containing approximately 25 per cent of the Canadian population). Thus, despite a growing interest in the use of EM over the past 20 years, today, EM is still not employed by all provinces to monitor the community supervision of offenders. Although Quebec has declined to introduce the new technology, EM has expanded to include other populations. Table 2.1 summarizes the current use of EM across Canada as of 1 December 2009.

Application of EM to federal prisoners

As noted earlier in this chapter, prisoners in Canada fall under the jurisdiction of provincial correctional authorities if they have been sentenced to terms under two years' duration. Longer terms of custody are served in federal penitentiaries and come under the jurisdiction of the federal correctional authorities. Until recently, EM applied only to 'provincial' prisoners – those serving terms of custody of under two years' duration. However, in 2008 the federal government announced a one-year pilot that would be capable of monitoring up to 30 federal parolees in the Ontario region (Public Safety Canada 2008). Like the provinces of Nova Scotia and Manitoba, the federal government is testing the use of GPS technology as an additional supervision tool to complement normal case man-agement practices. It is expected that monitoring offenders using GPS technol-ogy will improve correctional authorities' ability to supervise offenders since their whereabouts can be determined at any time. Currently it is being used with a small number of federal parolees to ensure compliance with conditions such as curfew or location restrictions, as an alternative to a residency condition or as an alternative to revocation or suspension if the offender's risk to public safety is considered to be manageable with the increased supervision afforded by GPS supervision.[7] Normally revocation or suspension of parole for a condition viola-tion would result in a return to custody. Referral to EM is not based on offence type but is determined on a case-by-case basis.

Table 2.1 Use of EM across Canada

Province	Conditional sentence of imprisonment	Temporary absence	Parole/community supervision order	Bail	Other application[a]
British Columbia	A				
Alberta	A				A
Saskatchewan	A			A	
Manitoba		Y	Y	Y	Y
Ontario	A	A	A		A
Nova Scotia	A				
Newfoundland & Labrador	A	A		A/Y	A/Y

Notes
A = adult; Y = youth.
a Other application includes other dispositions such as intermittent sentences of imprisonment, peace bond, etc.

Security-related applications

Besides sentencing and corrections there is one other use for EM with GPS technology currently being employed by the federal government. The Canada Border Services Agency is authorized under section 77 of the Immigration and Refugee Protection Act to use security certificates to arrest, detain, bring to hearing and remove permanent residents or foreign nationals who are found to be inadmissible to Canada. This finding is based on grounds related to national security, a violation of human or international rights, serious criminality or organized crime. EM is used in these cases to ensure compliance with the conditions of their release ordered by the Federal court. As of July 2008, however, only four individuals were subject to security certificates.

Young offenders

Until recently, EM in Canada has been reserved for adult offenders. Concerns regarding social, cognitive and moral development have been raised when considering electronically monitoring young offenders (e.g. Finlay 2001). A review of Canadian correctional services in 2004 indicated that Saskatchewan was the only jurisdiction to electronically monitor youth (Calverley and Beattie 2005) at that time. However, in April 2007 Manitoba announced a small-scale pilot project to assess the effectiveness of using GPS technology to supervise high-risk, young vehicle thieves. Up to 20 juvenile offenders would be electronically supervised at one time. EM begins once they reach a point in their sentence where they must be released into the community (Government of Manitoba 2007). An evaluation of the first six months of the youth EM programme revealed that the monitoring had mixed results (Government of Manitoba 2008). EM worked in the sense that correctional authorities had been able to establish the location of all monitored individuals at all times. It had failed in the sense that several individuals had committed further vehicle thefts – although monitoring permitted the authorities to re-arrest and charge these individuals (Government of Manitoba 2008).

The future of EM in Canada

No government across Canada has contemplated making EM a separate sanction, as has been proposed in some European jurisdictions. For the foreseeable future EM in this country will remain a condition of a community-based sanction, or some form of release from custody either pre- or post-conviction. However, we do envisage an increase in the volume of individuals being subject to this form of monitoring. In our view, there are two reasons to expect an expansion in the use of EM within the next few years in Canada.

Political pressure and its likely impact on EM

One cause of this expansion is political in nature. The re-election of a conservative federal government in 2008 changed the criminal justice climate to a significant degree. The new government made criminal justice one of its policy priorities, and has taken a rather punitive 'law and order' approach to penal reform. When he announced the expansion of EM to federal (i.e. longer term) offenders, the then Ministry of Public Safety noted that: 'We have listened to police and victims groups who have been requesting this for years' (Public Safety Canada 2008). Although federal justice officials have no direct influence on the treatment of offenders under provincial jurisdiction, historically there has been considerable tension between the two levels of government with respect to criminal justice issues. Provincial governments have sought to avoid being 'shown up' by their federal counterparts in terms of being tough on offenders. Consequently, we expect a number of provincial governments to widen the application of EM, particularly with respect to offenders serving community-based sentences for violent crimes.

Expansion of EM to reduce the number of remand prisoners

To date, the imposition of EM as a condition of judicial interim release has been rare. However, it seems likely that EM will in the future be applied more frequently to high-risk individuals granted bail while awaiting trial. Although discussion of the use of custody generally focuses on sentenced admissions, there is considerable concern across the country about the fact that admissions to remand now account for a significant and rising proportion of the custodial population. Average remand counts have risen by 26 per cent since 1997/1998. As a proportion of the total provincial/territorial supervised offender population this represents an increase from approximately one-third to one-half over the course of ten years. Remanded admissions to custody in 2006/2007 (the most recent year for which data are available) represented almost two-thirds (64 per cent) of admissions to provincial/territorial custody (Babooram 2008). One possible solution to lessen the pressure on prison populations is to place higher-risk accused persons under EM as a condition of bail. With the remand population nearing a state of crisis in some jurisdictions, consideration is sure to be given to introducing EM for accused persons charged with serious offences and who to this point would have been denied bail.

Conclusion

As can be seen, EM has developed in Canada in a rather haphazard fashion. There has been no national debate about the utility and propriety of subjecting offenders to this form of surveillance. Indeed, there is a rather limited amount of empirical or legal scholarship exploring the issue. A special issue of the *Canadian Criminal Law Review* published in 2001 contains an interesting collection of articles, but there is little else. The country needs to examine more closely the way that EM currently operates, and to undertake an exploration of the question of the legitimacy of the practice – as suggested by Allan Manson (2001) in his contribution to that special issue. As well, we need to develop a coherent 'EM policy' – one which can be applied nationally (see discussion in Doob 2001). And perhaps most importantly, correctional agencies across the country which use EM need to conduct systematic research into its costs and benefits – at present our knowledge is founded upon research from a decade ago (e.g. Bonta *et al.* 1999), or studies from other jurisdictions where EM is implemented in very different ways and is used for different purposes.

Notes

1 The EM programme in Ontario was not included in the evaluation since data collection was already underway by the time it was implemented in 1996.
2 Bill C-41 received Royal Assent on 13 July 1995 and was proclaimed in force on 3 September 1996.
3 The other prerequisites are the following: the offence may not carry a mandatory sentence of imprisonment; the court must be satisfied that the offender's presence in the community does not represent a risk to the community; and the imposition of the CSI must be consistent with the codified purpose and principles of sentencing.
4 If the response is not swift and punitive, the sanction fails to reflect the image that is always attributed to it – the so-called 'Sword of Damocles'.
5 *R.* v. *Proulx*, [2000] 1 SCR 61, [2000] SSC 5, 140 CCC.
6 *R.* v. *Oliver* [1997] NJ, [1996] NJ.
7 At the time this chapter was prepared the pilot was complete but the evaluation report had not yet been publicly released.

References

Andrews, D. and Bonta, J. (2003) *The Psychology of Criminal Conduct*, 3rd edn (Cincinnati, OH: Anderson Publishing Co.).

Baboorram, A. (2008) 'The changing profile of adults in custody, 2006/2007', *Juristat*, 28:10. Online. Available at: www5.statcan.gc.ca.

Bonta, J., Wallace-Capretta, S. and Rooney, J. (1999) *Electronic Monitoring in Canada: User report* (Ottawa: Solicitor General Canada). Online. Available at: ww2.ps-sp. gc.ca/publications/corrections/em_e.asp.

Bonta, J., Wallace-Capretta, S. and Rooney, J. (2000a) 'Can electronic monitoring make a difference? An evaluation of three Canadian programs', *Crime & Delinquency*, 46, pp. 61–75.

Bonta, J., Wallace-Capretta, S. and Rooney, J. (2000b) 'A quasi-experimental evaluation of an intensive rehabilitation supervision program', *Criminal Justice and Behavior*, 27, pp. 312–329.

Borgida, A. (2001) 'Electronic monitoring in Ontario', *Canadian Criminal Law Review*, 6, pp. 311–314.

British Columbia Corrections Branch. (1995) 'B.C. Corrections Branch manual of operations adult institutional services: electronic monitoring program', in K. Schulz (ed.) *Electronic Monitoring and Corrections: The policy, the operation, the research* (Burnaby, BC: Simon Fraser University), pp. 59–68.

Calverley, D. and Beattie, K. (2005) *Community Corrections in Canada 2004* (Ottawa: Statistics Canada).

Canada (1996) *Corrections Population Growth: Report for Federal/Provincial/Territorial Ministers responsible for justice* (Ottawa: Solicitor General Canada).

Clements, L. (2001) 'Electronic monitoring in Saskatchewan', *Canadian Criminal Law Review*, 6, pp. 309–311.

Doherty, D. (1995) 'Impressions of the impact of the electronic monitoring program on the family', in K. Schulz (ed.) *Electronic Monitoring and Corrections: The policy, the operation, the research* (Burnaby, BC: Simon Fraser University), pp. 129–140.

Doob, A.N. (2001) 'If electronic monitoring is the answer, what is the question?', *Canadian Criminal Law Review*, 6, pp. 363–366.

Finlay, J. (2001) 'Should young offenders be electronically monitored?', *Canadian Criminal Law Review*, 6, pp. 344–346.

Foran, T. (1992) 'Trends in custodial counts and admissions: provinces and territories', *Juristat*, 12:9. Online. Available at: www5.statcan.gc.ca.

Gomme, I. (1995) 'From Big House to Big Brother: confinement in the future', in N. Larsen (ed.) *The Canadian Criminal Justice System* (Toronto: Scholars' Press), pp. 489–516.

Gouvernement du Québec (2000) *Surveillance électronique: solution ou panacée?* Québec: Ministére de la Sécurité publique. Direction de l'administration et des programmes.

Government of Alberta (2005) 'Pilot project to electronically monitor low-risk offenders', news release, 28 September. Online. Available at: http://alberta.ca/home/NewsFrame. cfm?ReleaseID=/acn/200509/18821C810738A-E58E-4AD5-A30BE839E172D6B0.html.

Government of Alberta (2008/2009) 'Annual Report'. Online, available at: www.solgps. alberta.ca/Publications1/Annual%20Reports/2009/2008%20-%202009%20Solicitor%20General%20Annual%20Report.pdf.

Government of British Columbia (1987) *Electronic Monitoring Systems for Offender Supervision: Discussion* Paper, 2nd edn (Victoria, BC: Ministry of Attorney General, Corrections Branch).

Government of Manitoba (2007) 'GPS monitoring next step to auto theft crackdown: electronic monitoring devices to track highest-risk thieves during one-year pilot – Chomiak', news release, 18 April. Online. Available at: http://news.gov.mb.ca/news/index,print.html?archive=2007-4-01&item=1474.

Government of Manitoba (2008) 'Electronic monitoring mid-project results released by Manitoba justice', media bulletin. Online. Available at: www.gov.mb.ca/chc/press/top/2008/10/2008-10-30-092300-4675.html.

Government of Ontario (1991) *An Evaluation of the Electronic Monitoring Pilot Project: Mimico Correctional Centre – April, 1989–October, 1990* (North Bay: Ministry of Correctional Services of Ontario).

Government of Ontario (2005) *Electronic Supervision Program: Information Package – Adult Community Services* (North Bay: Ontario Ministry of Community Safety and Correctional Services).

Government of Saskatchewan (2010) 'Intensive supervision/electronic monitoring'. Online. Available at: http://cpsp.gov.sk.ca/Intensive-Supervision-Electronic-Monitoring.

Hill, B. (2001) 'What are the real costs of electronic monitoring?', *Canadian Criminal Law Review*, 6, pp. 353–359.

John Howard Society of Ontario (1996) 'Fact sheet 7: electronic monitoring 1–4', April.

Lang, T. (1996) 'Electronic monitoring's place in corrections: A Canadian perspective', in American Correctional Association, *Correctional Issues: Community Corrections* (Lanham, MD: American Correctional Association), pp. 123–126.

Maidment, M.R. (2002) 'Toward a 'woman-centered' approach to community-based corrections: A gendered analysis of electronic monitoring (EM) in Eastern Canada', *Women & Criminal Justice*, 13, pp. 47–67.

Mainprize, S. (1995) 'Social, psychological, and familial impacts of home confinement and electronic monitoring: Exploratory research findings from British Columbia's pilot project', in K. Schulz (ed.) *Electronic Monitoring and Corrections: The policy, the operation, the research* (Burnaby, BC: Simon Fraser University) pp. 141–187.

Manson, A. (2001) 'Who's in the net? Electronic monitoring: who's minding the net?', *Canadian Criminal Law Review*, 6, pp. 335–344.

Marth, M. (2008) 'Adult criminal court statistics, 2006/07', *Juristat*, 28:15. Online. Available at: www5.statcan.gc.ca.

Martin, D. (2001) 'Gender implications of electronic monitoring', *Canadian Criminal Law Review*, 6, pp. 346–353.

Neville, L. (1989). *Electronic Monitoring System for Offender Supervision: Pilot Project Evaluation* (Victoria, BC: Ministry of Solicitor General, Corrections Branch).

Nova Scotia Department of Justice (2005) 'New corrections act for safer, stronger Nova Scotia', news release, 19 October. Online. Available at: www.gov.ns.ca/news/details. asp?id=20051019006.

Public Safety Canada (2008) 'Governments of Canada and Nova Scotia sign an agreement for electronic monitoring technology', press release, 11 August. Online. Available: Available at: www.publicsafety.gc.ca/media/nr/2008/nr20080811-eng.aspx.

Roberts, J.V. (2004) *The Virtual Prison: Community custody and the evolution of imprisonment* (Cambridge: Cambridge University Press).

Roberts, J.V. and Cole, D.P. (1999) *Making Sense of Sentencing* (Toronto: Toronto University Press).

Roberts, J.V. and Melchers, R. (2003) 'The incarceration of aboriginal offenders: An analysis of trends, 1978–2001', *Canadian Journal of Criminology and Criminal Justice*, 45, pp. 211–242.

Roberts, J.V., Hutchison, C. and Jesseman, R. (2005) 'Supervising conditional sentence orders: The perceptions and experiences of probation officers in Ontario', *Criminal Reports*, 29, pp. 107–119.

Scoville, J. (2001) 'Electronic monitoring: the Newfoundland experience', *Canadian Criminal Law Review*, 6, pp. 314–317.

3 'Parallel tracks'

Probation and electronic monitoring in England, Wales and Scotland

George Mair and Mike Nellis

Introduction

The UK likes to see itself as a leader in penal policy and practice; it is, for example, proud to claim its importance as the originator of probation (despite the rather more accurate claims of the United States, or in Europe, the Netherlands) and it is notable that as Eastern Bloc countries moved to Westernize themselves after the fall of the Berlin Wall and the collapse of the Soviet Union, many of these countries followed the advice of academics and probation officers from England and Wales about how to modernize their probation services (despite the often retrograde managerial and cultural changes 'our' Probation Service was undergoing from 1991 onwards). Another development where England and Wales led the way for Europe was in the piloting of electronic monitoring (EM) as a criminal justice tool, although it went about it in ways which reflected the government of the day's particular sense of penal crisis, and their preferred solutions, which others in mainland Europe neither shared nor fully wished to emulate. This chapter will focus on the origins and development of EM in England and Wales, concentrating particularly on research and policy, and touch more briefly on its later development in Scotland, which was slightly different.

'Punishment in the community' and policy transfer

While the existence of EM in the United States was a necessary factor in its adoption in England and Wales, it was not a sufficient one. The presence of an innovative policy initiative in one country is no guarantee that it will be copied in another, but there is no doubt that the use of EM house arrest in a significant number of American states (and four Canadian provinces) was significant in leading to its transfer across the Atlantic (Mair and Nee 1990). EM was pushed onto the policy agenda in England and Wales in two main ways. First, by Tom Stacey, a journalist who had independently thought up the idea of remote monitoring as an alternative to custody (initially envisaging tracking more than house arrest), and founded the Offenders Tag Association in 1981 (in effect, the origin of the word 'tagging' to denote EM) to promote it (Nellis 1991, 2000). Stacey, who was well networked in the Conservative Party, tried to interest two Home Secretaries – William Whitelaw (1979–1983) and his successor Leon Brittan (1983–1985) – in US developments without success, but his efforts did mean that EM was brought to government attention quite early. Second, the organizations that made and sold electronic equipment in the United States saw their next market as the UK – members of the Home Office Research and Planning Unit (RPU) attending criminological conferences in the United States were told so quite openly, and senior staff met with Home Office officials in London in order to push their product.

As a result of high-level Home Office interest, a member of the RPU was tasked to keep in touch with the development of EM in North America and several briefing papers were written for policy-makers setting out the findings of research. Members of the Home Office also attended a small conference on EM in Canada, held in London in 1987. In the same year, a House of Commons Home Affairs Committee report recommended that the Home Office should examine the use of EM of offenders in the United States to see if it had any possible application to England and Wales (House of Commons 1987); the government response noted that a Home Office minister of state had visited the United States recently and had looked at how 'tagging' (a term not current in America) was used there (House of Commons 1987). Official interest in EM was thus encouraged.

At the same time, the Conservative government was under considerable pressure due to the size of the prison population, and a great deal of effort had gone into the development of alternatives to custody during the previous 10–15 years. All the evidence suggested that the various probation-based disposals (community service, probation centres and other requirements that could be added onto the probation order) had not been successful in diverting offenders from custody. The government response was increasingly to criticize the social work ethos of the Probation Service, claiming that it was too soft on offenders, with the implication that tougher 'punishment in the community' – as the government strategy came to be called – would finally make reduced prisoner numbers possible. EM was claimed as just such a tough punishment.

A further ideological commitment on the government's part was cutting the costs of public service. One way of doing this was by privatizing public sector jobs and processes wherever possible. While the privatization of criminal justice was, understandably, viewed with some apprehension by those who worked in the sector, the government proceeded piecemeal to do this with some aspects of police work, and with some prisons. The latter was encouraged by the Home Affairs Committee report mentioned above (House of Commons 1987), while EM was perceived as a way of introducing privatization (and, by implication, some badly needed managerial rigour) into what were about to become known as 'community penalties'. This signalled to a number of security, construction and telecommunications companies, national and international, that a new market might soon emerge (Nathan 2003).

It is often forgotten that non-electronic curfews (introduced as 'night restriction orders' in the Criminal Justice Act 1982) and even the 'tracking' of offenders were being used in England and Wales – albeit controversially and sporadically – prior to the introduction of EM. These methods were used in intensive supervision schemes developed by a few probation areas (see Nellis 2004). While the great majority of probation officers were opposed to such schemes for adults – they were better accepted in youth justice services – it is important to note their existence. One of the acknowledged limitations of such schemes was that it was almost impossible to effectively monitor offender compliance with curfews via personal check-ups. Remote monitoring offered a more reliable approach.

These were the background factors to the development of EM in England and Wales. In 1988 a Green Paper was published, setting out the government's ideas for punishment in the community (Home Office 1988) and both tracking and curfews were suggested. Crucially, EM was now suggested as a means of monitoring these:

> Electronic monitoring might help to enforce an order which required offenders to stay at home. It is used for this purpose in North America. Less restrictively, it could help in tracking an offender's whereabouts. By itself, electronic monitoring could not prevent reoffending, though it might limit opportunities to a degree which a court would consider justified diversion from custody.
>
> (Home Office 1988: 12)

The Home Office spent the first part of 1988 hastily putting together a pilot project to test tagging in the field. This was the brainchild of John Patten, a junior minister in the Home Office who was keen to push tagging as a high-profile policy (that could, of course, advance his political career). Despite a lack of enthusiasm on the part of key Home Office officials, three trials of EM were initiated in August 1988, using private companies Chubb and Marconi as technology providers, and Securicor staff as monitoring officers. The focus was on bail (an alternative to pre-trial detention) because, unlike a pilot focused on sentencing, it did not require legislation and time-consuming Parliamentary debate, in which further opposition might have been aired. This did not exactly replicate how EM was used in the United States (as a sentence and condition of early release from prison), but it was hoped that the experience would inform plans for the use of EM as part of a curfew order. Well before the trials had been completed and evaluated, the government made clear its intention to introduce an EM curfew order (Home Office 1990).

EM was thus introduced in England and Wales on the basis of what were assumed to be vote-winning politics rather than a fully thought-out response to crime reduction or rising prison numbers. EM had the sheen of new technology (which was presumed appealing to the public); it offered the possibility of introducing privatization into the Probation Service by the back door; and its proponents saw it as a tougher approach to dealing with offenders. Arguments that suggested greater caution were simply marginalized: 'The research evidence in criminological terms was limited and unreliable; the economics of tagging were ignored; and the moral or ethical arguments were scarcely noted' (Mair 2005: 264).

EM under the Conservatives, 1988–1997

The first trials (carried out in three court divisions in England – Nottingham City, North Tyneside and Tower Bridge in London) proved difficult to organize as the bail/remand decision requires input from a wide range of criminal justice organizations. Local Probation Service involvement in the pilots was minimal and the views of both the Association of Chief Officers of Probation (ACOP) and the National Association of Probation Officers (NAPO) were negative: EM was 'seen as controlling, oppressive, an infringement of civil rights and not something that the Probation Service should be involved with' (Mair 2001: 170). Indeed, NAPO explored whether EM breached the European Convention on Human Rights (and to its chagrin found it did not) (Nellis 1991). Each of the trials lasted for only six months and EM could be imposed on individuals for up to 24 hours per day. Despite Home Office expectations of 150 defendants, in the event only 50 were tagged: 29 of these violated their curfew or were charged with another offence. Initial equipment problems were resolved over the course of the trials. Overall the results were equivocal – at best they suggested that EM 'worked' in the practical sense, but key unknowns remained: how confident were sentencers in tagging? What was the appropriate target group? What did it cost? Did it have any impact on re-offending? Could the Probation Service get involved with EM (see Mair and Nee 1990 for a full report of the first trials).

NAPO hoped that the trials would mean the end of tagging, but provisions for curfew orders had already been inserted in the Bill that was going through Parliament and that became law as the Criminal Justice Act 1991: curfews were to be restricted to a six-month maximum and to between two and twelve hours per day. Confident that tagging was coming, four invitation-only annual conferences (1989, 1990, 1991, 1992), sponsored by some of the companies involved, were organized at Leicester Polytechnic (later de Montfort University) by criminologist Ken Russell, where Tom Stacey and a number of American EM practitioners further acquainted selected British criminal justice professionals with the possibilities and pitfalls of EM (Russell and Lilly 1989; Lilly and Himan 1993). In policy and practice terms, however, nothing happened for several years, while a drafting error in the 1991 Act was corrected to allow for further piloting, rather than an immediate national roll-out.

EM may well have languished had the political situation not changed in the early to mid-1990s. A distressing child murder in Liverpool in February 1993 sparked a new wave of public anxiety about crime; a new Home Secretary, Michael Howard, was appointed, stridently demanding a more punitive penal system, and the Labour opposition under Tony Blair set about outbidding Howard's proposals on law and order. Howard was instrumental in taking EM forward despite the resistance of his officials, sentencers and the Probation

Service (an organization whose time, he felt, was over). And so EM was revived as offering a tough and restrictive way of dealing with offenders, and once again as a means of threatening the Probation Service (Jones and Newburn 2007). The 1994 Criminal Justice and Public Order Act permitted the phased introduction of curfew orders.

Three trials sites were again selected. The city of Manchester, the borough of Reading and the county of Norfolk were selected for their different geographical characteristics, and each trial was intended to run for nine months from July 1995. Uptake by the courts was again slow; six months into the trials only 18 curfew orders had been made, suggesting some reluctance on the part of sentencers to use them and on the part of probation officers to propose them in pre-sentence reports. In response to this, the trial areas were widened to cover the whole of Greater Manchester and all of the county of Berkshire for the Reading courts. Despite this, as well as regular Home Office exhortation to use EM curfews, there were only 83 orders during the first 12 months. In a further effort to boost use, the trials were extended to the end of March 1997 and other courts in Manchester and Berkshire were permitted to make use of curfew orders.

Low uptake remained a problem, but completion rates were high at 82 per cent, although these varied depending upon the court where the order had been made: at Crown Court the rate was 97 per cent; at magistrates' courts 82 per cent; and at the Youth Court 69 per cent. EM curfews could be made jointly along with a community sentence, on their own and where a pre-existing community penalty was already in force. Completion rates also varied according to how they were made: joint orders had a rate of 77 per cent; those with a pre-existing community penalty had a rate of 80 per cent; and the rate for stand-alone orders was 86 per cent. Probation's attitude towards EM seemingly softened during the trials, perhaps more in acquiescence to policy than genuine enthusiasm, although there was some of that (Nellis 2003). Uncertainty remained, however, about exactly which offenders to tag – was EM meant to replace short custodial sentences, or was it intended to displace low-tariff community penalties? (See Mair and Mortimer 1996; Mortimer and May 1997; Mortimer *et al.* 1999 for studies of the trials).

The government's strong commitment to EM was evident as, in spite of the trials failing to show unequivocal success, EM curfews were extended to a further four English counties (Cambridgeshire, Middlesex, Suffolk and West Yorkshire) from 1997. In addition, the Crime (Sentences) Act 1997 made EM curfews available for three new groups of offenders: fine defaulters, persistent petty offenders and juveniles aged 10–15. Further pilots in Norwich and Manchester looked at EM curfews as a condition of bail in 1998. During this 'expansionist' period for EM, the Labour Party won the general election of 1997, wresting credibility on law and order from the incumbent Conservative government. Despite saying critical things about EM in opposition, it was soon clear that New Labour's interest in it was as strong as its predecessors, maybe more so. Sensing this, chief probation officer Dick Whitfield became ACOP's lead spokesperson on EM, and played an important part in fostering more constructive, less rejecting-on-principle probation attitudes towards tagging (Whitfield 1997, 2001). NAPO also pragmatically modified its hostile tone, but the delivery of EM by commercial organizations remained a permanent obstacle to the association's full acceptance of it.

EM under New Labour, 1997–2010

New Labour maintained the momentum that the Conservatives had given EM, continuing with the pilots, adding in projects on bail and young offenders (10–18). Using the same sites as previously – Greater Manchester and Norwich – where sentencers were knowledgeable about, if not entirely comfortable with, EM may not have been wise, but the assumption (not entirely perverse) was that familiarity would eventually win greater credibility for EM: 'Choosing Greater Manchester and Norfolk to pilot the orders meant we could expect take-up of curfew orders with electronic monitoring to be faster than in completely new areas' (Elliott *et al.* 2000: 2). The accumulated and evolving results of the various trials gave New Labour the confidence to believe that EM curfew orders could be rolled-out nationally in January 1999 without undue risk, although the real spur for a national scheme came from a rapidly rising prison population, and its EM-based early release scheme – Home Detention Curfew (HDC) – was launched at the same time without ever having been trialled, with a lead-in time of only six months.

HDC attempted to address the huge – 50 per cent – rise in the daily prison population from 44,566 in 1993 to 65,298 in 1998 (Home Office 2000). It allowed eligible prisoners (those serving sentences of three months or more, but less than four years, who passed a risk assessment, provided a suitable address and agreed to be tagged) to be released up to 60 days before the end of their sentence. As hoped, it produced a quantum leap in the use of EM (Dodgson *et al.* 2001). In all the previous trials only a few hundred individuals had been tagged, whereas during the first year of HDC 14,800 were subjected to EM. While this represents a considerable number of people experiencing remote surveillance, out of a total of 49,500 prisoners who had in fact been eligible for HDC, only 30 per cent were released. This suggests caution and indeed risk-averseness on the part of prison governors who authorized early release: only good risks were chosen. This seems to be confirmed by the fact that only 5 per cent of those released on HDC were recalled to prison following a breakdown in their curfew; two-thirds of these were for a breach of curfew conditions and one-quarter as a result of a change in circumstances, with only eight individuals 'returned to custody because they represented a risk of serious harm to the public' (Dodgson *et al.* 2001: iv).

HDC was viewed positively by those curfewed, their families and supervising probation officers, and a cost–benefit analysis suggested that almost 2,000 prison places had been saved alongside a net benefit of £36 million. Numbers on HDC remained high: in 2000 a total of 15,500 were released on curfew, while in 2001 the figure dropped slightly to 13,600. The scheme was considered so successful (and the need to free up prison places remained so pressing) that three changes to HDC were made in 2002 to increase its use. First, the Presumptive HDC scheme was introduced for inmates serving between three months and under 12 months who had not been convicted of a sex, violence or drugs offence during the past three years. These prisoners would be released subject to a satisfactory Home Circumstances Assessment unless there were 'exceptional and compelling reasons why release should not be granted' (Home Office 2003: 223). Second, a few months later, the exclusion from the presumptive scheme of those with convictions for drugs possession was lifted. Third, the maximum curfew period was increased from 60 to 90 days). As a result, in 2002 the number released on HDC increased to 20,500 and the release rate grew to 37 per cent. It should be noted, however, that the use of HDC has declined; only 12,250 were released on it in 2010, explained by the *Offender Management Caseload Statistics* (Ministry of Justice 2010) primarily in terms of greater risk aversion on the part of prison authorities. A complex statistical study of all short-term releases between 2000 and 2006 concluded that those released *early* on HDC were no more likely to re-offend over 12- or 24-month periods than similar offenders not released early – a politically reassuring finding, which also confirmed HDC's perceived cost-effectiveness (Marie *et al.* 2011). In 2010, 1,154 prisoners were recalled from HDC, 18 per cent for a new offence (NOMS 2010). Increased refusals of initial prisoner requests for HDC have seemingly led to increased complaints about this to the Prisons and Probation Ombudsman (2009).

No great controversy attended the expansion of EM to juveniles and bail, but enthusiasm – expressed once again by low uptake – was not great. In the study of EM curfews for 10–15 year olds (the maximum length of a curfew for this age-group was reduced from six months to three) only 155 orders were made in 24 months – a take-up rate that was acknowledged as 'relatively low' (Elliott *et al.* 2000: v). With regard to the use of EM bail curfews, 198 curfews were made on 173 individuals in 17 months and take-up was admitted to be 'lower than planned' (Airs *et al.* 2000: v). Where EM was available for fine defaulters, it was only used in 15 per cent of possible cases (community service was the preferred option in 73 per cent of cases, and driving disqualification in 12 per cent); and when applied to petty persistent offenders it was used in one-quarter of cases, while community service was used in the remaining 75 per cent (Elliott and Airs 2000).

Furthermore, researchers were hard-pressed to find many positives in the three pilot studies. In the case of fine defaulters and petty persistent offenders, EM was seen by sentencers as passive rather than active; community service, on the other hand, entailed doing something positive for the community. Tagging was thought expensive, and there was evidence of misunderstanding about when it might be most appropriately used. It had negligible impact on the use of custody, did not increase the number of fines paid and possibly led to net-widening and up-tariffing. There was 'serious concern in the Probation Services that the brevity of suitability assessments for EM might overlook possible risks to offenders' families in the event of domestic violence, or to Probation Service staff' (Elliott and Airs 2000: x). No adverse family effects were found with tagged juveniles, although sentencers found it difficult to identify suitable cases. They claimed nonetheless that EM curfews were a useful additional disposal – although there was no evidence that they were used as an alternative to custody (Elliott *et al.* 2000). 'There was no *consistent* evidence [in the bail pilots] that a bail curfew provided a true alternative to custodial remand' (Airs *et al.* 2000: vi; emphasis added): it was so used, however, in more than half of those in the trial. EM bail was extended to cover 12–16-year-olds in April 2002 and further extended to 17-year-olds in July. Lack of inter-agency communication was an issue, as it had also been for the 10–15-year-olds, compounded by the presence of private sector agencies who had not been part of the traditional criminal justice system.

All three studies published in 2000 demonstrated that technical problems with EM were now relatively rare, and there were few strong negative feelings about EM. There was a sense that familiarity bred acceptance of EM, if not necessarily enthusiasm. Nonetheless, EM was being rolled-out nationally despite the absence of positive research findings, suggesting that for New Labour ideological factors were important, as they had been for the Conservatives.

Within a year of roll-out, the Criminal Justice and Courts Services Act 2000 introduced further applications of EM. This permitted the use of EM to ensure an offender's compliance with *any requirement* of a community rehabilitation order (CRO) or a community punishment and rehabilitation order (CPRO), including a curfew. It also introduced EM curfews into Detention and Training Orders (a mix of custody and community supervision for young offenders). Such curfews were already being used as part of the Youth Justice Board's Intensive Supervision and Surveillance Programme (ISSP) for serious young offenders, and as part of the Probation Service's (less extensive) young adult (17–20) equivalent, the Intensive Control and Change Programme (ICCP). The ISSP was subject to an extensive evaluation by the University of Oxford, which questioned whether such intensive measures had a crime-reductive effect, whether 'support' and 'surveillance' were in fact as compatible as the measure's name implied, and whether EM was really being used in an 'integrated' way if it was merely serving as the 'punishment part' of a multi-component sentence (Moore 2005). A terrible murder committed by a young man subject to an ISSP, but whose youth justice social workers and private sector monitoring officers barely knew what each other was doing, resulted in considerable negative publicity for EM, somewhat unfairly, because the incident constituted local 'system failure' more broadly (Nellis 2006).

By this time, not only were the target groups for EM expanding, awareness of new EM technologies was increasing too. The CJ and CS Act 2000 actually legislated *in anticipation* of GPS tracking technology becoming available in England, following its introduction in the United States in 1997. Its inclusion in the Act was a response to the high-profile murder of an eight-year-old girl by a known sex offender, and, at a time of heightened media concern about such offenders, signalled Home Office readiness to consider 'out of the box' solutions.

Tracking technology (whose quality the Home Office considered inadequate in 2000, but likely to improve) enabled the continuous tracing of an offender's movements, rather than just pinpointing his location at a single site, overnight, which in turn facilitated the designation of exclusion zones (a former victim's home area, area of routine offending, etc.), whose perimeter could be remotely monitored (Nellis 2005).

The evaluation of the first 13 months of EM curfews that had been rolled-out nationally in December 1999 indicated, unsurprisingly, that take-up was lower than predicted, with this being attributed to 'lack of knowledge about and confidence in the penalty, and the fact that tagging had yet to become part of the established sentencing repertoire' (Walter 2002: 4). Given the number of initiatives using EM during the previous five years, lack of knowledge is rather surprising. The research also found a range of views about how EM might be used, and, as before, continuing liaison and communication problems between criminal justice agencies and EM contractors. Interestingly, many sentencers considered stand-alone curfews to be of little use; curfews were thought likely to be most effective when used *alongside* another community penalty (although this did not necessarily mean *fully integrated* with it).

The opportunity to test this hypothesis came quickly. The CJ and CS Act provision for EM to be used alongside a CRO or a CPRO, as well as the use of EM curfews on prisoners released on licence, was piloted and evaluated in three probation areas: the results were not encouraging. The pilots were poorly organized, and inter-agency communication remained problematic. Recording and communication failures made it impossible to accurately distinguish 'new' from 'old' uses of EM. This not only undermined the viability of the evaluation but, more importantly, had potentially serious consequences for the conduct of breach proceedings (different agencies being involved, depending on the order). Over two years it was estimated that there were only 65–75 cases of a curfew requirement with a community sentence, and cases where EM was part of a licence condition. These were yet again depressingly low numbers (Bottomley *et al.* 2004: 49).

Nonetheless, EM became more deeply embedded in policy, partly reflecting a broader 'techno-managerialist', explicitly modernizing ethos in New Labour, and its determination to break with probation traditions and structures (McLaughlin *et al.* 2001). It remained committed to private sector service delivery for EM (with re-tendering every five years), initially contracting with the three companies that had undertaken trials for the Conservatives – Securicor, Reliance and Premier – later reducing to two – G4S (Securicor merged with Group 4, another security company) and Serco (Premier without its former partner Wackenhut, a private prisons provider in the United States). The Carter Report (2003) on the future of correctional services was keen on the private sector, and anticipated the commissioning of more services from them. It recommended the creation of the National Offender Management Service (NOMS), the capping of the still-rising daily prison population at 80,000 and more use of EM, proposals that the government anticipated and embraced (Home Office 2004). At the same time – as part of a strategy to streamline and strengthen community penalties – the Criminal Justice Act 2003 introduced a generic community order and a new suspended sentence order, each with 12 requirements available. For both exclusion and curfew requirements EM was expected to be used. The offender's consent to these requirements was needed, but a pre-sentence report was not.

A significant seal of approval of EM was given in 2006 by the National Audit Office (NAO – a cost-monitoring body) report, which claimed that 'Electronic monitoring of a curfew has become an integral part of the criminal justice system' (2006: 1). It noted that the use of curfew orders had increased considerably from 9,000 cases in 1999–2000 to 53,000 in 2004–2005. EM was judged to be 'much cheaper than custody' (NAO 2006: 4) and re-conviction rates were 'considerably lower than the national re-conviction rates for all those discharged from prison … and slightly lower than the national re-conviction rate for those completing community penalties' (NAO 2006: 3). In Home Office eyes, such findings – although the NAO could not explain the lower re-conviction rates, and called for more research into EM's effects – were sufficient to justify EM, even if it still had no clear penal (other than space and cost-saving) or crime-reductive purpose. The problems identified by the NAO were primarily administrative and, it was implied, easily solved.

With the strong personal backing of the Home Secretary, David Blunkett (2001–2004), the Home Office initiated a three-site GPS tracking pilot in 2004 (the first in Europe, apart from a short-lived experiment in Bavaria a few months earlier) in Manchester, the West Midlands and Hampshire (all focused on persistent and prolific offenders, with Manchester and Hampshire, in addition, covering sex offenders and young offenders on ISSPs, respectively). Over a two-year period 336 offenders were tracked, the majority on release from prison rather than court orders. Of these, 58 per cent were breached, but 46 per cent said it helped keep them out of trouble. While much learning took place at the local level – sentencers and police, in particular, being impressed with its potential – the evaluation concluded that there were still too many technical difficulties with GPS equipment for it to be a reliable means of supervision, and that it was not at the time a cost-effective intervention (Shute 2007). It should also be understood that in the course of the pilot there was a change of Home Secretary and a shift away from the earlier commitment to capping prison numbers at 80,000, towards allowing the daily population to rise to 100,000 if necessary. In such a climate there was less of an incentive to develop GPS tracking, despite the potential it had been seen to have by involved agencies, particularly with persistent and prolific offenders, more so than with sex offenders.

In the same period as the tracking pilot, small-scale but controversial use of EM curfews, voice verification and GPS tracking was made with refused asylum seekers (offsetting the requirement that they attend reporting centres): the results were never published, but the practice ceased. Even more controversially, the Prevention of Terrorism Act 2005 introduced Control Orders for terrorist *suspects* whom English courts had been forbidden to imprison by a European human rights ruling; these could include a number of major restrictions on an individual's liberty, among them 24-hour EM house arrest (Nellis 2006). In 2007, the NOMS Bail Accommodation and Support Service was created, one element of which was to encourage the use of HDC for eligible prisoners who otherwise lacked a suitable home to go to on release. The 2008 Criminal Justice and Immigration Act made several changes aimed at encouraging further use of EM as a condition of bail, including discounting time spent on EM from any subsequent custodial sentence (as was the case for remand in custody), and a minimum curfew period of nine hours per day.

Towards the integration of EM and offender management?

Between 1999 and 2011 over 760,000 people had been monitored in England and Wales. Cases had gone up from 60,000 per year in 2005/2006 to 116,000 in 2010/2011. On any given day in 2011, some 23,000 offenders were on EM curfews: 34 per cent on bail, 52 per cent on a court-ordered community sentence and 14 per cent on release from prison on licence (Ministry of Justice Information Sheet – Electronic Monitoring: key facts 2011). The 52 per cent on community sentences reflected steady increases in EM's use between 2005 and 2010 (from 3,209 to 17,476 in community orders (3 per cent to 8 per cent of requirements) and 526 to 8,491 in suspended sentence orders (5 per cent to 9 per cent of requirements) (Ministry of Justice 2010: table 4.9). It is not possible to say from this whether EM was being used as a stand-alone requirement, or in conjunction with other requirements, but as Mair and Mills (2009) have argued, it does seem to suggest that community sentences are becoming more punitive, and that pressure was coming from within NOMS to use EM on a progressively larger scale.

In spite of the many official evaluations of EM's various manifestations, it has remained stubbornly unclear whether it is effective, for whom and why (and indeed, whether it works best as a stand-alone or an integrated measure, as Bonta, *et al.* (1999) had suggested it might). Anthea Hucklesby's (2008, 2009, see also this volume) research on the impact of EM on compliance and desistance (sponsored by G4S but undertaken independently) sharpened understanding a little in this respect, showing that even on stand-alone EM curfews offenders were sometimes prompted to contemplate desistance by the restrictive experience and by the influence of helpful family members, and were actively enabled to do so by being kept way from negative influences (people, peer groups or pubs), thereby breaking bad habits. Hucklesby sensed unused potential in EM but also warned that curfew orders could remove people from positive influences, particularly if they impeded employment.

Hucklesby's sense that the probable strengths of EM were being underutilized is echoed in the first, and arguably belated, Criminal Justice Joint Inspection (CJJI) of EM curfews, *A Complicated Business*, whose authors talked of 'the *potential benefits* that EM curfews could make to the supervision of offenders, particularly when used creatively to address particular patterns of offending, or as a sentence for breach of another form of community supervision' (CJJI 2008: 32; emphasis added). EM was portrayed as a measure with a *potential* for crime reduction which had not yet found its niche, implying that something had gone wrong with its implementation. It was not in the CJJI's remit to question the mode of service delivery for EM – the use of the private sector – but, far more astutely than the earlier NAO report, it recognized the intractable complexity of communicating and working across the statutory/private sector divide and it alluded by its very title to the fact that the service delivery infrastructure had perhaps become more complicated than it needed to be, if best use was ever to be got from EM (Nellis 2011).

The CJJI explicitly criticized 'a missed opportunity to integrate curfews into mainstream offender management practice' (CJJI 2008: 11), confirming that – despite the widespread use of EM – it had remained apart from the Probation Service and developed on 'parallel tracks'. The Ministry of Justice was initially stung by these unanticipated criticisms – it was the first time *internal* criticism had been made of EM's direction of travel – but under the rubric of 'offender management' it did begin a process of encouraging greater integration of EM with other supervision methods. In practice this amounted to little more than pressing probation officers to propose EM curfews more often, increasing its proportionate use as a requirement in a community order, and ironing out the striking regional variations in their use. This may possibly have gone further had New Labour remained in power – there had been plans to devolve EM budgets to the regional level within NOMS in the hope of incentivizing greater use – but a change of government in May 2010 presaged the rapid dismantling of NOMS regional infrastructure (largely on cost grounds) and a temporary loss of momentum in respect of 'integrating' EM into offender management (Nellis 2011).

While the new Coalition government (Conservative-led with Liberal Democrat partners) repudiated much of New Labour's organizational rhetoric surrounding NOMS, it remained committed to developing local Probation Trusts as commissioning bodies, and to the slow fragmentation of the statutory Probation Service via cheaper forms of service provision from the voluntary and private sectors (including Serco and G4S who were already involved in delivering EM). Although the Coalition's penal policy was packaged as a 'rehabilitation revolution', and initially hinted at a willingness to reduce the use of custody, its one intended change to EM has been – purely punitively – to increase the maximum daily length of a curfew from 12 to 16 hours (despite Hucklesby's evidence that implied that this may make offenders' compliance with it more difficult), and to increase the maximum length of a curfew order from six to twelve months (aligning with Scotland in this latter respect) (Clarke 2010; Ministry of Justice 2011).

Internally within the Ministry of Justice further thought was being given to the future of EM, initially as a result of drastic budget cuts imposed by the Coalition on all government departments, but also as the EM service contracts came up for five-yearly renewal. High expenditure on stand-alone EM requirements, mostly imposed on offenders who would not have been at risk of custody (and some of whom would have been fined) seemed dubious as value for money. Influenced in part by comparative experiences at CEP EM conferences, and by the lingering message of *A Complicated Business*, a sense emerged among

Ministry of Justice officials that apart from its 'public protection' use within Multi-Agency Public Protection Arrangements (MAPPA) (about which there was negligible EM-focused research), EM in England and Wales was not being used in as integrated or innovative a way as it was in some other European countries. Further stimuli for new thinking came from the development of two GPS tracking initiatives outside the auspices of the Ministry of Justice, one (in 2009) in a National Health Service secure unit for prisoners with psychiatric disorders in south London (where it was used to monitor home leave and temporary leave) and the other (in 2010) in a joint police–probation 'persistent and prolific offender' project in Hertfordshire (where offenders were given voluntary opportunities for tracking in order to demonstrate their commitment to desistance, and absence from known crime scenes). The latter, in particular, indicated serious police interest in the part tracking could play in public protection (an unlearned lesson from the original GPS pilots), which helped rekindle Ministry of Justice support for it.

Officials involved in the pre-procurement review of EM use in England and Wales toyed with the possibility of using EM *less* (fewer stand-alone orders) *but better* (more integrated use) but this seems unlikely to be the outcome. As happened before with EM, ideological considerations will supplant empirical ones. While an emphasis on more innovative use of technology remains (both GPS and voice verification), the sum of money – £1 billion – being made available to contracted-out services has apparently been increased rather than reduced, as part of a vast planned expansion of private sector involvement in criminal justice (and other former public services) (*Guardian*, 29 September 2011). Whether the existing contractor duopoly in EM provision – G4S and Serco – survives intact is moot (some 30 companies have expressed interest in providing EM), but at a time of financial austerity this level of investment in private sector monitoring technology can only be to the detriment of residual public sector expertise in offender supervision.

EM in Scotland, 1998–2011

Scotland has a separate criminal justice system from England and Wales. The development of EM there came a little later and while the same basic 'parallel tracks' pattern of policy development emerged, it diverged a little from the Anglo-Welsh model. It was introduced first under a Labour government, then under a Scottish Nationalist government, eventually (after the pilots) contracting with Reliance as a single national service provider, then Serco. Schemes for adult offenders (aged over 16) were first trialled in 1998–2000, in Hamilton, Aberdeen and Peterhead, and subsequently evaluated by Lobley and Smith (2000; see also Smith 2001), who did not make a strong case for its adoption, encouraging instead more and better use of existing community penalties as a means of reducing prison use. The Scottish Executive (2000) subsequently organized a public consultation with relevant stakeholders, including sentencers, local authorities and voluntary organizations, the results of which were largely positive, and in 2002 legislated EM as a Restriction of Liberty Order (RLO – the equivalent of an EM curfew), and EM as a condition of both a Probation Order and a Drug Treatment and Testing Order. Unlike England and Wales, Scotland's orders permitted both 'restrictions to a place' (the equivalent of a curfew) and 'restrictions from a place' – the equivalent of an exclusion zone, created by placing tag-sensitive equipment around its perimeter – though the latter were little used. Subsequent legislation in 2003 specified that RLOs could be used as a direct alternative to custody, and also introduced EM as a parole condition.

EM for juvenile offenders (8–16-year-olds) was introduced in a different political context in Scotland than it had been in England. In Scotland it was introduced as both a stand-alone RLO and as part of Intensive Supervision and Monitoring (ISM) programmes in 2004, which were in turn part of a larger 'anti-social behaviour initiative' that the ruling Scottish Labour party attempted to import from England in the hope of it proving similarly popular with tabloid media, police and citizens. In England, the use of stand-alone EM curfews for juveniles and the introduction of ISSPs were discursively and practically separate initiatives from the 'antisocial behaviour agenda', and untainted by liberal dislike of it. It is likely that EM for juveniles would in any case have been resisted by the many champions of the very welfare-oriented approach towards this age group that had been so strikingly sustained in Scotland since the 1960s, but coupling it with the explicitly punitive and controlling aspects of the 'antisocial behaviour agenda', which was even less well received than in England, intensified hostility to it (McAra 2006). The government considered 'movement restriction requirements' (as the EM provision was called) to be integral elements of ISMs, but in the pilots some children's panels (welfare tribunals rather than courts), while happy with all other aspects of the intensive support programmes, refused to include them. The Scottish government threatened to withdraw funding for ISMs as a whole unless the panels complied (but never in practice did so). The ISM evaluation did not find that young people whose mobility was restricted by EM fared any better on ISM in terms of re-offending than those whose was not, and when the scheme went national EM curfews became a discretionary element in it (Khan and Hill 2008). Deuchars (2012) later, more ethnographic, research on juvenile (and young adult) experiences of EM in Glasgow reaffirmed the resentment among those subject to it, and their families, that Khan and Hill had also noted.

Scotland introduced a HDC scheme in July 2006 to ease pressure on its rising adult prison population and to structure the early release process on much the same basis as it had been introduced in England and Wales. As there, it significantly increased daily numbers on EM – but unlike there, HDCs proportionate use has not declined, and remains higher than the use of court-ordered EM sentences. Perhaps the most striking operational difference between the two countries, however, is the much higher recall rate in Scotland – 25 per cent in 2010 as opposed to 11 per cent in England and Wales, which may possibly be explained by the fact that recall decisions are made by individual prisons in Scotland, but coordinated by a central office in England and Wales (Armstrong *et al.* 2011).

Faced with a rising remand population, Scotland did consider using EM as a means of strengthening bail, but after a four-site pilot (Glasgow, Stirling and Kilmarnock Sheriff's Court, plus Glasgow High Court) in 2005–2006 concluded that it was not a cost-effective measure, Scotland decided against using it nationally. Uptake was low – only 4.4 per cent of all 6,914 eligible cases in a 16-month period, and of the 306 applications for EM bail only 38 per cent were granted, mostly curfew restrictions *to* a place, with a minority restricted *from* a place, or both. The comparatively high cost of EM bail derived from the fact that there was no discount on any subsequent custodial sentence, as there was from a custodial remand, saving costs at that point in the process (Barry *et al.* 2007). The government decided against a national roll-out, but the cost finding may have influenced England and Wales to introduce sentence discounts in their EM bail scheme in 2008.

The most significant departure from Anglo-Welsh practice in the Scottish use of EM is the most recent. When Scotland introduced the equivalent of its generic community order – a Community Payback Order (CPO) – in February 2011 as part of a broader strategy to reduce prisoner numbers (by ending the use of custodial sentences of under three months) EM was *not* one of its requirements, as it had been in England and Wales. Stand-alone RLOs remained available, separate from the local authority services that constituted the CPO, reflecting the prevalent sense that social work and EM were in no way complementary. More interestingly, however, EM curfew (called a 'restricted movement requirement') was made available as a penalty for breaching the requirements of a CPO, as a possible way of forestalling (or delaying) the use of a custodial sentence. Given marked regional variations in the use of RLOs, it remains to be seen if sentencers are consistent in their use of this breach measure, which will raise issues of fairness if they are not.

Conclusion

The England and Wales EM scheme quickly became the largest in Europe because of its readiness to use stand-alone EM curfews on a large scale at progressively lower tariff levels, despite initial (but easily questioned) government claims that it would be a high-tariff alternative to custody. Given the circumstances of its introduction – as a means of threatening the Probation Service with displacement if it did not adopt a more punitive and controlling ethos – it was highly unlikely that it would ever be integrated effectively into other measures of community supervision, and continued service delivery by the private sector compounded the sense that it was a separate activity, running on parallel tracks to the probation service. Notwithstanding 'integrated' uses of EM in respect of ISSPs and MAPPA, the mainly low-tariff use of EM in Britain, given its potential to add constructive elements of control into targeted rehabilitation or reintegration programmes for offenders genuinely at risk of custody represents the worst of all possible worlds. Despite the amount and quality of research on EM undertaken in Britain, it was rarely used well, partly because government commitment to reducing the use of imprisonment, in the rare moments when this occurred, was never more than half-hearted.

Drawing on the plethora of meticulous research undertaken in England and Wales, and on extensive knowledge of international developments, probation manager Dick Whitfield sought to stimulate a serious debate about the modest and constructive uses to which EM might be put, but, unlike Sweden, because of England and Wales' service delivery infrastructure, and the Probation Service's continuing marginalization, it was never within the Service's ability (or inclination) to shape the way EM was used. Whitfield was, however, instrumental in encouraging the CEP to devote resources to successive EM conferences, and there is a certain irony in the way that recognition of better EM practices in some other European countries, borne of these conferences, has eventually impacted on English thinking, if only slightly, and with uncertain consequences.

The new Coalition government have distanced themselves a little from the (much-criticized) techno-managerialist obsessions that characterized New Labour, but have maintained a commitment to 'modernizing' public services and intensified efforts to contract-out 'offender management' services to voluntary and commercial organizations. Their vaunted commitment to a 'rehabilitation revolution' seems half-hearted, and their plans for further investment in EM – something of a 'Trojan horse' for the private sector – suggest that they are content with the large-scale use of purely punitive measures, as stand-alone EM has always been.

There is a tendency in England and Wales for penal reformers and probation services to sometimes look north to Scotland for more convivial, less punitive ways of organizing criminal justice services, and notwithstanding its comparably high rate of imprisonment, Scotland has indeed retained (because politicians have not actively stifled it) a slightly greater commitment to rehabilitative measures, strikingly so for juveniles, but to some extent even for adult offenders. In this climate, greater scepticism has prevailed towards EM. It never felt as embedded or accepted in the sentencing repertoire as it became in England and Wales, and certainly there has been only marginal interest in innovative uses of it (not even, as in England and Wales, in the run up to the renewal of the service contract). Nonetheless, there is no reason to think in either country, that EM will have no future. As one among many affordances of pervasive telecommunication networks – telehealth and telecare also have an increasing presence in the UK – remote monitoring of offender locations (and maybe movements) will continue to be seen as an appropriately and self-evidently 'modern' form of intervention. Worldwide, EM continues to grow, and the early adopters are unlikely to opt out.

Dystopian scenarios are easily conjured out of EM, but the real lesson of British experience with EM is how little difference the stimulus of technological innovation actually made to penal practice; if moral argument and political strategies alone cannot galvanize commitment to reduced prison use, the availability of a new technology (at least *this* technology, in *this* context) cannot, by itself, be of help. EM has earned a niche for itself in the British criminal justice system, created a new occupation of private sector monitoring officers (Hucklesby 2011) and given new penal/surveillant experiences to a large number of offenders, but it has not had even a modestly transformative effect on the enduring punitive traditions that ensure Britain's continuing place near the top of European league tables of prison use. It was absorbed early into these traditions, and despite the relentlessly modernizing rhetoric associated with the policies and structures through which it was implemented, political and professional inertia – and an increasingly transparent commercialism – has kept it there, with dispiriting penal consequences. In England and Wales, EM was not used to build on the best of what was happening in penal policy in the 1990s – in terms of an early (if shortlived) commitment to reducing custody and increased quality in probation supervision – and its relentless expansion in the twenty-first century as a stand-alone measure, parallel to two governments' deliberate fragmentation of the Probation Service into a multiplicity of third (and private) sector offender management services, is most aptly described in Stuart Hall's (1988) terms as 'regressive modernization'.

References

Airs, J., Elliott, R. and Conrad, E. (2000) *Electronically Monitored Curfew as a Condition of Bail: Report of the pilot* (London: Home Office).

Armstong, S., Malloch, M., Nellis, M. and Norris, P. (2011) *Evaluating the Effectiveness of Home Detention Curfew and Open Prison in Scotland: Research Findings 32/2011* (Edinburgh: Scottish Government).

Barry, M., Malloch, M., Moodie, K, Nellis, M., Knapp, M., Romeo, R. and Dhansiri, S. (2007) *An Evaluation of the Use of Electronic Monitoring as a Condition of Bail in Scotland* (Edinburgh: Scottish Executive).

Bonta, J., Capretta, S.W. and Rooney, J. (1999) *Electronic Monitoring in Canada* (Toronto: Solicitor General's Office).

Bottomley, K., Hucklesby, A., Mair, G. and Nellis M. (2004) 'The new uses of electronic monitoring: findings from the implementation phase in three pilot areas', in *Issues in Community and Criminal Justice Monograph 5* (London: NAPO).

Carter, P. (2003) *Managing Offenders, Reducing Crime: A new approach* (London: Strategy Unit).

CJJI (Criminal Justice Joint Inspection) (2008) *A Complicated Business: A joint inspection of electronically monitored curfew requirements orders and licences* (London: CCJI.).

Clarke, K. (2010) 'The government's vision for criminal justice reform', Speech presented at the Centre for Crime and Justice Studies, London, 30 June.

Deuchars, R. (2012) 'The impact of curfews and electronic monitoring on the social strains, support and capital experienced by youth gang members and offenders in the west of Scotland' *Criminology and Criminal Justice* (forthcoming).

Dodgson, K., Goodwin, P., Howard, P., Llewellyn-Thomas, S., Mortimer, E., Russell, N. and Weiner, M. (2001) *Electronic Monitoring of Released Prisoners: An evaluation of the Home Detention Curfew Scheme.* (London: Home Office).

Elliott, R. and Airs, J. (2000) *New Measures for Fine Defaulters, Persistent Petty Offenders and Others: The report of the Crime (Sentence) Act 1997 pilots* (London: Home Office).

Elliott, R., Airs, J., Easton, C. and Lewis, R. (2000) *Electronically Monitored Curfew for 10- to 15-Year-Olds: Report of the pilot.* (London: Home Office).

Hall, S. (1988) *The Hard Road to Renewal: Thatcherism and the crisis of the Left* (London: Verso).

Home Office (1988) *Punishment, Custody and the Community* (London: HMSO).

Home Office (1990) *Crime, Justice and Protecting the Public* (London: HMSO).

Home Office (2000) *Prison Statistics* (London: Home Office).

Home Office (2003) *Prison Statistics England and Wales 2002* (London: The Stationery Office).

Home Office (2004) *Reducing Crime, Changing Lives: The government's plans for transforming the management of offenders* (London: Home Office).

House of Commons (1987) *Third Report from the Home Affairs Committee: State and use of prisons*, Vol. 1. (London: HMSO).

Hucklesby, A. (2008) 'Vehicles of desistance? The impact of electronically monitored curfew orders', *Criminology and Criminal Justice*, 8, pp. 51–71.

Hucklesby, A. (2009) 'Understanding offender's compliance: A case study of electronically monitored curfew orders', *Journal of Law and Society*, 36:2, pp. 248–271.

Hucklesby, A. (2011) 'The working life of electronic monitoring officers', *Criminology and Criminal Justice*, 11:1, pp. 59–76.

Jones, T. and Newburn, T. (2007) *Policy Transfer and Criminal Justice: Exploring US influence over British crime control policy* (Maidenhead: Open University Press).

Khan, F. and Hill, M. (2008) *Evaluation of Includem's Intensive Support Services* (Glasgow: Includem).

Lilly, J.R. and Himan, J. (eds) (1993) *The Electronic Monitoring of Offenders* (Leicester: De Montfort University Law School Monograph).

Lobley, D. and Smith, D. (2000) *Evaluation of Electronically Monitored Restriction of Liberty Orders* (Edinburgh: Scottish Executive Central Research Unit).

McAra, L. (2006) 'Welfare in crisis: key developments in Scottish youth justice', in J. Muncie and B. Goldson (eds) *Comparative Youth Justice* (London: Sage), pp. 127–145.

McLaughlin, E., Muncie, J. and Hughes, G. (2001) 'The permanent revolution: New Labour, new public management and the modernisation of criminal justice', *Criminal Justice*, 1:3, pp. 301–318.

Mair, G. (2001) 'Technology and the future of community penalties', in A. Bottoms, L. Gelsthorpe and S. Rex (eds) *Community Penalties: Change and challenges* (Cullompton: Willan), pp. 168–182.

Mair, G. (2005) 'Electronic monitoring in England and Wales: evidence-based or not?', *Criminal Justice*, 5:3, pp. 257–277.

Mair, G. and Mills, H. (2009) *The Community Order and the Suspended Sentence Order Three Years On: The views and experiences of probation officers and offenders* (London: Centre for Crime and Justice Studies).

Mair, G. and Mortimer, E. (1996) *Curfew Orders with Electronic Monitoring* (London: Home Office).

Mair, G. and Nee, C. (1990) *Electric Monitoring: The trials and their results* (London: HMSO).

Marie, O., Moreton, K. and Goncalves, M. (2011) *The Effect of Early Release of Prisoners on Home Detention Curfew (HDC) on Recidivism* (London: Ministry of Justice).

Ministry of Justice (2010) *Offender Management Statistics: Quarterly bulletin* (London: Ministry of Justice).

Ministry of Justice (2011) *Green Paper: Breaking the cycle – effective punishment, rehabilitation and sentencing of offenders* (London: Ministry of Justice).

Moore, R. (2005) 'The use of electronic and human surveillance in a multi-modal programme', *Youth Justice*, 5:5, pp. 17–32.

Mortimer, E. and May, C. (1997) *Electronic Monitoring in Practice: The second year of the trials of curfew orders* (London: Home Office).

Mortimer, E., Pereira, E. and Walter, I. (1999) *Making the Tag Fit: Further analysis from the first two years of the trials of curfew orders* (London: Home Office).

NAO (National Audit Office) (2006) *The Electronic Monitoring of Adult Offenders* (London: The Stationery Office).

Nathan, S. (2003) 'Prison privatisation in the United Kingdom', in A. Coyle, B. Campbell and R. Neufeld (eds) *Capitalist Punishment: prison privatisation and human rights* (London: Zed books), pp. 162–178.

Nellis, M. (1991) 'The electronic monitoring of offenders in England and Wales: recent developments and future prospects', *British Journal of Criminology*, 31:2, pp. 165–185.

Nellis, M. (2000) 'Law and order: the electronic monitoring of offenders', in D. Dolowitz (ed.) *Policy Transfer and British Social Policy* (Buckingham: Open University Press), pp. 98–117.

Nellis, M. (2003) 'Electronic monitoring and the future of probation', in W.H. Chui and M. Nellis (eds) *Moving Probation Forward: Evidence, arguments and practice* (Harlow: Pearson Longman), pp. 245–260.

Nellis, M. (2004) 'The electronic monitoring of offenders in Britain: a critical overview', in *Issues in Community and Criminal Justice Monograph 5* (London: NAPO), pp. 53–91.

Nellis, M. (2005) '"Out of this World": the advent of the satellite tracking of offenders in England and Wales', *Howard Journal*, 44:2, pp. 125–150.

Nellis, M. (2006) 'The limitations of electronic monitoring: the tagging of Peter Williams', *Prison Service Journal*, 164, pp. 3–12.

Nellis, M. (2011) 'The 'complicated business' of electronic monitoring', in R. Taylor, M. Hill and F. McNeill (eds) *Early Professional Development for Social Workers* (Birmingham: Venture Press/BASW), pp. 293–302.

NOMS (2010) 'Prison population and accommodation briefing, 19th November 2010', National Offender Management Service.

Prisons and Probation Ombudsman (2009) *Annual Report 2008–2009* (London: Central Office of Information).

Russell, K. and Lilly, J.R. (eds) (1989) *The Electronic Monitoring of Offenders* (Leicester: Leicester Polytechnic Law School Monograph).

Scottish Executive (2000) *Tagging Offenders: The role of electronic monitoring in the Scottish criminal justice system* (Edinburgh: Scottish Executive).

Shute, S. (2007) *Satellite Tracking of Offenders: A study of the pilots in England and Wales* (London: Ministry of Justice).

Smith, D. (2001) 'Electronic monitoring of offenders: the Scottish experience', *Criminal Justice*, 1:2, pp. 201–214.

Walter, I. (2002) *Evaluation of the National Roll-Out of Curfew Orders*. Online. Available at: www.homeoffice.gov.uk/rds/pdfs2/rdsolr1502.pdf.

Whitfield, D. (1997) *Tackling the Tag* (Winchester: Waterside Press).

Whitfield, D. (2001) *The Magic Bracelet* (Winchester: Waterside Press).

4 Extending the electronic net in Australia and New Zealand

Developments in electronic monitoring down-under

Russell G. Smith and Anita Gibbs

Introduction

Australia and New Zealand, although far removed from the United States and Europe, have always shown a willingness to take on new European and American developments in crime control, especially those involving high technology. The first Pentonville-style prison in Melbourne in the 1830s, for example, installed an elaborate treadmill which, despite the best efforts of the authorities, was regularly out of order – much to the prisoners' approval (National Trust of Australia (Victoria) 1991). More recently, Australia has explored a variety of new technologies of crime control (Grabosky 1998). It was predictable, therefore, that Australia and New Zealand would experiment with EM as soon as it became available. EM programmes have been running since the early 1990s in New South Wales, Queensland, South Australia, Northern Territory and Western Australia (Aungles 1995). New Zealand's use of EM began in 1999 to support the introduction of home detention as an alternative to imprisonment (Gibbs and King 2003).

This chapter explores the use of EM in Australia and New Zealand, not only for correctional purposes following criminal prosecution and conviction, but also for surveillance of individuals deemed to be at risk of committing serious violent crimes or terrorist-related activities. We briefly examine the drivers that led to the development of EM in each country, then consider the legislative framework used to support these orders. We then review the structure and scale of programmes and issues of controversy arising from practice and research. We conclude with some thoughts on ethics and on the future of EM.

The development of EM

There are a number of reasons explaining why electronic monitoring (EM) has developed in Australia and New Zealand, and why EM has now attained the status of 'here to stay', rather than being viewed as just another techno-fashion which will diminish over time. Mainprize (1996) suggested that EM established itself internationally in a context of fiscal control and restraint, as well as the ideological imperative that rehabilitation was not working, and therefore 'getting tough' with the use of new surveillance technology was what politicians and criminal justice policy-makers needed to do. Another important aspect was that the technologies of remote communication and control were ready and so could easily be applied to a whole range of criminal justice control strategies. There were other drivers – for example, in both Australia and New Zealand prison overcrowding was used as a reason for introducing EM of prisoners released early on home detention or parole (Richardson 1999; Bagaric 2002; Gibbs 2004), as was the idea of cost-effective intermediate sanctions for people who would have otherwise gone to prison. The aggressive marketing of private companies was also instrumental in the growth of EM (Maxfield and Baumer 1990; Liverani 1998).

According to Albrecht (2003: 250), EM is not house arrest but 'is a restriction of freedom through enforcing precisely defined or structured time schedules through technology'. The way in which Australia and New Zealand have used EM reflects this structuring of time. Authorities in the two countries have wanted to control or monitor the location of an individual without resorting to imprisonment, and EM fits as the means to achieve these goals. For example, EM can be applied before a criminal trial, while a defendant is bailed, or after conviction to ensure limits have been placed on an offender's freedom without resorting to a full-time custodial sanction. Also, upon release from prison, a Parole Board may want to impose restrictions on an offender and EM can be used to monitor the offender's movements at home. Finally, and most contentiously, after completing a sentence, authorities have tried to use EM as a crime-prevention tool, particularly in situations where serious violent offences may occur.

In 1987 the eminent Australian sentencing scholar, Richard Fox, reviewed the policy considerations applicable to the use of EM in Australia (Fox 1987). In the state of Victoria, an inquiry into sentencing law reform had already identified the potential for EM (Victorian Sentencing Committee 1987), although Fox was less enthusiastic, preferring a more cautious approach that would be based on the outcome of evaluative research. The mid-1980s was also a time at which the use of conditional sentencing dispositions increased greatly and EM was seen to be an efficient way in which correctional administrators could assess compliance with orders quickly and cheaply. When Fox (2001) reviewed the topic in 2001, he renewed his call for vigorous debate over the ever-expanding use of surveillance technologies in Australia, which has extended far beyond using EM on offenders.

In New Zealand, a small pilot study between 1995 and 1997 introduced passive monitoring to support paroled prisoners by using telephone calls and voice verification to identify offenders. The evaluation of the pilot showed that during an 18-month period only 37 offenders were released on monitoring conditions and of these about 30 per cent re-offended within two years (Church and Dunstan 1997). The pilot was not viewed as a success, but this did not stop the then National Government introducing a full home detention scheme with active EM in 1999 (Gibbs and King 2003).

Legislation and EM practice in Australia

Generally in Australia and New Zealand, sentencing legislation has been sufficiently broad to permit the use of EM as one of a variety of conditions attached to bail, probation or parole orders. The Standard Guidelines for Corrections in Australia (Western Australia Department of Justice *et al.* 2004) state that the level of surveillance be proportionate to the assessed risk level and the minimum level needed for compliance, that the monitoring regime be minimally intrusive for co-inhabitants and that monitoring devices be as unobtrusive, practical and robust against the signalling of false violations (Western Australia Department of Justice *et al.* 2004: § 2.3–2.5). The current legislative regime in Australia can best be understood by considering the various stages in the criminal justice system at which EM may be used, the different technologies – radio frequency and GPS, and their passive and active modes of use – and their three main rationales. First, EM can be used to ensure that the individual offender remains in a designated place, typically at home during established curfew hours (Mukherjee 1999; Crowe 2002). Alternatively, it can be used to prohibit entry to proscribed areas, or approach of particular people, such as complainants, potential victims or even co-offenders (Marien 2002; *Economist* 2002). Finally, EM may be used so that authorities can continuously track a person, without actually restricting their movements.

A range of monitoring systems are used in Australia. For example, an active monitoring system has been used in South Australia for the past five years, in preference to the earlier passive system. This system has a drive-by facility which allows a supervisor to drive past a place where an offender is supposed to be, removing the intrusive nature of personal visits, which can disrupt a household or workplace (South Australia Department for Correctional Services 2009). Similarly, in the Australian Capital Territory (ACT) an active monitoring system was previously used, through a fixed unit commonly placed in the offender's residence. In the Northern Territory a modified version of active EM is used. An electronic device is worn by the offender in the post-release stage; however, its purpose is to record face-to-face interactions with surveillance officers rather than obtaining the individual's whereabouts (Henderson 2006). At present New South Wales mostly uses passive monitoring, with visits to the home and phone calls to check the location of the individual in question.

In Australia, correctional agency statistics are collected for 'restricted movement orders', which includes home detention with or without EM. Data do not, however, exist solely for orders which entail EM, although in some jurisdictions, such as Victoria, all restricted movement orders are accompanied by EM. Restricted movement orders are available in all jurisdictions except Tasmania, Queensland and the ACT. Community corrections also include post-custodial programmes (for example, parole, release on licence, pre-release orders and some forms of home detention), under which prisoners released into the community continue to be subject to corrective services supervision (Productivity Commission Report 2005: ch. 7.18). Data from 1999 to 2009 are presented in Table 4.1. Overall,

Table 4.1 Restricted movement orders (home detention) in Australian jurisdictions, 1999–2009: average daily number of persons and average completion rates (in parentheses)

Jurisdiction	1999–2000	2000–2001	2001–2002	2002–2003	2003–2004	2004–2005[2]	2005–2006	2006–2007	2007–2008	2008–2009[3]
New South Wales	188 (75.5%)	184 (74.7%)	175 (76.4%)	229 (81.9%)	200 (75.9%)	192 (78.7%)	211 (83.5%)	213 (82.8%)	152 (87.5%)	175 (79.7%)
Victoria	N/A	N/A	N/A	N/A	2[1] (100%)	20 (91.2%)	22 (98.4%)	24 (94.9%)	34 (98.9%)	32 (97.7)
Queensland	112 (88.7%)	103 (89.8%)	78 (80.3%)	75 (83.2%)	63 (66.8%)	69 (84.0%)	77 (89.2%)	4 (84.5%)	N/A	N/A
Western Australia[4]	89 (83.4%)	85 (82.2%)	83 (79.5%)	81 (79.1%)	80 (74.8%)	15 (57.3%)	16 (73.0%)	5 (75.1%)	7 (50%)	4 (70.6%)
South Australia	132 (66.3%)	171 (69.9%)	185 (65.4%)	219 (70.7%)	278 (61.1%)	307 (65.4%)	376 (67.8%)	380 (69.3%)	359 (70.5%)	423 (75.2%)
Tasmania	N/A	N/A	N/A	N/A	N/A	N/A	N/A	N/A	N/A	N/A
Australian Capital Territory	N/A	N/A	2 (100%)	2 (66.7%)	3 (50.0%)	6 (83.3%)	1 (100%)	N/A	N/A	N/A
Northern Territories	18 (95.5)	33 (93.5%)	34 (85.7%)	51 (83.2%)	58 (86.4%)	56 (92.2%)	42 (88.7%)	38 (86.1%)	34 (88%)	31 (92.3%)
Australia (total)	539 (78.6%)	576 (78.4%)	558 (75.3%)	657 (78.2%)	684 (72.3%)	792 (72.1%)	866 (77.2%)	772 (76.4%)	586 (78.6%)	665 (78.2%)

Source: Productivity Commission 2004–2009.

Notes

1 According to Productivity Commission (2005): restricted movement orders (home detention) were introduced in Victoria on 1 January 2004; in the six months to the end of the financial year, 25 offenders had received these orders.

2 According to the SA Correctional Services Annual Report 2004–2005, 'Almost 95% of Intensive Bail Supervision Orders include EM' (*n* = 652 new orders).

3 Restricted movement orders were available in all jurisdictions except Queensland, Tasmania and Australian Capital Territory for 2008–2009. In QLD restricted movement orders were removed as a sentencing option following the introduction of the Corrective Services Act 2006 with only those currently serving the orders continuing until their completion. Home detention was removed as a sentencing option from ACT legislation as of 30 June 2005.

4 The definition of a restricted movement order was revised in 2008, only to include those conditional bail orders which enforced EM. The figures for WA must therefore be interpreted with caution when making comparisons between jurisdictions.

the numbers of persons on restricted movement orders (home detention) increased steadily between 1999/2000 and 2006/2007, before dropping in 2007/2008. An increase occurred again in 2008/2009.

Data are also published with respect to certain demographic characteristics of offenders on restricted movement orders. Of the 175 people on restricted movement orders in New South Wales, on average, for example, in 2008–2009, 148 were males (84 per cent); 28 were females (16 per cent); 16 were indigenous (9.1 per cent) and 154 were non-indigenous (88 per cent) (Productivity Commission 2010). In terms of successful completion rates, the principal evaluative criterion for community corrections orders in Australia, it appears that there are few differences between successful completion of supervision compliance orders and restricted movement orders in Australian jurisdictions (Productivity Commission 2006). In 2008–2009, successful completion of restricted movement orders ranged from 98 per cent in Victoria to 75 per cent in South Australia, with the Australian average at 78 per cent (Western Australia had the lowest completion rate of 71 per cent, but this relates to a very small sample size compared with other jurisdictions). Since 1999, each Australian state and territory for which data are available has shown similar completion rates from year to year, with Victoria having the highest rates of any jurisdiction since restricted movement orders were first introduced in January 2004.

Pre-trial

Both Western Australian and South Australian legislation provide for EM at the pre-trial stage. The Bail Act 1982 (Western Australia) allows home detention to be imposed on an accused person aged over 17, but only by a judicial officer. A suitability report must first be obtained from a corrections officer and then the accused person may be required to wear a device or to permit the installation of a device in the place where the person is required to remain. Similarly, South Australian legislation provides for home detention EM as a court-imposed condition of bail and the courts have significantly increased their use of this option in recent years (Productivity Commission 2007: 7.35). The courts have significantly increased their use of this option in recent years and, as a result, South Australia manages the largest home detention EM programme nationally (Productivity Commission 2007: 7.35). A recent study into remand in South Australia, however, found that there was perceived to be a severe limitation in the number of available electronic devices to support bail, and that magistrates indicated that if more electronic devices were available home detention would be more frequently utilized as a bail alternative (King *et al.* 2005: 101).

Primary sentencing

Two Australian jurisdictions have specific legislative authority for home detention with EM as a primary sentencing option. The Northern Territory Sentencing Act provides that a 'court which sentences an offender to a term of imprisonment may make an order suspending the sentence on the offender entering into a home detention order'. Offenders on a home detention order may be required to 'wear or have attached a monitoring device'. The programme is a direct alternative to imprisonment (Department of Justice 2002). The court first sentences an offender to imprisonment and then, if the offender consents and is assessed as suitable, the term may be served through monitored home detention. In Western Australia the Sentencing Act 1995 provides that a court may impose an intensive supervision order with a curfew requirement. This requires the offender to 'submit to surveillance or monitoring as ordered' and to wear a device or have a device installed in his or her home. EM 'may only be imposed for a term of 6 months or less'. In addition, the Young Offenders Amendment Act 2005 provides courts with the option of extending the application of curfews with EM to juveniles. It is now used with young offenders in metropolitan areas and in some regional areas of Western Australia (Western Australian Department of Justice 2009). New South Wales law does not specifically authorize EM, but the Crimes (Sentencing Procedure) Act 1999 (NSW) gives courts the power to sentence certain offenders to home detention with 'such conditions as it considers appropriate'. In practice, EM is used to enforce these home detention orders (Keay 2000; Studerus 1999; Jarred 2000). In Victoria, both the courts and the Adult Parole Board may direct offenders to undergo home detention. During submissions to a court on sentencing, the offender or his or her legal representative may suggest home detention as a sentencing option for appropriate offenders. Similarly, home detention can be requested during an application for parole. In the ACT, restricted movement orders (home detention) were first introduced in October 2001, and became available as a sentencing option in October 2002. They were removed as of 30 June 2005.

Custodial monitoring

In the ACT, the Corrections Management Act 2009 (ACT) permits the use of radio frequency identification (RFID) to track prisoners, staff and visitors within the Alexander Maconochie Centre, the ACTs new correctional facility. The Corrections Management (Radio Frequency Identification) policy seeks to increase prisoner accountability for incidents and to facilitate the resolution of disputes between inmates. During muster or lockdown times, the RFID system will decrease the time spent accounting for prisoner whereabouts and therefore will increase the efficiency of security processes, allowing for the allocation of on-ground staff to other tasks. Ongoing evaluative research is needed to determine the extent to which these objectives are being realized.

Post-prison

Legislation in two jurisdictions contemplates the use of EM in post-prison administration of sentences. In Western Australia, the Sentence Administration Act 1995 allows certain prisoners to be released on home detention. These offenders may be required to wear a monitoring device or to have a device installed in the place where they are required to live. Similarly, the Queensland Corrective Services Act 2000 provides that offenders released on community-based release orders (including parole and home detention) may be required to wear a device that monitors the offender's location. In November 2006 the New South Wales government passed an amendment to the Dangerous Prisoners (Sexual Offenders) Act 2003, allowing courts to impose EM on offenders as part of extended supervision orders following completion of prison terms. A new probation and parole service was launched in Queensland in 2006 to undertake monitoring of those offenders serving sentences in the community (Queensland Corrective Services 2007). A total of A$4 million was allocated in budgets for 2007–2011 to implement the EM system. By August 2007 EM had become a standard feature of all new orders, allowing Queensland correctional officers to impose curfews and EM as required (Queensland Corrective Services 2007).

In Victoria, in February 2005, the government passed the Serious Sex Offenders Monitoring Act 2005 (Vic) to allow EM of sex offenders following their release from prison, house arrest, reporting requirements and bans on mixing with children. An extended supervision order is now able to be applied to a serious offender who is unresponsive to treatment, will not partake in rehabilitation or does not show remorse for his or her actions. The idea behind extended supervision is to help released prisoners become stable, while also safeguarding the public. The Act allows for restrictions to be imposed on where serial sex offenders may live and work, what contact they may have with children, as well as determining the circumstances in which they may move house or leave the state without permission. Orders are subject to appeal and may be revised or extended on application to a court, but can be imposed for up to 15 years following the completion of a prison term. The legislation was used first in July 2005 to monitor the movements of a convicted paedophile (see discussion below; Shiel 2005). In Victoria, the home detention programme commenced on 1 January 2004 pursuant to the Corrections and Sentencing Acts (Home Detention) Act 2003 (Vic). It is targeted at carefully selected non-violent, low-security offenders who serve part of their sentence by way of home detention after they have served two-thirds of their minimum term of imprisonment. Offenders may serve a maximum of six months on home detention. Home detention enables low-risk offenders to maintain the employment, family and community ties necessary for rehabilitation and reintegration. Under the programme, the Board can revoke court orders and its own orders in cases where orders are breached. It is a core condition of a home detention order in Victoria that the offender submit to EM (including voice recording) of compliance with the order (§ 18ZZB(i) Sentencing Act 1991 (Vic); § 60J(i) Corrections Act 1986 (Vic)).

During 2004–2005, the Victorian Parole Board received a total of 293 applications from offenders wishing to participate in the programme. This result compares with 233 applications received in the first six months of the programme. The board assesses applications carefully to ensure that the offender is eligible. In determining an application, the board assesses information relating to the offender's criminal history; past and current sentence structure; psychological, psychiatric, medical and intervention order history; accommodation arrangements; prison conduct; and programme participation (Adult Parole Board of Victoria 2005: 22).

Once the board's home detention staff have determined that an applicant is eligible for the programme, they request the Home Detention Unit to provide an assessment report for the board. Before making a decision to grant home detention, the board interviews every offender by video conference or in person and explains the requirements of the programme. Of the 293 applications received, the board determined that 162 applications were ineligible for the programme and made 131 assessment requests to the Home Detention Unit for a report (Adult Parole Board of Victoria 2005: 22). In 2004–2005, the board made 57 home detention orders and the courts a further eight, totalling 65, all of which employed EM. An evaluation of this programme in 2006 revealed low breach and revocation rates (Corrections Victoria 2006). Overall, there were five serious breaches that led to revocation and 15 minor breaches. These rates were lowest for the post-prison stage rather than when orders were handed down at initial sentencing. The Victorian home detention programme returned $1.80 in benefits for every $1 spent on the programme in 2006, therefore yielding superior outcomes for less cost than the alternative of imprisonment (Corrections Victoria 2006). The evaluation also revealed overwhelming support from family members, despite suggestions in the literature that home detention with monitoring can have adverse effects on the families residing with detainees (Martin *et al.* 2009; Martinovic 2007).

In South Australia, EM is available in the final six months of a prison sentence (Jarred 2000). The prisoner is released into the community with an EM condition and will then either progress onto a traditional parole order or finish the sentence. A radio frequency (RF) system is used which automatically checks a detainee's presence at their residence every 11 seconds, which is arguably less intrusive to the offender and other residents than systems which make random telephone calls to the home. The monitoring device records and stores all movements and alerts the on-call duty officer if the offender moves out of range or there is tampering with the equipment. At any given time up to 175 people can be monitored electronically. The system also provides for checks on detainees attending a place of employment, educational institution, etc. (South Australia Department of Correctional Services 2004: 3).

In Queensland a trial of 74 offenders on home detention with EM was undertaken in the southeast corner of the state in 2001. It was found, however, that the electronic bracelets did not add any statistical significance to the successful completion of the orders. The Queensland Department of Corrective Services found no great advantage to the use of EM and found it to be quite an expensive technology. On its own, the department believed that EM did nothing to assist offenders to integrate into the community or to be successfully under surveillance (evidence of Ms Kathryn Holman, Executive Adviser, Correctional Operations, in the Office of the Deputy Director General, Queensland to the Inquiry into *Back-end Home Detention* (New South Wales Parliament, Legislative Council, Standing Committee on Law and Justice 2005)).

In December 2005, the Queensland government indicated an intention to introduce legislation later in 2006, similar to that which exists in Victoria, which would enable convicted paedophile offenders to be subject to EM if a risk of re-offending is established. The proposal was sparked by a case in which a convicted paedophile was charged with sex offences against two girls in Queensland. Under the proposed laws, police would be able to apply to the courts for child sex offender prohibition orders which could restrict where paedophiles can live, and even who they can associate with. This could mean a paedophile is prevented from going within 200 metres of parks or movie theatres where children congregate, entering shopping centres when school children could be there or even associating with anyone aged under 16 (Odgers 2005).

GPS technology has been piloted or mooted in several states. New South Wales promoted it as part of the 'serious sex offenders monitoring program' which would keep the community safe by detecting the exact location of sex offenders after their prison term has ended (New South Wales minister for corrective services and public sector reform 2009). In 2006 Western Australia's minister for corrective services, reporting on a trial of three GPS devices conducted between January and March 2006, was disappointed that the technology only traced wearers' movements retrospectively, not as they actually moved through the community in real time (Western Australia minister for corrective services 2006). Similarly, the Queensland police minister stated that using GPS-based supervision systems for sex offenders had not been ruled out, but that the systems were not yet 'fool proof' (Australian Broadcasting Corporation 2009). Trials in Victoria (and New Zealand) have found that the GPS signal can be blocked by buildings and the location of the offender falsely identified (Multimedia Victoria 2009).

Terrorism prevention

> Australia now has legislation that enables, inter alia, control orders, which may include EM, to be made in respect of persons in situations in which such orders will substantially assist in preventing a terrorist act, or where it is suspected on reasonable grounds that a person has provided training to, or received training from, a listed terrorist organisation (Criminal Code Act 1995 (Cth), Division 104). The Australian Security Intelligence Organisation Act (1979) also allows for the use of electronic tracking devices on anybody suspected of being involved in 'activities prejudicial to security'.
>
> (ASIO Act 1979)

Although the use of EM in this context would entail similar issues to its use in correctional settings, the manner in which the legislation has been framed in Australia has raised numerous legal and human rights concerns (see, for example, Byrnes *et al.* 2005). These questions relate principally to the legal protections that govern the making of orders, their constitutionality, their compliance or otherwise with international human rights protections and their likely effectiveness. It remains to be seen whether EM control orders will be used, and to what extent, and whether or not these human rights concerns will eventuate.

Other applications

There are two other possible applications similar to pre-trial usage. The first concerns the monitoring of refugees while their applications for asylum are being processed. At present most such applicants are held in detention (Brennan 2002). The Human Rights Council of Australia (Sidoti 2002) has suggested EM as an alternative to detention. The second context concerns restraining orders, which a court may impose to prevent a potential offender from approaching a complainant (Legal Aid NSW 2003). EM is not currently used in either of these settings in Australia, although modern restriction and surveillance capabilities may raise the possibility for consideration.

Legislation and EM practice in New Zealand

New Zealand's legal framework is focused on two Acts, the Sentencing Act 2002 and Parole Act 2002, which provide the authority for the use of EM of offenders in a range of situations. Primarily these Acts have allowed for home detention to be used as an alternative means of imprisonment (i.e. prison in the home instead of prisons), and after 1 October 2007 as a sentence option in its own right. Before October 2007 offenders coming to court and receiving a sentence of less than two years imprisonment were given 'leave to apply' for home detention by a sentencing judge. About 10 per cent of these offenders received home detention to be served at home, but it was still viewed as a custodial sentence and breaches would mostly result in a return to prison (this was known as front-end home detention). Prisoners serving sentences of over two years and eligible for parole also could apply for home detention up to five months earlier than when their parole would have begun. This meant that after assessment they might get out of prison three months earlier than they would have done on parole. Again, about 10 per cent of these eligible long-term inmates got out early in this way (this was known as back-end home detention).

In October 2007 the New Zealand Labour-led government introduced home detention (with EM) as a sentence in its own right rather than just as a custodial option (Department of Corrections 2007b). They also introduced community detention (EM curfews). The effect of both of these has been to substantially increase the numbers of offenders under electronic surveillance (Department of Corrections 2009).

New Zealand legislation also allows for the electronic monitoring of serious sexual offenders in the community while they are on a variety of court orders, most notably the extended supervision order introduced by the Parole (Extended Supervision) Amendment Act 2004, which can last for up to ten years after they have left prison – in order to prevent serious sexual crimes occurring. A pilot

GPS scheme was trialled in New Zealand during 2005/2006 for offenders on home detention with mixed success. As in Victoria's GPS scheme, the technology was not deemed fully reliable. Plans are in place for it to be used on a small number of offenders, but only as a supplement to active EM rather than as a replacement (Department of Corrections 2006, 2007a).

As far as use in New Zealand is concerned, EM has mainly been a tool to monitor offenders on home detention, although satellite tracking has been piloted. The published statistics reveal limited information about home detention orders and the data that is available is for 2003 and 2004, depending on the source of information. In 2003 and 2004 some 1,950 home detention orders were made (Department of Corrections 2005), with an average daily population of detainees (as they are called) at 595 (see Table 4.2).

The demographic information on home detainees shows that 10 per cent of detainees are aged between 16 and 19 years; 29 per cent between 20 and 29 years; 47 per cent between 30 and 49; and 13 per cent over 50 years (Department of Corrections 2004). In the detainee population there are 19.8 per cent females and 80.2 per cent males, which is relatively high for females given their usual prison proportion of 5–6 per cent, and their community sentence proportions of 18 per cent (Department of Corrections 2004). The ethnicity data shows that 46 per cent of the detainee population are European, 4 per cent are European and Maori, 35 per cent are Maori, 8 per cent are Pacific Peoples, 1 per cent are Maori and Pacific, and 6 per cent are unknown (Department of Corrections 2004). The length of time that people spend on average on home detention in New Zealand is about 13 weeks (Gibbs 2004).

Data on successful completions show that completion rates for all kinds of home detention are very high, ranging from 82 per cent to 90 per cent (Department of Corrections 2009). Data from the Department of Corrections (2008) show two-year re-conviction rates varying between 26 per cent and 37 per cent

Table 4.2 Home detention in New Zealand, 2003: average daily number of persons

Region	Number	Per cent
Auckland	53	8.9
Christchurch	113	19
Dunedin/Invercargill	39	6.6
Hamilton	34	5.7
Hawkes Bay/Gisborne	46	7.7
Manakau	54	9.1
Nelson/Marlborough/West Coast	21	3.5
Northland	37	6.2
Taranaki/Whanganui/Tararua	37	6.2
Bay of Plenty	84	14.1
Waitemata	36	6.1
Wellington	41	6.9
New Zealand total	595	100

Source: Department of Corrections (2004).

for offenders on home detention. This compares favourably with people released on parole (44 per cent re-conviction rate) and community-based sentences (43 per cent) (Department of Corrections 2008). There seems to be no doubt that home detainees, by virtue of the extra surveillance that EM imposes, do appear to offend less while on the orders (Gibbs 2004).

The home detention scheme is operated by the Department of Corrections with involvement from private sector companies for the actual monitoring equipment and compliance with conditions. The Community Probation Service has a remit to provide intensive supervision to those offenders on home detention orders. This means a fairly high level of intervention. Each home detention order progresses in a series of phases, and offenders on phase one, for example, may have to see or be visited by a probation officer up to three times each week for up to half of their sentence, which could mean many months. They will also have conditions to attend programmes for substance misuse, anger management, counselling, offending behaviour courses and possibly employment-related training. Offenders are very restricted in phase one as to what they can do; they are allowed to go grocery shopping, attend medical appointments, attend funerals, attend and observe religious activities, and attend employment or study. Otherwise they are required to remain at home, although probation officers do have some limited discretion to give permission to permit leave. For women at home with young children, phase one can prove extremely stressful. In phase two, detainees might be allowed to attend one social function each month and some leisure time. Phases 3 and 4 progressively allow more social outings. The overall aims of home detention, aside from early release from imprisonment, are reintegration and rehabilitation, and the intensive supervision and programmes are therefore viewed as the means to achieve these.

All offenders subject to home detention are also subject to electronic and security personnel monitoring 24 hours a day, seven days a week. Electronic surveillance equipment provides monitoring through a dedicated telephone line or cellular network using RF monitoring. The offender wears a security anklet, which continuously emits a signal that is received by the equipment installed at the residence. Should the offender leave the property without prior consent from their home detention officer, an alarm is triggered immediately. Security personnel check the violations and report them to probation staff for follow up. Additionally, there are random checks by the private surveillance company to monitor if the offender is where he or she is supposed to be. No action is taken if the violation is found to be a technical problem with the EM equipment. In some parts of New Zealand there are still problems providing adequate coverage of cellular monitoring – because of this the equipment has not always been 100 per cent reliable.

Offenders on home detention must consent and be willing to abide by the conditions of home detention. Home detention orders may include both statutory and special conditions imposed by the Parole Board and courts on release to home detention. Any violation of these conditions will incur enforcement procedures by the home detention probation officer, including penalties, court action or a recall to prison.

Controversies, advantages and disadvantages of EM

In both Australia and New Zealand, little public debate about EM has occurred, other than for specific incidents or about high-profile public figures being monitored. The *New Zealand Herald* ran a full feature explaining home detention in 2003 because a national TV3 newsreader was given home detention with EM for drugs-related offences (*New Zealand Herald* 2003). Otherwise there has been little of interest to the media and use of electronic surveillance to monitor offenders is a non-issue for the New Zealand public at large (Gibbs and King 2003).

In Victoria (Australia) in July 2005 considerable media attention was given to a case involving the use of EM. The case concerned an offender who had served 12 years for sexual abuse of six children, and who was released on parole and monitored with an electronic anklet. The conditions of his monitoring, which lasted for 15 years, after which the offender would be 73 years of age, required him to seek permission to leave his accommodation, a prohibition on associating with minors, a requirement to live alone, a ban on living near schools, kindergartens or child-care centres, a requirement to receive treatment and regular reporting to authorities several times each week. A curfew was applied at night and he was banned from leaving home at times when he was likely to encounter children. A corrections officer also supervised him on outings. The offender was dubbed 'Mr Baldy', arising from his habit of kidnapping young boys, shaving their heads and molesting them sexually (Shiel 2005). He served eight years in the 1980s for crimes involving six boys, but re-offended almost immediately after his release, sexually assaulting two more boys which led to a further conviction and sentence of 14 years' imprisonment.

Upon his release on parole, his former victims as well as various victim support advocates expressed their concern at his release and the risk of re-offending. Criticism was not, however, specifically levelled at the use of EM, but rather the fact of his parole generally (Milovanovic 2005). Media reporters were able to locate his residence and he was subjected to a campaign of harassment, which resulted in correctional officers relocating him to a residence on the perimeter of a country prison. He was living in what is known as 'the village of the damned', a separate village just outside of Ararat prison in Victoria, which houses serious offenders on extended supervision orders and under constant surveillance. Just prior to Christmas 2005, concerns were again raised that he was living close to the prison where a children's Christmas event was scheduled to occur. He was relocated away from the prison during the party in order to quell concerns (Dowsley and Hodgson 2005). Further, he was found to have been 'off the air' and not electronically monitored between 30 November and 15 December 2008 after he disconnected the mains power in his unit, disabling the monitoring station in his house (Wilkinson 2010a). The ankle bracelet was picked up instead by the monitoring units installed in other residences as he travelled around the village. Because he was still within the 40-metre range of any given monitoring unit, no alarm was raised.

Another example concerns a rapist who, in January 2010, fled the same village in Ararat (Wilkinson 2010b). Authorities were alerted that he had breached the perimeter; however, the bracelet could not be used to locate him. These incidents have highlighted the need for GPS monitoring to be coupled with current electronic surveillance techniques in order to locate offenders when such breaches of security occur.

There are a variety of potential advantages and disadvantages associated with the use of EM. One of the major advantages is the possibility of reduced prison populations. This is most likely where monitoring is used as an alternative to prison, rather than to enhance existing non-custodial orders. Reduced prison populations have so far not been demonstrated in spite of reasonable numbers released to EM (Gibbs 2004). There appears to be, however, no overall consensus as to the ability of EM to reduce prison numbers. It depends upon whether monitoring is used to enhance existing community-based sentences or as an alternative to prison.

EM can, however, contribute to substantial cost savings (Richardson 1999). This has been the experience in a variety of jurisdictions, including New Zealand, New South Wales, the United States and the UK (Maxfield and Baumer 1990; Richardson 1999; Jarred 2000). Cost savings are obviously enhanced even further if a user-pays system is used. In the ACT, however, the introduction of home detention in October 2001 led to a marked increase in recurrent expenditure on community corrections from A\$3,126 in 2000–2001 to A\$5,861 in 2002–2003 (Productivity Commission 2004). Similarly, there are now many studies demonstrating that EM can have positive effects in respect of maintaining employment and family ties, which can in turn contribute to rehabilitation (see, for example, Liverani 1998; Bonta *et al.* 1999; Gibbs and King 2001; Mortimer 2001; Payne and Gainey 2004).

A perceived disadvantage of EM is the lack of incapacitation. EM does not physically restrain a tracked person and dangerous offenders may still offend before authorities can intervene. Also, the less onerous conditions of home detention with EM may result in some victims and the public perceiving some offenders as being dealt with too leniently. Research suggests that offenders themselves do not view EM as a soft option (Payne and Gainey 1998; Gibbs and King 2001). Families of home detainees also experience extra burdens and stresses as a consequence of the orders (Doherty 1995; Jarred 2000).

In both countries a specific issue for families of offenders is that of 'sponsorship', whereby a family member agrees to sponsor a detainee living at their home. They are required to sign a form agreeing to accommodate detainees, to accept EM equipment in their homes and to agree that they recognize the rules and conditions of home detention, which the detainee has to comply with. The felt sense of obligation that sponsors feel places a pressure on them to adopt a supervisory role towards spouses, sons or daughters, ensuring they stick to their monitoring conditions. This can impose extra 'burdens' on families (mainly women) – for example, extra finances to feed detainees, extra time to ferry detainees to appointments and extra stress from having the detainee under their feet more than usual (Gibbs 2004).

There have also been concerns that EM as a primary sentence may actually increase the severity of some sentences (Jarred 2000). For example, it is possible that EM may be used where mere suspension or probation would have been used previously: 'Sentencers will be readily tempted to order electronically enforced home detention for offenders not truly facing an immediate prospect of imprisonment' (Fox 1987: 141–142). Net widening may occur if offenders breach conditions of monitoring, leading to periods of actual imprisonment being served.

Ethical concerns

The use of EM in the criminal justice system also raises a number of ethical, legal and practical issues. As monitoring is predominantly applicable in correctional contexts, so the question of punishment arises because of the power of modern monitoring technologies to achieve purposes of restriction and surveillance. Although not a punishment in itself, EM has the potential to enforce restrictions upon a person's liberty in connection with a judicially imposed punishment such as home detention.

Systematic research in Australia has yet to evaluate offenders' experiences of EM (Richardson 1999; Studerus 1999); however, anecdotal evidence suggests that it is a negative experience, although clearly without the 'violence, intimidation and degrading punishment' of some prison experiences (Keay 2000). In New Zealand, however, research by Gibbs and King (2001, 2003) showed instances of psychological distress and extra burdens to both offenders and their families while on home detention and EM. EM is both physically and psychologically invasive: a person's every move can now be tracked, other than when the device is programmed to be off – these days that rarely happens. The experience of constant surveillance, particularly via devices fixed to their body, or even surgically implanted beneath the skin (as has been mooted, *The Economist* 2002; Bright 2002; see also Fabelo 2001 on miniature video cameras), raises serious civil liberties issues.

Complex questions arise concerning the scope, application and delivery of EM. Is the use of force acceptable when attaching a device? If the offender is subject to a curfew, should authorities have any right to track his or her movements outside curfew hours? To what uses should information about the offender's movements be put? One system in the United States, for example, correlates the wearer's movements with crime reports and alerts authorities if he or she appears to have been present at a crime scene (Scheeres 2002). In many jurisdictions, including Australia, private sector firms operate EM systems on behalf of statutory agencies (Maxfield and Baumer 1990; Richardson 1999), raising the same contentious issues about commercial motivation and accountability as have been raised in respect of private prison management (Harding 1998).

Some offenders involved in monitoring programmes are required to pay a fee towards the cost of the equipment and the monitoring (Maxfield and

Baumer 1990; Scheeres 2002), although this has not occurred to date in Australia or New Zealand. This is partially justified by the argument that offenders who remain in the community can continue in employment (if they are able to find suitable work). The logical extension is, however, that all offenders on community-based programmes should be required to contribute to correctional costs. This could place hardship on those with low incomes and high family maintenance costs.

The future of EM

The use of EM has the potential to improve the cost-effectiveness of correctional programmes, provide enhanced opportunities for offender rehabilitation and extend the range of sentences available to the courts. Despite the fact that EM has been in use for at least two decades, there are still many legal, ethical and practical issues to resolve. In Australia and New Zealand, community corrections agencies have embraced the technologies without waiting for the results of evaluative research to appear – a phenomenon not unusual in connection with the introduction of new technologies. Renzema and Mayo-Wilson (2005), who liken EM to an aspirin that is being touted as a potential cure for all ailments, insist that it is as yet unproven in its effectiveness at reducing re-offending and question whether it should therefore be used.

There are already adequate alternatives to EM in both Australia and New Zealand and supervision sentences are under-utilized. Better targeting of lower-risk offenders for these options rather than EM should be pursued as the evidence shows that it is higher-risk offenders who benefit by being monitored when they are also subject to other good-quality intervention programmes (Bonta *et al*. 1999). Any new EM programmes also need to take account of gender bias and ensure the needs of women offenders, children and women family members of male offenders are catered to, reflecting differences of responsibility for childcare and employment (Maidment 2002; King and Gibbs 2003).

Although the latest EM technologies are far less invasive and more efficient than in the past, their surveillance potential creates concerns of over-regulation and infringement of human rights. We should ensure that if such technologies continue to be adopted they are used in the most productive and ethical ways. The pressure to make greater use of EM will arise, particularly if the technologies develop in efficiency and sophistication. It would be desirable, however, for any increased implementation of EM to be delayed until the outcomes of intensive evaluative research have been undertaken. The following cautionary observation of Casella (2003: 92) is worth recalling in the present context:

> The longer a technology is used, the more entrenched in life it becomes. When technologies are new, or are used in newer ways ... their uses are easier to modify and their consequences easier to control.... If we wish to question the unintended consequences of these developments, now is the time to do so.

Note

1 The views expressed in this chapter are those of the authors alone and do not represent the policies of the Australian or New Zealand governments. We are grateful to Rachel Hale, PhD candidate at Monash University, for her assistance in the preparation of this chapter.

References

Adult Parole Board of Victoria (2005) *Annual Report 2004–05* (Melbourne: Adult Parole Board of Victoria). Online. Available at: www.justice.vic.gov.au/CA256902000FE154/Lookup/DOJ_CORRECTIONS_PART3/$file/APB_Annual_Report_0405.pdf.

Albrecht, H.J. (2003) 'The place of EM in the development of criminal punishment and systems of sanctions', in M. Mayer, R. Haverkamp and R. Lévy, (eds) *Will Electronic Monitoring Have a Future in Europe?* (Freiburg: Max Plank Institute), pp. 249–264.

Aungles, A. (1995) 'Three bedroomed prisons in the Asia Pacific region: home imprisonment and electronic surveillance in Australia, Hawaii, and Singapore', *Just Policy*, 2, pp. 32–37.

Australian Broadcasting Corporation (ABC) News (2009). 'Government considering GPS tracking of sex offenders', 16 June. Online. Available at: www.abc.net.au/news/stories/2009/06/16/2599424.htm.

Bagaric, M. (2002) 'Home truths about home detention', *The Journal of Criminal Law*, 66:5, pp. 425–443.

Bonta, J., Wallace-Capretta, S. and Rooney, J. (1999) *EM in Canada* (Canada: Solicitor General Canada).

Brennan, F. (2002) 'Australia's refugee policy: facts, needs and limits'. Online. Available at: www.ceo.parra.catholic.edu.au/pdf/sjustice/fb_paper.pdf.

Bright, M. (2002) 'Surgical tags plan for sex offenders', *The Observer*. Online. Available at: http://society.guardian.co.uk/children/story/0,1074,842393,00.html.

Byrnes, A., Charlesworth, H. and McKinnon, G. (2005) 'Human rights implications of the Anti-Terrorism Bill 2005', Letter of advice to Mr John Stanhope, 18 October. Online. Available at: www.chiefminister.act.gov.au/docs/_20051018.pdf.

Casella, R. (2003) 'The false allure of security technologies', *Social Justice*, 30:3, pp. 82–93.

Church, A. and Dunstan, S. (1997) *Home Detention: The Evaluation of the Home Detention Pilot Programme 1995–1997* (Wellington: Ministry of Justice).

Crowe, A.H. (2002) 'Electronic supervision: from decision-making to implementation', *Corrections Today*, 64:5, pp. 130–133.

Department of Corrections (2004) *Census of Prison Inmates and Home Detainees 2003* (Wellington: Department of Corrections).

Department of Corrections (2005) *Corrections News March 2006* (Wellington: Department of Corrections).

Department of Corrections (2006) *Department of Corrections Annual Report 2005/6*, (Wellington: Department of Corrections).

Department of Corrections (2007a) *Corrections News September 2007* (Wellington: Department of Corrections).

Department of Corrections (2007b) *Corrections News November 2007* (Wellington: Department of Corrections).

Department of Corrections (2008) *Department of Corrections Annual Report 2007/8* (Wellington: Department of Corrections).

Department of Corrections (2009) *Department of Corrections Annual Report 2007/8* (Wellington: Department of Corrections).

Department of Justice (2002) *Annual report 2001–2002* (Perth: Department of Justice). Online. Available at: www.department.dotag.wa.gov.au/_files/DOJ_AnnualReport_Full.pdf.

Doherty, D. (1995) 'Impressions of the impact of the EM program on the family', in K. Schulz (ed.) *EM and Corrections: The policy, the operation, the research* (Canada: Simon Fraser University), pp. 129–141.

Dowsley, A. and Hodgson, S. (2005) 'Mr Baldy spoils party: evil cloud over kids' Christmas', *Herald-Sun* (Melbourne), 1 December, p. 4.

The Economist (2002) 'Something to watch over you: surveillance', 17 August.

Fabelo, T. (2001) ' "Technocorrections": promises and uncertain threats', *Crime & Justice International*, March, pp. 11–12/30–32.

Fox, R.G. (1987) 'Dr Schwitzgebel's machine revisited: EM of offenders', *Australian and New Zealand Journal of Criminology*, 20:3, pp. 131–147.

Fox, R.G. (2001) 'Someone to watch over us: back to the panopticon?', *Criminal Justice*, 1:3, pp. 251–276.

Gibbs, A. (2004) 'A letter from New Zealand: home detention – emerging issues after the first three years', *Crime Prevention and Community Safety*, 6:3, pp. 57–64.

Gibbs, A. and King, D. (2001) *The Electronic Ball and Chain? The Development, Operation and Impact of Home Detention in New Zealand* (Dunedin: Community and Family Studies, University of Otago).

Gibbs, A. and King, D. (2003) 'The electronic ball and chain? The operation and impact of home detention with EM in New Zealand', *Australian and New Zealand Journal of Criminology*, 36:1, pp. 1–17.

Grabosky, P.N. (1998) 'Technology and crime control', *Trends and Issues in Crime and Criminal Justice*, No. 78 (Canberra: Australian Institute of Criminology).

Harding, R. (1998) 'Private prisons in Australia: the second phase', *Trends & Issues in Crime and Criminal Justice*, No. 84, Australian Institute of Criminology.

Henderson, M. (2006) 'Benchmarking study of home detention programs in Australia and New Zealand', Report to National Corrections Advisory Group. Online. Available at: www.justice.vic.gov.au/wps/wcm/connect/DOJ+Internet/Home/Sentencing/Home+Detention/JUSTICE+-+Benchmarking+Study+of+Home+Detention+Programs+in+Australia+and+New+Zealand.

Jarred, W. (2000) 'EM: Corrective Services Bill 2000', Legislation Brief 11/00, Queensland Parliamentary Library.

Keay, N. (2000) 'Home detention: an alternative to prison?', *Current Issues in Criminal Justice*, 12:1, pp. 98–105.

King, D. and Gibbs, A. (2003) 'Is home detention in New Zealand disadvantaging women and children?', *Probation Journal*, 50:2, pp. 115–126.

King, S., Bamford, D. and Sarre, R. (2005) 'Factors that influence remand in custody: final report to the Criminology Research Council', Social Policy Research Group.

Legal Aid NSW (2003) 'Apprehended violence orders'. Online. Available at: www.lawlink.nsw.gov.au/lac/lac.nsf/pages/avoapply.

Liverani, M.R. (1998) 'Slow take-up for home detention: magistrates cool, many lawyers unaware of the option', *Law Society Journal*, February, pp. 42–48.

Maidment, M.R. (2002) 'Toward a women-centred approach to community-based corrections: a gendered analysis of EM in Eastern Canada', *Women and Criminal Justice*, 13:4, pp. 47–68.

Mainprize, S. (1996) 'Elective affinities in the engineering of social control: the evolution of EM', *Electronic Journal of Sociology*. Online. Available at: www.sociology.org/content/vol. 002.002/mainprize.html.

Marien, M. (2002) 'Recent developments in criminal law legislation in New South Wales'. Online. Available at: www.lawlink.nsw.gov.au/clrd1.nsf/pages/Recent%20 Developments%20Speech.

Martin, J.S., Hanrahan, K. and Bowers, J.H. (2009) 'Offenders perceptions of home arrest and EM', *Journal of Offenders Rehabilitation*, 48, pp. 547–570.

Martinovic, M. (2007) 'Home detention: issues, dilemmas and impacts for co-residing family members', *Current Issues in Criminology*, 19, pp. 90–105.

Maxfield, M.G. and Baumer, T.L. (1990) 'Home detention with EM: comparing pretrial and postconviction programs', *Crime & Delinquency*, 36:4, pp. 521–536.

Milovanovic, S. (2005) 'Mr Baldy released: but under strict watch', *The Age* (Melbourne), 14 July.

Mortimer, E. (2001) 'EM of released prisoners: an evaluation of the Home Detention Curfew Scheme'. *Research Findings* No. 139, Home Office.

Mukherjee, S. (1999) 'Intermediate sanctions: EM and house arrest', in G. Newman (ed.), *Global Report on Crime and Justice* (New York: Oxford University Press), pp 89–102.

Multimedia Victoria (2009) 'Smart SME's Market validation program technology requirement specifications: EM of high risk offenders'. Online. Available at: www.mmv.vic.gov.au/Assets/2289/1/MVPTRS_DoJ_MonitoringHighRiskOffenders.pdf.

National Trust of Australia (Victoria) (1991) *The Old Melbourne Gaol* (Melbourne: National Trust of Australia – Victoria).

New South Wales minister for corrective services and public sector reform (2009) 'Sex offender monitoring program doubled', media release, 30 August. Online. Available at: www.dcs.nsw.gov.au/information/media_releases/30%20Aug%202009%20-%20 Sex%20offender%20monitoring%20program%20doubled.pdf.

New South Wales Parliament, Legislative Council, Standing Committee on Law and Justice (2005) 'Back-end home detention', Report No. 28, Legislative Council, Standing Committee on Law and Justice.

New Zealand Herald (2003) 'Home is where the prison is', 16 September.

Odgers, R. (2005) 'New laws to restrict pedophile movement', *Courier Mail*, (Brisbane) 13 December. Online. Available at: http://couriermail.news.com.au/printpage/0,5942, 17545290,00.html.

Payne, B.K. and Gainey, R.R. (1998) 'A qualitative assessment of the pains experienced on EM', *International Journal of Offender Therapy and Comparative Criminology*, 42:1, pp. 149–163.

Payne, B.K. and Gainey, R.R. (2004) 'The EM of offenders released from jail or prison: safety, control, and comparisons to the incarceration experience', *The Prison Journal*, 84:4, pp. 413–435.

Productivity Commission (2004) *Report on Government Services 2004* (Canberra: Steering Committee for the Review of Government Service Provision).

Productivity Commission (2005) *Report on Government Services 2005* (Canberra: Steering Committee for the Review of Government Service Provision).

Productivity Commission (2006) *Report on Government Services 2006* (Canberra: Steering Committee for the Review of Government Service Provision).

Productivity Commission (2007) *Report on Government Services 2007* (Canberra: Steering Committee for the Review of Government Service Provision).

Productivity Commission (2008) *Report on Government Services 2008* (Canberra: Steering Committee for the Review of Government Service Provision).

Productivity Commission (2009) *Report on Government Services 2008–2009* (Canberra: Steering Committee for the Review of Government Service Provision).

Productivity Commission (2010) *Report on Government Services 2009–2010* (Canberra: Steering Committee for the Review of Government Service Provision).

Queensland Corrective Services (2007) 'Fact sheet 1: EM'. Online. Available at: www.correctiveservices.qld.gov.au/About_Us/The_Department/Probation_and_Parole/Electronic_Monitoring/documents/factsheet_1_Electronic_Monitoring.pdf

Renzema, M. and Mayo-Wilson, E. (2005) 'Can EM reduce crime for moderate to high-risk offenders?', *Journal of Experimental Criminology*, 1:2, pp. 215–237.

Richardson, R. (1999) 'Electronic tagging of offenders: trials in England', *The Howard Journal*, 38:2, pp. 158–172.

Scheeres, J. (2002) 'GPS: keeping cons out of jail', *Wired News*. Online. Available at: www.wired.com/news/privacy/0,1848,55740,00.html.

Shiel, F. (2005) 'Ankle bracelet to monitor pedophile', *The Age* (Melbourne), 14 July.

Sidoti, C. (2002) *Refugee Policy: Is There a Way Out of This Mess?* (Canberra: Racial Respect Seminar).

South Australia Department for Correctional Services (2004) *Community Corrections* (Adelaide: Government of South Australia).

South Australia Department for Correctional Services (2009) *Community Corrections* (Adelaide: Government of South Australia).

Studerus, K. (1999) 'Home detention: two years on', *Corrective Services Bulletin*, No. 454, p. 4.

Victorian Sentencing Committee (1987) *Discussion Paper* (Melbourne: Government Printer).

Western Australia Department of Justice (2009) 'Reducing juvenile offending in Western Australia'. Online. Available at: www.correctiveservices.wa.gov.au/_files/Reducing_juvenile_offending.pdf.

Western Australia Department of Justice, New South Wales Corrective Services, South Australia Correctional Services, Australian Capital Territory Corrective Services, Tasmania Department of Justice, Queensland Department of Corrective Services, Victoria Department of Justice and Northern Territory Department of Justice (2004) 'Standard guidelines for corrections in Australia'. Online. Available at: www.justice.vic.gov.au/wps/wcm/connect/DOJ+Internet/resources/file/eb511243e812e33/National_Standard_Guidelines_For_Corrections_In_Australia_2004.pdf

Western Australia Minister for Corrective Services (2006) 'Minister "disappointed" after offender tracking devices fail trial conditions', media release, 21 July. Online. Available at: http://www.mediastatements.wa.gov.au/Lists/Statements/DispForm.aspx?ID=126500.

Wilkinson, G. (2010a) 'Losing track of Mr Baldy', *Herald Sun*, 1 February. Online. Available at: www.heraldsun.com.au.

Wilkinson, G. (2010b) 'Two thirds of Victorian sex offenders released from prison are protected by suppression orders', *Herald Sun*, 30 January. Online. Available at: www.heraldsun,com.au.

5 From voice verification to GPS tracking

The development of electronic monitoring in South Korea

Younoh Cho and Byung Bae Kim

Criminal justice and probation in Korea

There are many recognizable Western aspects to the contemporary criminal justice system in the Republic of Korea, but probation for adults is a relatively new development, and many of the measures which were introduced intermittently in the West over the course of the twentieth century – basic probation orders, attendance centres, community service orders and electronic monitoring, including GPS tracking – have all been introduced into Korea over the last 25 years. Korea has been a keen observer of international developments in criminal justice, but there is no long-established adult probation tradition against which EM may seem anomalous or misguided.

The Ministry of Justice was formed in 1948 as part of a vast reform of government organization. According to a recent official source it has 'mostly retained its original structure and functions while it continues to make necessary adjustments to adapt to the contemporary demands in legal affairs' (International Legal Affairs Division 2009: 5). It has six major departments – planning and coordination, criminal affairs, legal affairs, corrections, immigration and human rights and crime prevention – all of which owed something to Western models of practice in these areas, reflecting Korea's openness to the transfer of policy ideas from Western Europe and the United States. It nonetheless retains the death penalty, but has not used it for more than a decade. Special youth courts and probation supervision for juvenile offenders (understood as 12–20-year-olds) have existed in Korea since the 1960s, and largely had a welfare and humanist orientation, although it has always been possible to deal with juvenile offenders between the ages of 14 and 20 who commit serious violent crimes in adult courts. The government body responsible for this work (and later adult probation) – the Social Protection and Rehabilitation Bureau, formed in 1981 – has always had a public protection remit, but understood it initially in terms of meeting the welfare needs of those under its supervision, rather than punishing and controlling them.

The creation of an adult probation service (and the revitalization of its youth services) is associated with the ending of military rule in Korea and the subsequent emergence of demands for more democratic, Westernized social forms.

Democratization coincided with a period of massive economic growth and vast migrations from the relatively orderly countryside to the cities, in which crime rates inevitably and inexorably rose. A major financial crisis in the late 1990s brought the boom years to an end, deepening the impoverishment of the urban poor and creating a climate of insecurity in which both crime and media and public concern about it intensified (Neary 2003). As Chung (2002) notes, the probation services for adults that developed in the 1990s were 'deeply grounded in western philosophic assumptions', and derived from a period of academic and legal reflection on criminal justice issues in Korea which began a decade earlier:

> The major rationale behind the reflection on our criminal justice system seemed to be associated with the wide range of disillusion on the current exercise of our criminal justice sanctions such as penal servitude and confinement as the basic penal sanctions. More specifically, by the late 1980s, it had become widely recognized that custodial sentences were generally ineffective as a deterrent against further reoffending and the rehabilitative efficacy of institutional treatment was increasingly questioned. Imprisonment had moreover been recognised as having detrimental effects upon individual offenders and their families and concern was being expressed at this time both about the levels of overcrowding in penal institutions and the high cost of maintaining the prison system.
>
> (Chung 2002: 214)

This was not, however, the only Western reasoning that was affecting the development of the nascent probation service. Rising crime and public concern about it – particularly sex crime against women and children, which had a high media profile – led the Korean government to push the probation service towards a more overly public protection role, alongside a rigorous form of sex offender notification (Palermo 2005). The contours of a welfare-oriented service remained: of the 204,000 convicted persons in Korea in 2002, two-thirds were under probation supervision, and one-third doing community service (which, as in the West, is a separate measure from probation itself, and has been said to have reduced the prison population somewhat). The distribution of custodial and non-custodial penalties remained broadly similar in 2009 – 185,000 people were under probation supervision, but the approach to supervising them was changing. There had arguably never been sufficient numbers of designated probation officers for the tasks required of them – there were still only 1,100 in 2009, working long hours with large caseloads, supported by large numbers of volunteers who assist with reintegration into the community. Although Chung (2002) (a social work professor) complained that probation officers were not well trained compared to some of their Western counterparts – they were required to study social science, criminal law and correctional administration but lacked important theoretical understanding of what the effective treatment of offending requires – it may not be social work skills that are most valued in the emerging Korean probation service, in which new surveillance technology plays a significant part.

From voice verification to GPS tracking

The Korean Ministry of Justice followed international developments in electronic monitoring (EM) technologies for a number of years, but did not adopt any of them until the twenty-first century, and in a strikingly different order from the way they were introduced in the West. Unlike most other countries, which used a traditional radio frequency (RF) system to enforce home confinement, the Korean Ministry of Justice first experimented with voice verification for juvenile offenders, them moved straight to a satellite tracking system for adults (Cho 2008, 2010). Although curfews (usually to a home address) are an integral part of the voice verification programme, and can be a part of the satellite tracking programme, Korea has had no experience of the ordinary house-arrest versions of EM that are so dominant in other countries, and in that sense it reflects a new departure in the 'evolution' of EM.

The Automated Voiceprint Recognition Supervision (AVRS) programme for high-risk juvenile offenders was piloted in Seoul between 2003 and 2005 as part of a broader commitment to developing more intensive, relatively low-cost, non-custodial measures. Youth crime, which was only 5.5 per cent of all crime in Korea in 2002, was declining overall, especially among 18–19-year-olds, though it was rising among 14–15-year-olds. The programme required no ankle tag. It used the biometric of an individual's unique voiceprint, captured at the point of sentence, and aimed to regulate and reduce criminal behaviour, particularly at night, by making random automated phone calls to curfewed young people, which had to be answered by them in order to prove that they were present in their home. Custody was available for proven breaches. The programme was run by the Probation Service and was understood as a form of situational crime prevention – keeping young people away from peers with whom they might offend at night, as well as increasing parental contact and influence. It extended the range of a probation officer's influence without needing to increase probation officer numbers. An initial evaluation of the AVRS pilot (Kim 2005) influentially claimed that it did reduce recidivism and improved child–parent relationships, and between 2003 and 2006 the numbers of juveniles given AVRS by youth courts increased across the country from 251 to 2,857. Cho's (2008) later, more methodologically sophisticated study, which will be discussed below, was more sceptical.

The introduction of satellite tracking in Korea was generated by public, media and official concern about offences of sexual violence in the context of a society with a strong and widespread commitment to optimizing the potential of electronic communication technology, including use of the internet. The law governing EM through the Global Positioning System – the GPS Electronic Monitoring Act for Specific Sex Offenders – was enacted in April 2007 and implemented in September 2009 (Ministry of Justice 2009b). There had been a striking increase in the rate of sex-related crimes in Korea in the past ten years. The recorded rate of sex crimes increased by 83.4 per cent from 1997 to 2006, as the number of sex offences per 100,000 people jumped from

15.1 in 1997 to 27.7 in 2006 (Legal Research and Training Institute 2007). Specifically, the enactment of the legislation was directly triggered by the widely publicized rape and murder of an 11-year-old girl from an elementary school in Young-San, Seoul in 2006 although it was not the only crime of this kind. The legislation facilitated the real-time, 24-hour tracking of sex offenders in the community who were placed on probation or parole (Ministry of Justice 2009a).

The public outcry against sex offenders – in which the use of the death penalty was canvassed (without success) – was strong enough to dent confidence in the conventional forms of probation and parole supervision in the community, and to warrant the use of the harsher and more effective penalties which Korean technology appeared to make possible. Perceived scope for the implementation of EM grew and the number of sex offenders under probation and EM combined have dramatically increased. After the relatively limited use of EM with GPS during September 2009 (53 sex offenders), the number of probation supervision orders with EM rose rapidly, with EM GPS being imposed upon a total of 518 sex offenders between 1 September 2008 and 31 December 2009.

GPS monitoring for sex offenders on probation or parole is not a 'stand-alone' penalty in so far as it is also linked with probation or parole supervision, but it can be the dominant aspect of these orders. Tracked sex offenders are not necessarily subject to home detention or curfew orders when they are under such surveillance. It is the ability to track movement over a 24-hour period that is considered of prime importance. It is optional that courts impose additional conditions, such as an exclusionary order, home confinement, a curfew order, a restraining order or a treatment attendance order, on designated higher-risk offenders who are thought to require even stricter supervision while on electronic monitoring, according to Section 9 of the GPS Electronic Monitoring Act for Specific Sex Offenders.

The GPS programme targets convicted offenders who have sexually abused children under the age of 13 and repeatedly committed sex crimes, with a view to deterring further offences. There are three different types of sentences which require the wearing of the electronic device after a judge endorses the request from prosecutors (Ministry of Justice 2009a). First, EM with GPS can be applied as an additional condition of probation, as a suspended sentence for sex offenders (Section 28). Second, it can be imposed as a parole condition to enable sex offenders to be released early from prison (Section 23). While EM for those who are placed on probation for a suspended period is optional, the use of EM to enforce sentences following release before the official end of their imprisonment period is mandatory. Third, EM with GPS can be imposed on specific sex offenders who have a high-risk of re-offending (Section 5). Even sex offenders who have completed their prison sentences can still be sentenced to GPS EM if they are categorized by the courts as high-risk offenders who are likely to commit further crimes in the community. Such GPS monitoring can legally be imposed for up to ten years.

Delivering the GPS programme

When the GPS programme was first introduced, the Korean Probation Service in the Ministry of Justice set up a consortium with the Samsung Data Systems (Samsung SDS) company in order to develop an innovative tool for the EM system. Samsung is one of Korea's largest conglomerate companies and most prestigious brands, which, through a network of affiliated companies, has interests in global construction, aerospace technology and insurance, as well as electronics and telecommunications. G4S, who were at one time considered as potential suppliers of GPS technology, were never really serious contenders, given Samsung's high standing and commercial/political influence in Korea. The state-of-the-art technology of the tracking programme was based on the combination of four different location-determination technologies, all loaded into a single portable tracking device, which between them enable tracking outside (GPS), inside buildings in towns and cities (P-CELL), inside buildings in rural areas (CELL-ID) and in the subway (BEACON). To call the Korean tracking programme a 'GPS system' is thus a kind of shorthand – it is in fact something much more sophisticated. This reflects the extent to which modern Korean society is 'wired' for locatability and mobile communication among its citizens: it also makes it one of the most comprehensive offender tracking systems in the world. It enables the monitoring centre to maintain constant and stable communication with sex offenders, who wear the tag attached to their ankle, which can be made to vibrate automatically if it exceeds the range of the portable tracking device, reminding the offender not to stray far from it. Whether sex offenders stay at home or leave their designated location, the satellite tracking system, using the multiple position-determination technologies combined with GPS, permits sex offenders to be tracked 24 hours a day.

Unlike some European countries and American states, the Korean Ministry of Justice has not made a service contract with a private security company to manage EM. When electronic monitoring with GPS was first introduced, staff and technicians from Samsung SDS did play a major role in implementing the programme in South Korea. However, once the U-Guard software (for processing and coordinating the tracking data) and Central Control Tower were installed in the Seoul Probation Office in 2009, probation officers replaced the Samsung employees in managing the programme, making it easier to combine the GPS monitoring with other aspects of supervision, and to ensure that all conditions are being enforced. A special probation unit – called the Central Control Tower for GPS Electronic Monitoring – undertakes this work (Ministry of Justice, 2009b). They are able to watch the movements of sex offenders live in real time on large TV screens mounted high on the walls of this unit. They are able to detect EM breaches or probation condition violations very quickly, and also to respond to any technical problems with an EM device. The GPS system undoubtedly provides the Probation Service with better information about sex offenders in the community than they would otherwise have, and a better opportunity to understand their routine lifestyle (see Elzinga and Nijboer 2006 in respect of the

Netherlands). In addition, it makes it possible to collect and submit more reliable circumstantial evidence regarding suspected offenders' comings and goings to judges if the offender under EM is being investigated. In fact, a sex offender who committed an additional rape while on the GPS programme was arrested on the basis of the information concerning his movements recorded by the U-Guard software. The court trying the case accepted the GPS-derived information as significantly decisive evidence in determining a guilty verdict.

Probation officers undertake assessments for the GPS programme. Before offenders are referred to them, officers can submit an investigation report to the court or the prosecutor, which addresses potential risks of re-offending, suitability of EM tracking, offender–victim relations and psychological characteristics of the criminal. This pre-sentence investigation report is designed to help judges or prosecutors determine whether or not EM is appropriate for specific offenders. This report is expected to offer comprehensible information in identifying high-risk sex offenders by using well-known assessment tools such as the Psychopath Checklist-Revised (PCL-R). The Ministry of Justice mandates the use of the Korean Sex Offender Risk Assessment Scale (KSORAS), a 15-item risk-assessment tool that was developed from 2007 to 2008. In this assessment, offenders who score more than 13 are regarded as high-risk offenders.

There are some operational difficulties with the programme. The probation officers in charge of the GPS are required to check up on all tracking data collected on the previous day, and to review the reliability and validity of the information obtained from the GPS tracking system. They are required to make four face-to-face contacts every month, and to pay occasional unscheduled visits to the offender's home and work place. They may also refer monitored sex offenders to counselling and treatment programmes, if necessary, in order to prevent further crime in the community. However, there are not enough officers to supervise tracked offenders properly. The workloads of probation officers who supervise tracked offenders are the same as those who supervise regular offenders. While there are more than 300 sex offenders subject to the round-the-clock monitoring programme, Central Control Tower has less than 20 staff. A further significant drawback with the programme has been a lack of cooperation between the probation service and the police. When tracked offenders abscond from GPS supervision, cooperation between the two agencies is crucial to their re-arrest. However, there is no multi-agency arrangement among different criminal justice organizations for managing monitored sex offenders in South Korea, although the case of a 29-year-old man who removed the anklet and escaped from probation supervision in November 2009 stimulated significant debate about this. Strategic collaboration between community correction and police departments is vital to programme improvement (Cho 2009b).

Public debate about the GPS programme

There has been public and professional debate about the use of GPS tracking in Korea. It is seen to have numerous technological advantages, and to augment other forms of probation supervision. Both the electronic communication infra-structure in Korea and the GPS equipment itself are thought to be reliable. Although mountainous areas account for approximately two-thirds of Korean territory, the multiple position-determination technologies function relatively well wherever the offender is in the country. Additionally, it is possible for pro-bation officers to map out an individualized surveillance strategy by program-ming an exclusionary zone, which is defined as a forbidden area by judges. In this way, electronic tracking can protect vulnerable crime targets, such as chil-dren and specific female victims, more efficiently, while offenders can maintain their job and social life in the community. However, the effectiveness of GPS tracking has not yet been entirely proven in South Korea, although research is underway (Cho 2010).

The Korean Ministry of Justice applied electronic monitoring using GPS in order to provide an immediate response to the demands of the public and stake-holders for punitive sanctions towards sexual criminals in 2008, despite the absence of available evidence on effectiveness. The absence of any perceived problems with the programme nonetheless makes it likely that the use of GPS EM will increase significantly and be expanded in the near future in South Korea to include other types of dangerous offenders who commit felonies such as armed robbery and kidnapping (Ministry of Justice 2009a).

However, there remains an underlying concern as to whether the GPS pro-gramme is in fact sufficient to guarantee public safety and effective enough to prevent or deter sex offenders from pursuing illegal activities. Reviews of research on other, non-GPS, EM programmes do not show significant impact on participants' recidivism (Renzema and Mayo-Wilson 2005; Gainey *et al.* 2000). This is the basis of an ongoing debate in Korea as to how significantly real-time EM with GPS does affect offenders' situational thinking and deter further sexual crimes. The limited evidence gathered so far is promising. A small number of sex offenders were re-arrested for additional offences while on EM from 1 Sep-tember 2008 to 31 December 2009 when EM was first implemented nationally (Ministry of Justice 2009b). From a total of 518 sex offenders placed on EM using GPS, only three offenders were re-arrested for additional crimes while on EM, which is an estimated recidivism rate of about 0.6 per cent. Specifically, only one sex offender among them was sent back to prison because he commit-ted a sexual offence; the other two sex offenders committed non-sexual offences. Considering the general recidivism rate of 3.2 per cent for sex offenders who were not electronically monitored in South Korea, the likelihood of re-offending while under GPS EM seems very low (Legal Research and Training Institute 2008).

However, it might be said that the current means of estimating the recidivism rate will have to be revised because it does not include enough 'crime-breeding time' to calculate the true number of re-offences (Cho 2010). If insufficiently long follow-up periods are used to measure recidivism, any perceived deterrent effect might simply result from a temporary suppression effect due to the other components of probation supervision. While short-term suppression is good and desirable in itself, the recidivism rate should be measured after a lengthy period, at least one year after the completion of EM, in order to see if there is a genuinely long-term deterrent effect from the EM programme. In their Florida-based study of recidivism, Padgett *et al.* (2006) found that both RF and GPS monitoring had a high probability of reducing re-offending for the duration of the programme, but less so afterwards. In South Korea it is too early to collect and analyse more than one year of recidivism data since the GPS EM programme began only on 1 September 2008. The effectiveness of the programme in reducing recidivism will be considered in future longitudinal research.

There is, in addition, a debate about the extent to which the 24/7 tracking system can be applied without significantly violating an offender's human rights. Korea established a Human Rights Bureau within the Ministry of Justice in 2006 – but had been concerned with human rights throughout its post-military period – which, among other responsibilities, is concerned with preventing and remedying human rights abuses in law enforcement and corrections. Opponents of the EM programme among the public and in the media in South Korea have usually asserted that there are obvious violations of human rights inherent in EM – the invasion of a criminal's human right to privacy. In this context, when EM first began, the Ministry of Justice and Congress did their best not to inflame controversy with critics in terms of human right violations. They tried to forestall human rights violations by adopting a very strict offender selection and targeting process. This had a significant impact on both the Electronic Monitoring Act and the programme implementation process, which resulted in rather complicated EM restrictions being imposed on specific offenders, and also in numerous limitations on the utilization of GPS tracking data. Some of the solutions to the potential stigma of wearing an EM device are merely technical: a desire to develop 'the worlds smallest sized GPS units' has been seen as a way of minimizing human rights infringements (Ministry of Justice 2009c). There is as yet no clear agreement as to the full range of matters that should be regarded as human right infringements in implementing EM.

Evaluating EM in Korea

Kim's (2005) one-year follow-up study of the AVRS programme for juvenile probationers, mentioned earlier, is relevant to understanding the potential application and practicability of other intensive supervision programmes in South Korea. Although the AVRS curfew programme does not function in exactly the same way as the GPS EM programme – one restricts offenders to a single location, while the other maps their movements over 24 hours – there are some common goals and a shared logic in the two programmes regarding the intensity of face-to-face contacts with probation officers and the intended reduction of recidivism.

Kim (2005) compared the recidivism rate of young offenders in a curfew programme and that of juvenile probationers in regular probation by testing a one-year follow-up data set. He found that the AVRS curfew programme had significance in reducing the re-conviction rate as well as in increasing opportunities for establishing positive relationships between juvenile probationers and their parents. With this result, he recommended that the government enforce the EM programme in order to provide high-risk offenders with increased levels of accountability and diversion from prison (Kim 2005). Kim's comparison group, however, was not sufficiently representative, and for this methodological reason the conclusions were suspect. In a quasi-experimental design study, researchers need to utilize an equivalent comparison group to minimize the risk of sampling bias (Lullen *et al.* 2005; Imbens 2000). Using such an approach, Cho (2009c) found that, in fact, the AVRS curfew programme is not a statistically significant factor in affecting the probability of re-arrest. Although six potential co-variates were controlled by creating propensity scores, the result of the logistic regression showed that the AVRS curfew programme for juvenile probationers was not a significant predictor of recidivism over a one-year follow-up period (Cho 2009c). Instead, this study showed that the AVRS curfew programme actually increased the chances of juvenile probationers receiving warning tickets and revocation of probation during the programme period.

Even if the intensive supervision programme increases the likelihood of violating technical conditions and of being caught by probation officers for the breach, there may be other possible advantages to an EM programme. Despite inconclusive results so far concerning recidivism and EM, it can still be asked whether a GPS monitoring programme actually has the potential to be a factor in causing sex offenders to change their criminal behaviour, or at least to contribute to such change. In the long term, changing sex offenders' behaviour is the ultimate goal that EM is supposed to achieve, by decreasing their opportunities for crime and increasing the risks of detection of violations, reflecting the 'routine activity approach' and theoretical background of 'situational crime prevention' (Clarke and Homel 1997). Furthermore, forcing offenders to be away from their potential victims for a sustained period may produce structural changes in the routine of sex offenders. Whether the monitoring of movement changes attitudes – as opposed to shaping patterns of behaviour – is debatable, although treatment and counselling programmes may be better able to do this than technology.

A recent provisional evaluation report on Korea's GPS monitoring programme found that it has had a positive effect in changing the routine and lifestyle of sex offenders who are placed on EM (Cho 2010). More than two-thirds of the participants (67 per cent) from a total of 186 sex offenders with experience of being on EM through GPS said the programme encouraged them to return home earlier after work and stay away from trouble or delinquent peers while maintaining positive relationships with their family members. Furthermore, over half (65 per cent) of sex offenders interviewed said that GPS electronic monitoring affected their behaviour in a good way and that it motivated them to give up their criminal impulses while on EM. However, when the participants were asked about the onerousness of EM as a punishment, 31 per cent said they would have preferred to serve their time in prison rather than wearing the electronic anklet. Taken as a whole, the EM participants' overall attitudes towards GPS monitoring are negative – they experience it as a punishment – but they accept that it has a positive impact on changing their lifestyles and family relationships while being at liberty in the community.

Conclusion

With the exception of Singapore, which was an early adopter of EM house arrest but was little studied (and not easy to get data on), the study of EM has largely been a Western preoccupation, and the emergence of South Korea as a leading user is further evidence of the technology's potential for expansion. It is significant, however, that Korea never used RF EM for house arrest – preferring voice verification for this purpose with juveniles – and that it moved so quickly to GPS tracking, which can of course monitor curfews as well as movement more widely. This represents a different pattern of evolution in EM to Western countries, which may well be followed by others who will see no need to use 'first-generation technology' when 'second-generation technology' is so much more versatile. It is clear also that general Korean confidence in GPS tracking for sex offenders reflects the wider enthusiasm and taken-for-grantedness of high-tech 'communication' solutions to the problems of urban living, even if it took a particular penal conjuncture – public outrage about sex crime – to stimulate its emergence. Once this had happened, adoption and expansion were extraordinarily rapid, despite some human rights objections. It meant a significant shift of culture within Korea's relatively new Probation Service, but there was no truly entrenched welfare culture in the service to hold it back, and there was a strong command-and-control ethos which drove it forward. It remains to be seen whether Korea's example is taken up by other Eastern countries.

References

Cho, Younoh (2008) 'Analysis of automated voiceprint recognition supervision programme in Korea', PhD, City University of New York.

Cho, Younoh (2009a) 'Empirical consequences of electronic monitoring with GPS and practical recommendation for application of EM in South Korea', *International Seminar Commemorating the 20th Anniversary of Korean Probation and Parole* (Seoul: Ministry of Justice), pp. 181–220.

Cho, Younoh (2009b) 'A study on the crime deterrent effect of GPS electronic monitoring programme', *Korean Journal of Public Safety and Criminal Justice*, 18:4, pp. 481–511.

Cho, Younoh (2009c) 'Analysis of the Automated Voiceprint Recognition Curfew for juvenile probationer in Korea', *Korean Association of Criminology*, 21:1, pp. 9–36.

Cho, Younoh (2010) *An Analysis of Electronic Monitoring with GPS for Specific Sex Offenders* (Seoul: Korea Probation Journal Press).

Chung, Woo-Sik (2002) 'The community service order in Korea', *The 121st International Training Papers Conference* (Seoul: Ministry of Justice).

Clarke, R.V. and Homel, R. (1997). 'A revised classification of situational crime prevention techniques', in S.P. Lab (ed.) *Crime Prevention at a Crossroads* (Cincinnati, OH: Anderson), pp. 134–161.

Elzinga, H.K. and Nijboer, J.A. (2006) 'Probation supervision through GPS', *European Journal of Crime, Criminal Law and Criminal Justice*, 14:4, pp. 366–381.

Gainey, R.R., Payne, B.K. and O'Toole, M. (2000) 'The relationship between time in jail, time on electronic monitoring, and recidivism: an event history analysis of a jail-based programme', *Justice Quarterly*, 17:4, pp. 733–752.

Imbens, G.W. (2000) 'The role of propensity score in estimating dose-response functions', *Biometrika*, 87:3, pp. 706–710.

International Legal Affairs Division (2009) *Criminal Justice in Korea* (Seoul: Ministry of Justice).

Kim, I.S. (2005) *Research on Electronic Monitoring in Korea: Validity of the Introduction of the Programme and Guideline for the Legalization* (Seoul: Korea Probation Journal Press).

Legal Research and Training Institute. (2007) *White Paper on Crime* (Seoul: The Ministry of Justice).

Legal Research and Training Institute. (2008) *White Paper on Crime* (Seoul: The Ministry of Justice).

Lullen, J., Shadish, W.R. and Clark, M.H. (2005) 'Propensity scores: an introduction and experimental test', *Evaluation Review*, 29:6, pp. 530–558.

Ministry of Justice. (2009a) *The Guideline of Electronic Monitoring through GPS in Korea* (Seoul: Korean Crime Prevention Policy Division).

Ministry of Justice. (2009b) *Promotion Material for Understanding of Electronic Monitoring Programme with GPS* (Seoul: Korean Crime Prevention Policy Division).

Ministry of Justice. (2009c) *High Risk Offenders: GPS Tracking Programme in Korea* (Seoul: Ministry of Justice).

Neary, M. (2003) *Korean Transformations: Power workers, probation and the politics of human rights* (Seoul: Sungkonghoe University).

Newman, G., Clarke, R.V. and Shoham, S.G. (1997) *Rational Choice and Situational Crime Prevention* (Gower House: Arena-Ashgate Publishing).

Padgett, K., Bales, W. and Blomberg, T. (2006) 'Under surveillance: an empirical test of the effectiveness and implications of electronic monitoring', *Criminology and Public Policy*, 5:1, pp. 61–92.

Palermo, G. (2005) 'Reflections on sexual offender notification laws', *International Journal of Offender Therapy and Comparative Criminology*, 49:4, pp. 359–361.

Renzema, M. and Mayo-Wilson, E. (2005) 'Can electronic monitoring reduce crime for moderate to high-risk offenders?', *Journal of Experimental Criminology*, 1:2, pp. 215–237.

6 High level of support and high level of control

An efficient Swedish model of electronic monitoring?

Inka Wennerberg

History

Sweden was one of the first countries in Europe to introduce electronic monitoring (EM) within the criminal justice system, as a 'front door' scheme – part of a strategy to find credible alternatives to shorter prison sentences. Intensive supervision with electronic monitoring (ISEM) was piloted in 1994 in six probation districts, extended after two years to cover the whole of Sweden, and became a permanent part of the Swedish Penalty Code in 1999. The main aim was to create a solid alternative to prison that could satisfy criminal justice requirements without resulting in the negative consequences associated with imprisonment; a secondary motivation was to reduce the costs of imprisonment. The target group of the scheme were offenders sentenced to a maximum of three months' imprisonment, who could apply to serve their prison sentence by means of ISEM rather than entering custody (Brottsförebyggande rådet 1999a). It was considered vital to avoid using EM in isolation merely as a form of house arrest, as it had been in the United States, and as it was in England and Wales. For that reason it was linked from the start to a treatment programme, which meant specific conditions: no use of alcohol or drugs; a motivational programme arranged by the Probation Service; and intensive control, both personal and electronic. A further basic requirements was also an approved form of employment. It was the close link between EM and treatment programmes organized by the probation service that made the scheme one of 'intensive supervision' (Whitfield 1997).

In 2001 a 'back door' programme, using EM as part of a prison-release programme, was piloted as a result of the positive experiences with ISEM, and in response to a growing prison population. The objective of the pilot was to lower the risk of recidivism by providing an opportunity for long-term prisoners to spend a period of time in the community with more support and control than they would normally have received following the discharge from prison. The target group for EM release were prisoners serving a minimum of two years of imprisonment, who could apply to serve the last months of their sentences before conditional release with EM release. The characteristics of the new back door scheme were quite similar to the front door programme (Brottsförebyggande rådet 2003, 2005a).

In 2005 a pilot scheme was launched to expand the use of both ISEM and EM release to include larger target groups, as a result of the still-rising prison population and because of the positive results from previous evaluations. The target group for ISEM was expanded to include sentences of a maximum six months and the target group for EM release was expanded at the same time to include sentences from 18 months of imprisonment or more. The maximum time for EM release was simultaneously lengthened to a maximum of six months. The most recent expansion of EM took place in January 2007, when two new release initiatives were introduced: halfway houses and extended parole (Bill 2005/2006: 123). Extended parole has replaced EM release as the back door programme, in effect extending it to include prisoners serving over six months of imprisonment. This makes it possible for long-term prisoners to serve a much longer part of their sentence with EM, to a maximum of one year. As with earlier schemes, it requires the offender to have employment. The new scheme makes it possible to gradually decrease the degree of control over a released prisoner: so long as there have been no breaches of programme conditions the curfew and EM can cease completely, and be replaced by supervision alone. The Correctional Treatment Act also makes it possible to combine halfway houses with EM (Brottsförebyggande rådet 2007a).

Since 2005 EM has also been used as a means of supervision within Swedish prisons. The first prison to implement EM was Kolmarden, a low-security (open) prison with a maximum capacity of 185 inmates. The objective of using EM within prison was to increase security at a limited cost by monitoring the presence of the prisoners within prison and preserving the open atmosphere. The monitoring system is based on radio frequency (RF) and built on the same type of technology used in the front door and back door programmes. All inmates are tagged with an electronic device and the prison is divided into inclusive and exclusive zones. The technology makes it possible to ensure that a particular inmate is in a certain area at a certain time. The Kolmarden experience with EM was considered successful and since 2008 three other low-security prisons have been equipped with EM (Carlsson 2009).

Integrating EM and probation

The majority of EM cases in Sweden are on the front door programme. In 2008 there were 3,087 individuals who began a period of ISEM compared to 786 individuals who started the EM release programme. The number of offenders serving their sentence by means of ISEM peaked in 1998, but has declined since because, at the same time as ISEM became permanent in 1999 another new sentence was introduced – a suspended sentence combined with community service. This quickly became popular with sentencers and focused more or less on the same target group as ISEM, producing a substantial reduction in the numbers of offenders subject to the latter. Figure 6.1 shows the numbers of offenders who began ISEM or EM release since 1997.

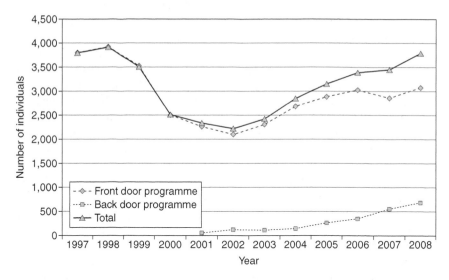

Figure 6.1 The number of individuals beginning a period of EM – ISEM or EM release – between 1999 and 2007.

At both a strategic and practical level, the Swedish approach to using EM has been characterized by close involvement with the Probation Service. Private sector involvement has been limited to provision of the equipment, and technical back-up services. There were several reasons why the Swedish Prison and Probation Administration favoured Probation Service provision rather than, as in England and Wales, for example, contracting service delivery to the private sector. It wished to create a reliable and secure programme by keeping strict control over the way EM was used. In addition, because of its deep commitment to a rehabilitative approach to offenders, the Administration wished to create a high level of interaction between EM and probation, rather than see them used separately (Carlsson 2003). The decision to let the Probation Service operate all stages of EM has, in my view, proved successful. The model has led to a trustworthy and reliable scheme. The low involvement of the private sector has also meant that the rehabilitative approach has been kept in focus and that EM is seen as part of a rehabilitative strategy.

In terms of practice, with both the front door and back door schemes, the offender applies to the Probation Service. The service conducts an assessment to see if the offender meets the requirements and is suitable for the programme, and decides whether to accept or reject. The basic requirements for both ISEM and EM release are: a suitable place to live, a telephone and an approved form of occupation. Consent is required both from the offender and for any fellow occupant in order to grant the application. Once an application has been approved, the Probation Service is responsible for the implementation of the whole scheme; arranging for temporary work, installing the equipment, running the monitoring centre, reacting to breaches and, at the end of the programme, de-tagging the offenders. The idea behind ISEM is that applications from as many eligible offenders as possible will be accepted, but the decision of EM release entails a more careful selection method, including a risk assessment. If there is a risk that the offender will abscond, re-offend or abuse alcohol or drugs during the time of the sentence, the application will not be granted. The offenders who are serving their prison sentence by ISEM must pay a daily fee of 50 SKr to the victims' contingency fund, if it is justified by their possibility of having a viable income (Brottsförebyggande rådet 1999a, 2003, 2005a). The fee was originally introduced using the argument that offenders who were granted ISEM would have significant economic advantages in comparison to offenders serving their sentences in prison. When EM release was introduced a fee was also considered, but the suggestion was not approved, on the basis that the target group of long-term prisoners, unlike the ISEM target group, had a very poor economic situation, and also because the other release programmes did not require a special fee (Bill 2000/2001: 76).

The Swedish model of EM supervision is also characterized by combining a high level of control with a high level of support. Intensive supervision with EM means that the offender is confined to the home and only allowed to leave when he or she is taking part in the obligatory occupation, which normally means studies or work, or in other scheduled activities required by the sentence, such as taking part in a treatment programme. Electronic tagging is used to regulate the presence or absence of the offender at home by clearly specifying the times when he is expected to be home, and the times when he can be elsewhere. In addition to control by electronic monitoring, the Probation Service also makes unannounced home visits several times a week. Due to the fact that the offender is serving a prison sentence, the programme also includes a prohibition to use any alcohol or drugs, and in conjunction with the home visits alcohol testing is done. Drug testing is done at the beginning of each sentence and thereafter whenever it is judged necessary by the supervisor. The level of control at work has in earlier evaluations been considered as the weak link in the programme, although it requires an appointed contact person at the place of employment who can inform the Probation Service of any breaches from the conditions (Brotts-förebyggande rådet 1999a). It is also possible for the probation officer to make unannounced visits or phone calls to the workplace.

Face-to-face supervision is an important part of the overall scheme, which is carried out by probation officers or external supervisors.[1] The offender has to meet with the supervisor a couple of times a month during the programme. The scheme has a low tolerance for misconduct. Serious breaches, such as any use of alcohol or drugs, require that the programme is discontinued and the offender recalled to serve the remainder of the sentence in prison. The level of control for EM release has been criticized as too high. The amount of 'free time' at the start of the scheme was less than in other alternative release programmes[2] or in the prison leave offered by low-security prisons. This lack of free time and the strict schedule made the community alternative seen unattractive to many prisoners. In order to make EM release more attractive the amount of free time was later increased to correspond more with the alternatives. In my view, this development was necessary in order to give long-term prisoners a proper opportunity to readjust to the freedoms of life back in the community.

The programme supports offenders in order that they may make full use of the EM schemes. If the offender does not have a job or is unable to arrange employment of their own, the Prison and Probation Service will offer assistance to arrange this, which usually means an occupation similar to community service. Offenders who apply for EM release can also be provided with economic benefit payments by the Probation Service if an income cannot be secured by other means. In ISEM, a majority of the offenders take part in crime-reduction or addiction-related programmes. These motivation-to-change programmes are mainly directed at offenders on the front door programme, since those on the back door programme are expected to have been offered equivalents while still in prison. The offenders in the EM release programme will nonetheless often take part in other rehabilitation measures, such as treatment or external contact with psychiatric or addiction-recovery services (Brottsförebyggande rådet 1999a, 2004, 2007a; Whitfield 1997). The linking of EM to a treatment programme is vital if there is to be a genuinely rehabilitative element in the scheme and not just a requirement to cut costs. The combination of high levels of control and high levels of support has made the schemes into credible alternatives to prison, and specifically for EM release has provided an effective tool for resettlement.

Controversies and debates

The use of EM in Sweden has not been particularly controversial in comparison to some of the other European countries, although in the early 1990s when it was first introduced it generated a good deal of debate in the media and among the public. EM was seen as too soft compared to imprisonment and was considered applicable only to offenders with a stable social situation. Some media commentators feared that the technique would replace human contact and the rehabilitative approach with a mechanistic process, as Whitfield (1997) had suggested it could do. Initially, there was also resistance within the Probation Service to EM. It was seen as too repressive and not something that the Probation Service should manage. To overcome this resistance the hand-picked team of supportive probation officers who worked on ISEM became a separate part of the organization, seeking to prove its worth before it was made mainstream.

The image of EM in the media soon became quite positive, and has remained so. There are several reasons that might explain why EM has not been particularly controversial in Sweden. When it was introduced, the Probation Service had a clearly defined media strategy and had personnel with special training to handle the media. Furthermore, the target group was low risk, and there have never been any serious incidents involving EM reported in the media. Both front door and back door programmes were introduced gradually, and began with a regional pilot, followed by a national pilot. The target groups have only been gradually extended and each phase has been subject to several rigorous evaluations.

Even in political debate the use of EM has been relatively uncontentious. Most parties have been positive about it as an alternative to prison. When the front door scheme was introduced in 1994 it was supported by a right-wing government, but by the time EM release was introduced in 2001 Sweden had a left-wing government. Such political differences as there are distil down to a right-wing focus on the ability to lower penal costs versus a left-wing emphasis on supporting rehabilitation.

Research on EM

There has been quite extensive research into the use of EM in Sweden. The research consists mainly of evaluations done by the National Council for Crime Prevention on commission from the government. The implementation of both ISEM and EM release has been carefully evaluated, as has the extended use of both the front door and back door programmes.

Implementing ISEM

When ISEM was introduced the pilot was evaluated (Brottsförebyggande rådet 1999a). One of the hopes behind the ISEM evaluation was a desire to show that it was a viable and credible alternative to prison. The results of the evaluation showed that almost half of all prison sentences up to three months were indeed served on ISEM. Those selected for ISEM were often offenders sentenced for drink driving who had a somewhat more favourable social background and current social situation than the offenders who served their sentences in prison. The Probation Service's work on investigation and assessment for ISEM was judged quite positively. The level of personal supervision was high, with regularly scheduled face-to-face contact and several unannounced home visits each week. The offenders spent on average 30 hours per week at their occupation, although interviews with the appointed contact persons showed that they tended to deal with rule violations themselves instead of reporting them to the Probation Service. Only 6 per cent of the offenders had to leave the programme as a result of violations, which were mostly caused by using alcohol. The concern in some quarters that ISEM would simply become an unrehabilitative form of house arrest was not confirmed by the evaluation.

The evaluation concluded that ISEM is a form of sentence implementation that seems to be at least as intrusive as prison when it comes to limiting an offender's freedom of movement, but without being encumbered by the negative consequences associated with imprisonment. It also yields substantial economic gains for society since it is considerably cheaper than prison and the offender can continue working during the time of ISEM.

Implementing EM release

The evaluation of EM release asked if the new release programme could be a useful means of facilitating inmates' readjustment into society before full release from their status as prisoners (Brottsförebyggande rådet 2003, 2004, 2005a). It described offenders selected for EM release, their social situation for the six months after finishing the EM programme and the pattern of re-offending. The results showed that almost 40 per cent of all inmates with more than two years of imprisonment applied for EM release. About half were granted EM release, which corresponds to approximately 20 per cent of the total population of long-term prisoners. As with the front door programme, the offenders who were granted EM release had a more favourable background than other long-term inmates. They were better educated and had a substantially better social situation. The evaluation questioned whether the target group was the right one and suggested extending it to include inmates with a somewhat higher-risk profile. The study found a small group of offenders who fulfilled the criteria for EM release, but who did not apply, giving as their reason the view that EM release involved too many regulations and controls. In several cases offenders thought that work release was a better alternative than EM. The figure for breaches of EM release was pleasingly low: only 6 per cent of the offenders breached the conditions and were returned to prison. In most of these cases breach was the result of using alcohol or other drugs. Although the selected offenders had a more favourable social background, the study showed that half of them had received assistance from the Probation Service to fulfil the requirements of EM release, mostly in relation to occupation or income. Some were provided with an occupation akin to community service and received an income from the Prison and Probation Administration. Others were assisted to find places on labour market schemes.

One of the objectives of the evaluation was to study the effect of EM release on the social situation. The social situation (occupation, accommodation and income) of offenders at the beginning of the EM release programme was compared to their social situation six months after their final conditional discharge from prison. The results showed a clear improvement. The proportion of offenders with regular jobs improved from 31 to 56 per cent and the proportion with a home of their own had increased from 52 to 72 per cent. The study did not, however, have a matched control group, making it impossible to know with certainty whether the improvements were the result of attending the EM release programme. It is reasonable to assume that the improvements have to some extent to do with a selection effect, which has to do with the high demands to get an EM release. It could be that the offenders who are granted EM release consist of more motivated offenders, who would have improved their situation even without attending the EM release programme. Even so, the study gives a positive picture compared to other research on resettlement for long-term prisoners. It concluded that even if the offender attending EM-release is highly motivated they may still need help from probation to readjust to society after release from prison, and that control and support can be constructively balanced (Brottsföre-byggande rådet 2004).

Evaluations of EM in the reform of the prison release mechanisms that were introduced in January 2007 appeared shortly afterwards (Brottsförebyggande rådet 2008, 2009). The reforms entailed replacing the first EM release pro-gramme with a more flexible arrangement involving parole. Its effect was to increase the number of individuals released on EM. The study showed that the group selected for the new EM release programme are still offenders with more favourable backgrounds, with low-risk profiles for recidivism and substance abuse. The revocation rate remained low and even decreased from 5 per cent in 2006 to 2 per cent in 2007. One-third of the offenders were able to cease the EM completely before the end of the supervision programme due to good behaviour. It is difficult to know if the low revocation rate has more to do with the imposi-tion of external control or whether the selected offenders are simply more dis-posed to behaving well. The study infers that the revocation rate is so low because the selection process is too strict and risk-averse, and suggests that offenders with a slightly higher-risk profile should be considered for extended work release with EM. Subsequent research into an EM early release scheme (whose participants were in employment and subject to offending behaviour pro-grammes and regular sobriety controls) proved to have significantly lower levels of recidivism than a control group, especially among offenders with 'intermedi-ate levels of previous criminality' (Marklund and Holmberg 2009: 41).

The experiences of the ISEM and EM release from participants and their families

When the front door scheme was introduced, 1,600 offenders who had fulfilled the programme filled in a questionnaire of how they felt about their time on the programme (Brottsförebyggande rådet 1999a, 2005a). Data were also collected from 104 adult fellow occupants who were interviewed. The experiences described by the offenders and the fellow occupants were predominantly posi-tive regarding the way they had been dealt with by the Probation Service. The special requirements that EM programmes involve – i.e. prohibition of using alcohol or drugs, meeting the requirements of an occupation, unannounced home visits and wearing the electronic bracelet – were in most cases not perceived as hard to cope with. It was quite common for the offenders to find it difficult to attend their daily routines – e.g. to maintain normal contact with friends and to participate in leisure activities. In spite of this, most offenders and fellow occu-pants perceived the time on the EM programme to be a milder sanction than a prison term. A great majority also would apply for the EM programme if they were given the opportunity to choose again.

The experiences of the offenders were also explored in the evaluation of EM release and interviews with 55 offenders who were attending the programme (Brottsförebyggande rådet 2003, 2004). Most offenders were satisfied with their time on EM release. They appreciated the fact that EM release made it possible to spend time with their families. Regarding their social situation, the offenders emphasized the importance of having some form of occupation when leaving prison and the combination of control and support which EM release provided. What were perceived as less positive were the strict schedule and the lack of free time. Almost all of the offenders would have applied for EM release if they were put in the same situation again. Interviews were also carried out with 28 family members in order to examine their experiences from the EM release. Those interviewed were generally positive, especially those who had children. Several family members felt that life became easier when the inmate returned home, but others felt it restricted their own freedom.

When the length of the front door and the back door programmes was extended in 2005 a small number of interviews were carried out in order to get an understanding of how the offenders perceived being tagged for a longer period of time (Brottsförebyggande rådet 2007a). Even when the period of electronic tagging was extended, the offenders were still predominantly positive about their experience with the programme. They thought that the longer time gave them an opportunity to adjust to the strict daily routines. Because of the limited material it is not possible to draw safe conclusions, but the positive picture matches the results of earlier studies in both Sweden and other countries (Brottsförebyggande rådet 2003, 2004; Bonta *et al.* 1999; Dodgson *et al.* 2001; Spaans and Verwers 1997).

Effects on re-offending

According to meta-analyses there are few studies that have provided evidence of EM having an effect of re-offending, and the few studies made often have a number of shortcomings. There is a Swedish study on EM release, however, that showed some positive effects.

ISEM

One of the objectives with ISEM when it was introduced was that it would contribute to reduce the risk of re-offending. To study the effects of ISEM on re-offending the first evaluation included an analysis based on 600 offenders who were granted ISEM in 1994 and 1995 (Brottsförebyggande rådet 1999a). ISEM was, at the time of the study, a pilot limited to certain regions in Sweden. The ISEM group was compared with a matched control group from other parts of the country to study the differences in criminal recidivism up to three years after conditional release. The control group included offenders of the same sex and age, who lived in the same type of community with the same nationality and the same type of criminal history and earlier prison experience as the ISEM group. The results show no significant differences between the ISEM group and the control group concerning the rate of offenders sentenced to supervision or imprisonment up to three years after the original sentence. Although there were no general differences between the groups, the analysis shows that the offenders who were sentenced for drink driving committed the same crime significantly less in the future. Because of several unsure factors when constructing the matched control group and the fairly low statistical significance, any conclusions have to be drawn carefully. The conclusion from the study appears to be that the re-offending rate is the same if the offender serves the sentence by ISEM or in prison. At the same time, the results indicate that ISEM can have a positive effect on offenders who are sentenced for drink driving.

EM release

A study of EM release in Sweden has showed some positive results on re-offending (Brottsförebyggande rådet 2005a, 2007b; Marklund and Holmberg 2009). The study compared a group of 260 inmates who concluded their prison sentences by means of an EM release with a corresponding (matched) control group in order to study possible differences in criminal recidivism. Both groups had a minimum sentence of two years' imprisonment. The EM release group was compared with the matches to study any differences in criminal recidivism after a three-year follow-up.

The results show no differences between the two groups after one year of follow-up, but three years after conditional release there were significant differences between the EM release group and the control group. After three years the EM release group was re-convicted less than the comparable control group – 26 per cent compared to 38 per cent in the control group (Table 6.1). There is also a significant difference between the groups considering re-conviction and subsequent prison sentences, which is an indication of more serious crimes.

The average time to re-conviction was one year and four months after conditional release. The result points out that the difference in re-conviction is predominantly in the second year of follow-up, which can be explained by the factor that the EM release group, which consists of long-term prisoners, have one year of supervision after conditional release.

Further analysis shows that EM release seems to have the greatest positive effect on criminal recidivism with individuals who have one or two previous

Table 6.1 Proportion re-convicted during the three-year follow-up period; proportion sentenced to a new prison term and mean numbers of convictions and offences

	EM release group (N = 260)	*Control group (N = 260)*
Proportion re-convicted during follow-up period	26**	38**
Proportion sentenced to prison during follow-up period	13**	21**

Source: Brottsförebyggande rådet 2007a: 19.

Note
* $p < 0.05$; ** $p < 0.01$.

convictions and with older people (>37 years old). The results might indicate that the older people and the offenders with one or two previous convictions are more open to the support that EM release can offer. It is possible that among the group with no previous convictions the risk is already low, which makes it difficult to affect the rate in a positive direction. On the other hand, the situation for the group with several previous re-convictions might be too difficult for EM release to have a positive influence on criminal recidivism.

In summary, the study indicates that the Swedish EM release programme has positive effects on re-offending among those offenders who are participating in the EM release programme and a comparable control group at a three-year follow-up. However, the results must be carefully interpreted because the design of the study is not randomized and there might be factors that influence the results that are not controlled for. The results seem to provide support for the Swedish model of EM embedded in a programme with high levels of control and support.

Crime victims' views on ISEM and EM release

Most research on EM has been focused on the offender or the practitioner's perspective and very seldom on the victim's view. The international studies that have been carried out are interviews with victims of domestic violence involved in cases at a pre-trial stage (Erez *et al.* 2004; Erez and Ibarra 2007). The crime victim's perspective, however, has become more the focus of the criminal justice debate over the last decades. The question of how victims felt about offenders serving their prison sentence with EM was investigated in one of the evaluations made by the National Council for Crime Prevention (Brottsförebyggande rådet 2007a). Forty-one victims of violent crimes, sexual crime or robbery were included in the study.[3] It was not possible to produce a quantitative picture of victims' views of ISEM and EM release because the non-response group probably included a larger proportion of people who are negative towards electronic tagging than found among the victims that participated in the study. Among the interviews, the majority were positive. One conclusion that can be drawn from the study is that victims are more accepting of ISEM than of EM release. The results indicate that victims of serious crimes are more negative towards EM than victims subjected to less serious offences, regardless of how much time has passed since the trial. The overall picture was that the views of the victims differed very much and the victims with the strongest feelings, both positive and negative, were victims of domestic violence.

Among the interviewed crime victims where the offender had been placed on EM release, the proportions with negative views and positive views were equal. Victims who were negative felt that the sentence was too short in relation to what they had experienced during the offences. The victims who were positive saw the programme from the offender's perspective and thought that it was a better alternative to prison, because it increased the chances for the offender to get back into society.

When studying the victims of the less serious crimes, most victims had a positive view of ISEM. The victims who were negative thought that EM was too lenient and did not fit the crime and the suffering caused. The majority of the victims were positive and felt that the sentence was in proportion to the crime that was committed. Some of them thought that being on a tag could also be as bad as being in prison. Other victims felt that the most important thing was the trial and the imposition of a sentence, not the sentence itself. The victims of domestic violence were, as noted above, those with the strongest feelings, in some cases negative, but in most cases positive. They were positive because the offender could maintain his social status and was able to keep his job. Some of them also thought that EM would reduce the risk of the offender getting vindictive and hateful.

Future developments

From tagging to tracking

The technology used in the front door and back door programmes has, since their introduction, been based on RF technology in order to assess whether the offender is at home at a certain time according to a schedule. In 2010 the Prison and Probation Administration undertook a pilot using tracking technology on the EM release group. The purpose of the pilot is not to replace the RF technology, but rather to explore if the new technology can be used for a new target group with a slightly higher risk than the target group for the back door programme today. The goal is to make it possible for more offenders to have a gradual release from prison. In Europe most countries still use the RF technology, but the development of tracking is slowly increasing (Wennerberg and Pinto 2009). The introduction of tracking within the front door and back door programmes in Sweden can be seen as a natural development and was probably expected at some time or another, but RF technology has a great advantage of being a much cheaper alternative to prison in comparison to tracking.

EM and restraining orders

The development of tracking has offered new possibilities and arenas for using EM. It is likely in the near future that the new arena for using EM in Sweden will be in relation to restraining orders.[4] The objective of using EM in relation to restraining orders is to prevent the offender making contact with the victim and to help discover any breaches. Already in the 1990s it was suggested by the government in Sweden to look into the possibilities of using EM with restraining orders in order to create a safer situation for the victims of domestic violence. At the same time it was questioned whether EM could deter any offender who had already breached the order several times.

Earlier studies showed that EM for restraining orders was used in a few places in the United States in the 1990s (Brottsförebyggande rådet 1999b). The system for bilateral EM was RF-based (usually referred to as reverse tagging) and meant that a receiver was placed at the victim's home and the offender was carrying an electronic device. When the offender got closer than 150 metres from the victim's home, the alarm went off at the monitoring centre and made it possible for the police to intervene. The results of the report showed that the technique would make it possible to provide proof of breaches of restraining orders and that it could work as a deterrent to the offender, but that the technical equipment was at the time insufficient to provide reliable security for the victims who were exposed to threats and violence. The development of the ability to track the offender with GPS has produced new possibilities for the use of EM for victim protection. Tracking makes it possible to create exclusion zones around the victim's house, work or other places where the offender is not supposed to visit, which would make it possible to discover any breaches of the order. The National Council for Crime Prevention established in a report that there are several limitations to the use of EM as a crime-preventive measure and that there is a difficult balance between the efficiency of the technique and the credibility of the measure (Brottsförebyggande rådet 2005b). Except for the technical limitations, there have also been difficulties finding a legal solution to using EM in relation to restraining orders in Sweden. Since restraining orders in the Swedish legal system are a preventive measure, it has been hard to find a legal solution which will justify the infringement of the private integrity for the offender.

In 2007 the government gave the police force the assignment of performing practical testing of electronic monitoring in relation to restraining orders. The pilot was based on experiments with technical equipment on volunteers (Rikspolisstyrelsen 2007). Three basic types of bilateral electronic monitoring were identified and tested: reverse tagging, tracking of the offender (single tracking) and tracking of both offender and victim (dual tracking). Dual tracking was considered to be the most expensive method and still in its infancy. The conclusion reached was that the technique made it possible to act as a deterrent, constitute technical proof of breaches, warn the victims and to stop ongoing threats. At the same time it was pointed out that EM could never provide 100 per cent protection for the victim and therefore is unsuitable in cases of a high risk of violence. The size of the exclusion zone was also considered to be important. If the exclusion zones are large enough it makes it possible for the police to act in a preventive way to stop any ongoing threats, whereas small exclusion zones only make it possible to warn the victim and to provide technical proof of any violation.

The Stalking Inquiry, in October 2008, submitted a report including, among other things, a legal proposal for the use of EM with restraining orders (Swedish Government 2008). EM is proposed to be targeted at people who have already breached the conditions of the restraining order and should be based on a risk assessment. It is suggested perpetrators with a high risk of breaching the order should not be selected. The proposal suggests the use of hybrid tracking of the offender in combination with exclusion zones – for example, around the victim's house. This means that the position of the perpetrator will not be known to the monitoring staff unless the offender enters an exclusion zone. The victim will, according to the proposal, be offered complementary technical equipment to carry outside of their home. Since the restraining order is not a sentence in Sweden, the police service has been recommended as the authority to be in charge of EM and to follow up breaches. The decision to enforce EM with the restraining order will be suggested by the court. There is a risk that the expectations of the technique will be too high and that any mishap will mean a lack of faith in the scheme. It is therefore important that the implementation of EM as a preventive measure should be introduced gradually and followed by an evaluation. EM also needs to be followed by well-developed routines for information on the conditions for both the offender and the victim and how to react to any violations in order to be an efficient crime-preventive tool. However, with setting the right expectations and using the technique in collaboration with well-developed routines, the use of EM will provide the victim with better protection than the use of a restraining order alone.

Notes

1 External supervisors are laypersons appointed by the Probation Service. They meet regularly with the offender, but are not entitled to change the order or handle breaches.
2 Work release constitutes an alternative pre-release programme and involves the inmate carrying out work, studies or some other form of occupation outside prison during working hours. Work release includes a programme of prison leave, which EM-release did not have in the beginning.
3 Originally 73 victims were selected for the study; 60 per cent of them were located and agreed to answer questions about how they perceived the offender being placed on EM.
4 A restraining order is a preventive measure decided by the Prosecutor in Sweden. The target group is mainly domestic violence offenders or stalkers. It means that the offender is not allowed to make any contact with the victim, physical or otherwise. Breaches of the order are punishable.

References

Bill 2000/01:76 *Från anstalt till frihet* (From prison to liberty).
Bill 2005/06:123 *En modernare kriminalvårdslag* (A Modernized Correctional Treatment Act).
Bonta, J., Rooney, J. and Wallace-Capretta, S. (1999) *Electronic Monitoring in Canada* (Ottawa: Public Works and Government Services Canada).
Brottsförebyggande rådet (1999a) 'Intensivövervakning med elektronisk kontroll. En utvärdering av 1997 och 1998 års riksomfattande försöksverksamhet' (Intensive supervision by means of electronic control: an evaluation of the 1997 and 1998 national trial project), Brå-report 1999:4, Brå. Fritzes.
Brottsförebyggande rådet (1999b) 'Elektronisk övervakning vid besöksförbud. Teknikens möjligheter och begränsningar' (Electronic monitoring with restraining order: the possibilities and limitations with the technique), Memorandum, Brå.
Brottsförebyggande rådet (2003) 'Fängelse i frihet. En utvärdering av intensivövervakning med elektronisk kontroll' (Prison at liberty: an evaluation of intensive supervision by means of electronic control), Brå-report 2003:4, Brå. Fritzes.

Brottsförebyggande rådet (2004) 'Ett steg på väg mot frihet. En beskrivning av intagnas sociala situation efter intensivövervakning med elektronisk kontroll – IÖV-utsluss' (A step on the road to freedom: a description of the social situation of inmates subsequent to intensive supervision by means of electronic control – EM-release), Brå-report, EditaNorstedt.

Brottsförebyggande rådet (2005a) 'Electronic tagging in Sweden', Brå-report 2005:8, Brå. Fritzes.

Brottsförebyggande rådet (2005b) 'Reinforcing restraining orders using electronic monitoring' Brå.

Brottsförebyggande rådet (2007a) 'Extended use of electronic tagging in Sweden: The offenders and victim's view', Brå-report 2007:3, Brå. Fritzes.

Brottsförebyggande rådet (2007b) 'Utökad användning av elektronisk fotboja inom kriminalvården' (Extended use of electronic tagging within the Prison and Probation Service), Brå-report 2007:19, Brå. Fritzes.

Brottsförebyggande rådet (2008) '2007 års reform för bättre utslussning inom Kriminalvården. Vilka blev effekterna under det första året?' (2007's legal reform for better release within the Prison and Probation Service: What were the effect during the first year?), Brå-report 2008:19, Brå. Fritzes.

Brottsförebyggande rådet (2009) '2007 års reform av utslussning i kriminalvården'. (2007's legal reform for release within the Prison and Probation Service), Brå-report 2009:18, Brå. Fritzes.

Carlsson, K. (2003) 'Intensive supervision with electronic monitoring in Sweden', in M. Mayer, R. Haverkamp and R. Lévy (eds) *Will Electronic Monitoring Have a Future in Europe?* (Freiburg: Max Planck Institut für ausländisches und internationales Strafrecht), pp. 69–76.

Carlsson, K. (2009) 'EM in Swedish low security prisons.' Presentation at CEP Electronic Monitoring Conference 2009. Online. Available at: www.cepprobation.org.

Dodgson, K., Goodwin, P. Howard, P., Llewellyn-Thomas, S., Mortimer, E., Russell, N. and Weiner, M. (2001) 'Electronic monitoring of released prisoners: an evaluation of the Home Detention Curfew scheme', Home Office Research Study 222, Home Office Research, Development and Statistics Directorate.

Erez, E. and Ibarra, P.R. (2007) 'Making your home a shelter: electronic monitoring and victim re-entry in domestic violence cases', *British Journal of Criminology*, 47, pp. 100–120.

Erez, E., Ibarra, P.R. and Lurie, N.A. (2004) 'Electronic monitoring of domestic violence cases: a study of two bilateral programs', *Federal Probation*, 68:1, pp. 15–20.

Marklund, F. and Holmberg, S. (2009) 'Effects of early release from prison using electronic tagging in Sweden', *Journal of Experimental Criminology*, 5:1, pp. 41–61.

Rikspolisstyrelsen (2007) *Förstärkt besöksförbud genom elektronisk övervakning* (Reinforced restraining order by electronic monitoring) (Stockholm: RPS).

Spaans, E. and Verwers, C. (1997) *Electronic Monitoring in the Netherlands: Results and experiment*, English summary (The Hague: Netherlands Ministry of Justice).

Swedish Government (2008) *'Stalkning: ett allvarligt brott'* (Stalking: a serious crime), Official Report, SOU 2008:81, Fritzes.

Wennerberg, I. and Pinto. S. (2009) 'Summary of questionnaires'. Paper presented at the CEP Electronic Monitoring Conference 2009. Online. Available at: www.cepprobation.org.

Whitfield, D. (1997) *Tackling the Tag: The electronic monitoring of offenders* (Winchester: Waterside).

7 From tagging to tracking

Beginnings and development of electronic monitoring in France

René Lévy

Instituted in December 1997 but effectively put into operation only in October 2000, electronic monitoring (EM), whether in the form of 'tagging' or 'tracking' has experienced at least six major reforms, in 2000, 2002, 2004, 2005, 2008 and 2009, with the objective of broadening the scope of its utilization.[1] Thus, long as its preliminaries may have been, it was able to gain a foothold, law after law, in all the various phases of the penal process. Today, tagging can be enforced during the pre- and post-trial phases, but also by the court, applicable as much to minors as to adults, and, since 2005, through the tracking device, applied as a safety measure to convicts once they have served the greater part of their sentence or even after they have served it.

The aim of this chapter is to take an in-depth look at these measures. After a review of the legal framework of EM (up to 2010) in the first section, the circumstances of its genesis and the principal stages of its evolution, I will, in the second section, attempt to circumscribe its application and the characteristics of the target population.

Genesis and evolution of tagging

A laborious start

EM made its first appearance in an official text in France in 1989, in socialist deputy Gilbert Bonnemaison's report on 'The modernization of the public correctional services' (Bonnemaison 1989).[2] The measure was linked to a *numerus clausus* for confinement, aimed at limiting prison overcrowding. The idea was to select those inmates suitable to being placed under EM so as to leave room for new arrivals, be they in pre- or post-trial detention (as a probationary measure in the latter case). The report also considered the possibility of using EM to replace short prison sentences.

Inspired by what was done in Florida (and by projects then under study in Great Britain), the report argued that EM was 'an effective sanction, whereas it is too often thought that prison is the only real punishment' (Bonnemaison 1989: 28),[3] but at the same time enabled offenders to maintain family ties, keep their job or get training, and that its cost would be 'considerably lower than the cost of confinement'.[4]

The Bonnemaison report briefly outlined what was to become initially the French scheme, but received no immediate follow-up. The issue was raised again in 1995–1996 in another parliamentary report, prepared by a right-wing senator, Guy-Pierre Cabanel, this time, under the title 'For improved prevention of recidivism' (Cabanel 1996). The Cabanel report reviewed the experiments under way in other countries (Great Britain, the Netherlands, Sweden) and also came to the conclusion that EM was an effective, financially advantageous tool for preventing recidivism, and a way of combating prison overcrowding. The scheme proposed aimed essentially at using EM to replace short prison terms and for probationary purposes at the end of longer prison sentences: it expressed serious reservations as to the use of EM in the pre-trial phase.

In accordance with his report, the senator attempted to have a bill voted in, introducing EM. He finally succeeded, with the 19 December 1997 Act,[5] which set up EM as a mitigating measure for a prison term of less than one year or when less than one year remained to be served (Kuhn and Madignier 1998: 676; Pradel 1998; Couvrat 1998).

An evolution spurred by prison population pressure and political competition

However, close to three years went by between when the 1997 Act came into force and the implementation of EM in October 2000. Why this unusual hiatus? I believe the reasons for the lag are, first, the unpreparedness of the corrections administration (the *Direction de l'Administration Pénitentiaire*, or DAP, a division of the Ministry of Justice), and possibly the reluctance of the Left (then in power) to apply EM. The relative inertia of the DAP authorities can probably be seen in the evolution of the prison situation. As shown in Figure 7.1, not long after the bill was passed, a reversal occurred in the demographic of prisons. From the early 1980s to 1996, the prison population had risen steadily, although not at a constant pace. But a reversal occurred in 1996 and the downward trend continued until the second semester of 2001. At the same time there was a tremendous increase in non-custodial sentences, with about 100,000 people in 1994 and 141,000 in 2002. In other words, and irrespective of the causes of these changes, the DAP, not very much in favour of EM to begin with, was clearly in no hurry to look into an additional community-based measure, since the inflationary pressure on prison populations was declining.[6]

Conversely, the new interest in EM and the ambitious objectives later set for it by the DAP coincide perfectly with the 2001 upswing, which has produced a staggering rise in the prison population. But the reversal also roughly corresponds to political change, when the Left lost first the presidential and immediately after the parliamentary elections of April–May 2002. Since then the government and the criminal justice system are confronted with a major contradiction. On one hand, the increased punitivity of the criminal policy of the Right since 2002 has caused a serious crisis of prison overcrowding which affects facilities hosting short-term sentences.[7] This has led, on the other hand, to frantic efforts to limit prison populations by increasing the use of existing alternatives to imprisonment or getting detainees released before the end of their term. EM appeared uniquely suited to these objectives and this is the main reason for its recent developments, which I will examine in the following sections for the various stages of the criminal justice process.

The pre-trial phase

A veritable Sisyphus' rock of the French justice system (Robert 1992), for two centuries pre-trial detention has been a constant source of concern in France, and innumerable reforms have been initiated (in vain) towards reducing its use. The frequency of the application of pre-trial detention is a determining factor in the variations in the penitentiary population: the number of incarcerations due to pre-trial detention currently represent approximately 60 per cent of all incarcerations and between one-quarter and one-third of detainees, at a time when the prison population has reached levels unprecedented in the last 30 years. Thus, it is not surprising that EM was seen as a possible remedy. Tagging was extended to the pre-trial sphere by the law of 15 June 2000, 'reinforcing the protection of the presumption of innocence and the rights of the victims'. From this perspective, tagging was only applicable to offences carrying a sentence of at least three years imprisonment, but this never took hold. After the right-wing government returned to power in 2002, the law of 9 September 2002 abolished this provision and in its place instituted tagging as an alternative to pre-trial judicial supervision, which could be enforced whatever the sanction imposed (Pitoun and Enderlin-Morieult 2003).[8] Again this

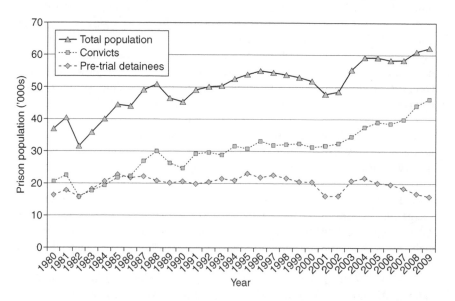

Figure 7.1 Evolution of the prison population since 1980 (number on 1 January).

failed, with only about 100 measures in force each month in 2009. A new attempt was made with the law of 24 November 2009: according to this law, offenders awaiting trial and those incurring two years of imprisonment or more can be subjected to home confinement under tagging, or can be subjected to tracking if they incur a seven-year imprisonment sentence with 'socio-judicial supervision'.[9] In such cases, EM cannot last more than two years, with renewals every six months.

The trial phase

The ensuing reforms express the government's concern at the slow take-off of the measure, which they attempted to stimulate in various ways, even if it entailed renouncing its underlying philosophy and ignoring the arguments advocating caution. Thus, in 2004 tribunals were authorized to order tagging, and the public prosecutors authorized to propose it within the framework of a new procedure aimed at the quick settlement of cases modelled on *plea bargaining*. We have thus progressed from a back-door measure to a front-door measure, which earlier had been rejected because of its inherent tendency to favour *net-widening*.[10]

The post-trial phase

The post-trial phase has not been neglected. On the contrary, the post-trial procedure was modified so as to leave more initiative with the probation services vis-à-vis the penalty enforcement judge (PEJ), thus partially going back on the provisions of the 15 June 2000 law.[11] Whereas this law had strongly stressed the jurisdictional nature of the procedure for the adjustment of sentences in the name of the defendant's rights, the law of 9 March 2004, on the contrary, reinforced the role of the correctional and probation services in the procedure.[12]

It would, however, be simplistic to view these vacillations merely as the expression of the classic opposition between a 'Left' concerned with liberty and therefore inclined to reinforce the judge's powers, and a more authoritarian 'Right', which preferred to reduce these same powers in favour of the Executive. In fact, the Right did not oppose the earlier 2000 reform, but abstained because they felt that the law did not go far enough with regard to the protection of the individuals concerned. If there is no doubt that the 2004 reform was to a great extent dictated by the fact that the statutory independence of the PEJ rendered him less susceptible to the injunctions of criminal policy on the part of the government, in contrast to the correctional services, it also follows from the desire to explore more systematically the possibilities of the adjustment of sentences, especially in their final phase, so as to limit unconditional discharge from prison, i.e. without any post-discharge support. The correctional services are henceforth obliged to examine the situation of all the detainees from this perspective. There is thus no real break with the ideology of rehabilitation, but rather a more pragmatic way of implementing it.[13]

This trend has been reinforced by the law of 24 November 2009, which has raised the threshold of eligibility to tagging to two years instead of one (except for recidivists): those sentenced to two years' imprisonment or less, or those whose remaining prison sentence is two years or less (provided, in this case, that they had not been sentenced to more than five years' imprisonment) may now benefit from tagging.

Moreover, following the British example, those detainees who have not benefited from any adjustment measure of their prison sentence will, in principle, automatically be released under EM for the final four months of their sentence (or two-thirds of their sentence if the total sentence is less than six months). This may well give a major boost to tagging, given the potential number of eligible detainees. This new measure has been cast in rehabilitative discourse as a way not to let anyone leave prison without some kind of support. However, given that it will be too brief to implement any meaningful social support scheme, it should rather be seen as a revolving door scheme, in the British fashion, aimed at alleviating prison overcrowding somewhat.

Safety measures and tracking

On the other hand, another element in the field of EM is of a completely different order, both in intention and means. Even if some of the official justifications continue to draw upon the rehabilitation discourse, it is the misgivings towards the latter that have incited politicians to take the decisive step in 2005 towards tracking and to further development of it afterwards. Crime and insecurity has been high on the political agenda ever since Jean-Marie Le Pen, the leader of the extreme Right National Front party overtook the Socialist party leader Lionel Jospin, the actual favourite, making it second to Jacques Chirac in the presidential race of 2002. In the following years, when Nicolas Sarkozy fought against Chirac for the control of the majority party to secure his own candidacy for 2007, the two factions vied to outdo each other on toughness on crime. And once Sarkozy finally succeeded in controlling the party at the end of 2004, he devised a (successful) strategy to deprive Le Pen of his voters in the next election by constantly stressing issues that were important to them, like immigration and crime, a strategy he has consistently pursued since his 2007 election until today.

In this context, fuelled by several spectacular criminal affairs calling into question repeat offenders and serial killers, and backed by a series of ad hoc official reports (Clément and Léonard 2004; Fenech 2005; Garraud 2006; Lamanda 2008),[14] a seemingly unending string of legal reforms aimed at repeat offenders have been devised (some yet to be passed), and recidivism has reappeared as the 'creative obsession' it was in the late nineteenth century.[15]

As a consequence, tracking is now present in four different schemes aimed at controlling dangerous and repeat offenders once they have served their prison sentences:

1   A probationary measure within the framework of parole (which was already the case for tagging).[16]

2   A temporary addition to an already existing surveillance and support measure called *socio-judicial supervision* for serious sexual or violent offenders sentenced to at least seven years' imprisonment. Tracking can only be used for two years, renewable once in case of misdemeanour and twice in case of felony, subject to, each time, a medical expert certifying the degree of dangerousness of the individual in question, who has also to consent to the measure (albeit under threat of severe reincarceration).[17]

3   An addition to another safety measure called *judicial surveillance of danger-ous persons* in the case of those sentenced to ten years' imprisonment or more and released without parole. Its duration is limited to the total reductions of sentences from which the offender has benefited; in case the obligations are not respected, the PEJ can cancel the reductions fully or partially and re-imprison the accused for the corresponding duration. However, due to the technicality that this is a safety measure, not a penalty, the offender cannot be subjected to social or educational support measures, not obliged to work.[18]

4   An addition to yet another safety measure called *safety surveillance* for offend-ers who, having been initially sentenced to 15 years' imprisonment or more, and having already served either *socio-judicial supervision* or *judicial surveil-lance*, are still considered 'particularly dangerous' and presenting a 'very high probability of recidivism'. *Safety surveillance* is used for one year, indefinitely renewable, subject to review by a specialized court and medical assessment. As of 1 October 2009, one person was under *safety surveillance* and 33 would be eligible within one year (Ministère de la Justice 2009a).[19]

Tracking was tested between June 2006 and May 2008, and then implemented on a national scale. Penitentiary staff are responsible for fitting and removing the tags, as well as dealing with the alarms. A private service company is being used for the maintenance of the system and for the technical aspects of remote moni-toring.[20] According to the Ministry of Justice, as of 1 October 2009, there were 38 people under tracking, of which 34 were also under the *judicial surveillance* scheme (Ministère de la Justice 2009a).[21]

A further extension of tracking was announced in November 2009. Inspired by the Spanish experience, the government is considering tracking violent hus-bands/partners in order to protect their victims.[22] A test was to be launched in 2010.

The implementation of EM

A limited private–public partnership

Tagging and tracking are currently organized on the basis of a division of tasks between the official agencies and the providers of equipment, with small differ-ences between the two schemes. In the case of tagging the provider's role is limited to the leasing and maintenance of the material supplied. The entire range of operations, including remote monitoring, is the responsibility of the penitentiary staff. Monitoring is carried out by 12 regional surveillance centres in metropolitan France (and one in Martinique) (Cour des Comptes (Revenue Court) 2006, p. 111).[23] This structure is greatly oversized compared with that of Great Britain, which has only three (one per private supplier), and Florida, which has only one with two permanent staff. In 2004–2005 there was some talk of reducing the number of centres to three. This reform was to be accompanied by a redefinition of the respective roles of the administration and the service providers: the administration would have retained only the 'sovereignty' functions (placing and removing the tags, keeping files, follow-up, intervening in the event of an alert), but the task of monitoring would have been privatized. However, although the legal framework of tagging was accordingly re-modified, this project has not been implemented since an initial call for tenders was withdrawn in March 2005. The reason for this withdrawal seems to be an uncertainty about what functions could legally be delegated to private contractors.[24]

The organization is somewhat different for tracking, with only one national monitoring centre, operated by a private operator, which redirects the alarms to the regional centres.[25]

The cost of EM

The low cost of tagging in comparison with imprisonment is one of the arguments most commonly advanced by the supporters of this measure.[26] Without entering into a discussion of this argument, which is more difficult than it appears, it should however be noted that the most diverse information can be found in the various official reports on its implementation.[27] Table 7.1 summarizes the available information.

The disparity of these figures is striking and their sometimes exaggerated apparent accuracy gives pause. The comparison between these estimates is

Table 7.1 Estimates of the unit cost per day of the various sanctions or penal measures (in euros)[28]

	Warsmann Report (2003)	Fenech Report (2005)	Court of Accounts (2006)	Correctional services (2006)	Senatorial Report (2009)
	22	11	10	–	13.75
Tracking	–	Approx. 60	–	30	30
Semi-liberty	20–30	–	27.63	–	–
External placement	12–18	–	–	–	–
Jail	55.80	60	39	60	80

Source: Warsmann 2003: 444; Fenech 2005: 23–34; Luart 2009.

rendered difficult by the fact that the bases of the calculations are not clearly specified or are disparate. Warsmann thus compares the per day cost of the tagging 'material' – that is the hiring charge – 'in the current launching phase' (the deployment not having yet been completed) with the cost of imprisonment in a jail 'calculated on the basis of the standard number of prisoners in the establishment, and not taking into consideration the employers' contributions and amortization costs'.[29] The latest Senatorial Report of 2009 also indicates that its estimates do not take account of labour costs. In addition to which, the halving of the cost of tagging in the other reports cannot be explained by the steady growth of the measure, as the rent of the equipment has to be paid, notwithstanding the number of tags effectively in use. Furthermore, the cost indicated by the *Cour des Comptes* is based on the 2003 data, – the year the Warsmann report was written. In the last analysis, the source of all this data happens to be the corrections department!

The growth of tagging since its inception

As we have seen, EM is henceforth omnipresent in the criminal process, at least on paper. Does the ground reality bear this out and how is it actually used? I have already indicated that tracking is used very parsimoniously at present. This is due in part to the fact that some of the new provisions are not retroactive. From a quantitative perspective, it is unlikely that post-detention use grows to more than a few hundred cases, but domestic violence may be a more promising area of development.

The situation is different regarding tagging, for its growth has been significant in recent years and recent measures will increase its use. To assess the current situation we must rely both on official and research data. Official data are actually very sparse. The DAP only publishes monthly statistics of the number of tags, which doesn't inform on the characteristics of those tagged.[30] To specify who the targets of tagging are, we must depend on the sole research available, namely the study undertaken by CESDIP in collaboration with the research unit of the DAP, a study which – although it gives a lot of information – does not answer all the questions.[31]

Figure 7.2, based on the DAP statistics, indicates a rapid growth starting in 2004. At the time of writing there are around 4,000 tags in use at any given time (the peak was 4,838 in July 2009). Between 2000 and 2006, tagging was employed as a substitute for a short prison term in 90.9 per cent of cases (hereafter: 'substitute tags'); in 9.1 per cent of the cases tagging was used on completion of a sentence (hereafter: 'released tags') or as a probationary measure accompanying parole (hereafter: 'parole tags'). In other words, nine times out of ten, tagging was used as a means of avoiding imprisonment, and only one out of ten times as a means of early discharge.[32] Among back door alternatives to imprisonment, tagging is now the most frequent.[33]

These numbers must be compared to those of other types of sentences: when EM started to rise, at the beginning of 2004, there were 59,000 prisoners (up

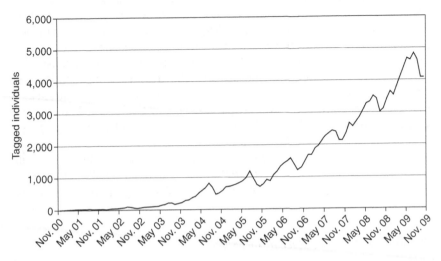

Figure 7.2 Number of tagged individuals as of the beginning of each month (November 2000–October 2009).

from 48,000 in 2001, the lowest year since 1990) and 123,500 non-custodial measures (down from 141,500 in 2001). At present, there are about 62,000 detainees and about 159,000 non-custodial measures. As shown in Figure 7.1, this rise is entirely due to a growing number of convictions, while the number of pre-trial detentions remained stable over the period. It is thus doubtful that EM has had a serious impact on the prison population.

Socio-demographic and penal profile of the persons under EM?[34]

As shown in Table 7.2, not all differences between those who benefit from EM as an alternative to imprisonment ('substitute tags') and those who benefit from an early release ('released tags') on EM are significant statistically. The significant differences pertain to age, life as a couple and employment. 'Substitute tags' are younger, less frequently living as a couple and more frequently employed than 'released' and 'parole' tags. They are also more frequently sentenced for drink driving, other driving offences or drug offences, whereas the former prisoners are more frequently sentenced for sexual assault or drug offences.

Kensey and Narcy (2008) have also compared their sample of tagged individuals ('substitute tags' only) with a sample of prisoners having served the same time.[36] The results are shown in Table 7.3. It shows major – and statistically significant – differences between these two groups: tagged individuals are more frequently employed at the time of sentencing, have a much higher rate of literacy, are less frequently of foreign citizenship, live more frequently as couples and

Table 7.2 Socio-demographic characteristics of tagged persons according to legal situation

	Substitute to imprisonment ≤1 year	Completion of sentence ≤1 year	Total
Female	5.2%	4.6%	5.2%
Foreigner	7.7%	5.4%	7.5%
Married/couple*	42.1%	48.4%	42.6%
One or more children	46.5%	45.4%	46.4%
Average age at begin of EM (years)	34.4	33.2	34.3
Less than 20 years old	(Std dev. 11.6) 2.3%	(Std dev. 11.9) 4.2%	(Std dev. 11.7) 2.5%
Employment*	63.6%	53.7%	62.7%
Illiterate/elementary school	17.5%	20.6%	17.8%
N	2,404	240[35]	2,644

Note
* t-test statistically significant at 0.10 level.

have more children. They are also slightly more frequently female. The type of offence is also different: theft (in its various forms) is twice as frequent among prisoners, while all other offences are more prevalent among tagged individuals. According to a probit model analysis, when socio-demographic attributes and type of offence are held constant, employed persons, females and those having committed a drug offence, drink driving or sexual assault have a slightly higher probability to benefit from tagging rather than imprisonment.

Duration of sentence

The average duration of tagging in the sample is two and a half months, but while 'substitute tags' are (understandably) close to this average with 2.4 months, 'released tags' serve on average 3.4 months. The difference is largest for tagging lasting more than six months, which concerns 15 per cent of 'released tags' but only 4.1 per cent of 'substitute tags'.

Place and timetable of house arrest

Kensey and Narcy (2008) have not examined this place and timetable of house arrest. However, according to an earlier study (Hazard *et al.* 2005), in practically all cases (99 per cent), house arrest takes place at the residence of the convicted person; the existence of a permanent place of residence thus seems to be an unwritten condition for tagging, though legally other places of residence are conceivable – a hostel, for example, or even the workplace.

In three-quarters of the cases this compulsory residence order only applies to working days (Monday to Friday) and in one-sixth of the cases it also applies to weekends. In nearly 10 per cent of the cases the matter is more complicated. This

Table 7.3 Comparison of tagged persons and prisoners having served six months or less

Characteristics	Substitute tags	Imprisonment
Female	5.3%	3.3%
French citizenship	92.4%	76.6%
Couple	*42.1%*	*23.4%*
Average age	34 years *(Std dev.: 12.0)*	29.4 years *(Std dev.: 9.9)*
Number of children	1.1 *(Std dev.: 1.4)*	0.6 *(Std dev.: 1.2)*
Illiterate or elementary	18%	50.1%
Employed (at time of sentence)	71.7%	34.5%
Type of offence (%)		
Drugs	13.2	7.1
Violence	19.1	15.4
Theft or receiving	6.4	14.8
Theft or receiving (aggravated)	10.6	19.2
Sexual assault	4.4	1.5
Fraud	6.2	3.3
Drink driving	22.4	10.4
Driving	6.6	5.3
Robbery	2.3	4.6
Other	8.7	1.8
N	1,921	21,111

Note
All differences are statistically significant.

signifies that most convicts are not housebound during weekends, which considerably lightens the constraints that EM has on family life. However, released offenders tend to be relatively more controlled during weekends than non-detainees.

The conditions imposed

The conditions imposed can theoretically vary enormously (Table 7.4). Apart from the conditions implicit in the provision, the magistrate can impose all those conditions stipulated in articles 132-44 and 132-46 of the Code of Criminal Procedure (CCP) – that is to say, conditions of probation. They can apply to monitoring measures that oblige the convict to comply with the various convocations and inform the authorities of any changes in his situation (art. 132-44 CCP). It can also involve obligations or bans that could be imposed on the offender, particularly with regard to his residence, his professional and other occupations, the company he keeps and his financial obligations (art. 132-45 CCP); and lastly to the 'support measures' of a social or material nature that could be proffered to the convict, and which are not specified in the Code (art. 132-46 CCP).

As the obligations are very diverse, they lend themselves to multiple combinations; in our earlier study we encountered 55 in our sample. However, on the other hand, this extreme individualization of the measures in reality concerns only one-quarter of the convicted individuals. As a result, in three-quarters of cases, EM is reduced to its simplest form.

Table 7.4 Overview of the conditions of implementation of the different modalities of tagging and tracking

Phase of procedure	Situation	Offences	Legal conditions	Other conditions	Type	Decision maker	Duration	Successive laws or decrees	Reference codes
Pre-trial	Pre-trial detention; home confinement	Tagging for misdemeanours or felonies amenable to at least two years' imprisonment; tracking if amenable to at least seven years' imprisonment, plus socio-judicial supervision	Duration has to be specified by a judge Consent of the accused and his co-habitants[37] Presence of lawyer mandatory EM duration to be deducted from imprionment sentence	Profession Studies Training Medical treatment Family	Tagging Tracking	Court or judge	Six months renewable, up to two years	L. 2002-1138, 9 September 2002; D. 2004-243, 17 March 2004; L. 2009-1436, 24 November 2009	Art. 137 and 142-5 ff. CCP Art. R 57-33 CCP
Judgement	Ab initio	All	Sentence or remaining prison sentence less than two years (one if recidivist) Consent of the accused and his co-habitants Presence of lawyer optional (mandatory for juveniles)	Profession Studies Training Medical treatment Family	Tagging	Court	Until end of sentence	L. 2004-204, 9 March 2004; L. 2009-1436, 24 November 2009	Art. 132-26-1 PC and ff. Art. 723-7 ff. CCP
	Guilty-plea	Misdemeanours incurring a penalty of maximum five years' imprisonment	Sentence or remaining prison sentence less than one year Consent of the accused and his co-habitants Presence of lawyer mandatory	Profession Studies Training Medical treatment Family	Tagging	Proposition Prosecutor decision PEJ	One-year maximum	L. 2004-204, 9 March 2004	Art. 495-8 CCP

continued

Table 7.4 Continued

Phase of procedure	Situation	Offences	Legal conditions	Other conditions	Type	Decision maker	Duration	Successive laws or decrees	Reference codes
Post-trial	Alternative to imprisonment (person not detained)	All	Sentence or remaining prison sentence less than two years (one if recidivist) Consent of the accused and his co-habitants Presence of lawyer optional	Profession Studies Training Medical treatment Family	Tagging	PEJ	Until end of sentence	L. 97-1159, 19 December 1997; D. 2002-479, 3 April 2003; L. 2009-1436, 24 November 2009	Art. 723-7 and 723-15 ff. CCP
	Completion of sentence (person detained)	All	1 Remaining prison sentence less than two years (one if recidivist), if sentence less than five years Consent of the accused and his co-habitants Presence of lawyer optional 2 Sentence less than five years: final four months under EM 3 Sentence less than six months: final two-thirds under EM Case 2 and 3: except if materially impossible, refusal of peron or incompatibility with personality or risk of recidivism Offences incurring SJS: subject to psychiatric examination	Profession Studies Training Medical treatment Family	Tagging	Case 1: Correctional Services under control of PEJ Case 2 and 3: Correctional Services under authority of prosecutor	Until end of sentence	L. 2004-204; 9 March 2004 L. 2009-1436, 24 November 2009	Case 1: Art. 723-19 ff. CCP Case 2 and 3: Art. 723-28 CCP

Measure	Persons / Offences	Conditions	Profession Studies Training Medical treatment Family	Tagging	Correctional Services PEJ	Duration	Law	Article
Parole	All	Ongoing sentence Consent of the accused and his co-habitants Presence of lawyer optional				One-year maximum	L. 97-1159, 19 December 1997	Art. 723-7 ff. and 720-5 CCP
Parole	Sexual offences (incurring socio-judicial supervision)[38]	Ongoing sentence Consent of the accused Presence of lawyer optional		Tracking	PEJ	One-year maximum	L. 2005-1549, 12 December 2005	Art. 723-7 CCP
Socio-judicial supervision	Sexual offences (incurring socio-judicial supervision)	Over 18 Imprisonment more than seven years Consent required Presence of lawyer optional Medical expertise (dangerousness)		Tracking	Court PEJ	Misdemeanour: Two lots of two years; Felony: Three lots of two years	L. 2005-1549, 12 December 2005	Art. 131-36-9 à 131-36-13 PC Art. 763-10 à 763-14 CCP Art. 763-3 CCP
Post-release safety measure Judicial surveillance	Sexual or violent offences (incurring socio-judicial follow-up)	Imprisonment more than ten years Consent required Presence of lawyer mandatory Medical expertise (dangerousness)		Tracking	PEJ	Duration equal to reductions of penalties	L. 2005-1549, 12 December 2005	Art. 723-29 à 723-37 CCP
Safety surveillance	Sexual or violent offences (incurring socio-judicial follow-up)	Imprisonment more than 15 years Consent required Presence of lawyer mandatory Medical expertise (dangerousness)		Tracking	Special court	One-year renewable (no maximum)	L. 2008-174, 25 February 2008	Art. 763-8 CCP

Kensey and Narcy's (2008) study sheds additional light on this issue by showing that while employment is the foremost condition imposed on tagged offenders, it is less so for released tags. Conversely, the latter are more frequently under condition to get additional education or training, or to take a temporary job or internship.

However, a local study tends in fact to show that social support is practically non-existent and contact with social workers non-existent when tagging is incident-free, so EM is reduced to surveillance. This view is shared by a recent report commissioned by the National Consultative Commission for Human Rights, which recommended that EM should always be accompanied by social work (Donnet 2006; CNCDH 2007).

Incidents and revocation of the measure

The great majority of taggings reach completion normally. In fact, according to an earlier DAP statistic, the failure rate, measured by the withdrawal of the order, comes to 5.5 per cent for the totality of tags imposed since their inception (453 out of 8,217 tag authorizations completed by 1 March 2006). There have been 33 cases of destruction of the tag followed by flight (0.4 per cent).

But as we can ascertain, the extreme measure that withdrawal represents is rare; moreover, according to Kensey and Narcy's study, a majority of cases have been without incident (56.4 per cent); in 30 per cent of cases there have been one or two incidents; and in 13.6 per cent more than two. However, incidents are more frequent for 'released tags', perhaps due to longer sentences.

Conclusion

What can we add in conclusion to this brief overview? First, that EM, after a laborious start, has become the most popular among adjustment-of-sentence measures. Until now, however, tagging was applied more as a means of avoiding imprisonment than as an instrument for reducing the existing prison population. This is likely to change in the near future, as tagging has now been established as the normal way to complete the final stages of imprisonment, when no other adjustment measure has been decided. This new provision is likely to bring about a differentiation in the composition of the population under tagging, with 'alternative tags' aimed at a relatively socially integrated population resembling those serving community sentences, while 'released tags' will come closer in outlook to the prison population than they are now. Another consequence will be increased pressure on already overloaded probation services in charge of EM. Whether this will have negative consequences for the outcome of tagging remains to be seen.

Whatever the case, these recent changes, and also the development of tracking, which is specifically aimed at dangerous offenders, are likely to modify the perception both of EM and of imprisonment. Whereas in the first decade of its existence tagging tended to be used as a more intensive community sentence, nowadays the authorities cannot but insist on its punitive character if they wish to 'sell' EM as an effective substitute to imprisonment or a safe way to control dangerous predators. By doing so, they instil the idea that imprisonment is not the ultimate punishment. In a powerful essay published a few years ago, the lawyer Thierry Lévy, former president of the International Observatory of Prisons, an organization dedicated to the defence of prisoners, pleaded for EM as a true alternative to prison. He wrote: 'This measure being capable of rendering the same services as prison, it still needs to be perceived as a real penalty, that is to say an irksome and painful punishment' (Lévy 2006, p. 77). An unexpected stand, which reminds one – although coming from the opposite political plank – of that taken by the founder of the Offender Tag Association, the journalist and visitor of prisons, Tom Stacey, who was induced by his hatred of prisons to become, in the early 1980s, the principal promoter of EM in England (Nellis 2000, 2001). It would indeed be an irony in the history of punishment that increased punitivity would bring about the demise of prisons.

Acknowledgements

The author wishes to thank Annie Kensey for providing him with statistical data on EM and Bessie Leconte for revisions. The translation was made by Pryia Sen.

Notes

1 EM is not an isolated case of compulsive law-making: according to Danet (2008b), between 2002 and 2007, 40 laws have introduced changes in the Code of Criminal Procedure and 30 in the Criminal Code, and this 'legislative frenzy' remains unabated to this day, with several major reform bills being currently discussed. See also Robert and Zauberman (2010).

2 On the creation of this report, see Froment (1998: 281–286).

3 This echoed criticism commonly heard in the United States, alleging that measures outside of prison are only 'a slap on the wrist' for offenders (Tonry 1990: 184).

4 The Bonnemaison report did not conceal the disadvantages of EM – namely the risk of greater social control through net-widening as well as of social discrimination and of being an offence to the person's dignity – but relativized or refuted them (pp. 29–30).

5 Act no. 97-1159 dated 19 December 1997, recognizing EM as a mode of custodial sentence-serving.

6 For a detailed analysis, see Lévy and Pitoun (2004) and Lévy (2005). Kaluszynski and Froment (2003) disagree, arguing that the DAP had favoured EM for some time, but had come up against a lack of political determination, and that the intervention of Senator Cabanel enabled it to get around that obstacle. This argument does not seem compatible with this administration's blatant unpreparedness.

7 This trend has been increased by the decision of president Sarkozy to abandon the French habit of amnesties and massive pardons which were customary until then (see Lévy 2007).

8 Judicial supervision is an alternative to pre-trial detention that enables the accused to be subjected to controls, curbs on freedom of movement and bail.

9 Socio-judicial supervision is a surveillance and support non-custodial measure for serious sexual or violent offenders.

10 On this point see Lévy (2003), in particular p. 18 and following.

11 The PEJ is a sitting judge responsible for the execution of penalties and their amendment according to circumstances and the personal situation of the accused. To accomplish this task he is helped by the Penitentiary Services of Reinsertion and Probation attached to each tribunal.

12 Law no. 2004-204 of March 2004 on the adaptation of Justice to the evolution of criminality, also known as Perben 2 Law, after the UMP law minister (right-wing).

13 This procedure draws on the report of the deputy Jean-Luc Warsmann, who although close to the minister of justice, Dominique Perben, was highly influenced by the rehabilitation ideology (Warsmann 2003). See Cardet (2005a).

14 Another official report focusing on mentally ill dangerous offenders was published, recommending the use of EM upon release, but remaining cautious about tracking (Burgelin 2005); on the same subject, similar cautiousness was voiced in a later parliamentary report (Goujon and Gautier 2006). For a discussion of these reports, see Herzog-Evans (2005) and Lazerges (2006).

15 This expression was coined by Schnapper (1991) in his seminal article on late nineteenth-century criminal policy. On the renewed importance of recidivism and dangerosity in current criminal policy, see Danet (2008a), Mucchielli (2008), Robert (2009) and Robert and Zauberman (2009).

16 Law no. 2005-1549 of 12 December 2005.

17 Socio-judicial supervision (SJS, in French: *suivi socio-judiciaire*) was instituted in 1998 and was initially restricted to sexual offenders; tracking was added by law no. 2005-1549 of 12 December 2005, which also expanded the list of eligible offences to a range of violent crimes. SJS can be awarded as the main penalty, or as a safety measure in addition to imprisonment. Standard duration is ten years for misdemeanours and 20 years for felonies, but it can be extended. As the study by Carrasco (2007: 4–5) indicates, the number of measures of this type are few: they have gone up from five in 1998 to about 1,000 in 2005, or about 10 per cent of the convictions against eligible sexual offenders at the time. According to the Ministry of Justice, 1,404 measures were pronounced in 2008 (Ministère de la Justice 2009a). The application of this measure is handicapped by a dearth of psychiatrists in the public sector, so the measure cannot be implemented in many of the tribunals, in addition to which it has met with strong doctrinal resistance in medical circles.

18 In French: *surveillance judiciaire des personnes dangereuses (SJPD)*, established by law no. 2005-1549 of 12 December 2005. As of October 2009, 233 persons were subjected to judicial surveillance, but only 34 to tracking (Ministère de la Justice 2009a). The first offender subjected to tracking under this new measure was sentenced to 18 years of imprisonment for numerous sexual offences and rapes on minors; he has been assigned to live in Paris, a city he doesn't know, in a room provided by an NGO; he may leave his room between 9 a.m. and 6 p.m., but is restricted from leaving the block of his home; he is also under a restraining order forbidding him to appear in any public space where minors are habitually present (public gardens, schools, swimming pools, etc.); see Herzog-Evans (2009).

19 In French: *surveillance de sûreté*. Those who fail to meet their obligations can be reincarcerated under a measure called *safety detention* (in French: *rétention de sûreté*), also renewable for one year. *Safety detention* can also be meted out directly instead of safety surveillance. This measure was established by law no. 2008-174, 25 February 2008. A new bill, introduced by the government in November 2008, is currently being examined in Parliament. It corrects a number of defects of previous legislation and introduces a provision required by the Constitutional Court, whereby no one can be subjected to *safety detention* if not given adequate support during imprisonment. It would also authorize tracking for those who are released while their case is reviewed for suspicion of miscarriage of justice (an extremely rare situation).

20 For lack of candidates, the first tracking assignment took place on 1 August 2006. The subject was a parolee having spent 14 years in prison. No other details have been given, because the Ministry did not want that person identified. The first tracked offender under the socio-judicial surveillance scheme was released in September 2007 (he had raped an 11-year-old girl and had been sentenced to 14 years of imprisonment); he was re-arrested in June 2008 for failing to respect his obligations (http://tempsreel.nouvelobs.com/actualites/20071011.OBS9294/?xtmc=psem&xtcr=5).

21 It is not indicated whether the four remaining cases were under *socio-judicial surveillance* or parole.

22 http://abonnes.lemonde.fr/societe/article/2009/11/25/la-france-va-experimenter-le-bracelet-electronique-pour-les-conjoints-violents_1271747_3224.html.

23 There have been separate calls for tender for each regional surveillance centre; the vast majority of contracts has been awarded to the Elmo-tech company.

24 On the outsourcing of monitoring from a legal perspective, see Cardet (2005b).

25 According to corporate sources, the monitoring centre is operated by ADT, while Elmo-tech provides and maintains the equipment (www.dmatek.com/default.asp?PageID=39&YearID=54&ItemID=69).

26 See the press releases prepared by the Ministry of Justice during the launch of the experiment in September 2000.

27 For cost estimations issues, see Lévy (2003: 23–25).

28 Fenech gives this estimate, but indicates, with regard to tracking, prices varying from €8 to €150, depending on the suppliers interviewed, whereas the cost in the UK is €98.70 and $10–13 in the United States (Cour des Comptes 2006: 108) (2003 data). This last report is especially critical of the cost estimation methods employed by the DAP, in particular by penitentiary establishments under joint management (where some of the tasks are entrusted to private companies, as for example catering, maintenance, cleaning, prison work) – see p. 172 and following. The Correctional Services' estimates for tracking and jail appear in their in-house magazine, *Étapes* (August 2006, 131, p. 1). The source for the Senate figures is Luart (2009).

29 Nor, moreover, the acknowledged over-population of these establishments destined for pre-trial detention and short-term prison sentences.

30 The DAP publishes an extremely rudimentary statistical instrument, which indicates only how many tags are in operation in each of the nine regional districts of the DAP. In other words, the DAP does not specify either the characteristics of the people targeted, or their legal status, nor the outcome of this measure. This surprising deficiency is not merely limited to tagging; the Clément-Léonard report observed that in relation to the socio-judicial supervision, neither the Health Ministry nor the DAP were in a position to indicate how many of these cases were accompanied by a medical care injunction (in principle supervised by the Correctional Services); the latter were not even able to indicate the number of 'coordinating doctors' entrusted in principle with these medical procedures, nor a fortiori, to provide statistical details of their work (Clément and Léonard 2004: 57). An internal report of the Ministry of Justice indicates that, due to incompatible computing systems in the various segments of this agency, and also to an imperfect knowledge of the possibilities of existing software by the people in charge, it is impossible to assess precisely either how many cases are being processed at the penalty enforcement stage, or the duration and/or dates of termination of this process (Crépin-Mauriès 2006: 31).

31 This study was started in 2000 when EM was first being tested (Kensey *et al.* 2003; Lévy and Pitoun 2004; Lévy 2005); there were several follow-up studies: Hazard *et al.* (2005); Lévy and Kensey (2006); Kensey and Narcy (2008). A study of recidivism by former tagged offenders is currently under way (Benaouda *et al.* 2010).

32 In an earlier study, based on a more limited number of cases between 2000 and 2003, the corresponding figures were: 88.8 per cent as a substitute for short prison terms;

10.5 per cent as completion of sentence; and 7 per cent as a probationary measure accompanying parole (Lévy and Kensey 2006). These data do not pertain to pre-trial use of tagging.

33 In 2008 there were 7,494 EM measures, 5,928 semi-detentions and 2,608 external placements. All these measures were on the rise, and taken together they rose by 42.5 per cent between 2007 and 2008 (Ministère de la Justice 2009b: 29).

34 This section, and Tables 7.2 and 7.3 are based on Kensey and Narcy (2008), who have analysed 2,680 cases of tagging between October 2000 and November 2006, i.e. 21 per cent of all tags during this period. I wish to thank Annie Kensey and Mathieu Narcy for giving me access to an unpublished draft report of this study; a previous study based on the first 580 tags produced very similar results (see Hazard *et al.* 2005; Lévy and Kensey 2006); we will rely on the latter for topics not examined by the more recent study.

35 Including 21 'parole tags'.

36 This sample comprises individuals imprisoned and released in 2002. As the period of reference for the two samples is different, it is assumed that detainees' characteristics remained constant between 2001 and 2006.

37 Co-owner or co-tenant of his residence; if the place of house arrest is not the residence, the consent of the person in authority is necessary (employer, for instance).

38 This category includes a very large number of indictments. It mainly involves: (1) various forms of assault, aggravated by rape; (2) sexual assault (rape or other acts) or attempts; (3) procuring of minors or vulnerable persons; (4) corruption of minors, pornography involving minors; (5) sexual assault on minors aged 15 years or less (especially incest). For details on these offences see Lavielle and Lameyre (2005: Table 43.21A, pp. 437–438).

References

Benaouda, A., Kensey, A. and Lévy, R. (2010) 'La récidive des premiers placés sous surveillance électronique', *Cahiers d'études pénitentiaires et criminologiques*, 33, pp. 1–6.

Bonnemaison, G. (1989) *La modernisation du service public pénitentiaire. Rapport au Premier ministre et au Garde des Sceaux, ministre de la Justice* (Paris: Ministère de la Justice).

Burgelin, J.-F. (2005) *Santé, Justice et Dangerosité: pour une meilleure prévention de la récidive. Rapport de la Commission Santé-Justice* (Paris: Ministère de la Justice, Ministère de la Santé et des Solidarités).

Cabanel, G.-P. (1996) *Pour une meilleure prévention de la récidive. Rapport au Premier ministre* (Paris: La Documentation française).

Cardet, C. (2005a) 'L'extension du domaine du placement sous surveillance électronique par les "lois Perben I et II"', *Revue pénitentiaire et de droit pénal*, 1, pp. 195–209.

Cardet, C. (2005b) 'L'externalisation de la mise en œuvre du placement sous surveillance électronique', *Revue pénitentiaire et de droit pénal*, 2, pp. 313–324.

Carrasco, V. (2007) *Les condamnations à une mesure de suivi socio-judiciaire. Analyse statistique à partir des données extraites du Casier judiciaire* (Paris: Ministère de la Justice (DAGE/SDSED)).

Clément, P. and Léonard, G. (2004) *Rapport d'information (...) sur le traitement de la récidive des infractions pénales* (Paris: Assemblée nationale).

CNCDH (Commission nationale Consultative des Droits de l'Homme) (2007) *Sanctionner dans le respect des droits de l'Homme II, les alternatives à la détention* (Paris: La Documentation française).

Cour des comptes (2006) *Garde et réinsertion. La gestion des prisons. Rapport théma-tique* (Paris: Cour des comptes).

Couvrat, P. (1998) 'Une première approche de la loi du 19 décembre 1997 relative au placement sous surveillance électronique', *Revue de science criminelle*, 2, pp. 374–378.

Crépin-Mauriès, R. (2006) *Rapport sur l'exécution et l'application des peines* (Paris: Ministère de la Justice).

Danet, J. (2008a) 'La dangerosité, une notion criminologique, séculaire et mutante', *Champ Pénal*, 5, pp. 2–27.

Danet, J. (2008b) 'Cinq ans de frénésie pénale', in L. Mucchielli (ed.) *La frénésie sécurit-aire. Retour à l'ordre et nouveau contrôle social* (Paris: La Découverte), pp. 19–29.

Donnet, E. (2006) *Sous surveillance électronique: le vécu des placés d'Eure-et-Loir. Cer-tificat d'aptitude aux fonctions de conseiller d'insertion et de probation* (Agen: ENAP).

Fenech, G. (2005) *Le placement sous surveillance électronique. Rapport de la mission confiée par le Premier ministre à Monsieur Georges Fenech, député du Rhône* (Paris: Ministère de la Justice).

Froment, J.-C. (1998) *La république des surveillants de prison (1958–1998)* (Paris: LGDJ).

Garraud, J.-P. (2006) *Réponses à la dangerosité. Rapport sur la mission parlementaire confiée par le Premier ministre à Monsieur Jean-Paul Garraud, député de la Gironde, sur la dangerosité et la prise en charge des individus dangereux* (Paris: Premier ministre). Online. Available at: http://lesrapports.ladocumentationfrancaise.fr/BRP/064000800/0000.pdf (accessed 31 May 2012).

Goujon, P. and Gautier, C. (2006) 'Rapport d'information (...) sur les mesures de sûreté concernant les personnes dangereuses', Sénat, Report no. 420. Available at: www.senat.fr/rap/r05-420/r05-4201.pdf (accessed 31 May 2012).

Hazard, A., Kensey, A. and Lévy, R. (2005) 'Le placement sous surveillance électron-ique: une mesure désormais prise en compte', *Cahiers de démographie pénitentiaire*, 16, pp. 1–6.

Herzog-Evans, M. (2005) 'Récidive: surveiller et punir plus que prévenir et guérir', *Actu-alité Juridique Pénal*, 9, pp. 305–314.

Herzog-Evans, M. (2009) 'Le premier placé sous PSEM à Paris restreint à un pâté de maisons', *Actualité Juridique Pénal*, 12, pp. 509–510.

Kaluszynski, M. and Froment, J.-C. (2003) *Sécurité et nouvelles technologies. Évaluation comparée dans cinq pays européens (Belgique, Espagne, France, Grande-Bretagne, Suisse) des processus de recours au placement sous surveillance électronique* (Greno-ble: CERAT-IEP).

Kensey, A. and Narcy, M. (2008) 'Les caractéristiques sociodémographiques des person-nes sous PSE (2000–2006)', *Cahiers d'études pénitentiaires et criminologiques*, 21, pp. 1–6.

Kensey, A., Pitoun, A., Lévy, R. and Tournier, P.V. (2003) *Sous surveillance électron-ique. La mise en place du 'bracelet électronique' en France (octobre 2000-mai 2002)* (Paris: Ministère de la Justice, Direction de l'administration pénitentiaire).

Kuhn, A. and Madignier, B. (1998) 'Surveillance électronique: la France dans une per-spective internationale', *Revue de science criminelle*, 4, pp. 671–686.

Lamanda, V. (2008) 'Amoindrir les risques de récidive criminelle des condamnés dan-gereux. Rapport à M. le Président de la République'. Online. Available at: http://lesrap-ports.ladocumentationfrancaise.fr/BRP/084000332/0000.pdf (accessed 31 May 2012).

Lavielle, B. and Lameyre, X. (2005) *Le guide des peines* (Paris: Dalloz).

Lazerges, C. (2006) 'L'électronique au service de la politique criminelle: du placement sous surveillance électronique statique (PSE) au placement sous surveillance électronique mobile (PSEM)', *Revue de science criminelle*, 1, pp. 183–196.

Lévy, R. (2003) 'Electronic monitoring: hopes and fears', in M. Mayer, R. Haverkamp and R. Lévy (eds) *Will Electronic Monitoring Have a Future in Europe?* (Freiburg im Breisgau: edition iuscrim), pp. 13–35.

Lévy, R. (2005) 'Electronic monitoring in France: the present situation and perspectives', in C. Emsley (ed.) *The Persistent Prison: Problems, Images and Alternatives* (Milton Keynes: Open University Press), pp. 173–195.

Lévy, R. (2007) 'Pardons and amnesties as policy instruments in contemporary France', in M. Tonry (ed.) *Crime, Punishment, and Politics in Comparative Perspective* (Chicago, IL: Chicago University Press), pp. 551–590.

Lévy, R. and Kensey, A. (2006) 'Le placement sous surveillance électronique en France: comment? Qui? Pour quoi?', in R. Lévy and X. Lameyre (eds) *Poursuivre et punir sans emprisonner. Les alternatives à l'incarcération* (Bruxelles: La Charte), pp. 71–89.

Lévy, R. and Pitoun, A. (2004) 'L'expérimentation du placement sous surveillance électronique en France et ses enseignements (2001–2004)', *Déviance et Société*, 28:4, pp. 411–437.

Lévy, T. (2006) *Nos têtes sont plus dures que les murs des prisons* (Paris: Grasset).

Luart, R. du (2009) *Rapport spécial, fait au nom de la commission des finances, sur le projet de loi de finances pour 2010* (n° 100 (2009–2010) – Justice (n° 101 tome 3 annexe 16 (2009–2010)). Online. Available at: www.senat.fr/rap/l09-101-3-16/l09-101-3-1619.html#toc153 (accessed 19 November 2009).

Ministère de la Justice (2009a) 'Prise en charge des délinquants et criminels sexuels', *L'ActuJUSTICE. La Lettre du porte-parole du ministère de la Justice et des Libertés*, n°3. Online Available at: www.presse.justice.gouv.fr/index.php?rubrique=11598&article=18245 (accessed 31 May 2012).

Ministère de la Justice (2009b) *Les chiffres-clés de la justice* (Paris: Ministère de la Justice).

Mucchielli, L. (2008) *La frénésie sécuritaire. Retour à l'ordre et nouveau contrôle social* (Paris: La Découverte).

Nellis, M. (2000) 'Law and order: the electronic monitoring of offenders', in D.P. Dolowitz (ed.) *Policy Transfer and British Social Policy: Learning from the USA?* (Buckingham: Open University Press), pp. 98–118.

Nellis, M. (2001) 'Interview with Tom Stacey, founder of the Offender's Tag Association', *Prison Service Journal*, 135, pp. 76–80.

Pitoun, A. and Enderlin-Morieult, C.-S. (2003) 'Placement sous surveillance électronique', in *Encyclopédie juridique Dalloz, Répertoire de droit pénal et de procédure pénale* (Paris: Dalloz).

Pradel, J. (1998) 'La "prison à domicile" sous surveillance électronique, nouvelle modalité d'exécution de la peine privative de liberté. Premier aperçu de la loi du 19 décembre 1997', *Revue pénitentiaire et de droit pénal*, 1:2, pp. 15–26.

Robert, P. (ed.) (1992) *Entre l'ordre et la liberté, la détention provisoire. Deux siècles de débats* (Paris: L'Harmattan).

Robert, P. and Zauberman, R. (2010) 'Crise sécuritaire et alarme à la récidive. Entre étude savante et fébrilité législative', in J.-P. Allinne, and M. Soula (eds) *Les Récidivistes: Représentations et traitements de la récidive XIXe-XXIe siècles* (Rennes: Presses universitaires de Rennes), pp. 211–225.

Schnapper, B. (1991) 'La récidive, une obsession créatrice au XIXe siècle', in B. Schnapper (ed.) *Voies nouvelles en histoire du droit. La justice, la famille, la répression pénale (XVIe-XXe siècles)* (Paris: PUF), pp. 313–351.

Tonry, M. (1990) 'Stated and latent functions of ISP', *Crime & Delinquency*, 36:1, pp. 174–191.

Warsmann, J.-L. (2003) 'Rapport de la mission parlementaire auprès de Dominique Perben, Garde des sceaux'.

8   Is the sky the limit?

Eagerness for electronic monitoring in Belgium

Kristel Beyens and Dan Kaminski

A remarkable political eagerness for EM

Electronic monitoring (EM) emerged in Belgium in 1998 as a local pilot scheme in a Brussels prison in the context of the preparation of early release of prisoners serving a maximum prison sentence of 18 months. In 2000, with very limited experience of its implementation, and without any evidence of its potential effects or benefits, the minister of justice decided on a nation-wide implementation. This decision was taken without either any legal provision for the regulation of EM or any discussions in Parliament on the desirability of this novelty. EM was thus quietly smuggled into the Belgian correctional system. Since then, several proposals and attempts to extend the use of EM to other phases of the criminal justice system have been made, but in Belgium to date EM is still used solely as a way of serving a prison sentence. Nevertheless, despite a slow start, the use of EM has increased rapidly since 2006. In the first part of 2010 about 1,000 prisoners were subject to EM in Belgium.

Right from the start, there was a great political openness, and even greediness, towards the use of this penal innovation in Belgium. National implementation was rapidly decided, quantitative targets have been put forward and a number of studies have been funded to investigate this penal measure. Before the local pilot scheme was launched, researchers from the Criminal Justice Policy Service, De Buck and D'Haenens (1996), were assigned to conduct a study of the international literature on the opportunity of introducing EM in Belgium. Stassaert *et al.* (2000) investigated the experiences of people being made subject to EM in the early stage of implementation. Goossens *et al.* (2005) were commissioned to explore the possibility of introducing EM as an autonomous penalty imposed by the sentencing judge. Devresse *et al.* (2006) conducted an evaluation of the organization of EM and De Man *et al.* (2009) were asked to explore the possibility and added value of the introduction of EM as an alternative to remand custody (see also Maes *et al.* 2012).[1] All these studies were commissioned by the minister of justice, which is rather extraordinary for Belgium, which does not have a vast tradition of investing in penological research financed by the government.

Mainprize (1996) introduced the Weberian concept of 'elective affinity' as a framework to understand better the introduction of EM into American correctional control practices. In the Belgian context, Dobry's (1986) metaphor of the 'window of opportunity' seems to be more suitable, because Belgian EM seems to have developed affinity with all rationalities and opportunities, and does not seem be so 'elective'. Its introduction has just waited for the opportunistic opening of a window. This opening can be recognized in Belgium in the conjuncture of specific political, technological, economic and ideological powers, penal conditions and interests that have encouraged the introduction of this particular practice at this particular moment. The market was ready for it, the technique was looking for possible applications and the penal practice and penological thinking were open to technological innovation that offered so many possibilities and met the many needs of the penal system. Last but not least, the Belgian policy-makers were looking desperately for a ready-made and cheap solution to a rising prison population they could not bring under control. The idea of EM thus landed on very fertile soil, which guaranteed its implementation. Moreover, the introduction of EM in Belgium cannot be dissociated from the context of 'policy transfer' of control and punishment and of the tradition of Belgian policy-makers to look abroad for solutions to local penal problems. No matter how striking the parallels with developments abroad may be or appear to be – such as the penitentiary and budgetary crisis and the search for more controlling alternatives for imprisonment – in order to understand the development of a penal practice, it is crucial to look at the particular political and local context in which 'alien' or 'new' ideas and practices are implemented.

A short history of EM in Belgium

EM was first mentioned in 1995 by a member of parliament of the extreme-Right party Vlaams Blok, in a parliamentary question to the minister of justice asking whether Belgium intended to follow the Netherlands in its experiments with EM. The answer was ambivalent. Although the minister of justice did not like the idea, the possibilities for experimenting were there (Beyens 1996). The Belgian Criminal Justice Policy Service was asked for advice and formulated some rather unfavourable advice about the possible introduction of EM (De Buck and D'Haenens 1996). However, interest in EM increased, and in 1996 it emerged in a White Paper by the minister of justice, De Clerck, titled 'Penal policy and prison policy' (Minister of Justice 1997, originally 1996) as a possible substitute for a prison sentence that could help to reduce the prison population. To date, however, no public debate on the expediency of EM in the Belgian penal context, its penal objectives and other fundamental ethical issues has ever been held. On 1 April 1998 an experiment with EM began in a Brussels prison (Bas 1999) and a study was promptly ordered to investigate the experiences of the people being made subject to EM and to evaluate the experiment.[2] Due to very strict eligibility criteria in the early stage of implementation, EM was only a moderate success from a quantitative point of view. Very soon it was decided to extend the experiment by a year. To get more prisoners under EM, the eligibility criteria were widened and the number of prisons that were involved increased.

EM emerged again in a White Paper of the next minister of justice, (Verwilghen 1999) and it was soon decided that, from October 2000 onwards, EM would gradually be introduced nation-wide. In 2000, a separate National Centre for Electronic Monitoring (NCEM) was established to organize the day-to-day implementation of EM. The initial objective of increasing the daily EM population to 300 was realized in November 2000, but in September 2002 the Council of Ministers decided that the EM population should be increased to 600 at any given time. At the government summit of 30–31 March 2004 it was stated for the first time that EM should be introduced as an autonomous sentence for offences that are eligible for an unconditional prison sentence of between six months and three years. The Criminology Department of the National Institute for Criminology and Criminalistics was ordered to study and prepare for the introduction of EM as an autonomous penalty by making a list of possible offences that would be eligible for a sentence of EM (Goossens *et al.* 2005; Goossens 2006; Goossens and Maes 2009). The study showed, however, that the judiciary was not demanding its imposition, in particular, and the advice to the minister was not favourable regarding the introduction of EM as an autonomous sentence option.

It took until October 2006 to arrive at a daily EM population of 600. This rise was initiated under heavy political pressure and was a direct result of a political fight between the Flemish Catholic opposition and the French-speaking socialist minister of justice, Onkelinx. Various incidents forced the then socialist Onkelinx to justify her policy regarding EM (even if sometimes those events had nothing to do with EM itself): the murder of Joe Van Holsbeek; the racist assassination in Antwerp; the massive escape from the prison of Termonde; and, last but not least, record-breaking prison overcrowding. The government's coalition agreements of July 2003 to achieve the goal of 1,000 prisoners under EM were recalled and the minister's political position was challenged, because this quantitative goal was still not realized. From then it was a major aim to expand the EM population from about 350 up to 600. From May 2006 onwards, the staff of the NCEM were put under enormous pressure to realize these numbers in a short period of time. Due to considerable and rapid transformations in the organization of the implementation of EM to realize these increased numbers of offenders having to be put under EM, a period of instability in its implementation practice was ushered in (Devresse *et al.* 2006; Beyens and Devresse 2009).

The expansion of the EM net re-appeared in the coalition agreements of Prime Minister Leterme (2008) and in the White Papers of his successive ministers of justice, Vandeurzen (2007–2008) and De Clerck (2010). Although the studies that were ordered by the then ministers to evaluate the possible added value of EM as an autonomous sanction (Goossens *et al.* 2005; Goossens and Maes 2009) or as an alternative for remand custody (De Man *et al.* 2009; Maes *et al.* 2012) are not univocally favourable and even doubt the added value of EM in the sentencing and pre-sentencing phase, the coalition agreement of 2008 states that EM shall be extended to these areas of criminal justice in order to increase the opportunities to use EM and to increase the number of people subject to EM to 1,500. In the latest White Paper of Minister of Justice De Clerck (2010), the target of 1,500 was repeated and the decision to extend its implementation to the sentencing phase was confirmed. Referring to the economic, legal and practical problems that were raised in the evaluation research by De Man *et al.* (2009), and the fact that the researchers had found that the use of EM in the phase of remand would only have a very small reductive effect on the number of remand prisoners, it was stated in the White Paper that the possibility to introduce EM in the pre-sentencing phase as an alternative to remand would be further explored after consultation with the actors in the field. Two additional groups were added to the list of possible candidates for EM: mentally ill offenders and convicted persons who were put at the disposal of the Sentence Implementation Court after having served their prison sentence. It was stated, however, that the extension of the number of people under EM in the execution phase of prison sentences would remain the highest priority.

There have been numerous attempts to extend the use of EM to other phases of the criminal justice system. However, to date EM is still only used as a way of implementing a prison sentence in Belgium. The use of the Global Positioning System (GPS) technology and voice verification were already possible in the first contract, but haven't been used to date. The new contract with 3M Electronic Monitoring (previously Elmo-Tech) will deliver more and more modern equipment, enabling GPS and voice verification.[3]

It is clear that the eagerness to introduce EM in Belgium is inseparably linked with the enduring penitentiary crisis, fuelled by prison overcrowding and industrial action by the prison guards' union related to this prison overcrowding. On a political level, EM is promoted as a 'quick fix' solution or a panacea for the penitentiary problems and has become an frequent topic in government policy statements. All this has resulted in an unrivalled flow – at least to Belgian standards – of short-term initiatives aiming to extend the target group of people liable to be subject to EM. Although the struggle against the rising prison population is an important motivation for the government to pursue EM, the general prison population has not decreased with the introduction of EM. In 1999 the Belgian prison population counted 7,889 detainees in prison and ten under EM (FOD Justitie 2009: 50); in June 2009 there were 10,519 detainees in prison (De Clerck 2010: 21) and about 1,000 prisoners serving their sentences under EM. This means that the total number of people serving a prison sentence has increased by 45 per cent in ten years, thanks to the additional capacity provided by EM. With approximately 11,500 detainees in prison or under EM, Belgium has a detention rate of about 100 per 100,000 inhabitants (compared with 77 in 1999).

The overview also shows that EM is a measure that has been encouraged by governments and ministers of the three main political families – the conservative-catholic, liberal and socialist parties – and that it cannot be regarded as favoured by a particular political party. This shows the malleability of EM, being able to satisfy different sets of values and penological aims.

'Legal' provisions and regulatory framework

EM has been introduced in the execution phase of the criminal justice system and it is still only used as a way of implementing a prison sentence. For the first six years, the implementation practice was regulated by numerous successive ministerial circular letters. In 2006 the execution of prison sentences was legally regulated[4] and some articles in the relevant Act are also devoted to EM. However, it should be said that the regulation of the execution of sentences by ministerial letters (so-called pseudo-legislation) is characteristic of the execution of punishment in general in Belgium. In the past this practice has been strongly criticized from a judicial point of view. An important criticism is that this legislation of 2006 smuggled EM noiselessly into the Belgian punishment structure and thus confirmed and legalized a by now established practice. No specific legislation has been dedicated to EM to date. Fundamental questions on whether EM should be introduced, for whom and for what purpose have never been discussed in Parliament.

Article 22 of the Act of 17 May 2006 defines EM as

> a form of execution of a liberty-depriving sentence, by which the convicted serves the entire or a part of his liberty-depriving sentence outside prison, according to a particular implementation plan, whereby the compliance is, *amongst others*, controlled by electronic means. [our italic]

It does not specify, however, which type of technical control is allowed (active or passive, pursuing traceability or not, etc.) and there is no reference to any limits to the use of technical control with regard to fundamental rights. In other words, the possibility to adapt the measure to technological innovation is left open (Devresse *et al.* 2006: 245). The practical regulations about the selection and the daily course of EM are described in the ministerial circular letter of 25 July 2008, which uses the same definition of EM as the Act of 2006.

Assignment

The assignment regulations and implementation practices are determined by the length of sentence and are based on the distinction between prison sentences of up to three years and more than three years' imprisonment. Over the years the application possibilities have been systematically extended and, today, for prisoners with a prison sentence of up to three years, the application of EM has almost become a routine matter. A system has been installed to offer almost all sentenced prisoners the possibility of serving at least part of, if not their full, prison term[5] under EM.

Today, the circular letter of July 2008 is the main guide for the assignment of EM to prisoners with a sentence of up to three years and for the operation of all EM measures (see Figure 8.1). It replaces all the previous regulations that have been in force over the years.[6] The Act of May 2006 defines the assignment criteria for sentences of more than three years.

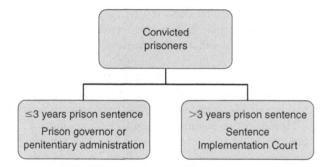

Figure 8.1 Eligibility criteria and decision-making bodies for EM in Belgium since 2007.

After a long history of extensions of the application criteria, to date two main categories of eligibility for EM can be distinguished.[7] For prison sentences of three years or less, the prison governor decides autonomously about the conversion of a prison sentence into an EM measure. There are only two exceptions to this rule: the Detention Management Service of the Penitentiary Administration decides about the assignment of EM for persons who are convicted of sexual abuse and for prisoners without a valid residence permit. It should be noted that these two categories have long been excluded from EM, which explains the option to take away this responsibility from the prison governor and to refer this decision to the Detention Management Service. At the start of the execution of the prison sentence – on his or her first day in prison – the prisoner is offered the option of serving his or her prison sentence in the community under EM. If the prisoner agrees, the execution of the prison sentence is immediately interrupted and the convicted person can return home until the assignment procedure is terminated.

Since February 2007, multidisciplinary Sentence Implementation Courts have been given the jurisdiction to decide on the assignment of EM to convicted prisoners with a sentence of more than three years and up to life imprisonment.[8] In Belgium, all prisoners can be considered for EM six months before the date they become eligible for conditional release.[9] EM is thus used as a transitional measure between imprisonment and conditional release (the so-called process of 'graduality') and not as an extra condition of conditional release.

With regard to prisoners serving a sentence of more than three years, general counter-indications are formulated in Article 47 §1 of the Act of 2006 and relate to the absence of reintegration perspectives, the risk of committing new serious offences, the risk that the person under EM will importune the victims of previous offences and the attitude towards the victims during the course of his imprisonment. The psycho-social service of the prison is mandated to assess these risks and write a report for the Sentence Implementation Court, which decides about the assignment of EM.

With regard to prisoners serving a prison sentence of three years or less, the ministerial circular letter of 2008 mentions counter-indications for eligibility for EM that are related to the refusal of adult co-habiting persons of the prisoner, the incompatibility of the family context with the EM measure, the residence and its environment, the nature of the offence, the risk of committing new serious criminal offences, the risk of a serious threat to the physical integrity of third parties, the risk of non-compliance and the attitude of the offender towards the victim(s).

Although the overall use of EM is encouraged, all these counter-indications strongly indicate that it is thus not an automatic 'right'. The imposition of EM in Belgium is always coupled with certain general conditions, which are similar for all categories of prisoners: no re-offending; having a fixed abode; responding to the directives of the justice assistants; and complying with the daily schedule. It is explicitly stated that persons being made subject to an EM, and the adult family members with whom they live, have to give their consent to serve the EM period in the same house. With regard to the aim of reintegration, the person under EM has to work out a daily occupation schedule, which can be employment, domestic tasks, training, therapy or preparation for one of those activities. The offender is not liable to any financial guarantee to be put under EM.[10]

Up to July 2006, social enquiry reports were written by justice assistants to prepare all EM assignments. To speed up the assignment procedure, the July 2006 circular letter abolished this obligation for assignments of EM to prisoners with a prison term of one year or less. This social enquiry report, however, is not only an important source of information for adequate decision-making – its abolition also meant that personal contacts to obtain the consent of the family members were abandoned, which might have negative consequences for the daily implementation of EM. The abolition of social enquiry reports for this growing category of individuals under EM was clearly dictated by considerations of rationalization and economic reasons. Moreover, this far-reaching decision was taken before the results of the evaluation study of the implementation of EM by Devresse *et al.* (2006), commissioned by the minister of justice, were known. This research, which was terminated in September 2006, clearly showed the crucial value of the social enquiry reports with regard to preparation for the assignment of EM, and with regard to the information required by all the actors involved in the implementation of EM. The circular letter of 25 July 2008 reintroduced the obligation of social reports to prepare the assignment procedure for all EM decisions, and this seems to have had an effect on the selection. However, it seems that the decision to impose EM for short-term prisoners is taken in a quasi-automatic way by prison governors, who are under pressure to relieve prison overcrowding.

The legal status of being subject to an EM measure is a source of ambivalence: prisoners who are serving their sentences in the community under EM maintain their legal status, and thus also their social status, of prisoner. In practice this mixed status of 'unfree, detained citizen in society' excludes them from legal access to social security benefits. They can, however, claim a substitute allowance from the Justice Department, which is lower than the rate of social security benefits. From a social and reintegrative point of view, however, it can be regarded as a responsibility of society to provide for the necessities of life of all citizens, especially for a vulnerable group in society such as prisoners. Rombaut *et al.* (2003) rightly point out that this situation deprives them of general social rights and reinforces the marginal position of those subject to an EM measure, which can be regarded as a perverse effect of their legal position of still being a prisoner.

Execution and management of EM

Since the start of implementation of EM in Belgium, the equipment has been supplied by Elmo-Tech (now 3M Electronic Monitoring), a private company that is active around the world.[11] To date (only) the presence of the offender in a pre-defined perimeter around his home is monitored by a continuously signalling system attached to an ankle bracelet. Monitoring data transfer can be performed over landlines (PSTN) and, since March 2005, over cellular (GSM) networks for prisoners without a fixed telephone line, thus avoiding the costs of installation of a landline. All equipment costs are covered by the Federal Government Justice Service. As the Act of 2006 does not specify the type of technological control, swift introduction of GPS is possible and expected.

Since its introduction in 2000, two periods can be distinguished in the short but turbulent history of the execution and management of EM. Between 2000 and May 2006, the implementation of EM could be described as being character-ized by a thorough – penitentiary-style – preparation and selection of the candi-dates eligible for EM. There was a strict follow-up, consisting of electronic control combined with social supervision. This first period has clear characteris-tics and has become known as the 'Belgian model', having three major charac-teristics: a strong coherence of control and penitentiary discipline; a rather intensive and intrusive form of social supervision; and a requirement for the offender to have a 'useful activity' (e.g. employment, education or training, house keeping) (Kaminski and Devresse 2010).

Since May 2006 the political pressure to increase the number of people under EM necessitated changes in the (careful) selection of EM candidates and the fol-low-up of offenders during the implementation of EM. This ushered in a transi-tion period and the following key moments can be distinguished. First, the transition of the social supervision of EM from the NCEM to the Directorate-General of the Houses of Justice and the reduction, not to say erosion, of the role of the NCEM. Second, with the establishment of the Sentence Implementation Courts in February 2007, they became responsible for the assignment and control of the follow-up of EM for prisoners with prison sentences of more than three years. Third, in July 2008 a new ministerial circular was introduced to regulate the day-to-day execution of all sentences subject to EM. Since the transition period started, the day-to-day practice has become more fragmented than before and there are still many aspects that remain unclear. To date no systematic research has been done on the current execution practice.

Devresse *et al.* (2006) studied the first implementation period, up to May 2006 (the period of the so-called 'Belgian model'). In that period, the NCEM was the major actor in the execution of EM in Belgium and it was responsible for the production of the social reports to prepare the assignment of EM, for the daily follow-up of the EM measure (social supervision and electronic control) and for making decisions on recalls. This rather centralized form of organization entailed swift communication of information on the offender between the different levels and actors involved in the implementation practice, which is especially interesting when crucial decisions in the follow-up of the offender have to be taken. The NCEM was established as a special facility within the Prison Administration[12] and as such it could be regarded as a kind of additional, 'virtual' prison. However, the status and place of the NCEM has always been ambiguous and a source of discussion.[13] It is hard to dissociate the establishment of this centre from the conflicts on the interpretation of the supervision and control of persons who were placed under EM. The NCEM was an answer to the deadlock that arose in the debate on the relation between social supervision and control and the task and the role of the probation officer in this. The probation officers,[14] who initially were in charge of the supervision and the follow-up of those subject to EM, refused to be involved in prompt surveillance on the spot when, for instance, the offender's time schedule was violated.[15] As a consequence, a separate facility was created and, from 2000 onwards, specially created officers, 'NCEM-social assistants',[16] were made responsible for the social supervision of people under EM.

Technical monitoring process

The central computer at the NCEM detects all alarms on a 24-hour basis, and the data are processed daily from 6 a.m. to 10 p.m. by the NCEM monitoring service staff. There is thus no immediate control during the night. The monitoring staff have telephone contact with the offenders in case of alarm, or in case of other questions with regard to the pre-set time-schedule.

Supervision

Following the ministerial circular of 2008, the justice assistant – formerly known as social assistant – must visit the offender in his home within a period of 48 hours after the installation of the equipment. In practice this is not always possible, however. The justice assistant sets up an individual time-schedule in consultation with the offender, taking into account the individual and general conditions with which the offender has to comply. The offender must return home every day, which implies that certain professional activities might be excluded or hampered. Every violation of the schedule has to be justified with certificates and written proof of all kind. Under certain conditions, changes of the time-schedule can be requested in advance and with the required certificates. Always having to ask for permission brings a lot of time pressure, stress for the offenders and red tape for the organization, and adds an important administrative dimension to the EM measure.

According to the period someone is under control[17] and assuming his good behaviour, between 8 and 25 hours of free time can be assigned per week. This time can be used for shopping for groceries, leisure, family activities, etc. In case of breach of the conditions, the number of hours of free time can be reduced as a form of 'pay back' for the hours or minutes one is too late arriving home. From this point of view, giving more free time in the course of the measure can also be used as a favour or a 'carrot' to stimulate the person under EM to comply with the strict daily schedule and the imposed conditions. In addition to their regular free time, offenders also receive free time for official holidays. As prisoners, people under EM also have the right to 'penitentiary leave', which is assigned to prisoners who are within one year before their eligibility date of conditional release. This penitentiary leave gives three times 36 hours of free time per trimester (Ministerial Circular 2008).

EM in Belgium consists of more than merely checking alarm reports behind computer screens. As well as the strict observance of the daily time-schedule, people under EM have to comply with a number of conditions – for example, looking for a job if they are unemployed, paying penal fines, debts or civil damages, abstaining from drugs, following therapy, avoiding contact with certain individuals, etc. However, no intensive therapy or, for example, cognitive behavioural programmes, have to be followed during the EM period. With decreasing frequency, the justice assistant visits the offender at home and has regular contact with him on the phone. To manage the case load of the justice assistants, since 2007 home visits have become less frequent and, instead, the offender is summoned to the office of the justice assistant. Devresse *et al.* (2006) see the combination of control and supervision as an important and vital element that compensates for the cold technicality of the surveillance aspect. Since 2007, with the shift of the supervision of EM to the justice assistants of the Directorate-General of the Houses of Justice, this task is also included in their 'global Business Programme Reengineering Plan', systematizing the general procedure, the frequency of contacts and the reporting process (Jonckheere 2009a, 2009b). The rationalization of contacts and the standardization of the follow-up might be regarded as a gain in terms of fairness and management, but fewer possibilities for individualization entail also a loss of human judgement versus pure surveillance (Beyens *et al.* 2007b). This new public management movement fits in a broader reorganization and rationalization of the functioning of the Federal Government Justice Service.

Breach

Justice assistants have to report regularly to the commissioners of EM, that is, the prison governors for prison sentences of three years or less or to the Sentence Implementation Courts for sentences of more than three years. In case of non-compliance, there is room for negotiation between the person subject to EM and the justice assistant. A first sanction can be a recalculation of the number of hours of free time, but in cases of serious or recurrent problems, the procedure is different for offenders with a prison sentence of three years or less and of more than three years. For the first category, the prison governor has the power to decide about recall to prison. In practice the prison governors are very hesitant to recall on account of prison overcrowding. In certain circumstances the director of the NCEM can request the police, via an arrest warrant, to proceed with a recall to prison. This procedure is, however, in contradiction with the legal and deontological powers of the NCEM, which since 2007 has been part of the Directorate General of the Houses of Justice. For prisoners with a sentence of more than three years, the procedure is more in conformity to the law: either the Sentence Implementation Court receives a negative report from the justice assistant and consequently decides about recall, or the director of the NCEM informs the Crown Prosecutor, who may order the arrest of the person under EM and inform the Sentence Implementation Court. The Sentence Implementation Court can decide to recall or to grant a conditional release (Kaminski and Devresse 2010). To date, no systematic research has been done on the recall policies and their motivations.

The EM period is terminated as soon as the offender is provisionally released (sentences of three years or less), conditionally released (sentences of more than three years) or has served the full prison sentence. In the case of conditional release, the EM period is not fixed, because the Sentence Implementation Court has the discretionary power to decide about the conditional release and about the extension of the EM period.

Statistics

Figure 8.2 shows that it took three years to reach the government's target of 350 detainees under EM. The period 2002–2006 shows a rather stable EM population around 300–350, and after 2006 the numbers rise abruptly to 600 in 2007 and to 1,084 in December 2009.[18]

With regard to gender distribution, 7.2 per cent (230) of all new EM mandates in 2009 were for female offenders, which is slightly higher than the proportion of females in the prison population.

Looking at the proportion of EM in the reference population of convicted prisoners, it can be calculated that in March 2009 the group of prisoners under EM ($N=749$) formed 13.7 per cent of the group of convicted persons in prison ($N=5,433$). In 2010 the EM population formed about 8–9 per cent of the total prison population, which can be regarded as a considerable proportion. Given the plans of the Belgian government to expand the scope of EM, it can be assumed that the proportion and thus the importance of EM in the penal landscape will only increase in the near future.

In addition to those who are actually subject to EM, there is also a waiting list of candidates for EM. According to the SIPAR database,[19] in December 2009 there were 1,014 convicted offenders waiting at home to serve their prison

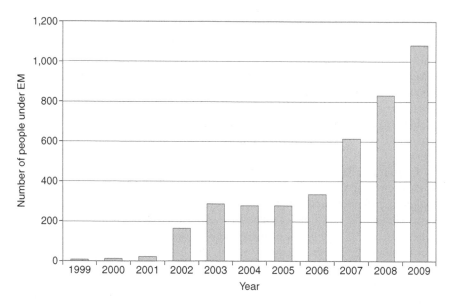

Figure 8.2 EM daily population: 1999–2009 (sources: 1999–2007: FOD Justitie (2009); 2008–2009: PROGSEET).

sentences in the community. Of these, 46 per cent (469) had already received a approval for EM and were waiting to serve their sentence at home; 54 per cent (545) were waiting for the social enquiry report to be produced. This waiting list has almost doubled in 2012 and is thus caused by a combination of lack of staff and shortage of technical equipment due to budget problems. It leads to an unwanted extension of the duration of the punishment period and thus to more 'pains' of punishment.

Looking at the distribution of the number of people under EM according to the two main categories of sentence length, we see a growing proportion of offenders with a sentence of three years or less. Of all the new mandates in 2009, only 15 per cent were for prisoners with a longer sentence and 85 per cent were for prisoners with a sentence of three years' imprisonment or less. Looking at the data with regard to the daily EM population, we see 30 per cent of prisoners with a sentence of more than three years versus 70 per cent with a sentence of three years or less in December 2009 (PROGSEET). This shows that EM in Belgium is increasingly used to relieve prison overcrowding by letting prisoners with a sentence of three years or less serve their (full) sentence in the community. This group is even larger than these proportions suggest, because we also know that the waiting list consists mainly of short-term prisoners who are waiting for their ankle bracelet at home. Because the long-term prisoners are obliged to wait in prison for their EM term, priority is given to this group.

In 2005 the average period under EM was 102 days (Beyens *et al.* 2007a) and there were only small differences between the two groups. In 2008 and

2009 the average length had slightly increased, to 111 and 113 days, respectively. In 2009, 72 per cent of all EM sentences lasted no longer than 150 days and 96 per cent no longer than 300 days. The longest EM period lasted for more than 720 days, or two years. It is remarkable that 14 per cent of all EM periods did not last longer than 30 days. The provision that the EM period should last for a minimum of 15 days has been abolished, leading to very short periods of EM (sometimes a couple of days). One could question the stated objective of reintegration and wonder about the relevance of starting up this kind of complex sentence implementation procedure for such a short time.

From the perspective of reintegration, which is explicitly stated in the ministerial circular no. 1746 of 9 August 2002 as being the main aim of EM in Belgium, offenders under EM are supposed to have a useful day-time occupation. This useful day-time occupation was the core of the Belgian EM model: unless there was a problem of unavailability for the labour market (e.g. invalidity), looking for or having a useful day-time occupation was explicitly included in the individual conditions. From the data shown in Table 8.1, we see that about 60 per cent of the 344 people under EM were employed or engaged in (vocational) training, and nearly 28 per cent of them were actively looking for a job. The data in Table 8.1 are from 2006. These statistics are unfortunately no longer available. With regard to the termination of the EM measure, we have data for 2005 and 2009, but originating from different sources and thus not fully comparable. However, a recalculation is shown in Table 8.2.

Compared with 2005, the completion rate fell in 2009, but at 75.7 per cent of all cases is still rather high. Taking into account the different registration systems and the big differences in total numbers between the two reference years, it could be stated that there are no indications that there have been significant changes in the completion rates and recalls. We do not possess adequate data on escapes annually to compare the years 2005 and 2009, but to date there have not been any disturbing escapes that have shaken public opinion or have been mentioned in the media.

Table 8.1 Day-time occupation during EM period on 21 March 2006

Day-time occupation	N	%
Employment	139	39
Volunteer work	6	2
Education/formation	69	20
Looking for a job	98	28
Illness/invalidity	32	9
Pension	6	2
Other	4	1
Total	344	100

Source: NCEM, PROGSEET.

Table 8.2 Reasons for terminating the EM period in 2005 and 2009

Reasons for termination	2005		2009	
	N	*%*	*N*	*%*
Completed	944	81	2320	75.7
Recall to prison	212	18	418	13.6
Deceased	1	0	8	0.002
Miscellaneous	7	1	317	10.5
Total	1,164	100	3,063	100

Sources: 2005: Beyens *et al.* (2007); 2009: SIPAR.

Discussion

EM as an uneasy compromise between substantive penological and regulatory goals

EM can be regarded as an intermediate sanction between rehabilitation-oriented first-generation alternatives and imprisonment (Morris and Tonry 1990). By offering stricter and more immediate control it meets the criticism of first-generation alternatives of being too soft and not controlling enough. The additional possibility of technical control increases its punitive bite and probably its credibility. Its potential to meet divergent penological objectives, such as reintegration, retribution, deterrence, neutralization and restoration, increases its appeal for politicians, penal actors and the public. Also, from a socio-historical point of view, EM can be considered as an intermediary, a sort of compromise of two types of conflicting if not contradictory aims.

The first type of aims EM is supposed to serve is substantively penological and has a social dimension, aiming to limit the damage caused by detention, to maintain the prisoner's familial, social and economic ties and to support their reintegration (Kaminski 2009). This social-rehabilitative reasoning reflects the ideas of the (active) welfare state, which gives high value to objectives of social reintegration and recently also of activation. In this respect the circular letter of 9 August 2002 states that the basic idea of rehabilitation in the context of EM is translated into 'the restriction of the harm of detention by offering the detainees the opportunity to spend (part of) their sentence in their familiar surroundings in order to thus continue their family life and their social and economical contacts'. This rehabilitative approach connects with the use of social inquiry reports, the demand for (having to look for) a useful day-time occupation and the involvement of justice assistants in social guidance during the EM period. The '*Homo criminalis*' of modernist, positivist criminology or the so-called old penology (Feeley and Simon 1992) is still the starting point of this inclusive penal enterprise, believing in the pliability and changeability of individuals (Hudson 1996; Young 1999).

The second type of aim is of a systemic or regulatory nature, underpinned by the promise of a reduction of prison overcrowding. From this point of view, EM practice is shaped by administrative and organizational concerns, guided by cost reduction and putting forward ever-increasing quantitative quotas, from 300 to 600, to 1,000 and recently up to 1,500. This rather 'actuarial' (Feeley and Simon 1994) systemic 'corporate' logic, aiming to 'fill' the reserved places of the virtual prison, brings along a radical change of penal policy.

Uniting these two kinds of logic, i.e. the substantive penological-social one and the systemic one, makes EM an ambivalent compromise. On the one hand, we find a historically resistant, but fragile and ever more attacked, aim for social integration, based on a (warm) regime of trust and individualization (old penology). On the other hand, there is the potential rise of an actuarial tendency, i.e. the introduction of a (cold) regime of surveillance and control, based on technologies and modalities of new public management (new penology). This dual approach shapes EM into a multifunctional vehicle to reactivate modernist objectives or illusions in a late modern, managerial context (Kaminski 2009). Moreover, it is an ambivalent mixture, because EM is certainly not representative of the resocialization ideal of the 1960s. The EM regime transforms the classical resocialization ideal into a reintegration that is supported by technical control and based on disciplining the offender through strict compliance with a time-schedule. The primary underlying image is that of a rational offender who has to submit himself and adapt to increasing forms of technological and social control. Moreover, in Belgium, the objective of reintegration is combined with requirements to fulfil towards the victim as part of the conditions being imposed, and the attitude towards the victims has become an element that has to be taken into account when deciding about the eligibility for EM. This referral to a restorative approach is, however, a kind of chameleon-like objective that, since the Dutroux case, systematically pops up in penal reforms or new legislation and is symptomatic of the sacralization of the victim in post-Dutroux penal policy. (The infamous Dutroux case involved the alleged abduction, rape and murder of several children and young girls while the suspect was under parole. It shocked society in Belgium and abroad.)

The compromise is clearly unequal and the pressure for quantitative goals gains priority. With the slogan 'quality first, then capacity', this quantitative priority is strangely enough denied in the two last White Papers. However, it shows the gap between the official discourse and the possibilities for penal practice.[20]

EM from a reductionist perspective

The systemic arguments, i.e. the lower cost of virtual imprisonment compared with detention in prison and the potential reductive effect of the use of EM on the size of the prison population, clearly dominate the EM policy and political debate in Belgium. Strictly speaking, the argument of cost effectiveness cannot be denied. And although detailed data are not available, roughly speaking it can be stated that with an estimated cost of €38.65 per day, EM is almost three times cheaper than one day in prison (estimated cost from €110 to €127). The theory of reducing the prison population cannot be confirmed, however. On the contrary, the introduction of EM has created the opportunity to execute more prison sentences, but at a lower cost per head. Thus the global cost reduction can be questioned.

We have already pointed out that the total prison population has increased by 45 per cent since the introduction of EM in 2000. Taking into account that in June 2010 about 11,500 prisoners were serving their sentences in prison or under EM, and that there was a waiting list of about 1,000 people waiting to serve their sentences under EM, we can only conclude that the Belgian penal web is continuously growing. On the other hand, short-term prisoners (less than one year) have almost totally disappeared from prisons, which means that EM is a genuine alternative for imprisonment for this group. From the perspective of net-widening it could be stated that, due to the fact that EM can (still) only be imposed in the execution phase, EM is a real alternative to imprisonment for the category of short-term prisoners.

Despite all lip service to the reductionist policy by consecutive ministers of justice, and despite the claim that imprisonment should be an ultimate punishment, in Belgium EM is mainly used as an instrument, willingly or not, to serve an expansionist policy. Another explicit confirmation of this expansionist option is the penitentiary master plan that was adopted by the federal government on 18 April 2008, which foresees an increase of prison capacity by more than 2,235 new cells (Beyens and Janssens 2009: 9).

Additionally, the fact that a certain capacity quorum that has to be filled is being put forward by the government can be regarded as a remarkable shift in the Belgian penal logic and discourse. The foreseen EM capacity is increasingly used to keep prisoners with a sentence of three years or fewer out of prison (85 per cent in 2009). These places are, however, quickly filled up by prisoners with a prison sentence of more than five years, which is the fastest-growing group in Belgian prisons. They are eligible for EM at six months from their possible early release date, and their mean period under EM is about three months. Being made subject to EM is thus just another step in their penal trajectory, which is more and more designed as a succession of gradual inflections. This policy of graduality or progressiveness raises two considerations. First, for reasons that are often related to specific characteristics of the offender, but also to their residence and family, some offenders are capable of conforming to the requirements of a conditional release but not to the requirements of EM. Without any doubt, this kind of progressiveness is a 'safe' option and enhances the penal credibility and safety of the early release decision (everything will have been done, in a finely regulated way, so that the release is 'without risk'), but it is therefore not conceived according to the 'needs' of the offender. Second, from our observations of the prison practice, we know that (some) Sentence Implementation Courts consider the period under EM as a test period that can easily be extended in case of doubts of the risk of the release. Subsequently, this might lead to a deferral of the release date and therefore to an (additional) extension of the effective detention period, which can be interpreted as a kind of net-widening. However, this is not an automatic result; the opposite decision is also possible.

The controlling work and the controlled life

Besides questions about penality and its objectives, EM also raises issues concerning the work of the professional actors and the life of the person being made subject to the EM measure. These features are connected, because controlling work and controlled life are interdependent and they are presented by a double proposition: EM has minor added value and therefore needs to offer heavy compensations.

The use of electronic control entails a radical distinction from other community-based penalties, such as the work penalty and probation. However, the question of the real surplus value of EM should be raised: What is the penological benefit of this additional electronic control? How can the qualitative value be defined? The major 'advantages' are strictly regulatory (or systemic) and not penological. And for those who are subjected to it, the real difference produced by the technique is the physical reminder of prison (see Robert and Stassaert 2009: 26–27) – in other words, by wearing the anklet they experience a physical (and not virtual) penal marking, and no more. We believe that the substantial benefits of EM primarily depend on the human supervision that could be promoted without recourse to any electronic device. With regard to reintegration, how can the gain of technological control be assessed? We refer here to situations where the person being made subject to EM always has to prove his probity and legitimize certain unforeseen circumstances or incidents that are part of daily life (returning home too late because of having to work overtime or because of traffic jams, abandoning purchases at the check-out of the supermarket because the queue is too long, etc.). The use of the technological device assumes the integration of the convicted offender into a free world, but it is a virtual (or ideal) free world, where the trains have no delays, where there are no traffic jams, where CEOs don't expect flexibility from their employees, where everything is absolutely predictable. It could be stated that with the electronic supervision the convict is rather moved to a virtual free world instead of to a virtual prison (De Hert 2000). Therefore, the art of the controllers exists in incorporating or reducing this technological coercion in a more reintegrative way appropriate to a flexible and contingent society.

The technique is neither autonomous nor self-sufficing, and it does not work without regular human supervision and support (Devresse *et al.* 2006; Kaminski and Devresse 2010). Without this human compensation, EM loses credibility or effectiveness and is even counterproductive: the human control on the electronic control – albeit objectively 'optional' and considerably reduced since the abandonment of the disciplinary model – ensures coherence, rationality and effectiveness of the enforcement of the EM measure. Without the least nostalgia, we think that the removal of EM to the Directorate-General of the Houses of Justice has reversed the disciplinary logic and practices of the so-called Belgian model. The role of the Directorate-General of the Houses of Justice is to give concrete rehabilitative content to a penal measure and to ensure the compliance of the conditions imposed by a judicial authority, but not to sanction the breach of conditions (contrary to the penitentiary model developed until 2006). Consequently, the information provided through the technology is used to follow-up the person subject to EM by the justice assistants. Since 2007 EM can thus more than before be compared with the other community sanctions for which the Directorate-General of the Houses of Justice is responsible. This evolution from a penitentiary approach to more of a community-sanctions perspective questions in an acuter way the relevance of the use of an electronic form of control.

EM operates in a remote punishment setting, which increases the risk of depersonalization of the offender subject to EM. This risk especially applies to the monitoring staff who never meet the offenders they control and with whom they have frequent contact on the phone. While carrying out the measure, the controllers are required to manage, organize, plan and check the activities of a person located far from them. The telephone and fax are indispensable devices in this operation at a distance and the EM monitoring staff, who are incessantly on the phone, are confronted with commonplace questions of all kinds ('I cannot find my keys anymore'). The anklet and the tight control are at the same time sources of difficulty and levers of communication: the technological control itself imposes a specific mode of interaction and raises frequent problems, not all of which can be solved remotely.

Conclusion

In ten years EM has become a vested ingredient of the Belgian penal landscape and the government took several initiatives to expand its use even further. The sky seems to be the limit. The short and turbulent history of EM shows two important shifts. In the first period of the so-called Belgian model, EM was part of the prison system and combined penitentiary and rehabilitative elements in its implementation. This first period was characterized by a careful selection of the EM candidates, a thorough and individualized follow-up and control by social workers, encouraging the activation of the offender. If these characteristics were not fully abandoned, they were supported by a *correctional* ideology and a strong disciplinary spirit. The NCEM was a small-scale, centralized organization where communication between the different actors involved was encouraged. However, due to the political pressure to rapidly increase the number of offenders placed under EM, this organization came under attack in May 2006 and a period of instability began. To realize the increasing numbers called for, the NCEM was reorganized and the social follow-up of EM was transferred to the Directorate-General of the Houses of Justice in 2007. As a result, most of the pioneering and experienced staff who had been involved in the establishment of the Belgian model quit the service. This transfer from one directorate-general to another was thus not only a geographical move or a purely organizational change, but it also entailed another penological approach to the implementation of EM. With the introduction of the ministerial circular of 2008, there has been an attempt to return to the initial approach – e.g. by re-introducing the obligation of a social report as part of the selection of all EM candidates.

Today's political discourse on the implementation of EM is dominated by the demand for efficiency and credible punishment. This is not only the case for EM, but it fits within a general transformation in Belgian penality.

The use of EM restricted to the phase of the execution of prison sentences is the best guarantee against net-widening. In the future it may be expected, however, that the use of EM will be extended to other phases of the criminal justice system, such as the sentencing and even the pre-trial phases. GPS tracking and a system of voice verification will be introduced. With the broader use of EM, the numbers will increase and thus the pressure to rationalize the implementation and reduce costs per head. Although in its first years there was a great willingness to invest in criminological research to evaluate practices and proposals, with the rising use of EM, this interest seems to be fading away.

With regard to the knowledge or popularity of EM with the public, no survey has taken place. The exposure of EM in the media has, however, been rather limited, because there have not been any disturbing incidents, disappearances or recidivisms. This probably explains why the discourse on EM has not been impregnated by concerns about public protection or risk in Belgium.

Acknowledgements

We thank Ralf Bas, who is a pioneer of EM in Belgium, for sharing his knowledge and experiences with us about the establishment and organization of EM in the early years. Bas played a crucial role in shaping the so-called Belgian model. Pierre Reynaert and Sabine Riguel from the Directorate-General of the Houses of Justice contributed to our comprehension of the most recent practices and changes in the implementation of EM. Anabelle Rihoux, statistical analyst at the Directorate-General of the Houses of Justice, provided us with the statistical data. Last but not least we thank our colleagues Marie-Sophie Devresse (UCL) and Heidi Luypaert (VUB) for their collaboration on the empirical research we did together.

Notes

1 For an overview of the Belgian EM research, see Daems *et al.* (2009).
2 For the results of this research, see Stassaert (2000) and Robert and Stassaert (2009).
3 See the journals *De Morgen* and *La Libre Belgique*, 3 June 2010.
4 Acts of 17 May 2006 creating the Sentence Implementation Courts and with regard to the 'External legal position of the sentenced prisoner and the rights of the victims', respectively. See Bas and Pletincx (2005) for a first critical discussion with regard to EM.
5 In Belgium almost all prisoners are eligible for early release. E.g. in 2007, only 6.1 per cent of all prisoners served their full sentence (Snacken *et al.* 2010: 89). Also, prisoners whose prison sentence is converted into an EM measure are eligible for early release.
6 For a comprehensive review of the complicated history of the subsequent regulations, see Goossens (2009).

7 Previously there were up to six different categories, but the ministerial circular letter of 2008 has simplified the assignment of EM.

8 The Act of 17 May 2006 with regard to the 'External legal position of the sentenced prisoner and the rights of the victims' also foresees that a sentence implementation judge should decide about all EM assignments of prison sentences of three years or fewer. Due to financial constraints, the establishment of the figure of the sentence implementation judge has been postponed to at least 2012. In the meantime, the Penitentiary Administration and the prison governors take these decisions.

9 In Belgium, conditional release is not an automatic process, but is dependent on the fulfilment of certain conditions. For a full description of early release in Belgium, see Snacken *et al.* (2010).

10 Initially, the offender was obliged to pay a guarantee fee of €124, although those who absolutely could not pay this amount could be exempted from payment (Rombaut 2006).

11 http://solutions.3m.com/wps/portal/3M/en_US/ElectronicMonitoring/Home/Industry Leader/GlobalPresence/ (accessed 9 June 2012).

12 Because the Prison Administration has changed its name several times, we do not go into details and prefer to use the generic term 'Prison Administration'.

13 Personal communication with Ralf Bas, prison governor and (former) director of the NCET between 2000 and 2007.

14 With the establishment of the Directorate-General of the Houses of Justice in 2007, the probation officers became known as 'justice assistants'.

15 For an extended discussion of this question, see Beyens (2000) and Daems (2000).

16 They were explicitly not called 'probation officers' but 'social assistants' to emphasize symbolically the difference between the two. The EM social assistants were thus assumed to be less reluctant towards control in general and were prepared to be involved in a more controlling position in community-based punishment.

17 The periods of free hours are gradually extended throughout the EM period.

18 Since 2007, different numbers are produced depending on the source used.

19 The SIPAR database is the database of the Directorate-General of the Houses of Justice, which centralizes the statistical data on the implementation of community-based sanctions in Belgium.

20 E.g. in December 2008 there was a demonstration by the justice assistants, protesting against the long delays in the reimbursement of their transport costs.

References

Bas, R. (1999) '20 maanden elektronisch toezicht in België: Een eerste kwantitatieve analyse', *Winket*, 4, pp. 78–89.

Bas, R. and Pletincx, P. (2005) 'Vuil water blust ook vuur: naar een (rechts)positie voor elektronisch toezicht', *Orde van de dag*, 32, pp. 37–43

Beyens, K. (1996) 'Elektronisch toezicht. Een oplossing voor de Belgische strafrechtsbedeling?', *Panopticon*, 17:5, pp. 473–499.

Beyens, K. (2000) 'Toezien op elektronisch toezicht', *Orde van de Dag*, 10, pp. 23–32.

Beyens, K. and Devresse, M.-S. (2009) 'Elektronisch toezicht in België tussen 2000 en 2005: Een terugblik op de toekomst?' in T. Daems, S. De Decker, L. Robert and F. Verbruggen (eds) *Elektronisch Toezicht: De virtuele gevangenis als reële oplossing?* (Leuven: Universitaire Pers Leuven), pp. 61–74.

Beyens, K. and Janssens, F. (2009) 'Gevangenissen voor de eenentwintigste eeuw: De missie is helder – meer capaciteit. Maar waar is de visie?' *Orde van de Dag*, 48, pp. 7–20.

Beyens, K., Bas, R. and Kaminski, D. (2007a) 'Elektronisch toezicht in België: Een schijnbaar penitentiair ontstoppingsmiddel', *Panopticon*, 3:28, pp. 21–40.

Beyens, K., Devresse, M.-S., Kaminski, D. and Luypaert, H. (2007b) 'Over het "eigen" aardige karakter van het elektronisch toezicht in België', *Fatik, Tijdschrift voor Strafbeleid en Gevangeniswezen*, 116, pp. 4–15.

Daems, T. (2000) 'Wat met het rottweilergehalte van de gecontroleerde? Begeleiding én controle: rolonduidelijkheid in elektronisch toezicht', *Orde van de Dag*, 10, pp. 33–40.

Daems, T., De Decker, S., Robert, L. and Verbruggen, F. (eds) (2009) *Elektronisch Toezicht: De virtuele gevangenis als reële oplossing?* (Leuven: Universitaire Pers Leuven).

De Buck, K. and D'Haenens, K. (1996) *Electronic Monitoring* (Brussels: NICC).

De Clerck, S. (2010) *Politique Pénale et d'Exécution des Peines. Aperçu et développement, février 2010* Ministre de la Justice. Online. Available at: www.detentionalternatives.be/IMG/pdf/GetAttachment.aspx.pdf (accessed 6 June 2012).

De Hert, P. (2000) 'L'étranger en Ter Zake: Wijsgerig toezicht op nieuwe strafuitvoeringstechnieken', *Orde van de Dag*, 10, pp. 69–74.

De Man, C., Maes, E., Mine, B. and Van Brakel, R. (2009) *Toepassingsmogelijkheden van het Elektronisch Toezicht in het Kader van de Voorlopige Hechtenis/Possibilités d'Application de la Surveillance Electronique dans le Cadre de la Détention Préventive*. Unpublished report, NICC.

Devresse, M.-S., Luypaert, H., Kaminski, D. and Beyens, K. (2006) *Onderzoek Betreffende de Evaluatie van de Reglementering, van de Besluitvorming en van het Verloop van het Elektronisch Toezicht* (Brussels: UCL, VUB, FOD Justitie).

Dobry, M. (1986) *Sociologie des Crises Politiques: La dynamique des mobilisations intersectorielles* (Paris: Presses de la FNSP).

Feeley, M. and Simon, J. (1992) 'The new penology: notes on the emerging strategy of corrections and its implications', *Criminology*, 30:4, pp. 449–474.

Feeley, M. and Simon, J. (1994) 'Actuarial justice: the emerging new criminal law', in D. Nelken (ed.) *The Futures of Criminology* (London: Sage), pp. 173–201.

FOD Justitie (2008) *Reglementering Elektronisch Toezicht als Strafuitvoeringsmodaliteit (Regulations on Electronic Monitoring as a way of Sentence Implementation)*, Ministerial Circular letter nr. 1803, 25 July.

FOD Justitie (2009) *Justitie in cijfers*. Brussel: FOD Justitie.

Goossens, F. (2006). 'Elektronisch toezicht als autonome straf: De visie van de zetelende magistratuur', *Panopticon*, 27:5, pp. 43–57.

Goossens, F. and Maes, E. (2009) 'Elektronisch toezicht als autonome straf: het NICC –onderzoek in een notendop', in T. Daems, S. De Decker, L. Robert and F. Verbruggen (eds) *Elektronisch toezicht. De virtuele gevangenis als reële oplossing?* (Leuven: Universitaire Pers), pp. 35–59.

Goossens, F., Vanneste, C., Maes, E. and Deltenre, S. (2005) *Onderzoek met Betrekking tot het Invoeren van het Elektronisch Toezicht als Autonome Straf* (Brussels: NICC).

Goossens, S. (2009) 'Elektronisch toezicht: woelig verleden, wollige toekomst?', in T. Daems, S. De Decker, L. Robert and F. Verbruggen (eds) *Elektronisch Toezicht. De virtuele gevangenis als reële oplossing?* (Leuven: Universitaire Pers), pp. 75–83.

Hudson, B.J. (1996) *Understanding Justice: An Introduction to Ideas, Perspectives and Controversies in Modern Penal Theory* (Buckingham: Open University Press).

Jonckheere, A. (2009a) 'Les assistants de justice aux prises avec Sipar, un outil de gestion informatique', *Pyramides*, 17:1, pp. 93–109.

Jonckheere, A. (2009b) 'L'informatisation des maisons de justice: une réponse à l'enjeu d'uniformisation du travail social?', in B. Bernard (ed.) *Le Management des Organisations judiciaires* (Brussels: Larcier), pp. 137–152.

Kaminski, D. (2009) *Pénalité, Management, Innovation* (Namur: Presses Universitaires de Namur).

Kaminski, D. and Devresse, M.-S. (2010) 'De la surveillance électronique à la surveillance électronique: Réflexions sur le pouvoir mystificateur du baguage', in Y. Cartuyvels, G. Guillain and Fr. Tulkens (eds) *La Peine dans Tous ses États* (Brussels: Larcier), pp. 337–353.

Leterme (2008) *Regeerakkoord Gesloten door de Onderhandelaars van CD&V, MR, PS, Open Vld en cdH (Coalition Agreement).* Online. Available at: www.yvesleterme.be/sites/leterme/files/regeerakkoord.pdf (accessed 7 June 2012).

Maes, E., Mine, B., De Man, C. and Van Brakel, R. (2012) 'Thinking about electronic monitoring in the context of pre-trial detention in Belgium: a solution to prison overcrowding?', *European Journal of Probation*, 4:2, pp. 3–22.

Mainprize, S. (1996) 'Elective affinities in the engineering of social control: the evolution of electronic monitoring', *Electronic Journal of Sociology*. Online. Available at: www.sociology.org/content/vol. 002.002/mainprize.html?PHPSESSID=8e29eb0920aff4a54e82d134272830f3 (accessed 6 June 2012).

Minister of Justice (1997) 'Oriëntatienota Strafbeleid en Gevangenisbeleid (Penal policy and prison policy)', in, T. Peters and J. Vanacker (eds) *Van Oriëntatienota naar Penaal Beleid?* (Leuven: KUL), pp. 1–86.

Morris, N. and Tonry, M. (1990) *Between Prison and Probation: Intermediate Punishments in a Rational Sentencing System* (Oxford: Oxford University Press).

Robert, L. and Stassaert, H. (2009) 'Onder elektronisch toezicht gestelden aan het woord: krachtlijnen uit het eerste Belgische onderzoek', in T. Daems, S. De Decker, L. Robert and F. Verbruggen (eds) *Elektronisch Toezicht: De virtuele gevangenis als reële oplossing?* (Leuven: Universitaire Pers Leuven), pp. 9–33.

Rombaut, K. (2006) 'Cijfers over elektronisch toezicht', in E. Devroe, K. Beyens and E. Enhus (eds) *Zwart op Wit? Duiding van cijfers over onveiligheid en strafrechtsbedeling in België* (Brussels: VUBPress), pp. 359–374.

Rombaut, K., Pletincx, P. and Bas, R. (2003) 'Elektronisch toezicht onder de hamer: 300, 450, 1000, 2000 ... wie biedt meer?', *Fatik*, 21:99, pp. 14–16.

Snacken, S., Beyens, K. and Beernaert, M.-A. (2010) 'Belgium', in N. Padfield, D. van Zyl Smit and F. Dünkel (eds) *Release from Prison: European policies and practice* (Cullompton: Willan), pp. 70–103.

Stassaert, E. (2000) 'Kritische doorlichting van het elektronisch toezicht aan de hand van een belevingsonderzoek', *Orde van de Dag*, 10, pp. 45–52.

Stassaert, E., Peters, T. and Parmentier, S. (2000) *Elektronisch Toezicht: Een belevingsonderzoek bij de eerste groep van deelnemers. Eindrapport.* Unpublished report, Ministerie van Justitie and Katholieke Universiteit Leuven.

Vandeurzen (2007–2008) 'Algemene beleidsnota van de minister van Justitie' ('White Paper of the Minister of Justice'), *Parl. St., Kamer (House of Representatives)*, 2007–2008, no. 52-995/3, 6–8.

Verwilghen, M. (1999) 'Federaal veiligheids – en detentieplan (Federal safety and detention plan)', *Senate* 1999–2000, nr. 2-461/1.

Young, J. (1999) *The Exclusive Society* (London: Sage).

9   Bars in your head

Electronic monitoring in the Netherlands[1]

René van Swaaningen and Jolande uit Beijerse

Introduction

Electronic monitoring (EM) is currently widely applied within Dutch penal practice. Recent policy discussions suggest, moreover, a further expansion. Looking at the many different forms of electronic surveillance, one might think it must have a long tradition in the Netherlands. Though the possible introduction of EM has been a subject of political discussion since the mid-1980s, the first actual experiments only took place in 1995.

In this chapter we will situate the use of EM in the Netherlands in the context of the penal system's development as a whole. Though often presented as an alternative to custody, the question of whether EM has ever replaced any custodial sanction can hardly be answered, because its introduction coincided with an unprecedented expansion of the prison system and the gradual establishment of a culture of control (Downes and van Swaaningen 2007). In this chapter we will investigate whether, and if so, under what conditions EM could possibly resist this wider tendency of the last 15 years.[2]

In our analysis we consider four dominant paradigms in penology. We contrast a 'Foucauldian' perspective on EM as the panoptic technique par excellence in a 'carceral society' with an 'Eliasian' perspective in which it is interpreted as a sign that social control continues to move from *Fremdzwang* (external coercion) to *Selbstzwang* (self-discipline). In the first vision – to borrow Stanley Cohen's terms here – widening the net and thinning the meshes of social control are the dominant rationales. The Eliasian perspective is open to a more optimistic vision in which the rehabilitative potential of EM can be explored. Next to these two theories we will examine the role of actuarial and managerial considerations, which have become extremely influential in penological literature from the mid-1990s on.

After outlining its history in the Netherlands, we will describe the concrete forms through which EM is applied and its legal and political rationales. Evaluative research on the various modalities will be discussed in the next section. Since most of this research is available online, often with an English summary, we will be relatively brief about the research design here and concentrate on the results. Conclusions with respect to the role the different rationales of panopticism, rehabilitation, risk-management and cost efficiency play at different moments of the development of EM are the object of the last paragraph. Reflections about the question of how EM could contribute to a reduction of the use of imprisonment and to the rehabilitation of offenders conclude this chapter.

An ambivalent start

The apocryphal story is that EM has been introduced after the electronic bangle a 'bad guy' wore in a Spiderman comic inspired an American judge in the late 1970s. True or not, EM has quite a long history in the United States. There have been experiments since the mid-1960s, but its application really gained momentum in the early 1980s (Junger-Tas 1993: 34). The Dutch discussions started slightly later. The context here is an alleged 'lack of cell capacity' in the prison system and economizing measures in the justice budget the government had taken since the early 1980s. To prevent overcrowding, budgetary deficits and indeed a penal crisis if imposed sanctions could no longer be executed, more punishment was to be realized for less money. EM was put forward as a possible means to achieve this.

Some saw EM as a rather 'civilized' alternative to prison, but in those days there was also widespread technophobia. For many the sheer idea of controlling crime by electronic devices forecast the coming of the dystopic 'Big Brother' from George Orwell's *Nineteen Eighty-Four*. In March 1988, a committee of enquiry was established under the presidency of a professor of criminal law, Tom Schalken. The Schalken Committee had the task of investigating whether, in what cases, under which circumstances and to what extent EM could be used as an alternative to custody and indeed as a means to relieve the 'shortage of custodial capacity' that was still rising, despite the already strong expansion of the penal system that had taken place in the late 1980s. In December of that same year, the Schalken Committee (1988: 11) concluded that the time was not ripe for concrete experiments. The introduction of EM was socially not broadly based enough in the Netherlands; in fact, neither the public, the political or the scientific debate on the issue had taken shape. The Schalken Committee advised stimulating that debate first, before any concrete experiments could be started.

In response to this report, the minister of justice asked in June 1989 for the advice of the Probation Service, the police, the Council of Child Protection,[3] the Public Prosecutor's Office, the judiciary and the bar association. These were far from unanimous. The police were the only ones who were plainly positive, at least if EM was to be applied as an alternative to an unconditional prison sentence and not as an alternative to remand. The Council of Child Protection saw its potential as an alternative to custody, but was only in favour of EM if it would be combined with intensive social work. The Probation Service rejected EM altogether, because surveillance with only minimal human input would be incompatible with the rehabilitative ideal. The Public Prosecutor's Office was hesitant, and both the judiciary and the bar were too divided among themselves to present any unanimous advice. The Dutch League of Penal Reform, the

Coornhert Liga and the prisoners' organization BWO were not asked for their advice, but gave it nonetheless. They both rejected EM, mainly because it would probably just widen the net of penal control. They were also concerned about a 'Big Brother' state, excessive infractions of civil liberties, the 'punishment' of innocent family members, the commercialization of social control and the derailment of the Probation Service into a sheer control body (Scholten 1994).

In June 1990, the minister of justice initiated an expert meeting with 70 delegates from the judiciary, politics, the Probation Service, the academic world, the bar association and, of course, the Ministry of Justice itself. Only 15 per cent of the attendants were in favour of EM as an alternative to remand, some 20 per cent as a possible means to spend the last phase of a prison sentence under house arrest and some 30 per cent as an alternative to an unconditional prison sentence. The last model was seen to offer the biggest contribution to actually reducing the speed by which the prison system was expanding. The first two models would probably merely have net-widening effects. Another committee, the Committee of Consultation and Advice on Alternative Sanctions (OCAS) (OCAS 1990), was put to work in order to establish some unanimity. In October 1990, the OCAS committee advised abandoning the idea of experimenting with EM in the foreseeable future. The secretary of state for the penal system sent their negative advice to parliament, which was followed by years of silence on this issue.

But, the debate on how to solve the ever-souring political problem of a shortage of custodial capacity continued – and the arguments of nearly all penological experts that this alleged shortage was mainly caused by an increased length of custodial sentences was not listened to in the political arena of the late 1980s (Downes and van Swaaningen 2007). Between 1985 and 1990 the number of prison cells had increased by 50 per cent, and most penological experts argued that expansion should not continue at this rate. High imprisonment rates were still considered undesirable in a civilized society and penal expansionism would furthermore be an extremely expensive road to take. This argument persuaded some initial critics to choose the 'lesser evil' of EM as a possible way out.

The Probation Service, which was then confronted with major budget cuts, was put under pressure: if they remained unwilling to carry out a pilot on EM, the Ministry of Justice would be forced to look for other (i.e. private) partners. Since the Probation Service in the early 1990s was forced into a major transition anyway, in which their main task was changing from providing social work to offenders to supervising non-custodial sanctions, they finally accepted a supervising role in the proposed experiments with EM (van Swaaningen 2000). 'All of a sudden' they saw EM as a good contribution to the rehabilitation of offenders. The fact that the Probation Service had changed its opinion diametrically was a crucial argument for the government to start a pilot with EM (van Gestel 1998: 23).

Because the expansion of the prison system was so extremely costly, the Ministry of Justice continued to economize on nearly every 'welfare' component of the penal system, such as probation, aftercare, the quality of prison regimes, etc. In 1992 a ministerial working-group on the Reconsideration of the Subsidies for the Care of Delinquents and Juvenile Institutions concluded that the introduction of EM would reduce the costs of the prison system by 20 million Dutch guilders (approx €9 million). In advice to the government of 1993, EM was still mainly discussed in the context of alternatives to custody (Junger-Tas 1993), but soon financial arguments came to dominate the debate. Moreover, the actual introduction of EM did not put an end to the political debates on the need to solve the 'shortage of prison cells' by building still more prisons. In fact, the strongest expansion of the prison system, and the introduction of ever more 'austere' (that is, cheaper and more punitive) prison regimes were still to come (Downes and van Swaaningen 2007).

The first pilots

In 1995 a pilot with electronic surveillance was started in the three most northern provinces of the Netherlands. Next to the dominant argument of cost efficiency, the presumed possibility of combining a punitive and a rehabilitative rationale was also put forward as an additional reason to introduce EM. Some of the conditions put forward by the Schalken Committee of 1988 were included in the 1995 pilot. Electronic surveillance needed to be accompanied by 'meaningful activities' under the supervision of the Probation Service; it could only be applied with the consent of the offender; it should only signal whether the offender were present at a certain place and not imply the control over the content of someone's activities; and it should be limited to a period of six months. Two modalities were experimented with. First, electronic surveillance was used as a special condition, connected to a non-custodial sanction of 240 hours that replaced a suspended sentence – the so-called 'front-door variety' – and second, as a means to spend the last phase of one's detention outside the prison – the so-called 'back-door variety' (Spaans and Verwers 1997: 11, 15).

Basing her decision on positive experiences in the northern provinces, the minister of justice considered in 1997 a phased national introduction of electronic surveillance. She felt, however, that some additional experience was needed before a solid legal basis could be created.[4] With the introduction, in the new Penitentiary Principles Act of 1999, of so-called 'penitentiary programmes' in which the last phase of the detention period could be spent outside the prison walls under supervision of the Probation Service, the so-called back-door variety was given a formal legal status. In 1999 the front-door variety was regulated by an Indication of the Public Prosecutor's Office.[5]

From that time on, one pilot with EM followed another. In a Rotterdam pilot, EM was used as an alternative way of executing remand for juvenile offenders – those up to 18 years old – between 2000 and 2002. In an Amsterdam pilot from 2003 on, it was used as an additional condition to the non-custodial sanction ITB (*Individuele Traject Begeleiding*), in which habitual offenders between 18 and 25 years old receive an intensive training programme in social skills, in which they have to work on the problems that bring them continuously into contact with the police. In the Ministry of Justice's '*What Works?*' agenda of 2004, EM was put forward as a promising alternative to (1) remand; (2) a suspended prison sentence; and (3) an unconditional prison sentence. It also confirmed its use as a means of supervision during the above-mentioned 'penitentiary programme' outside the prison walls during the last phase of someone's prison term. EM during someone's parole period was proposed as well, but for this modality the law had to be changed, because at that time parole was quasi-automatically granted if there were no counter-arguments to deny it. The main rationale was, again, reducing the pressure on custodial capacity and on the Ministry of Justice's budget (Wartna *et al.* 2004: 17–18).

In 2004 a pilot with 'electronic detention' started as a means of executing an unconditional prison sentence of up to 90 days for offenders who were not a 'security risk', who reported themselves to the prison gate without any coercion – so-called 'self-reporters' (*zelfmelders*). The last developments were pilots with EM furloughs and the electronic tagging of prisoners. After a slow start in the late 1980s, the development of EM became very rapid once the experimental phases of the mid-1990s were over. Later we will deal with the actual experiences with the different modalities.

EM's place in the penal system: the back-door variety in the last phase of the prison sentence

Both advisory committees, the Schalken Committee of 1988 and the OCAS committee of 1990, argued that EM could not be solely motivated by economic and managerial arguments. Because it implies a serious infraction of civil liberties, including those of the people who live in the same house as the offender, there needs to be a sound legal rationale as well. Therefore, various conditions were connected to the introduction of EM. In order to see to it that electronic surveillance would really be used as an alternative to custody and not as a plain 'add on' that was only used in very minor cases that would otherwise have been dismissed (the net-widening argument), a court decision to incarcerate someone – whether on remand or as a penalty – was seen as a *conditio sine qua non*. Initially, this condition was observed.

However, with the first experiments of 1995 we also saw a new rationale coming up; a rationale characteristic of the general penological debates of that era. Though the actual expectations of rehabilitation had already been toned down drastically, the term still figures in every penal policy document. But, as it is called now, rehabilitative goals should not 'frustrate' (sic) the punitive character of a penalty: an offender should *feel* that he is punished for his wrongs and not merely 'helped' to reintegrate into society because he has had such a bad youth. Electronic surveillance could contribute to both if it were to be linked to a training scheme. The probation scheme provided a rehabilitative programme, but because the electronic surveillance also implied a deprivation of liberty, it would certainly be felt as a punishment as well (Spaans and Verwers 1997). The fact that EM is indeed experienced as a punitive sanction was confirmed in open interviews with participants to the first pilots, who described electronic surveillance as 'bars in your head' (van Gestel 1998).

Since 2003 it has been standard procedure to impose EM as part of the non-custodial penitentiary programme; prisoners can apply for the last part of their sentence if they meet certain conditions set by law and on advice of the prison governor (para. 7a of the Penitentiary Enactment). EM must be applied during the first one-third of the total length of that penitentiary programme, and can be expanded if the prison department and the Probation Service judge this to be necessary. Abandoning EM during a penitentiary programme is only possible in exceptional cases – for instance, if the anklet is, due to obligatory working clothes, so visible that it has a stigmatizing effect. Many participants to the first pilots saw so many disadvantages to EM that they preferred a stay in an open prison. Some were afraid of using the phone because this could activate the alarm. Others indicated they did not do any sport because than everybody could see the anklet, and that they would have to lie about coming late or leaving early (van Gestel 1998).

Figures from the Ministry of Justice's Prison Department show that only a few prisoners meet the conditions to follow a penitentiary programme. In 2009 there were 11,077 prisoners on a penitentiary programme *within* prison, but only 458 in a non-custodial setting. Just an – unspecified – part of these 458 is under electronic surveillance.[6]

In July 2008 the laws on parole were changed. Since that date parole has no longer been quasi-automatically granted if there are no counter-arguments to deny it, as was the case before; a prisoner has to 'earn' parole by good behaviour and it is accompanied by stricter conditions than before. When a convict has not participated in a penitentiary programme before his or her conditional release, that person will be monitored electronically for a part of the parole period.[7] This is another, new way to be subjected to EM.

We can conclude that, despite the rather bleak political arguments by which it was introduced, EM in its most common application – in the framework of a penitentiary programme – does have some rehabilitative potential. Yet this preparation for a safe return to society is due to the training schemes and social work activities during the penitentiary programme, rather than to EM as such. If this rehabilitative goal can also be achieved without EM, this would be preferable, argues penologist Jan Fiselier (1997: 68). His arguments are, first, that the penal principle of subsidiarity would demand this, and, second, that research shows that reintegration into society is more effective if people are enabled to take responsibility in their own hands. The question remains whether EM stimulates or rather frustrates someone's sense of responsibility.

The front-door varieties: a condition connected to a suspended sentence or suspended remand

Though the 'front-door' variety of EM – i.e. combined with a non-custodial sanction of 240 hours or a suspended sentence of up to six months – has existed since the first experiments in 1995, it has been applied much less frequently. WODC researchers Spaans and Verwers (1997: 14) propose that, because non-custodial sanctions become more intensive if they are combined with EM, a more serious group of offenders, which would in the present system not qualify for a non-custodial sanction, could be kept out of prison as well. Basing themselves on a small number of participants, they conclude that a non-custodial sanction combined with EM could replace an unconditional prison sentence of up to six months (Spaans and Verwers 1997: 33–34).

This variety has, however, hardly been applied. There are no official figures on this, but in an interview with the journal of the Public Prosecutor's Office, the coordinator of the first pilot with EM states that in 2000 there were only 14 applications of the front-door model.[8] When we checked later figures with the Probation Service, they came up with 37 such cases in 2002 and 2003, which is less than 3 per cent of the total number of times EM was applied over that same period. In 1997 the Liberal Democrat minister of justice, Winnie Sorgdrager, indicated that she wanted to further stimulate the front-door variety, notably for female offenders with children, also in order to create a wider knowledge about EM among the judiciary.[9] In 2002 the Christian Democrat minister of justice, Piet-Hein Donner, reinforced his predecessor's argument and estimated that in combination with EM non-custodial sanctions and suspended sentences could replace about 25 per cent of all custodial sanctions between 6 and 12 months.[10]

The most probable reason why the judiciary hardly applies the front-door variety is that the Indication of the Public Prosecutor's Office by which it is regulated is unclear about the length of the prison term that is to be compensated if EM is applied. The prosecutorial Indication (*Aanwijzing*) actually makes no distinction between a non-custodial sanction with or without electronic surveillance.[11] As long as it is not legally acknowledged that a non-custodial sanction *with* electronic surveillance is more intensive than without, the reductionist potential of EM in combination with a suspended sentence seems more realistic. The original goal of suspended sentences is to influence someone's behaviour by the threat of imprisonment, if an offender does not live up to certain conditions. As such, EM is not aimed at controlling specific behaviour, but as a safeguard that conditions imposed by the judge can be controlled. Nonetheless, the rationale of the prosecutorial Indication *is* behaviour control: it connects the front-door variety to a probation order that exists of work, education or (social skills) training for a minimum of 26 hours per week.

Since 2006 it is also possible to use EM as a condition under which remand can be suspended.[12] Lawyers have argued that because both front-door varieties imply a deprivation of liberty, new legislation should explicitly regulate *both*. A simple Indication of the Public Prosecutor's Office, which is after all not more than an internal guideline, is not good enough. Unlike a formal law, Indications do not have to be approved by Parliament (van Hattum 1995: 326; Boone 2000: 128–129).

From 'electronic detention' to 'electronic house arrest'

The linkage of electronic surveillance with a training scheme in social skills or (social work) supervision was dropped in 2000. The Green Paper 'Sanctions in perspective' from that year argued that EM was *as such* not a (non-custodial) sanction, but just a technical means of control that could be helpful with the execution of sanctions (Ministerie van Justitie, 2000: 60, 63). Herewith, the discussion on the necessity of a legal purpose and legitimation of EM was by-passed: if it was no sanction anyway, but a mere technical issue, there was no need for a penal rationale either. However, this argument is undermined by research that indicates that electronic surveillance is definitely experienced as an intensification of a sanction or a probation order (e.g. Spaans and Verwers 1997; van Gestel 1998).

An advisory committee on non-custodial sanctions from 2003, the Committee on the Deprivation of Liberty (*Commissie Vrijheidsbeperking*), proposed to differentiate between EM as a guarantee that conditions connected to a suspended sentence are actually obeyed, from cases in which EM is part of a sanction that already consists of punitive elements (Otte Committee 2003: 59).

The last variety was introduced by the Ministry of Justice in 2004 and is called 'electronic detention'. It is a means of executing an unconditional prison sentence of up to 90 days for offenders without a 'security risk' who report themselves to the prison gate without any coercion – so-called 'self-reporters'. This pilot is only open for convicts who agree to participate on a voluntary basis and with the consent of co-habitants. Moreover, the convict must have a fixed address where the electronic detention can be executed, speak either Dutch or English, should not have any problem with alcohol or drugs, no psycho-social or psychiatric disorder and cannot be subjected to deportation. The Probation Service has nothing to do with the pilot of electronic detention. The Prison Department carries out the surveillance itself. In a way, the judge who has imposed a custodial sanction is by-passed, because the prison department itself changes the way the sanction is executed.

As opposed to the 'back-door' and 'front-door' varieties described above, the sole purpose of electronic detention is to reduce the custodial 'capacity problem' and save money. It was announced in the 2000 Green Paper 'Sanctions in perspective' as a basic form of confinement without a further rehabilitative function that could annually save 115 million Dutch guilders (some €50 million) for the justice budget (Ministerie van Justitie 2000: 18, 59). The following Parliamentary discussions were on the question of which categories of offenders were to be placed in electronic detention. In a number of letters to Parliament, the minister of justice insisted on a swift introduction of electronic detention, because the high number of sentences that could not be executed could easily lead to a penal crisis. In October 2002 he announced an emergency measure that would make electronic detention possible, and in December of that same year he announced a pilot for people sentenced to custodial sentences of up to 90 days, who have to present themselves at the prison gate. With the proposed pilot, 200 prison cells were thought to be 'saved'.[13]

The pilot with electronic detention has been evaluated for the period from 1 November 2003 to 31 December 2004 (Post *et al.* 2005). In that period there were 3,391 intakes, of which 2,371 people have been selected for participation.

The vast majority of the participants – 93 per cent – finished their electronic detention successfully. Of the 7 per cent who were forced to stop, about 65 per cent were sent to prison and 35 per cent managed to escape. The costs per place were €40; that is one-third of the price of a cell in a minimum-security detention centre. Because electronic detention is seen as a form of detention, social security benefits are automatically stopped. This seems rather strange, because, unlike in prison, someone's costs of living remain the same if the 'detention' is carried out in their own home. Participants therefore receive compensation of €7.50 per day, but that is not sufficient for those who do not have an income. They will have to take on debt if they want to participate in the electronic detention pilot – with all the criminogenic risks that brings with it.

Participants in the electronic detention pilot were allowed to work, provided that it was every day at the same hours, at a fixed place and not during the night. The employer did not need to know about the electronic detention, but there was random control by sound-emitting transmitters or actual visits to see whether someone was present at work. Of the 60 participants who were interviewed, 25 had a job. Ten people lost their job during their electronic detention. In five cases this was really due to the electronic detention (e.g. because the employer found out about the offence); for the other five, their temporary contracts ended. Participants without a paid job have to spend 22 hours in their home and can spend two fixed hours outside. For people who are used to spending a lot of time indoors this is quite a bit easier than for those who would normally be outside with other people. Some preferred to do their time in prison, because that offered a more structured daily rhythm and the option to do sport and such. There is also urine control during electronic detention. The use of alcohol is allowed, but traces of illegal drugs lead to exclusion from the pilot. About 40 per cent of all participants complained about having gained weight due to a lack of movement.

Electronic detention is clearly experienced as punishment, but the advantages prevail in the research. Offenders experience less prisonization, less discrimination, less alienation from daily life and they can often keep their job. Put in criminological terms, they can maintain most of their attachment to society and are less institutionalized. Yet, the research of Post *et al.* does not speak of possible preventative, let alone rehabilitative effects in this respect. Cost-reduction and the prevention of overcrowded prisons are put forward as the major advantages. The main disadvantage mentioned is the mock security for society, because offenders are only virtually deprived of their liberty. They can commit new offences from their homes, where the supervision is less than in prison. The researchers therefore stress the importance of strict control and enforcement, because otherwise the credibility of electronic detention in the public and political debate will be undermined. This rather platitudinous conclusion is a good illustration of the central role 'control talk' plays in the political arena.

In 2005 the minister of justice announced the introduction of electronic detention on a permanent basis.[14] It will be codified as a principal punishment – i.e. not as a substitution for another penalty – and the legal term will be 'electronic house-arrest'. It is meant to be 'less intensive' and less 'total' than detention, and can be imposed in cases where fines or non-custodial sanctions are felt to be insufficient. It will also be used for offenders who are a nuisance at a particular place – e.g. shopping malls, football stadiums,[15] night clubs, swimming pools – or for offenders with a physical handicap that makes a stay in prison more difficult – e.g. someone in a wheelchair. It can also be used for fine defaulters, but only if the judge explicitly mentions this possibility in the verdict.

The punishment of electronic house-arrest as proposed in the new law will be more punitive than the pilot. The minister wants to deny offenders the possibility to work and he will reconsider the two hours of leisure time out of the home. Though it is plausible that these extra restrictions are mainly informed by financial reasons – i.e. controlling offenders outside the house implies more complicated and expensive equipment – the minister's main arguments are that they would broaden the areas of applying electronic house arrest,[16] and that work and leisure time would increase the danger of re-offending. Negotiations are underway with the Ministry of Welfare and Employment about the question of what to do with the withheld social security benefits of offenders under electronic house arrest.

In 2007 the bill to regulate this was proposed to Parliament. In the summer of 2007 the *Inspectie voor de Sanctietoepassing* (the committee that inspects the way penal sanctions are executed) commented that electronic detention seemed to be a good alternative to a short prison sentence. This committee criticized, however, the way in which electronic detention was executed at the time. According to the committee there was little central guidance, and because of that there were large differences in the way electronic detention was implemented and executed in different parts of the country (Inspectie voor de Sanctietoepassing 2007).

In the meantime, electronic detention was still applied on the basis of regulations of the Ministry of Justice. In 2008 it was applied to 2,031 people. This is a very small proportion of the total amount of people that entered the prison system in 2008: 41,599 – so not even 5 per cent! Because electronic detention does not last more than three months, there is only a very small number of people under it at any one time. In September 2008 there were 156 people under electronic detention (Kaladien and Eggen 2009: 531, 536).

In June 2009 some populist right-wing politicians demanded an emergency debate on this issue in Parliament. Although the practice of electronic detention had already existed for four years and had been evaluated officially, they argued that they had just found out about the existence of the phenomenon of electronic detention. They decried it in the media – that it was a shame that convicted criminals had the opportunity to undergo their punishment at home. Two of them, Teeven (neo-liberal party VVD) and De Roon (neo-nationalist party PVV), asked for a debate and proposed motions to stop this practice, but these were only supported by their own parties and overruled by Parliament.[17]

In March 2010 a new bill was announced in which 'electronic house-arrest' would not only be codified as a principal punishment, but also as a condition to suspend remand.[18] In advance of this bill, in June 2010, the minister of justice decided to end the practice of electronic detention as a means of executing an unconditional prison sentence.[19] In October of the same year the above-mentioned member of Parliament, Teeven, became the state secretary of security and justice. In February 2011 he decided that the bill on electronic house-arrest would not be submitted. His argument for this decision was that the new government thinks that electronic house-arrest is not a 'credible' form of punishment.

The most recent applications of EM

Since the new prosecutorial Indication of January 2006, EM can, as we have seen above, be used as a condition to suspend remand. This option was rejected earlier because it would lead to undesirable net-widening and because it would not have any rehabilitative potential, since the time to combine it with a meaningful training scheme would be too limited (Spaans and Verwers 1997: 13; OCAS 1990: 10). It is interesting to note that the Schalken Committee (1988: 28–29) argued that, because EM implied a less total form of deprivation of liberty than remand, which allows someone to keep his job, it could be used in a penal reductionist way and could well facilitate an offender's rehabilitation. This is in line with the rationale behind other means to suspend remand, in which defence lawyers draw up a proposal together with the Probation Service (uit Beijerse 2008: 485).

In a pilot that started in 2000 in Rotterdam, EM was used as an *alternative* way in which remand is executed (i.e. not as a means by which remand is *suspended*!) for juvenile offenders. Under Dutch juvenile criminal law, remand can be executed in a remand centre or in 'another suitable place' (para. 493, sub 3 Code of Criminal Procedure). A fixed address and a well-functioning family were needed in order to provide such a 'suitable place'. Evaluation research showed that the argument of the OCAS committee of 1990 – that the remand period was too short to develop a suitable training scheme – was not correct (Terlouw and Kamphorst 2002: 15). Though not unsuccessful, the experiment was not continued, because the entry conditions turned out to be so strict that only a very small number of juvenile offenders could participate. Moreover, many offenders *and* judges preferred the simultaneously introduced facility of 'night-detention' to electronic surveillance.[20]

Unlike a conditionally suspended sentence, remand is not a punishment, but a means to guarantee a just criminal procedure. If this can be guaranteed by less confining means than custody, the principle of subsidiarity demands that the 'lesser harm' is applied. Two legally described reasons to remand someone in custody – 'danger of escape' and 'danger of committing further offences' – may well be achieved through EM as well, but this may be more difficult with the other two legal grounds for remand – 'the necessity to prevent the defendant frustrating the collection of evidence' and the rather flexible concept of the 'shocked public order'. Though the necessity of combining EM with a training scheme may be less pressing in the case of remand, because it is not a sanction but a precautionary measure, the argument that the deprivation of liberty it implies necessitates a sound legal basis and not a simple prosecutorial Indication is equally valid here as with respect to the earlier mentioned modalities.

In January 2006 a pilot with a new detention concept started in Lelystad prison, in which detainees are electronically monitored.[21] The main rationale behind this new institution is that fewer staff are needed than in a traditional prison. Very unlike the – now abandoned – Dutch tradition of one prisoner to a cell, there are six to a cell in the new institution. The pilot concerns 150 prisoners who have a remainder of four months of imprisonment. Staff and inmates communicate via multi-functional TV screens, which are also used to phone, transmit the next day's activities programme, book visits, make appointments with the doctor and get information on the time one still has left in prison and on eventual new developments in one's case. Guards carry palm computers (so-called PDAs) with all the information on every inmate: personal data, verdict, date of release, photo and the whole 'penitentiary dossier' (in which all prisoners' 'good' and 'bad' behaviour is registered) that determines whether visits or furloughs are granted. It also has a transmitter with automatic aggression detection. The idea here is to: (1) provide the same level of security with fewer staff; (2) create safer working conditions for guards; and (3) create more security for offenders. There are some obvious inconsistencies in the combination of these three aims and it remains unclear how they are actually realized. An evaluation of the Lelystad pilot with the new detention concept appeared in 2007. One of the main conclusions was that there were many technical problems that had to be solved (Post *et al.* 2007). Quite a platitude, by which the conclusion 'it does not work (well)' is rephrased as 'we need to do more' in order to show that the direction taken itself has been the right one.

Over the last couple of years, there have also been two pilots in which the applicability of more mobile forms of electronic surveillance via GPS systems and mobile phones are tested. One pilot concerned an EM probation order (Elzinga and Nijboer 2006). In another pilot, the aim was to find out how treatment and social skills programmes for juvenile offenders and furloughs for inmates in a psychiatric detention centre could be monitored electronically (Miedema and Post 2006). The researchers of the pilot with an EM probation order argue that for a motivated offender this form of surveillance could have a rehabilitative potential, because it enables him to take more personal responsibility than would be possible under the direct supervision of a probation officer. But they are quite critical about the reliability of the Probation Service's risk-assessment system, *RISc*, that should provide the information on which the decision of whether or not an EM probation order poses security risks for society is based (Elzinga and Nijboer 2006). They also question the idea that it would require less work and reduce costs. Following offenders continuously in real time is indeed *extremely* labour intensive, and the necessary GPS equipment is very expensive and does not function everywhere equally well. But, their major concern lies in the often-failing software. Three out of four reported infractions were not due to actual breaches of the probation order – neither intentionally nor unwittingly – whereas 7 per cent of all intentional breaches were not registered by the system.

Research on EM treatment, training schemes and furloughs shows rather similar results. The devices are easy to sabotage, there are too many locations where no signal can be received, the frequently flat batteries frustrate the system and the costs of active monitoring are far higher than anticipated – up to €300 per day (Miedema and Post 2006). This is about the same amount – or even slightly more – that an average prison cell costs. For the time being these forms of EM will not be implemented, but new pilots are considered.

When the use of electronics is victim-oriented it is not reckoned to be EM: that term is reserved for the penal sphere. For similar reasons, camera surveillance (better known as CCTV), a very obvious electronic means of crime control that has been widely applied in the Netherlands since the late 1990s, is not reckoned to be EM: it would mainly have a preventative and not a penal goal. Research shows, however, hardly any of such preventive effects with respect to the offences it is aimed at – the largest positive effect is an increased subjective feeling of security. More objectively, cameras turn out to be mainly helpful in police investigations – if the quality of the camera is at least good enough to actually recognize somebody's face, which is often not the case (Geelhoed 2005).

Conclusion

In his influential book *Discipline and Punish*, Michel Foucault (1979: 304–305) argues:

> The carceral texture of society assures both the real capture of the body and its perpetual observation; it is, by its very nature, the apparatus of punishment that conforms most completely to the new economy of power and the instrument for the formulation of knowledge that this very economy needs.

Starting from this perspective, EM can well be seen as the ultimate realization of the panoptic dream. Though concrete references to Foucault's work are rare in the Dutch debate on EM, the idea of total control everywhere and at all times did dominate the debate in the 1980s. Looking at the development of 'control talk' over time, we can observe how the dominant vision of social control has actually turned around. Foucault was highly sceptical of panoptism – as was Stanley Cohen about widening the net and thinning the meshes of social control – and so were most Dutch critics in the 1980s. But with the emerging culture of control, the idea of intensified social control is rather seen as something positive, something worth striving for: the more control the better. That is the irony of history. The new detention concept in Lelystad, with EM prisoners, in particular, would be a perfect case for a Foucauldian analysis.

The dominance of control talk – either in its sceptical or its embracing variety – is all the more remarkable because the Eliasian analysis of a civilization process in which external coercion is transformed into self-discipline has been at least as influential in the Dutch penological debates as the work of Michel Foucault or Stanley Cohen. Herman Franke's (1995) socio-historical analysis of the Dutch prison system shows a process of 200 years in which prisoners have been increasingly 'responsibilized'. Instead of just sitting in a cell, more and more was actively expected of them. Franke calls this the 'emancipation' of prisoners. The introduction of EM can well be seen as a logical continuation of this Eliasian line of thought. But this analysis has not been made. This may be explained by the fact that the belief in penal reductionism and rehabilitation had already declined substantially when EM was introduced – though Franke has defended his 'emancipation thesis' by pointing at the increasing use that is (also) made of non-custodial sanctions. Yet a rehabilitative potential of EM cannot be fully discarded. This has, however, hardly ever been actively supported by the legislator or by policy-makers, and depended more on goodwilled practitioners and researchers – including those employed by the Ministry of Justice. As we have seen above, the rehabilitative potential of EM strongly varies from one modality to the other and largely depends on the question of whether or not it is combined with a training scheme. The one modality in which we see no rehabilitative goal at all is electronic house arrest.

A third central theory, actuarialism with its 'new penology' (Feeley and Simon 1992), has not been applied to the development of EM. Yet the parallel with, for example, Richard Ericson and Kevin Haggerty's book, *Policing the Risk Society*, from 1997 would be rather easy to draw. Their argument that policing has become 'risk communication' and information about groups of offenders and their surroundings has become more important than classical criminal investigation into a specific case can well be translated to new sanctioning practices. In the penal sphere, EM may well be the 'technological solution' *par excellence* to 'trace territories' and 'communicate risks' Ericson and Haggerty (1997) describe in the field of policing. No matter how popular the actuarial rationale of risk-management is in the penal sphere as a whole, EM has as yet hardly been used in this way. The above-mentioned pilots of the EM probation order and of monitoring furloughs from juvenile detention centres and psychiatric detention centres come the closest to the actuarial rationale. In both cases there were still too many technical problems, and in the first case the researchers were also sceptical because the Probation Service's risk-tracking instrument, *RISc*, is itself still in a developmental phase (Elzinga and Nijboer 2006).

The dominant rationale of EM in the Netherlands is far bleaker: reducing custodial capacity problems and cost efficiency. The arguments of rehabilitation and reducing the damaging effects of imprisonment were heard, notably from the side of the Probation Service, but they mainly played the role of a posteriori legitimizing the shift from a position contrary to a pro-EM position. Therefore it is easy to be pessimistic about EM in the Netherlands. But, that pessimism has more to do with the bleak penal culture in which it is embedded than with EM per se. The development of the Dutch penal system over the period 1985–2005 has been characterized as a dimmed beacon of tolerance (Cavadino and Dignan 2006: 113). It could even be on the road to dystopia (Downes and van Swaaningen 2007). In this context, plans for an expanded use of EM will also have to fit in this general penal rationale: more and cheaper punishment through more sophisticated techniques. With the current surplus of prison capacity – to such an extent that Dutch cells are rented out to the *Belgian* prison administration! – the political Right in particular regularly argues that we should start to punish 'properly' – i.e. imprisonment – instead of using EM and non-custodial sanctions as alternatives. As we have shown, the application of EM in non-custodial settings is very limited indeed.

But, as Stanley Cohen (1985) has reminded us, in his characteristic probing way, it makes more sense to cautiously reaffirm one's own beliefs and values than becoming a detached scientist. And that is what we have tried to do here: we have addressed what – penal and other – purposes we would like to see achieved with EM and investigated how they relate to valued legal principles and civil liberties. That implies a much broader discussion than we have now. Answering the central question of how EM could be used as a less intensive alternative to custody that would really reduce the use of prison may well be a common ground for policy-makers and critical penal scholars.

We must reconsider the legal goals of EM. As such, both the front-door and back-door varieties that have been applied since 1995 can be justified as contributions to penal reductionism and rehabilitation. As part of a wider training or rehabilitation scheme at the end of someone's detention, EM may be a means to facilitate a smoother reintegration into society for a wider group of offenders than if penitentiary programmes were applied without EM. Yet, if the penitentiary programme can be safely applied *without* EM, the legal principle of subsidiarity demands that it *is* applied without. The front-door variety, in which EM is used as a condition to a suspended prison sentence, does not only fit the legal goals of the suspended sentence – controlling someone's behaviour and special prevention – but it can also make a suspended sentence possible in cases where it would not be applied before. It can even be argued that the law *demands* the application of EM if it prevents remand: if the same legal goals – prevention of escape, recidivism and obscuring evidence – can be achieved by less confining means than custody, these are to be preferred. A similar thing can be said about the more recent use of EM as a condition to suspend remand. There is a clear danger of net-widening here. Therefore, a codification of EM that also describes the legal purposes it serves and the conditions under which it can be applied should replace its present regulation by a prosecutorial Indication. We place the biggest question mark over the introduction of electronic house arrest and the electronic so-called staff-extensive prison. These modalities are only motivated by managerial arguments. Because they are not combined with any training scheme, it is doubtful whether they will lead to a reduced use of imprisonment or contribute to rehabilitation. In this case, sheer net-widening is the most probable consequence.

Overall, the expectations of EM in the Netherlands have been high with respect to its contribution to reducing costs and pressure on the prison system. Yet, in practice hardly any costs were cut and in the meantime we have built so many new prisons that we currently have surplus prison capacity. There is hardly any expectation with respect to rehabilitation or actually reducing the use of imprisonment. Next to reconsidering the legal rationales by which EM is to be applied, as we did in the previous section, we also propose taking a look at the results from meta-evaluations on non-custodial sanctions. There is a tendency to expand the use of EM to a variety of new cases. Yet treating something new as a panacea has exactly been the problem with the effectiveness of some non-custodial sanctions. These were quite effective for the group of offenders they were originally intended for, but when applied to a wider category of more serious and more problematic offenders they 'worked' less well. A meta-evaluation into 'Halt', a reparative non-custodial sanction for juvenile offenders, shows that the personal commitment of the Halt staff, the fact that an offender shows remorse and has no personal or family problems is of more influence on the effectiveness than the actual content of the Halt programme as such (Ferwerda *et al.* 2006). These are lessons to bear in mind.

If questions on the legal purposes of EM are taken up, and a more specific analysis is made of the concrete cases in which it could contribute to these goals, and of the kind of rehabilitative schemes it is to be combined with, we can say something sensible about the potential impact of EM on penal developments in the Netherlands. As yet, the political discussion is too narrowly oriented at mere economic and managerial questions. In this way, EM will be just another companion on the road to dystopia. In this article we hope to have shown, however, that it is not the only road we can take.

Notes

1 This chapter was finished in March 2011. Later developments could not be included.
2 In this chapter we cannot deal with the dropping imprisonment rates since 2006. There is, however, little evidence that an increased use of EM has contributed to this recent development.
3 In Dutch: Raad voor de Kinderbescherming. This Council has a key advisory role in youth justice; see uit Beijerse and van Swaaningen (2006).
4 Minister of justice's letter to parliament, 30 October 1997, *Kamerstukken II* 1997–1998, 25712, nr. 1.
5 Aanwijzing elektronisch toezicht, 1 July 1999, *Staatscourant* 1999, no. 114, p. 18. An 'Indication' – *Aanwijzing* in Dutch – is a binding advice for prosecutors on a specific subject that functions as a kind of pseudo-law in the Dutch Criminal Justice System (Tak 2003).
6 www.dji.nl.
7 Para. 15a Criminal Code, Wet van, 6 December 2007, Staatsblad 2007, 500, implemented by: Besluit van 30 mei 2008, Staatsblad 2008, 194.
8 'Electronisch toezicht wordt nooit een massastraf', *Opportuun*, October 2000, online at: www.om.nl.
9 Minister of justice's letter to Parliament, 30 October 1997, *Kamerstukken II* 1997–1998, 25712, nr. 1, p. 3.
10 *Kamerstukken II* 2002–2003, 28600 VI, nr. 8, p. 9.
11 Aanwijzing elektronisch toezicht, *Staatscourant*, 1 July 1999, nr. 114, p. 18.
12 Aanwijzing elektronisch toezicht, *Staatscourant*, 1 June 2010, nr. 8001.
13 In a series of letters of the Minister of justice to Parliament: 16 October 2002, *Kamerstukken II* 2002–2003, 28600 VI, nr. 8, p. 7.; 9 December 2002, *Kamerstukken II* 2002–2003, 24587, nr. 87, p. 3; and 10 March 2003, *Kamerstukken II* 2002–2003, 24587, nr. 88, p. 5.

14 Minister of justice's letter to Parliament, 25 August 2005, *Kamerstukken* 2004–2005, 29800 VI, no. 167.
15 Later in 2006 a pilot with speech-recognition of hooligans was started. Hooligans with a stadium-prohibition injunction were called at their home (i.e. not on a mobile phone) and their voice was to be recognized by a computer.
16 In the pilot, electronic detention replaced a maximum of 90 days' imprisonment. This was strictly observed. A drink driver who had received several sentences, which together amounted to 91 days, was denied access to the pilot (*NRC Handelsblad*, 13–14 May 2006). Now electronic house arrest is an autonomous penalty and this substitution-maximum no longer exists. This is the rationale behind the minister's argument.
17 *Handelingen II* 2008–2009, 98, p. 7739–7740 and *Kamerstukken II* 2008–2009, 31700 VI, nrs. 139–140.
18 Council of Ministers press release, 22 March 2010.
19 *Staatscourant* 2010, nr. 10014.
20 State-secretary of justice's letter to Parliament, 7 March 2002, *Kamerstukken II* 2001–2002, 25712, nr. 3.
21 Minister of justice's letter to Parliament, 18 January 2006, Tweede Kamer 2005–2006, nos. 28979 and 24587.

References

Boone, M. (2000) *Recht voor commuun gestraften: dogmatisch-juridische aspecten van taakstraffen en penitentiaire programma's* (Deventer: Gouda Quint).
Cavadino, M. and Dignan, J. (2006) *Penal Systems: A Comparative Approach* (London: Sage).
Cohen, S. (1985) *Visions of Social Control: Crime, Punishment and Classification* (Cambridge: Polity Press).
Downes, D. and van Swaaningen, R. (2007) 'The road to dystopia: changes in the penal climate in the Netherlands', in M. Tonry and C. Bijleveld (eds) *Crime and Justice in the Netherlands* (Chicago, IL: Chicago University Press), pp. 31–72.
Elzinga, H.K. and Nijboer, J.A. (2006) 'Probation supervision through GPS', *European Journal of Crime, Criminal Law and Criminal Justice*, 14:4, pp. 366–381.
Ericson, R.V. and Haggerty, K.D. (1997) *Policing the Risk Society* (Oxford: Clarendon Press).
Feeley, M.M. and Simon, J. (1992) 'The new penology: notes on the emerging strategy of corrections and its implications', *Criminology*, 30:4, pp. 452–474.
Ferwerda, H., van Leiden, I., Arts, N. and Hauber, A. (2006) *Halt: Het Alternatief? De effecten van Halt beschreven* (Arnhem: Advies- en Onderzoeksgroep Beke). Online. Available at: www.wodc.nl/onderzoeken/onderzoek_113.asp?soort=publicatie&tab=pub (accessed 1 March 2011).
Fiselier, J.S. (1997) 'My home is my cell', *Sancties*, 2, pp. 65–69.
Foucault, M. (1979) *Discipline and Punish: The Birth of the Prison* (New York: Random House).
Franke, H. (1995) *The Emancipation of Prisoners: A Socio-historical Analysis of the Dutch Prison Experience* (Edinburgh: Edinburgh University Press).
Geelhoed, F. (2005) 'Verbeelde veiligheid: over effecten van cameratoezicht in het publieke domein', *Tijdschrift voor Veiligheid en Veiligheidszorg*, 4:2, pp. 3–27.
Inspectie voor de Sanctietoepassing (2007) *Uitvoering elektronische detentie* (The Hague: Ministry of Justice).

Junger-Tas, J. (1993) *Alternatieven voor de vrijheidsstraf: Lessen uit het buitenland* (The Hague: WODC).

Kaladien, S.N. and Eggen, A. Th. (2009) *Criminaliteit en Rechtshandhaving 2008* (The Hague: BJu).

Miedema, F. and Post, B. (2006) *Evaluatie pilot elektronische volgsystemen.* (The Hague: WODC) English summary online, available at: www.wodc.nl/images/1255_summary_tcm11–107975.pdf (accessed 1 March 2011).

Ministerie van Justitie (2000) *Sancties in perspectief: Beleidsnota inzake de heroriëntatie op de toepassing van vrijheidsstraffen en vrijheidsbeperkende straffen bij volwassenen* (The Hague: Ministry of Justice).

OCAS (1990) 'Advies van de Overleg- en adviescommissie alternatieve sancties betreffende Electronisch Toezicht'. Unpublished.

Otte Committtee (2003) *Vrijheidsbeperking door voorwaarden. De voorwaardelijke veroordeling en haar samenhang met de taakstraf, de voorlopige hechtenis en de voorwaardelijke invrijheidstelling* (The Hague: Ministry of Justice).

Post, B., Tielemans, L. and Woldringh, C. (2005) *Geboeid door de enkelband: evaluatie pilot elektronische detentie* (The Hague: WODC). English summary online, available at: www.wodc.nl/images/ob195_Summary_tcm11–4774.pdf (accessed 1 March 2011).

Post, B., Stoltz, S. and Miedema, F. (2007) *Evaluatie detentieconcept Lelystad* (The Hague: WODC). English summary, online, available at: www.wodc.nl/onderzoeksdatabase/1394a-pilotproject-detentieconept-lelystad-dcl-deelproject-1-dbm-v.aspx (accessed 1 March 2011).

Schalken Committee (1988) *Electronisch huisarrest: een boeiend alternatief?* (The Hague: Ministry of Justice).

Scholten, T. (1994) 'De gevangenis thuis: van Spiderman tot Hirsch Ballin', *Proces*, 73, pp. 51–61.

Spaans, E.C. and Verwers, C. (1997) *Elektronisch toezicht in Nederland: uitkomsten van het experiment* (The Hague: WODC). English summary, online, available at: www.wodc.nl/images/ob164_Summary_tcm11–24363.pdf (accessed 1 March 2011).

Tak, P. (2003) *The Dutch Criminal Justice System: Organization and Operation* (The Hague: WODC). Online. Available at: www.wodc.nl/onderzoeken/onderzoek_w00205.asp?qry=Tak&sqy=tcm0111%3CIN%3Ewebsite%3Cand%3Eoperationelestatus!='gaat%20niet%20door'&srt=wegingsfactor%20desc,%20datum%20desc&sta=3&soort=publicatie&tab=pub (accessed 1 March 2011).

Terlouw, G.J. and Kamphorst, P.A. (2002) *Van vast naar mobiel: een evaluatie van het experiment met elektronisch huisarrest voor minderjarigen als modaliteit voor de voorlopige hechtenis* (The Hague: WODC). English summary online, available at: www.wodc.nl/images/ob195_Summary_tcm11–4774.pdf (accessed 1 March 2011).

uit Beijerse, J. (2008) 'Naar een bij de onschuldpresumptie passend systeem van voorlopige hechtenis. De lessen van Europa en van de klassieke rechtsgeleerden', *Strafblad*, 6, pp. 465–487.

uit Beijerse, J. and Swaaningen, R. van (2006) 'The Netherlands: penal welfarism and risk management', in J. Muncie and B. Goldson (eds) *Comparative Youth Justice* (London: Sage), pp. 65–78.

van Gestel, B. (1998) 'Tralies in je hoofd: Over de psycho-sociale effecten van elektronisch huisarrest', *Tijdschrift voor Criminologie*, 40:1, pp. 21–38.

van Hattum, W.F. (1995) 'Van insluiten naar elektronisch aanlijnen: Het experiment met elektronisch toezicht', *Sancties*, 3, pp. 318–336.

van Swaaningen, R. (2000) 'Back to the 'iron cage' ': the example of the Dutch probation service', in P. Green and A. Rutherford (eds) *Criminal Policy in Transition* (Oxford: Hart), pp. 91–108.

Wartna, B.S.J., Baas, N.J. and Beenakkers, E.M. Th. (2004) *Beter, anders en goedkoper: een literatuurverkenning ten behoeve van het traject Modernisering Sanctietoepassing* (The Hague: WODC). Online Available at: www.wodc.nl/onderzoeken/onderzoek_347. asp?loc=/publicatie/perjaar/2004 (accessed 1 March 2011).

Part II
Debates

10 Surveillance, stigma and spatial constraint

The ethical challenges of electronic monitoring

Mike Nellis

Introduction

The introduction of electronic monitoring (EM) has not been equally controversial in all countries, but because it was so different in kind from pre-existing forms of community supervision, ostensibly threatening to some established probation service and penal reform interests (especially when delivered by the private sector), and easily cast as a step towards a Big Brother-style 'surveillance society', wariness, caution and hostility were perhaps inevitable among the more traditional penal reformers (Penal Affairs Committee 1988; Allchin 1989). EM's initial champions, on the other hand – Tom Stacey apart (Nellis 2010a) – were often technophiles in the security and communication industries who, while not wholly unversed in the ethical implications of new technologies, knew little or nothing of what probation at its best aspired to. Initially, the core debate among politicians and criminal justice professionals was between those who saw EM simply as an unacceptably intrusive form of surveillance, strikingly at odds with the humanistic impulses of traditional probation supervision, and those who saw it as a useful, necessary and arguably cost-effective way of enhancing the credibility of community supervision. Offenders themselves have tended to appreciate it from the start (Bettsworth 1989). The more recent view, periodically articulated in the British press, that it is a rather inconsequential, easily evaded, poorly enforced form of punishment was largely unthinkable then.

Norman Bishop (2003), the former English prison governor who pioneered the Swedish EM scheme, has indicated that the expert committee which drafted the European Rules on Community Sanctions and Measures in the early 1990s doubted the legitimacy of EM as a community sanction, and the resulting Rules questioned whether EM could be a 'meaningful' and constructive response to offenders (Council of Europe 1994: 56). A subsequent document on 'improving the implementation' of community sanctions accepted that EM was becoming widespread in Europe but, in anticipation of such obviously pernicious developments as satellite tracking (as it was then seen), argued that there was a pressing need to consider the implications of all EM 'for practical work with offenders and possible encroachments on personal integrity and human rights' (Council of Europe 2002: 31). Thus, very little attempt has been made to explore the ethics of EM from within the philosophy of punishment, or in terms of the ethics of surveillance, and this chapter is by no means comprehensive; it is merely a partial sketch of the conceptual territory. It reflects the author's Anglo-centric orientation to EM, but it will hopefully stimulate debate farther afield.

The several modalities of EM

To properly grasp the ethics of EM, one must have a clear understanding of what the technology permits, and the way it is used. EM is a generic term for several remote location-checking technologies which each make possible the micro-management of offenders' (or pre-trial detainees') locations and schedules at various points in the criminal justice process – pre-trial, as a community sanction or alternative to prison, or as a form of post-release supervision. Broadly speaking, these technologies facilitate three basic forms of spatial and temporal regulation.

First, *restriction to a specific place* for a specific number of hours per day (often, but not necessarily a night-time curfew), over a specific period of time. The place is usually an offender's home, or a relative's home, but it can be a hostel or halfway house. EM systems invariably combine different technologies to enforce such restrictions – radio frequency (RF) technology with either land-line or mobile telephony (GSM), voice verification with either of these, or RF, GSM and GPS satellites. A restriction *to* a place is as much a form of exclusion (from public space) as it is a form of confinement: while the offender is confined at home he is by definition prohibited from offending elsewhere. Semantically, the terms that have typically been used to describe restriction to a place – house arrest, home detention, home confinement, home incarceration – give the impression that confinement (in a punitive sense) is the purpose of restriction, but it is open to sentencers to use the sanction as a form of exclusion (in a punitive or a crime reductive sense) or, indeed, to have both purposes in mind. *Remote behavioural monitoring* can be an adjunct to restriction to a place, in that offenders who have been banned from using alcohol at home can be breathalized at a distance. Identity authentication (ensuring that a sober proxy does not use the machine) can be achieved using voice verification, or, where remote alcohol monitoring machines are equipped with a camera, video identification or, more recently, facial recognition

Second, EM enables restrictions (exclusions) from a specified place, temporarily, occasionally or permanently over a set period of time. The place (or places) can range from the home of a specific victim (e.g. of domestic violence) to an area in which the offender has offended regularly (an estate where he burgles) or an area in which he might subsequently offend (a park where a paedophile might meet children). RF technologies can be used to achieve exclusion by placing receivers at key entry points on the exclusion zone perimeter, but combinations of GPS satellites and GSM (the mobile phone system) enable exclusion more effectively, by continuously monitoring the whole perimeter of a designated zone.

Mobility monitoring entails keeping track of an offender's movements, inter-mittently or continuously, retrospectively or in real time, for a specified period. In some cases, for released sex offenders, the United States has proposed life-time tracking on GPS (in combination with GSM). By linking police and proba-tion/parole computers, an offender's whereabouts over a 24-hour period can be tallied with known crime scenes – this can exonerate as well as incriminate. There are other sorts of tracking, not involving GPS satellites. Voice verification (one brand of which is called 'Voice track') can be used to map the stages of an offender's daily journey, checking that he is where he is expected to be at agreed times, as he phones into a control centre from each stopping-off place.

Although the regulation of an offender's locations and schedules is not wholly new in community supervision – offenders have had to notify probation officers of address changes, or report punctually to offices or work sites at specified times – EM technologies massively increase the scale, precision and enforceabil-ity of such regulations. They add a new – remote surveillant – dimension to community supervision, and (potentially) – by restricting opportunities for unmonitored movement – broaden the kind and increase the intensity of control that can be imposed on an offender (without by any means making it absolute). In the past, the (non-electronic) regulation of movement was mostly a means to an end – an offender's required presence at a particular place and time was spec-ified to enable putatively crime reductive activities such as 'treatment' or 'com-munity service' to proceed. Without precluding the continuation of this 'old' approach, EM adds the possibility of structuring an offender's mobility – his locations and schedules – as a crime reductive strategy in its own right. This poses some new ethical challenges for those concerned with community supervi-sion, and perhaps penal policy more generally.

Ethics and the community supervision of offenders

Much is written about community sanctions which is not specifically flagged up as 'ethical' comment, but which is nonetheless concerned with the rightness or wrongness of applying different types and intensities of community supervision to different types of offender and offence. Discussions of 'net-widening', for example – the deliberate or negligent imposition of intrusive measures on offenders whose riskiness or offence seriousness does not warrant them, are ethical as much as technical (Cohen 1979). Legal reflections notwithstanding, surprisingly little is explicitly written about the ethics of community supervision, and three cursory (and by no means uncontested) points need to be made before proceeding with a more detailed argument.

First, given the general limitations of imprisonment as an effective and ethical means of ensuring rehabilitation, crime reduction and deterrence they need not be repeated here (see Mathiesen 1990: Sim 2009); it is morally and politically desirable to continue searching for constructive alternatives to prison for many types of offender, not only, but certainly including women offenders, low-risk petty persistent offenders, mentally ill offenders and juvenile offenders. Suffice to quote Nigel Walker, who captures part of what is wrong with using imprisonment (in many cases) while at the same time signalling what it is that community penalties might preserve: 'Custody may prevent people from harming others, but it also prevents them from doing things that are harmless. It prevents far more than is necessary' (Walker 1997: 614).

Second, a cautious case can be made for making community penalties more demanding of offenders in respect of crime reduction, and more capable of preventing harm to victims (Rex 2005). This is not a case for making them tough (painful) for their own sake, and not for routinely making them the 'virtual prison' or 'community custody' envisaged by Roberts (2004).

Third, non-custodial measures/community penalties in general cannot be justified in the abstract by the argument that they are intrinsically and necessarily less painful, less intrusive – or better than – imprisonment (for in some respects they may not be). Each particular type of alternative/community sanction requires justification in its own right, based on the kind of control it imposes and the affordances it offers. This is particularly true of EM.

The argument in this chapter draws on discussions of limiting retributivism, observations on the tension between parsimony and proportionality (Morris 1974; Tonry 1994; Dingwall and Harding 2002), communitarian insights into the symbolic and communicative aspects of punishment (Duff 1999; Lacey 2003) and specifically von Hirsch's (1990) reflections on the ethics of community penalties. Although he disdains utilitarian, crime reductive ends in sentencing, the criteria Hirsch identifies – (1) intrusiveness; (2) levels of interference with generic human interests (physical integrity, material support and amenity, freedom from humiliation, privacy and autonomy); (3) duration; and (4) the rights of third parties – are as vital to understanding parsimony as they are to understanding proportionality.

Exclusion and the spatial movement of offenders

One consequence of the situational crime prevention movement has been research interest in offenders' spatial decision-making – how they perceive, use and move about in given geographical areas. This has generated some knowledge of offenders' journeys to crime: the starting point, the direction of travel and the distance between the starting point and the site of the offence. Offenders' patterns of spatial use vary. Drug-using burglars, for example, tend to offend very locally; armed robbers go farther afield; and specialist car thieves travel long distances to find the required vehicle. Some offenders begin their journeys with a strong motivation to commit crime (e.g. to do a drug deal), others may simply take advantage of opportunities (unlocked cars, open handbags) that arise in the course of travel (whether aimless or purposive). Researchers who have examined 'distance to crime' tend to lean towards the assumption that offenders will offend as close to home as possible, in areas with which they are relatively or very familiar (even more so if they are young), simply for reasons of personal security: 'Since it requires more effort in time, money and distance to go a long distance rather than a short distance, all other things being equal, the rational criminal will choose the short distance' (Rengert 2004: 173). Researchers concluded from this that creating 'barriers to criminal spatial movement' (Rengert 2004: 176) would contribute to crime reduction, and Rengert (1989: 170) himself realized early that such knowledge may one day inform 'the expanding use of electronic tracking and monitoring devices'. While traditional personal exclusion strategies (bans from pubs or sports stadia) were readily encompassed by the situational crime prevention movement, its main strategies were forms of place-based protection, whose 'capable guardians' – CCTV, street lighting, fences and locked gates, concierges – were located on-site. EM – which in its tracking form might conceivably be characterized as a *mobile guardian* – creates the possibility of incorporating *and enforcing* spatial constraints within individualized supervision packages, to a degree unattainable in previous community sanctions.

But can exclusion from public space be justified, either as punishment or prevention? Von Hirsch and Shearing (2000) are largely hostile to the idea, grounding their resistance to it in a liberal theory of citizenship. Universal access to public space is important to citizenship for several reasons. It enables the utilization of goods and services, and facilitates the quality of life(style) they afford. Moreover, it actualizes the principle of 'membership [of] a free community', and helps sustain a subjective sense of belonging to such a community, or, more concretely, a neighbourhood, town or city. Order in public space can be maintained – as it traditionally has – by prohibiting harmful and undesirable behaviour and punishing perpetrators after it occurs; exclusion from the public space in question should form no part of a retributive punishment, nor should it be used preventively on the basis of predictions of behaviour (whether conduct-based or profile-based) that might occur there in the future.

Their argument hinges on the notion of illegitimate disqualification. Public space, they argue, is not something that offenders can morally be disqualified from using in the way that a dishonest professional who abuses public trust can be disqualified (or, they might have added, a dangerous driver can be temporarily banned from using the road). No special credentials are required by citizens to use public space in the way that they are required to become a professional public servant or to become a good, safe driver; there is thus nothing to rescind from a citizen if they abuse public space. 'The user of public or semi-public space', they say, 'does not entrust his interests to other users, in the manner that a patient or client entrusts his interests to his or her doctor or solicitor' (von Hirsch and Shearing 2000: 91). This is surely debatable. There is a very real sense in which ordinary users of public space entrust their interests (their safety) to others – they enter into the public domain with a reasonable expectation that their person and property will come to no harm, that mutual tolerance among lightly engaged strangers will safeguard them. This seems doubly true in respect of parents allowing or taking children into public space. There is a profound element of *entrusting* in the way we use public space, and a case – with both instrumental and symbolic elements – can be made for excluding those who abuse that trust. It is not a case that can be made lightly, and the *duration* of the exclusion, however, is crucial to its reasonableness: effort must be made, along-side electronic exclusion, to enable the offender to resume using public space at some agreed point on the understanding that he is capable of learning lessons and behaving better.

It is undeniable that exclusion from a public space – say, a city centre, a shop-ping centre, a harbourside, a housing estate, parks and school zones – interferes with key civil rights and impedes ordinary living. It may be experienced as shaming, but it is difficult to argue that such temporary exclusions impinge upon the dignity of a person in any fundamental sense (see Ward 2009). It indubitably inconveniences the offender, and may in addition increase the burden on those with whom the offender has a relationship. There have to be limits on the latter, both of severity and duration. Inconvenience and burden can be offset by allow-ing temporary access to the designated exclusion zones, enabling the offender to shop or socialize, and creating 'breathing space' for co-residents. Duration is crucial to the acceptability of certain exclusions: in so far as offenders dislike being excluded from a 'comfort zone', a promise to relax exclusion requirements at a specified point in the future can work as an incentive to ensure compliance with other aspects of supervision.

Using the home as a place of confinement

While the use of EM to enforce house arrest/home confinement has – to a greater or lesser degree – been particularly controversial (especially in countries with no tradition of house arrest as a criminal penalty), the ethics of it are far from simple. EM curfews are both forms of confinement and, simultaneously, by defi-nition, forms of exclusion; while under curfew one cannot enter or enjoy public spaces which, at certain times of the day or night, one might otherwise wish to access. It is arguably the exclusionary element which courts believe constitutes the most consistently punitive element of EM curfews: depending on the tem-perament, age and family circumstances of the tagged individual, confinement amidst the putative 'comforts' of home may not be an unpleasant experience. The fact of confinement, however, will inevitably impact on the offender in one of several ways, regardless of the court's intention. If the offender's home life is difficult the punitive element will be intensified (and may not in fact be tolerable, leading inexorably to violation and breach). If the period of confinement is used to strengthen bonds between an offender and his parent(s)/partner/children and/ or if it is used as a way of disrupting criminogenic routines (severing ties with the peers with whom one offends) or breaking criminal habits (reviewing where one is going in life) then it may be experienced as a welcome opportunity rather than deserved retribution.

Precisely because EM orders inevitably have collateral consequences for the offender beyond his exclusion, and for third parties with whom he may live, the question arises as to whether stand-alone EM orders are defensible in their own right or whether – even if they are defensible – it is still preferable that such orders are embedded in, and related to, rehabilitative programmes. In so far as a stand-alone EM order enables creative controls to be imposed on offenders which may in themselves have the ethical effect of crime reduction during the run of the order itself, a case can be made for the stand-alone model. If, however, a more long-term approach to crime reduction was being taken – beyond the end of the surveillance period – it makes greater ethical sense to involve the offender in programmes aimed at changing behaviour and sustaining desistance, and to harness the properties of EM which support them.

It should go without saying that a full 24-hour curfew, sustained over a period of days, would not be ethically acceptable. Such orders would impose too great a burden on an individual living alone, and even more so on third parties. The main objection is that any offender whom it was deemed necessary to keep in a particular place for a sustained period should in fact be in jail, or at least a hostel. The genuinely creative controls that EM affords derive precisely from its *intermittence*, the fact that it can be used for part of the day or night, with some precision, leaving the offender free to do other things outside the home (attend or seek employment, participate in rehabilitation programmes and mix socially). Intermittence gives respite to the offender from third parties, and, perhaps more importantly, vice versa. Arguably, the most conventional use of an EM curfew is as an evening and night-time restriction, say between 7 a.m. and 7 p.m. This approximates to a period when many people are indoors anyway, and part of the rationale of such an order is to impose stability and routine on offenders whose lives are otherwise chaotic. Implicit in this is the normative idea that it is conventional to be at home and asleep during the hours of darkness. The most punitive part of such an order is the curtailment of evening/night-time leisure activities – say those between 7 p.m. and midnight – and the loss of spontaneity in deciding to stay out – or stay elsewhere – overnight

An EM curfew, however, can be used much more flexibly – creatively – than this. The 12-hour maximum can be fixed differently on any given day, on different days and on weekdays and weekends. These variations can be used not merely to allow for different employment commitments, but also to address different temporal and spatial patterns of offending. It is possible to restrict offenders to their homes at times when they are known to have been involved in criminal incidents, or when they are likely to be so involved – e.g. at football matches. EM has been used in Scotland to restrict women to their homes in the later afternoon, when it was noted by sentencers that 4 p.m. was their peak time for shoplifting. Rengert's (2004) observation that 'the home is the anchor point that most people start from in the morning and return to in the evening' can form the basis of even more creative controls. The location of one's home, he writes, 'places constraints on how much territory an individual can utilize in a day given that he or she must return home in the evening, and the level of transportation technology available'. A 12-hour order can, for example, be split into two hour intervals, spaced over the 24-hour period. A Scottish sheriff did this in order to limit the distance a professional car thief could travel from his home, in effect preventing him from getting more than an hour away before he had to return. The issue of tagging juveniles who routinely split their accommodation between two separated or divorced parents is routinely solved by installing home receiver units in both houses.

The above uses of EM curfews can be considered 'creative' even if used as a stand-alone measure, but they are of limited efficacy. If EM is to make a contribution to sustained crime reduction and to viable alternatives to custody, such controls need to be integrated into intensive supervision programmes which makes significant demands on the offender's time and energy during the hours he is not subject to curfew, and challenge his thinking. The integration must be real and meaningful to the person subject to it – not, as in the case of Peter Williams, a young man who was subject to intensive supervision in England and Wales, experienced as an isolated, separately managed element in a programme whose administrators in the statutory and private sectors fail to communicate adequately with each other (Nellis 2006).

Then there is the question of severity. Probably because of an engrained sense within the civil libertarian tradition (whether Left or Right), that the very idea of EM house arrest violates the enduring symbolism of 'home' as a protected and inviolate space, it was initially understood as a rather intrusive penalty that should be reserved for serious, high-tariff offenders. If 'the home is where people are off stage, free from surveillance, in control of their immediate environment ... their castle ... where they feel they belong' (Saunders 1989: 184), the state's temporary use of it as penal space constitutes a significant (if not total) infringement of liberty. Even von Hirsch, reflecting on proportionality, seems to have accepted that EM home confinement is an intrinsically high tariff. Significantly, however, he does not distinguish between the several different ways in which stand-alone EM orders might be used, nor does he consider the complications (ethical and otherwise) that arise when EM is used as one (night-time or weekend) component among several in an intensive (day-time) supervision programme; the total package is surely more intrusive than night-time EM used alone.

The quality of the home in which the offender is confined, and the attitudes they hold towards it, together with the attitude other residents hold towards the offender, will affect the way severity is experienced. The size of the home (number of rooms) and the level of amenities – the ability of people to get out of each other's way when tempers are frayed – affect the nature of the offender's experience. There is every reason to think that enforced proximity may fray tempers and create resentment, but the archetypal white-collar offender, tagged and sitting by his pool sipping martinis is not in the same situation as the impoverished drug dealer in a tiny thin-walled flat in a high-rise tower block. There are, furthermore, age and gender dimensions to the meaning of home. It is arguable that because many adolescents lead less home-centred lives than small children or adults – preferring to be out with their peers – that they will experience home confinement more punitively than adults. Some feminists, for women, have seen the home as an exploitive workplace, not as a sanctuary, and in that sense already oppressive of women, without the state further using it as a place of confinement (Aungles 1994).

Mobility monitoring using satellite tracking

The use of GPS satellite tracking (augmented by various terrestrial tracking technologies) to monitor the movements of offenders – rather than just restricting them to a single place – has become relatively widespread in the United States and has been piloted in England and Wales and New Zealand and established on a small scale in the Netherlands and France. The technology can be used in a variety of different ways, to monitor movement on a 'wherever-you-go' basis, or more selectively, to prohibit entry into designated exclusion zones, either retrospectively or in real time. The exclusion zones can be designed around specific victims (of stalking, rape, domestic violence), around more general areas in which an offender has been known to offend (a harbourside, a housing estate, a sport stadium) or the type of area in which the offender might, on the basis of past experience, be likely to re-offend in the future (e.g. parks and playgrounds). Retrospective and real-time monitoring can be combined into a hybrid system, with the former used most of the time and the latter activated only when the perimeter of an exclusion zone is being approached (Nellis 2010b).

With retrospective tracking the agencies involved in the offender's supervision – probation and/or police – only learn of the offender's movements at some specified time later, say 24 hours, as a result of a download from the monitoring computer. The theory behind retrospective tracking is simple deterrence: offenders know that police/probation will acquire a computer print-out of his routes which will show if he was in the vicinity of a known crime or if he entered an area from which he had been prohibited. Clearly, this is of limited use if one wants to protect victims, but it is useful if one simply wants to manage an offender's spatial movements. With real-time tracking the offender's movements are known on a moment-by-moment basis: signals are passed from the tracking device worn by the offender, via the satellite, to the control centre on a continuous basis; dots representing the offenders can be followed live on a computerized map. In some versions of the technology, the offender can be contacted by text, pager or phone – for example, to issue warnings of proximity to a forbidden perimeter, or to instruct an offender that his signal has been lost, and to move to a space where the satellites can pick him up again. The hybrid strategy uses retrospective tracking on movement outside an exclusion zone, switching to real-time tracking if and when the offender enters an exclusion zone (assuming he is still wearing his tracking device).

The creation of exclusion zones to protect specific victims is not as simple an exercise as it seems. Too small a zone – too short a distance between the victim's home and the perimeter – would not allow the police sufficient time to respond once they had received notification that the perimeter had been violated. The size of the exclusion zone must take account of probable police response times, not just considerations of proportionality and what is fair to the offender. Depending on where the offender lives – and whether he has been given permission to pass through the exclusion zone en route to somewhere else – a large exclusion zone can be a serious inconvenience to him. With convicted child sex offenders, the intention behind exclusion may be to protect 'likely victims' rather than (or as well as) specific (previous) victims. The cost of excluding an offender from multiple sites – say, all the parks and playgrounds in a city region – would be excessively expensive, although this can be offset by prohibiting entry to them all, but creating electronic perimeters around only a few of them and not telling the offender which ones.

The creation of exclusion zones around areas where the offender has been known to offend is complex for different reasons, especially if the offending zone is in the immediate vicinity of the offender's own home. The rationale of such an exclusion zone is three-fold: (1) to give former and potential victims some respite from the presence of the offender; (2) to deny the offender the temptation to re-offend within a 'comfort zone' (a familiar place in which he finds it easy to offend and evade capture); and (3) simply to impose discipline on the offender by promising progressively more access to the exclusion zone as a means of incentivizing compliance with other aspects of the supervision programme. Where the offender lives 'within' or on the edge of the zone from which he is excluded, he is allowed one route in and out to his own home; he cannot approach or leave his home in any direction he pleases, whether on foot, by car or on public transport. This can be a huge inconvenience. One problem with being denied access to a place where one has regularly offended is that it also denies access to nearby family and friends – unless they come to you. One, perhaps paradoxical consequence of exclusion is that the offender, frustrated at not being able to go where he wants, simply stays indoors – an effect which could be achieved more easily, and more cheaply, by house arrest! There is a danger with this intensive micro-management of people's spatial behaviour of (as Nigel Walker said of imprisonment) preventing 'far more than is necessary'.

Some US states have legislated for lifetime GPS monitoring for certain sex offenders (mostly those who offend against children) and, as is customary there, to pay part costs of their monitoring (Doffing 2009; Waldo 2010). Empirically, lifetime monitoring is an unknown quantity – no-one has yet served long enough to judge its viability. The case for such a measure is usually made in terms of evidence which shows that for the duration of the period in which offenders are electronically monitored, they are less likely to offend (Padgett *et al.* 2006), but quite apart from the element of false extrapolation – what is bearable and even helpful for several months may not be bearable for several (or many) years – the ethical implications for citizenship of lifetime tracking are profound. By deeming people as forever untrustworthy, always suspicious, it fundamentally demeans them and denies their capacity for betterment. Lifelong imposition of EM does diminish dignity in a way that short-term use does not (Ward 2009).

Two further ethical/operational issues arise in respect of mobility monitoring, one relating to communication with the tracked offender, the other to the potential for linking such offenders to known crime scenes. Most GPS tracking equipment has a text facility: messages can be sent to an offender warning him that he is nearing the perimeter of an exclusion zone, or to summon him to a meeting with a probation officer. Some have a text-reply facility. Some equipment has a mobile phone built in, enabling verbal communication. Opinion varies (even among manufacturers) as to whether this is a good thing. If a tracked offender is seen (on a screen map) heading into an exclusion zone, the police will be called: is it also useful for the monitoring centre to be able to talk to him, assuming he even answers the phone? Would the purpose be to talk him down, counsel him, warn him, persuade him not to go through with whatever he has in mind? If he then did commit a crime, would the fact that communication had been attempted not make the monitoring authorities more accountable, having tried and failed? Is it not preferable just to send in the police? There seems at present to be no consensus on this, but such are the new dilemmas that tracking technology poses.

What of matching offender movement with crime incidents? The CrimeTrax program already does this and GPS monitoring may come to be seen as half-hearted and incomplete without such an affordance. It may well act as a further deterrent to the offender. Police forces many well find it a useful and efficient way to incriminate tracked offenders in the community, but it is not inconceivable that some legal pressure for the introduction of this technology will come from the wrongfully accused, people who believe that a combined record of their movements and crime scenes would exonerate rather than incriminate them.

Stigma, shame and the importance of dialogue

> An injury to human dignity is humiliation, and so even a criminal is entitled not to be humiliated. A decent society must not provide sound reasons for criminals to consider their dignity violated, even if their punishment gives them good reason to consider their social honour impaired.
>
> (Margalit 1996: 262)

Simply because it usually involves wearing visible technology – being marked – EM (even if one has consented to it) is potentially stigmatizing. Some American programmes have cultivated this: 'EM programmes that emphasise punishment', writes Meyer (2004: 116), 'tend to use bulkier devices that are harder to conceal and make calls to offenders, sometimes at annoying times.' Such approaches are not universal in America, however: STOP markets Bluetag, a one-piece GPS monitoring device, for example, as something that can be 'easily covered by a pants leg' (advert, *Journal of Offender Monitoring*, 19:1, 2006). In Europe there has been a marked preference for small anklets, as discreet as possible, but the issue of stigmatization is not wholly resolved by this – least of all by GPS tracking, which, until the use of one-piece units becomes the norm, requires the offender to carry a box as well as wear a tag, although these too are becoming smaller. The Penal Affairs Consortium (1997) in England considered tagging a 'uniquely stigmatising' community penalty for young people because they 'will have to attend school with a tag attached to their wrist or ankle, branding them as an offender'. Applying labelling theory, they warned that tagged youngsters 'will undoubtedly boast about their tag, and wear it as a badge of honour, adopting a "hard" image to live up to it' (Penal Affairs Consortium 1997). Undeniably, there are risks here: a young person would find it impossible to hide the fact of tagging in school sport or swimming sessions, and shame, resentment or pride – or indifference – are all possible reactions to this. Lucia Zedner has taken a clear position on the matter in respect of both juveniles and adults:

> The tag shames, but … it has none of the qualities of 'reintegrative shaming' promoted by Braithwaite and others. It labels the offender but provides no means for constructive dialogue with the offender's community, for the expression of remorse, or for the eventual reintegration back into civil society…. It may be imagined that this form of observation is ultimately dehumanising.
>
> (Zedner 2004: 221–222)

Although this captures something important, Zedner's criticism is overblown – she not only assumes that the tag *does* shame, but also that it shames *deeply enough* to be dehumanizing. As both von Hirsch (1990) and Whitfield (2001) have noted, there is nothing intrinsically intrusive about EM technology; some offenders may well regard it as *less intrusive* than frequent and uncongenial personal encounters with police or probation officers, and tolerate an element of shame for that reason. Shame is in any case harder to foster in offenders than is often supposed, and – what Zedner seemingly forgets – some degree of it is a prerequisite for the reintegration prescribed by Braithwaite (1989). Such shame as tagged offenders may feel about wearing the tag (as well as any frustration entailed by their exclusion) could be presented to (and accepted by) them as a legitimate 'penance' in Duff's (1999) sense of the term. However, this raises the question of *who* would encourage them to think in this way. Even in stand-alone EM schemes there are always monitoring officers (often working for private companies) who provide occasional human contact with tagged offenders (Jones 2003), but it is not their job as such to make the punishment 'meaningful'. There is indeed, as Zedner notes, nothing intrinsically dialogical about EM (and for Lindenberg (2003) that precludes any kind of rapprochement with social work practices and values), but at the same time there is nothing intrinsic to EM which prevents it from being embedded in, or linked to dialogical/communicative arrangements. In individual cases, EM may (like any punishment) prompt reflectiveness on the part of the offender; specifically, its constraints on movement may make as offender more amenable to, and available for, dialogue with families, neighbours and professionals than was previously the case. If it curtails offending, and if his visible presence in a community where he has caused trouble is reduced (by his compliance with a curfew or other exclusion), people may become less hostile to him. The progressive relaxation of exclusion (or confinement) may well foster reintegration back into society.

Stand-alone EM, however, backed up with the threat of imprisonment for non-compliance, leaves all of this to chance – it may or may not have a positive effect on an offender's behaviour. Given the milieu in which many socially disadvantaged offenders live, and the often dismal nature of their homes – and given all that is known about what actually does work to change offenders' behaviour – it seems unreasonable to expect EM alone to be constructive. The partnership – the entwining – of social work and tagging envisaged by Bishop and Whitfield is indeed the ideal, but for two reasons, not one. The use of EM to constrain offenders so that they can optimize the benefits of a rehabilitation programme is obviously important, but social work can also help the offender and his family cope with the onerousness entailed by EM itself, constructing and sustaining a narrative of legitimacy, mediating conflicts within the family and providing the kind of support that enables an offender to abide by the controls that have been placed upon him.

Conclusion

> How can a person with no knowledge of the future understand the meaning of the present? If we do not know what future the present is leading us toward, how can we say whether the present is good or bad, whether it deserves our concurrence, or our suspicion, or our hatred?
>
> (Kundera 2002: 143–144)

Knowing what we do about processes of commercial and technological innovation in criminal justice, we must take Kundera seriously, whether he is being ironic or not. In order to make rounded judgements about the ethical uses of EM technologies in the here and now, we need to discern (as best we can) where it could possibly and might probably lead. Many of the ethical arguments against EM, implicitly or explicitly, have in fact been of the thin-end-of-the-wedge variety, based less on anxiety about what the technology makes possible now (which may be acceptable), but what it might entail in the future (which may not be). This can lead to paralysing dystopian visions, which inhibit the development of useful technologies. But there are likely to be further politically and commercially induced technological developments in surveillance generally, and EM in particular, so the anxiety is not in itself ill-founded. The trouble with thin-end-of-the-wedge arguments in this context, however, is that they assume a 'sorcerer's apprentice'-like inability to restrain and channel technological development through ethical argument and political action; once unleashed, it can't be stopped.

Is there a way forward from this? Very broadly speaking, there are three discourses/traditions/social movements impinging on, indeed constituting, contemporary Western debate about crime: one emphasizing punitiveness, one managerialism (and risk management in particular) and the third rehabilitation, restoration and social justice (Rutherford 1993; Nellis 2005; Sparks 2006). While each can be depicted as an ideal type, in reality they overlap and interpenetrate, to different degrees and in different combinations, in different countries. Arguably, EM was conceptually rooted in rehabilitative thinking in the United States in the 1970s, but its subsequent expansion must be located within the managerialist movement, the aspiration to ever more meticulous regulation of offenders' lives and to the related advent of 'techno-corrections', the applications of technological innovations to crime control. The techno-correctional movement (which can have 'applications' in all three discourses) has been little analysed, and opinions inevitably vary as to the headway it is likely to make in the foreseeable future in respect of community supervision. Michael Tonry fears the worst:

> In the twenty-first century [the prison] may serve as a humane alternative to biochemical controls on behaviour and electronic controls on movement. The technological gap between drugs that allow deeply mentally disturbed people to function in the community and drugs that offset aggressive impulses or excitement is bridgeable. When that bridge is crossed, there will be those who regard the moral autonomy of offenders as less important than the prevention of harm to victims. Delayed delivery drugs and subcutaneous computer chips are available now. Some crime controllers will be happy to see them used. In the long term we cannot know how these debates will be resolved but for a time at least imprisonment may serve as a humane alternative to behavioural controls that may be much more deeply violative of human rights and liberties.
>
> (Tonry 2003: 4–5)

While this begs many questions about prison ever being a 'humane alternative' to community corrections, the logic of risk management in a culture of modernization does indeed point us in the direction of tight technical controls being applied to individuals in the community. Even if the presently used EM technologies come to be deemed failures – inadequate as forms of control and insufficient as punishment – the logic of efficient individualized control may well prompt the development and application of other, possibly more effective, technologies, which may well be biochemical rather than electronic, or mixtures of both. Leaving aside the vast expansion of telecare in the medical world, the development of remote alcohol monitoring – in particular GPS-enabled remote alcohol monitoring – already points, in a small way, towards a shift from *mere* spatial regulation towards behavioural-physiological regulation. Despite speculation in the early years of the twenty-first century (some serious, some ill-founded), sub-dermal implants using RFID chips are not a likely development in EM in the near future (Nellis 2011). Nonetheless, depending on the emerging technical affordances of new mobile communication systems, on wider political choices and penal priorities, on the continuing viability of humanistic forms of community supervision, and on levels of investment (both state and commercial) in research and development, this may change. The influence (and mutability) of 'the commercial–corrections complex' cannot be underestimated: private prison providers may network into pharmaceutical companies, as they networked themselves into telecommunications and EM companies.

The still-unfolding logic of risk management also points towards the further development of situational as opposed to dispositional measures. There is momentum behind the development of situational crime prevention which is entirely independent of the search for more controlling alternatives to prison, and the two are not mutually exclusive developments. But as surveillance and locatability technologies become a ubiquitous feature of contemporary urban – and increasingly rural – environments (via CCTV, speed cameras, RFID chips, biometric ID cards) – something akin to the surveillant assemblage depicted in the film *Minority Report* (d. Stephen Spielberg 2002) – it may be that there will be less need for the individualized surveillance packages currently represented by EM. The normalization of surveillance – and of personal locatability – in wider society may in fact diminish the apparent severity of EM as a penalty for offenders. If all citizens become electronically locatable via personal mobile communication devices, especially if they are GPS-enabled, the formal imposition of locatability on lawbreakers may not seem to be as punitive as it might once have seemed in a pre-electronic age.

Thus, for a range of reasons, EM is highly unlikely to displace imprisonment. Tonry's view that imprisonment might itself function as a sanctuary is not without precedent, and not without moral value, but in the present era it may possibly be wishful thinking. A society which implemented dehumanizing behavioural controls in the community would be highly unlikely to foster the existence of humane and constructive prisons. There are in fact EM technologies being used inside prisons, monitoring the location and movement of ankletagged prisoners within prison buildings in real time, undertaking online headcounts twice a day and guarding the perimeter. Such technologies save money on guards, and if the savings are then used constructively – say, to buy in more rehabilitative and educational staff – one may not find much to quarrel with. In extremis, however, such technologies may be the beginning of the automation of imprisonment – the creation of computerized penal environments in which the confined are regulated and tended only by machines, governed, perhaps, by an artificial intelligence. In some American supermaxes (super-maximum security prisons) staff are already expected to behave in an unemotional, robotic and uncaring way (Shalev 2009) – it is only a small step from this to real robots.

This, of course, is speculative – a way of taking Kundera seriously. There is no doubt that contemporary EM technologies, embedded in and expressive of the relentless onslaught of managerialism in criminal justice, could lead in the future to highly repressive forms of socio-technical crime control if nothing checks them (Landy 1996). Viscerally punitive sentiments can check them – and have already in the United States – because in the eyes of some the imposition of locatability is neither sufficiently punitive nor adequate as public protection, and brutal, low-cost penal dystopias can still be envisaged which are not high-tech at all. Humanistic ethics which place a high moral premium on reform and rehabilitation – on changing an offender for the better, respecting his rights and restoring him to citizenship, rather than merely controlling him – can also, in principle, shape and constrain the trajectory of EM's development – and in Europe have tended to do so. These penal ethics are precarious in late modernity, stronger in some countries than others, yet nowhere confidently ascendant – yet it is the affirmation and reaffirmation of such ethics which, history shows, sustains enlightenment and civility in penal policy, and which alone will ensure that EM is developed and used in ways which serve these ethics, rather than undermining and repudiating them.

References

Alchin, W. (1989) 'Chaperones, escorts, trackers and taggers', *The Friend*, 30 June.

Aungles, A. (1994) *The Prison and the Home: A Study of the Relationship Between Domesticity and Penality* (Sydney: Institute of Criminology).

Bettsworth, M. (1989) *Marking Time: A Prison Memoir* (London: MacMillan).

Bishop, N. (2003) 'Social work and electronic monitoring', in M. Mayer, R. Haverkamp and R. Lévy (eds) *Will Electronic Monitoring Have a Future in Europe?* (Freiburg: Max Planck Institute), pp. 227–236.

Braithwaite, J. (1989) *Crime, Shame and Re-integration* (Cambridge: Cambridge University Press).

Cohen, S. (1979) 'The punitive city: notes on the dispersal of social control', *Contemporary Crises*, 3, pp. 339–363.

Council of Europe (1994) *European Rules on Community Sanctions and Measures: Recommendation No, R (92) 16 and Explanatory Memorandum* (Strasbourg: Council of Europe).

Council of Europe (2002) *Improving the Implementation of the European Rules on Community Sanctions and Measures: Recommendation Rec (2000) 22 and Report* (Strasbourg: Council of Europe).

Dingwall, G. and Harding, C. (2002) 'Desert and the punitiveness of imprisonment', in C. Tata and N. Hutton (eds) *Sentencing and Society: International Perspectives* (Aldershot: Ashgate), pp. 308–328.

Doffing, D. (2009) 'Is there a future for RF in a GPS world?', *Journal of Offender Monitoring*, 22:1, pp. 12–15.

Duff, A. (1999) 'Punishment, communication and community', in M. Matravers (ed.) *Punishment and Political Theory* (Oxford: Hart), pp. 48–68.

Jones, A. (2003) 'The real tag team', unpublished Dissertation for BA Community Justice, University of Birmingham.

Kundera, M. (2002) *Ignorance* (London: Faber and Faber).

Lacey, N. (2003) 'Penal theory and penal practice: a communitarian approach', in S. McConville (ed.) *The Use of Punishment* (Cullompton: Willan), pp. 175–198.

Landy, M. (1996) *Scrapheap Services* (London: Ridinghouse Editions).

Lindenberg, M. (2003) 'From social work to control work: an observation on electronic monitoring of offenders and its impact on social work', in M. Mayer, R. Haverkamp and R. Lévy (eds) *Will Electronic Monitoring Have a Future in Europe?* (Freiburg: Max Planck Institute), pp. 119–202.

Margalit, A. (1996) *The Decent Society* (London: Harvard University Press).

Mathiesen, T. (1990) *Prison on Trial* (London: Sage).

Meyer, J.F. (2004) 'Home confinement with electronic monitoring', in G.A. Caputo, *Intermediate Sanctions in Corrections* (Denton, TX: University of North Texas Press), pp. 97–123.

Morris, N. (1974) *The Future of Imprisonment* (Chicago, IL: University of Chicago Press).

Nellis, M. (2005) 'Electronic monitoring, satellite tracking and the new punitiveness in England and Wales', in J. Pratt, D. Brown, S. Hallsworth, M. Brown and W. Morrison (eds) *The New Punitiveness: Trends, Theories, Perspectives* (Cullompton: Willan), pp. 167–188.

Nellis, M. (2006) 'The limitations of electronic monitoring: the tagging of Peter Williams', *Prison Service Journal*, 164, pp. 3–12.

Nellis, M. (2010a) 'Tom Stacey: founder of electronic monitoring in the UK', *Journal of Offender Monitoring*, 22:1, pp. 16–26.

Nellis, M. (2010b) 'Eternal Vigilance Inc: the satellite tracking of offenders in real-time', *Journal of Technology and Human Services*, 28, pp. 23–43.

Nellis, M. (2011) 'Implant technology and the electronic monitoring of offenders: old and new questions about compliance, control and legitimacy', in A. Crawford and A. Hucklesby (eds) *Legitimacy and Compliance in Criminal Justice* (Cullompton: Willan) (forthcoming).

Padgett, K.G., Bales, W.D. and Blomberg, T.G. (2006) 'Under surveillance: an empirical test of the effectiveness and consequences of electronic monitoring', *Criminology and Public Policy*, 5:1, pp. 61–91.

Penal Affairs Committee (1988) 'Electronic tagging: a briefing paper', *Quaker Social Responsibility and Education Journal*, 10:3, pp. 13–19.

Penal Affairs Consortium (1997) *The Electronic Monitoring of Offenders* (London: Penal Affairs Consortium).

Rengert, G.F. (1989) 'Behavioural geography and criminal behaviour', in D.J. Evans and D.T. Herbert (eds) *The Geography of Crime* (London: Routledge), pp. 161–175.

Rengert, G.F. (2004) 'The journey to crime' in G. Bruinsma, H. Elffers and J. de Jeiser J (eds) *Punishment, Places and Perpetrators: Developments in Criminology and Criminal Justice Research* (Cullompton: Willan), pp. 169–181.

Rex, S. (2005) *Reforming Community Penalties* (Cullompton: Willan).

Roberts, J.V. (2004) *The Virtual Prison: Community Custody and the Evolution of Imprisonment* (Cambridge: Cambridge University Press).

Rutherford, A. (1993) *Criminal Justice and the Pursuit of Decency* (Oxford: Oxford University Press).

Saunders, P. (1989) 'The meaning of "home" in contemporary English culture', *Housing Studies*, 4:3, pp. 177–192.

Shalev, S. (2009) *Supermax: Controlling Risk Through Solitary Confinement* (Cullompton: Willan).

Sim, J. (2009) *Prison and Punishment* (London: Sage).

Sparks, R. (2006) 'Anxiety, legitimacy and the shape of criminology'. Inaugural lecture, University of Edinburgh, 30 May.

Tonry, M. (1994) 'Proportionality, parsimony and the interchangeability of punishments', in A. Duff and D. Garland (eds) *A Reader on Punishment* (Oxford: Oxford University Press), pp. 112–160.

Tonry, M. (2003) (ed.) *The Future of Imprisonment* (Oxford: Oxford University Press).

von Hirsch, A. (1990) 'The ethics of community-based sanctions', *Crime and Delinquency*, 36:1, pp. 162–173.

von Hirsch, A. and Shearing, C. (2000) 'Exclusion from public space', in A. von-Hirsh, D. Garland and A. Wakefield (eds) *Ethical and Social Perspectives on Situational Crime Prevention* (Oxford: Hart Publishing), pp. 77–96.

Waldo, J. (2010) 'Electronic monitoring program and the offender funded option'. White Paper, BI Incorporated.

Walker, N. (1997) *Why Punish?* (Oxford: University Press).

Ward, T. (2009) 'Dignity and human rights in correctional practice', *European Journal of Probation*, 1:2, pp. 110–123. Online. Available at: www.ejprobation.ro.

Whitfield, D. (2001) *The Magic Bracelet: Technology and Offender Supervision* (Winchester: Waterside Publications).

Whitfield, D. (2005) 'Electronic monitoring', in T. Bateman and J. Pitts (eds) *The RHP Companion to Youth Justice* (Lyme Regis: Russel House Press), pp. 125–129.

Zedner, L. (2004) *Criminal Justice* (Oxford: Oxford University Press).

11 Commercial crime control and the development of electronically monitored punishment

A global perspective

Craig Paterson

Introduction

Electronically monitored (EM) punishment developed as a response to the problem of prison overcrowding as well as the enhanced focus placed upon re-introducing market values to the criminal justice sector and incorporating advances in information and communication technological (ICT) infrastructures to establish a new mode of crime control. The preference for market delivery of previously 'public' goods and services, initially described as 'privatization', became a feature of governmental projects in the (mainly) English-speaking countries that favoured neoliberal political and economic reforms during the 1980s and 1990s and enabled EM entrepreneurs in the United States, Canada, the UK, Australia and New Zealand to experiment with this new criminal justice tool. Thus, the evolution of EM as a penal innovation is best understood as an adjunct to broader developments in the commercial crime control market that laid its roots in the United States after the Second World War. This market, grounded in private security, benefited from growth spurts provided by the end of the Cold War, the liberalization of economic markets and rising concern about uncontrolled migration, global crime and international terrorism, to develop into a global market in commercial crime control and techno-corrections.

In many ways, the contours of the EM industry mirror those of the private prison industry that re-emerged out of the United States in the 1980s and spread to Australia and the UK during the 1990s before undergoing additional growth in Western Europe over the last decade. Similarities in market growth should not be over-emphasized though. EM was embraced in countries such as Canada and New Zealand that had rejected prison privatization. Because of this, developments in EM should be understood to have links with broader neoliberal processes of privatization while also being tied to the demand for enhanced surveillance capacity from late-modern nation states. This developmental process is incomplete. The establishment of second-generation EM technologies such as satellite tracking (or location monitoring as it is sometimes known) and biometrics is indicative of a developing market. Further, the commercial crime control industry, having laid its roots in countries that favoured privatization, has identified developing countries as future markets (Nathan 2003). This is evident in the growth in interest in EM from the post-Soviet countries (Kruusement 2007). Brazil has recently legislated for criminal justice reform in this area, while Argentina and Mexico already have established EM programmes. Criminal justice market reforms are also being promoted across Africa although, as yet, no country has adopted EM.

This chapter will provide an outline of the global EM market and identify the sources of its growth. A 2004 paper by Nossal and Wood commented on the 'raggedness' of prison privatization across five Western countries which had experienced similar neoliberal social and economic restructuring. This chapter uses a similar template to emphasize common themes in the development of EM across the globe while simultaneously acknowledging the raggedness of policy development at the local level. The chapter uses specific examples, drawn from the United States, Canada and England and Wales to illustrate the overall argument and augments the global focus through additional commentary from other nations. The chapter also looks at the role of the commercial sector as service providers of EM and reviews the history of EM alongside a debate about the nature of security in relation to the struggle for sovereign control over populations and territory. The chapter then moves on to focus on the way in which private security firms have become constituent parts of a new commercial–public hybrid mode of sub-contracted sovereign governance through which the state generates the market space for commercial organizations to enter the crime control system. The chapter subsequently outlines how multinational corporations have come to dominate the commercial markets in incarceration and techno-corrections. This raises questions about the role of commercial crime control in the development of public policy.

A brief history of EM

The market in EM punishment is both proliferating and expanding, thus providing analysts with a future vision of social regulation and control as seen through the eyes of commercial organizations, politicians and, more broadly, crime control systems. Many of the business areas where EM and commercial criminal justice now flourish are based upon original developments in the United States (Newburn 2002) that have inspired the development of new commercial crime control markets across the globe. Leaving aside the pioneering markets mentioned in the introduction, EM is now used in countries as geographically dispersed as Taiwan, Singapore, Hong Kong, South Africa, Sweden, Denmark, Norway, Finland, Russia, Poland, Germany, France, Belgium, the Netherlands, Portugal, Italy, Argentina, Mexico, Israel and Korea. Commercial crime control is an international business and EM, alongside other techno-corrections, has become a component of the international corrections–commercial complex identified by Lilly and Knepper (1992) two decades ago. The processes of globalization have prompted a period of reconstruction within many late-modern nation states since the 1980s and encouraged governments to shed peripheral functions to the commercial, voluntary and statutory sectors. These processes have provided added impetus to already substantial growth in the private security industry and aided the rise of multinational crime control conglomerates such as Corrections Corporation of America (CCA), Serco, Securitas, Sodexho, Wackenhut (now GEO), and Group 4 Securicor (G4S).

The last decade has seen the private security industry go through a multitude of mergers and acquisitions that has reduced competition in the marketplace and consolidated the dominant position of a select few multinationals in the global market. This is notable in the EM market, which is dominated by G4S and Serco in Europe and Australasia, while a more complex market in North America sees Serco provide EM equipment in Canada and G4S compete with a multitude of domestic manufacturers and service providers for contracts in the United States. These two organizations will be placed at the centre of a discussion about the role of commercial organizations in the development of criminal justice policy that takes place later in this chapter.

While technology manufacturers such as Elmotech, ProTech Monitoring and BI Incorporated have a global presence in the EM market, it is the intention here to outline the networks of governance that facilitated growth and competition in the global EM market for private security companies, acting as EM service providers and/or technology manufacturers, and, ultimately, consolidated the position of a select few multinationals as preferred bidders for EM contracts. These were the same commercial organizations that had been identified as constituent parts of the corrections–commercial complex that emerged out of the United States at the end of the Cold War and provided the foundations for the crime control industry that had already been established in the incarceration market by the 1990s (Christie 2000).

The growth of the private security industry in the period after the Second World War and within criminal justice since the beginning of the 1980s arose as the result of rising demand for security alongside the growing importance placed upon economic rationalities of crime control (Feeley 2002). The end of the Cold War in 1989 provided a further boost to the industry as private security companies were accompanied by defence contractors keen to maintain profit margins in the absence of a clearly defined threat against the Western world, and together they forged a new market in techno-corrections. The reassertion of the role of the market within criminal justice is representative of broad changes in societies that have moved from an inclusive focus upon welfarism towards strategies of social management associated with the neoliberal ethos of combining market competition, privatized institutions and sub-contracted, at-a-distance forms of social control. Within this context a growing emphasis is placed upon reducing the costs of crime control and encouraging other agencies that operate at a distance from central government to take a more direct role in the provision of security.

All EM programmes have an element of private sector interest, most commonly in the development and implementation of technology, yet England and Wales is the only jurisdiction to have sub-contracted all service provision to the private sector. Programme development is by no means uniform, with most other countries operating EM-based curfew orders through the public sector with varying degrees of commercial influence. Therefore, the development of EM should be viewed as a product of global forces that emphasize neoliberal rationales which are translated within each nation state's social, political and economic context. Further understanding of this context can be provided through a brief review of the historical development of EM in three of the pioneering markets: the United States, Canada, and England and Wales.

The United States

The first coordinated, Western house-arrest programme began in the United States in 1971 with the organized detention of juvenile offenders in St. Louis (Whitfield 1997: 31) followed by a plethora of schemes that appeared under the initial slogan of 'Community Control'. Unlike the first house-arrest programmes, EM developed in a commercial environment as a result of the perceived need for continuing technological innovation and, because of this, its development needs to be analysed alongside that of private prisons. The first modern private prison appeared in the United States in 1975 when the RCA Service Company set up the Weaversville unit in Pennsylvania for juvenile offenders, yet it was not until the 1980s that criminal justice privatization and EM became commonplace. The prison crisis of the 1980s led to an increase in the use of private prison facilities, which grew from housing 2,500 inmates in 1984 to containing 90,000 inmates in 1996 (Lotke 1996: 2); by 2002 private companies ran 153 facilities with an operational capacity of almost 120,000 (Tabarrok 2003: 77). Similarly, EM developed rapidly from its initial introduction in 1984 to providing around 75,000 EM units on 1,500 different tagging programmes by January 1998 (DeMichele and Payne 2009). Since the 1990s growth in first-generation EM technologies in the United States has slowed, but developments in second-generation technologies has ensured that market growth has been sustained. In 1997, Advanced Business Sciences and ProTech Monitoring introduced the first GPS systems to law enforcement agencies in Florida; this was followed by the innovative CrimeTrax software in 1998, which aimed to map offender locations against crime events reported to the police (Frost 2002). It is estimated that there were nearly 200,000 radio frequency (RF) and GPS units in use each day in the United States during 2009 (DeMichele and Payne 2009).

Canada

Despite having had minimal involvement in prison privatization, Canada became the first country outside of the United States to experiment with EM punishment, with the introduction of a pilot programme in British Columbia in 1987. Like other EM pioneers, Canada's involvement was driven by economic issues, not least the search for cheaper alternatives to rapidly rising incarceration rates (Bonta *et al.* 1999). The use of EM spread to other provinces. EM officers were seconded from correctional services and courts, which left the commercial organizations functioning solely as technology providers. While developments in EM in Canada have been much slower than the United States, there seems to be a consensus in the North American literature that the ongoing intensification of surveillance of offenders will eventually lead to a more efficient and effective mode of crime control (Renzema and Mayo-Wilson 2005; Padgett *et al.* 2006; Bottas 2007). This shift in thinking is evident in the academic and practitioner literature, which has moved on from legal and ethical debates to concerns about economies of scale (JHSA 2006; Bottas 2007), offender targeting and the incremental value of GPS technology when compared with first-generation EM technologies (Padgett *et al.* 2006). This runs contrary to developments in Europe, where the later development of the EM marketplace was, in part, a product of concerns about the role of new surveillance technologies in criminal justice, the potential for net-widening and the role of criminal justice privatization (Haverkamp *et al.* 2004: 42). Furthermore, a Canadian overview of the literature states that research on EM in Europe has generally been positive (Bottas 2007: 21) when broader reading provides much more mixed conclusions (Haverkamp *et al.* 2004). This is particularly evident in the literature from England and Wales (Mair 2005).

England and Wales

In England and Wales, the Offender's Tag Association, an organization with intimate connections to the Conservative Party, has been advocating the use of EM since 1982. In the mid-1980s the idea was picked up by John Patten MP, an ambitious junior minister in pursuit of an eye-catching policy to make his name; Patten's political drive led to the introduction of EM for the first time outside of North America, in the unsuccessful trials with bailees in 1989. Despite the failure of the original trials, Patten continued to advocate the use of EM as an effective alternative to imprisonment operated through the private sector, and in the mid-1990s new trials began. The evidence on the efficacy of EM-based curfew orders from the second set of trials was at best inconclusive (Mair and Mortimer 1996; Mortimer and May 1997) but, again, this only slowed development, and the Labour Party's election success in 1997 brought renewed growth to the EM industry at a time when stagnation seemed inevitable. From 1999 onwards, the number of offenders subject to EM-based restrictions grew exponentially as successive home secretaries encouraged its use and technological developments introduced biometric systems and satellite tracking. Despite this, there remained no clear evidence-base that identified what EM actually achieved (Mair 2005). Faced with this lack of supportive evidence from the three countries that pioneered the use of EM, it becomes essential to identify additional factors that drove growth in the EM market.

Commercial corrections and sub-contracted modes of governance

EM-based programmes have been born out of the long tradition of house arrest (Ball *et al.* 1988), an incapacitative measure that historically is linked more closely to political initiatives, and an increased focus upon the management (rather than the rehabilitation or reformation) of individuals and groups. From this perspective criminal justice systems concentrate upon the identification of risks, targeting offenders as aggregates rather than individuals, before assessing the means of their control and management, utilizing the most cost-effective measures (Feeley and Simon 1992). This approach encourages a process whereby the state sub-contracts or devolves its sovereign responsibilities to commercial organizations and emphasizes the role of the state as an auspice (Bayley and Shearing 2001) or commissioner (Fisher 2006) of governance rather than as a direct service provider. Thus, the provision of security is no longer seen principally as the function of the sovereign nation state and traditional large public sector institutions no longer maintain a privileged position in providing security; they are understood simply as one node of security among others in the commercial, voluntary and statutory sectors (Johnston and Shearing 2003).

Public sector reforms extend beyond the field of criminal justice and into the arenas of health, education and defence and are representative of global changes enacted through neoliberal political processes that encourage a process of sub-contracting sovereign responsibilities to the commercial, voluntary and statutory sectors. Therefore, similar patterns of growth in EM are evident in nation states such as the United States, Canada and the UK that had undertaken similar neo-liberal economic reforms alongside tough law and order policies and rising incarceration rates. The law and order politics of the 1980s, inspired by right-wing criminologists such as James Q. Wilson and Charles Murray, revived concern with the Victorian residuum, or underclass, and this influenced policy developments in the United States and, later, Canada and the UK. Right-wing think-tanks such as the Adam Smith Institute marketed criminal justice privatization in the UK as a solution to the problem of the urban poor, citing evidence provided by the Corrections Corporation of America (Coyle *et al.* 2003; Mattera *et al.* 2003) to advance the case for privatization.

This helps explain the arrival of EM in England and Wales in 1989 alongside a dearth of supportive research evidence but with key cheerleaders from the worlds of commerce and politics (Mair 2005; Paterson 2007). England and Wales, alongside early programmes in Sweden and the Netherlands, acted as a testing ground for Europe before EM technologies gradually established themselves across the continent from 2000 onwards. European countries have avoided the British model of EM policy implementation and its wholesale sub-contracting of service delivery to the private sector. Instead, programme delivery involves either a mixed commercial–public model where private companies provide and install equipment and a correctional agency provides supervision or, alternatively, a correctional agency takes sole responsibility. In Sweden the Probation Service deliver EM programmes, while in Italy this is the police's responsibility, and in Catalonia the Prison Service undertake this role (Haverkamp *et al.* 2004). The multitude of EM models and programmes that exist across the globe emphasize the raggedness of policy development at the local level, yet global policy convergence is evident from the presence of the multinational crime control conglomerates that were introduced earlier.

The global presence of commercial organizations in EM punishment makes them key objects of study, as do their links with the political establishment in late-modern states that are increasingly concerned with the problem of crime and disorder. In particular, the role of political and commercial figures in enacting policy reform requires further investigation. In the United States, rapid growth in the private security industry in the 1950s was driven by key figures that had transferred from the public sector to the private sector, such as former FBI agent George Wackenhut, and assisted the consolidation of the new industry. Similarly, prison privatization in the United States was inspired by Attorney General Meese's immigration detention experiment (Parenti 2003). Meese, now a member of a pro-privatization think-tank, provided CCA with their first detention centre contract. At the time, CCA's board comprised a former chairman of the Tennessee Republican Party, a former commissioner of the Virginia and Arkansas Departments of Corrections and a former director of the Federal Bureau of Prisons (Parenti 2003).

The first EM pilots in England and Wales were promoted by John Patten, while second-generation EM technologies were championed by the home secretary, David Blunkett. Having promoted the use of satellite tracking through his 'Prison Without Bars' slogan, Blunkett left his post to take up a job with Entrust, one of the many technology firms whose products he had promoted while in power. Similarly, John Reid was appointed group consultant for G4S in December 2008 after leaving his position as home secretary in June 2007. Having also run the Ministry of Defence until 2006, Reid courted public anger in the UK when, three months after starting his new position, G4S won a four-year contract to supply private security guards to around 200 Ministry of Defence sites across Britain (Hickley 2009).

Viewed through this lens, the birth and development of EM must be understood as the political construction of space for commercial organizations to enter the jurisdiction of traditional criminal justice agencies (Paterson 2009). In England and Wales resistance from the Probation Service to the introduction of EM allowed central government to invite commercial organizations into the jurisdiction of the Probation Service. This active market construction was also evident in the Criminal Justice and Court Services Act 2000, in which legislation for the satellite tracking of offenders in England and Wales was introduced in advance of the EM technology being ready for the programme (Nellis 2008). Thus, the development of EM cannot be understood solely as either governmentally inspired or as the product of market forces. Instead, it is important to recognize the political conflict experienced throughout its introduction and development as a contest over who delivers and administers justice. This helps to explain the wide range of EM-based programmes that exist internationally as a product of the ragged and uneven pattern of social and economic developments across the globe. While the global picture focuses on neoliberal economics and the expanding role of commercial organizations in criminal justice, a focus upon the contested struggle for sovereignty at the local level provides a more complex picture of rival agencies involved in shifting alliances with the state and the modes of governance this produces (Stenson 2005). Although the state generates the market space for commercial organizations to enter the crime control system as service providers, it also struggles to retain control over policy and strategies through short-term, formal contracts. This is why the state can be seen to act as the private security industry's pimp as much as its regulator (Zedner 2006) in creating commercial–public hybrid agencies whose positions in the market of crime control are legitimized and consolidated through national contracts and legislation while remaining only loosely regulated at the local level.

Constructing the market in crime control

Analysis of the commercial crime control market helps explain patterns of policy convergence, as embodied by the presence of global corporations in countries that have embraced criminal justice privatization, alongside a divergence of EM programmes at the local level. Most obviously, a pattern of initial policy exportation from the United States to other English-speaking countries can be identified, yet this is not translated into the existence of similar EM programmes. While New Right governments may embrace the ideology of privatization, this by no means guarantees that local power structures will follow suit. In England and Wales tight regulatory structures eventually scared off the American companies that originally trumpeted privatization in the 1980s and 1990s (Nossal and Wood 2004). CCA were key players in the initial lobbying of the UK government, yet their British franchise, UK Detention Services, had limited success in procuring services. Similarly, GEO Group played a significant part in the promotion of prison privatization, and subsequently within the construction of the EM industry, but ultimately all but withdrew from the European market.

The complexity of the policy process helps to explain the reticence of many European countries to embrace wholesale privatization of criminal justice services. Instead, many European nations have encouraged the role of commercial organizations as providers of innovative technology while maintaining control over service delivery. EM spread from the UK into Sweden in 1994 and the Netherlands in 1995, with both countries implementing EM through established criminal justice sectors. Across Europe, commercial organizations operate mainly as technology providers for programmes that monitor offenders in the community, yet the same commercial organizations retain their position as preferred bidders for state contracts. G4S and Serco are the sole providers across the three jurisdictions (England and Wales, Scotland and Northern Ireland) in the UK that run EM programmes and G4S have additional contracts in the Isle of Man and Jersey. The UK is the key European market for the commercial organizations. In 2005 England and Wales provided 82 per cent of European use of EM and a daily caseload of over 18,000 offenders (Wennerberg and Pinto 2009). Serco have an additional contract in Italy while G4S have contracts in the Netherlands, France and Austria. G4S's global reach extends to Australia and New Zealand and, in total, the organization electronically monitors over 40,000 subjects everyday (G4S 2010).

At the global level, the expansion of the commercial industry in criminal justice and other previously publicly provided services has been assisted by international trade agreements such as the General Agreement on Trade in Services (GATS) that came into operation in 1994, plus the influence of the World Trade Organization (WTO). GATS provides international corporations with a greater amount of freedom to open up markets, particularly in the public sector, while placing a set of legal limits on what governments can do to restrict private sector growth within a variety of industries. These rules encourage the liberalization of global trade by insisting that international corporations are entitled to the same subsidies and benefits as domestic businesses and by limiting other protectionist measures, such as tariffs. Under the GATS rules, public sector industries such as health, education and criminal justice are opened up to international competition through the creation of public–private partnerships (PPP), hence the presence of multinational corporations with global crime control interests in the EM market.

In 1989 it was Chubb and Marconi, two international defence contractors, who became involved in the EM bail trials in England as part of their pursuit of new markets. At the same time, new EM technology emerged out of countries such as the United States and Israel, where there was a long tradition of internal and external surveillance plus extensive military investment. Products that had initially been designed for military purposes were adapted for the new market in crime control, as we have seen with the recent development of the satellite tracking of offenders, which utilizes a combination of Global Positioning Satellite (GPS) and Global System for Mobile Communications (GSM) technologies.

In order to exploit potential new markets in commercial crime control the US government played an increasingly active role in lobbying foreign countries on behalf of American defence and private security contractors during the 1980s and 1990s (Lilly and Deflem 1996). The impact of this lobbying was felt in England and Wales, where the Prison Reform Trust obtained documents detailing private prison contracts between the government and international corporations such as the Corrections Corporation of America and Wackenhut, including an option to overcrowd prisons by almost 50 per cent (Lilly and Deflem 1996). Further evidence of the lobbying power of international corporations became evident at a privatization conference in the Netherlands when the director of UK Detention Services acknowledged, 'It took us two or three years to finally convince the government that this [privatization] was the way forward.... UK Detention Services was very much involved in bringing forward the arguments in favour of the case' (Hopkins 1993: 2, quoted in Beyens and Snacken 1996: 245).

Ultimately, this lobbying meant that the decrease in demand for military hardware at the end of the Cold War was partially offset by the development of new commercial markets in incarceration in the mid-1980s, in EM and other techno-corrections during the 1990s, and satellite tracking since 2000. A range of EM products are now available to private contractors, often with cost rather than technological development holding back the introduction of increasingly sophisticated systems. The global commercial drive behind expanding markets in surveillance and private security, aided by the presence of law and order lobbies, presents a clear challenge to the integrity of criminal justice systems. While the growth of first-generation EM in the United States has slowed since the latter part of the 1990s, this shortfall has been made up by growth in GPS location monitoring. Similarly, England and Wales have experienced a proliferation of EM-based programmes since Labour's 1997 election victory, although, after a short pilot programme, it was decided not to embrace satellite tracking technology. The Netherlands, Sweden and France have also piloted satellite tracking technology, but it is thought that substantial European growth in this area will be tied in with the launch of Galileo, Europe's system of satellites, when it is launched in 2014 (Nellis 2008). Hence, it is evident that market saturation is swiftly followed by penal innovation to sustain growth. This can be seen both in the role of political and commercial networks in policy transfer from the United States and also in the continuing technological innovations that ensure that the EM marketplace remains vibrant.

Politics, commerce and EM

The global embrace of techno-managerial strategies is evident across crime control systems through growth in technologies such as biometrics, CCTV and geographical information systems (GIS) that have developed in commercial environments that market the benefits of asocial technologies in monitoring and managing unruly and disruptive behaviour. This has proved problematic for surveillance technologies such as EM, CCTV and biometrics, whose development has often been driven by political and ideological agendas rather than evidence-based research (Groombridge 2008; Meek 2002; Muller 2005). Lilly's work in the United States has pointed towards the role of 'power politics instead of rational appraisal of evidence' (Lilly 2006: 93) in the EM industry. Canada has experienced extensive political and commercial lobbying for criminal justice privatization since the 1980s that assisted in the establishment of EM programmes and private prisons (Coyle et al. 2003: 14). The impact of lobbying in the United States and Canada is evident in both the lack of systematic evaluations of EM (Bonta et al. 1999; Renzema and Mayo-Wilson 2005) and the citation of commercially produced data as 'evidence' to support EM-based policies (Nathan 2003).

George Mair's research (2005) on the extent to which EM 'works' in England and Wales highlights the 'pick and mix' attitude taken by ministers and other Home Office officials with regard to the findings in official research. Good news is embraced and bad news is quietly ignored (Hope 2006). In 2003 a Home Office-commissioned evaluation on EM was aborted due to it not being cost-effective, although it eventually became apparent that the Home Office did not like the results that were coming out of the study (Mair 2005: 271). Similarly, in 2002, SNP politician John Swinney accused the Scottish Executive of providing evidence for increased privatization in the Scottish corrections system by subsidising Serco's profits at Kilmarnock prison. Nearly three-quarters of a million pounds of public money had been given to Serco in order to make the contracting-out process look more economically attractive to potential future bidders (Nathan 2002). As criminologists have warned (Loader 2000; Zedner 2006), contractually based, sub-contracted sovereign governance has developed in a way that *enables* the development of new markets in crime control as well as growth in systems of social control. This raises concerns about the future of crime control in an age of penal populism and mass incarceration. Moreover, recent EM policy developments in immigration, work and pensions and telecare for the elderly potentially provide the most significant developments yet in providing a clear extension of the remit of commercial influence beyond the crime control system.

Away from the official discourses of governmental savoir there is a dearth of information concerning the practices used by sub-contracted agencies in implementing governmental policy, as well as the means by which this is recorded and audited. This was finally acknowledged by the Audit Commission report on EM in England and Wales in January 2006. The evidence-base analysed by the Audit Commission on behalf of the Home Office is provided by the commercial contractors on an intermittent basis without any independent inspection. It is this same evidence-base that identifies how much the commercial contractors pay back to the Home Office in fines for not fulfilling obligations in their contract. The Audit Commission's report stated that future evaluations would require real-time access to the contractor's EM databases, as well as whole-case analysis in order to improve the 'rigour' with which the contractors were assessed. This statement amounted to a declaration of mistrust of the information being provided by the contractors and an acknowledgement that the regulatory systems used by the Home Office were not providing sufficient oversight.

Instead, a stream of audit-oriented evaluations has focused upon completion rates and levels of recidivism (Mair 2005). The Audit Commission's acknowledgement that the commercial contractors received insufficient monitoring from the Home Office presents an interesting irony when set against the Orwellian backdrop of EM and raises questions about the absence of any independent oversight of the EM industry, especially when one considers the clandestine nature of the commercial sector and the need for transparency and accountability in criminal justice. The importance of an independent regulator was further highlighted two months after the Audit Commission's report when Serco were questioned by the Committee of Public Accounts about the failure to report breaches on time. When questioned about the failure to report breaches, the boss of Serco's Home Affairs division, Tom Riall, admitted that they 'were not subject to performance deductions under the old contract for failures to report breaches on time' (House of Commons Committee of Public Accounts 2006). In other words, there were insufficient incentives to comply with the contract due to the absence of financial penalties.

Alongside Serco, the extensive commercial market in justice and security in England and Wales is dominated by two other significant players: G4S and

Sodexho (Kalyx). Despite the political emphasis being placed upon market-led 'contestability', the number of competitors in the field of commercial crime control has narrowed, leaving the big three to fight over the Home Office contracts. With EM, this has been reduced to a duopoly, with Serco and G4S as the only service providers. This raises significant questions about the quality of service provision in a market where competition has historically been defined by price rather than quality of service (Zedner 2006: 271).

There have been similar incidents in the United States, where attempts to expand the domestic market in EM have, at times, proved problematic, with initial growth in EM being accompanied by a multitude of scandals related to fraud, bribery and conflicts of interest (Lilly 1990). The confluence of political and commercial interests in commercial corrections makes the construction of clear and effective regulatory structures essential to ensure that the public interest is defended. Concerns about the duopoly of Serco and G4S in England and Wales are placed in context by the case of former Florida governor Bob Martinez. Martinez used his political position to promote the use of EM and satellite tracking technology in order to influence their adoption in Florida. ProTech Monitoring were the sole bidders for the first contract in 1997 and the recommended choice of the Florida Department of Corrections. Martinez, and his son Alan, were both partners in the Florida-based company, ProTech (Lilly 2006).

If criminal justice procurement is determined solely by cost, or opaque political–commercial networks, then the market in EM and other techno-corrections will become increasingly uncompetitive. This presents considerable concerns for public safety and the future effectiveness of commercial crime control. The cost savings produced by the re-tendering of the EM contracts in England and Wales in 2004, and in Scotland in 2005, were generated, in part, through a decrease in the levels of human support for offenders (Paterson 2007). This took place despite there being international evidence for increasing the amount of human support for EM-based sanctions in order to increase their effectiveness (Roberts 2004), and demonstrates the importance of cost in determining successful contract bids ahead of the quality of service provided. Within this performance-focused context, welfare practices are viewed as 'beyond the contract' (Cooper 2007) and as costs that should be minimized. This raises questions about whether EM-based programmes represent anything beyond the extension of commercial forms of social control into domestic spaces.

Evidence of success in commercial crime control in the United States has often been produced by industry-funded bodies and pro-privatization think-tanks. For example, the Association of Private Correctional & Treatment Organizations (APCTO) lobbies on behalf of private prisons and has been attempting 'to identify universities that have strong criminal justice programs ... about the prospects of conducting further research in the corrections and treatment fields' (APCTO 2003). The impact of these initiatives and their use of evidence to further global policy transfer has been felt both in Canada, where research produced and provided by vendors was used to support the introduction of policies (Coyle *et al.* 2003), and the UK, where evidence provided by CCA was used to promote the initial use of private prisons as well as the expansion of commercial criminal justice in both EM and community corrections (Carter 2001; Nathan 2003). More recently, G4S funded research at Leeds University that promoted the role of EM-based curfew orders as a community sentence (Hucklesby 2008).

Ultimately, the growth of EM in the United States, Canada and England and Wales, and subsequently across the globe, has taken place despite a lack of conclusive evidence that it 'works' in protecting the public and reducing re-offending (Bonta *et al.* 1999; Mair 2005; Lilly 2006; Renzema and Mayo-Wilson 2005). More recent evidence, outlined in this chapter, has shown that new and emerging questions about the future role of the private sector within the criminal justice system are yet to be answered. Thus far, consultation and 'evidence' have been used to legitimize rather than inform policy, which helps to explain the diverse use of EM technologies across jurisdictions. While this chapter has analysed the proliferation of EM in Western countries, G4S, Serco and Sodexho have subsequently targeted their expansionary endeavours at the developing world, most notably South America and Africa.

The lack of open, public debate surrounding the introduction, expansion and consolidation of the EM industry, and more generally commercial crime control, has been evident across the globe (Mair 2005; Lilly 2006). Lilly's early work on the corrections–commercial complex provided a warning about the clandestine role of commercial organizations in the development of public policy, highlighting concerns in the United States about the 'distinct overlap between the interests of for-profit companies, professional organisations and the interests of Federal agencies that is maintained by the flow of influence and personnel' (Lilly and Knepper 1992: 175). Lilly's later work (2006) continues with this analysis of the links between commerce, corrections and politics, yet, viewed from a global perspective, the role of commerce in crime control still remains a relatively arid area of study (Nellis 2003). This chapter has attempted to address some of these issues by: analysing the ragged nature of EM policy development across the globe and the prominent role of commercial crime control; highlighting the inter-changeable links between commercial and political figures throughout the policy development process; and identifying subsequent problems related to transparency and accountability.

Growth in EM has been driven by a fascination with the potential of new technologies to deliver managerialist solutions to complex social problems and the broader processes of neoliberal globalization that have developed the markets in incarceration and social control. The commercial market in crime control looks set to continue to expand and to present new opportunities for organizations linked into the outsourced justice sector to benefit from the imposition of market discipline into (commercial) criminal justice. The future mixed economy of justice has been promoted by the desire to slim down the state's functions and sub-contract its sovereign responsibilities. It is ideologically, politically and economically driven, often with little concern for the wider impact upon the crime control system and the public. As Cohen (1985) once noted, failure does not halt the spread of the net of social control; instead it perpetuates a search for new and more innovative forms of intervention.

Conclusion

The commercial markets in incarceration and social control have been driven by the dual forces of neoliberal globalization and insecurity that dominate the Western world in the twenty-first century. The market ideals of enhanced competition and service have consolidated the positions of multinational commercial organizations within the criminal justice system while costs have increased through a widening of the net of social control. By sub-contracting service delivery to the commercial sector, central government is able to expand the crime control system, and thus meet the political demand for enhancing security, while also deviating around fiscal restraints. This pluralization of governance presents new problems with regard to transparency and identifying lines of accountability within a fluid structure where relations between different agencies are perpetually negotiated and are part of an ongoing political contest.

This contest over the delivery of new forms of crime control is put into its historical context by Malcolm Feeley in his work on the legacies of privatization. Feeley (2002) highlights the important role played by private entrepreneurs in the development of new and expanded forms of social control, most clearly through the development of transportation and the prison in the eighteenth and nineteenth centuries, which were ultimately brought under state control. EM, and other forms of commercial surveillance, potentially provide a continuation of this historical trend. Recent policy developments in the United States present a potential future vision of social control beyond the prison and through surveillance. EM technologies are now being used to monitor the whereabouts of sex offenders who have completed their sentences. This presents a further extension to the remit of the industry in techno-corrections. The monitoring of offenders after the completion of their sentence represents a further proliferation in the use of EM-based programmes and a widening of the social control system through the lifelong surveillance of offenders. We will have to wait and see what legacy this leaves for future generations.

References

APCTO (Association of Private Correctional and Treatment Organizations) (2003) 'Partners in public service'. Online. Available at: www.apcto.org/e-news (accessed 10 March 2010).

Ball, R., Huff, R. and Lilly, J.R. (1988) *House Arrest and Correctional Policy: Doing Time at Home* (Newbury Park, CA: Sage).

Bayley, D. and Shearing, C. (2001) *The New Structure of Policing: Description, Conceptualization, and Research Agenda* (Washington, DC: National Institute of Justice).

Beyens, K. and Snacken, S. (1996) 'Prison privatisation: an international perspective', in R. Matthews and P. Francis (eds) *Prisons 2000* (London: MacMillan), pp. 240–265.

Bonta, J., Wallace-Capretta, S. and Rooney, J. (1999) *Electronic Monitoring in Canada* (Ottawa: Solicitor-General of Canada).

Bottas, S. (2007) *An Overview of Electronic Monitoring in Corrections: The Issues and Implications* (Ottawa: Correctional Services of Canada).

Carter, P. (2001) *Managing Offenders, Reducing Crime: A New Approach* (London: Cabinet Office).

Christie, N. (2000) *Crime Control as Industry* (London: Routledge).

Cohen, S. (1985) *Visions of Social Control* (Cambridge: Polity).

Cooper, C. (2007) 'Rehumanising social policy', paper presented at the Annual Conference of the British–Irish Section of the European Group for the Study of Deviance and Social Control, Institute of Historical Research, April 2007.

Coyle, A. Campbell, B. and Neufeld, R. (eds) (2003) *Capitalist Punishment: Prison Privatisation and Human Rights* (London: Zed books).

DeMichele, M. and Payne, B. (2009) 'Offender supervision with electronic technology'. Online. Available at: www.appa-net.org/eweb/docs/APPA/pubs/OSET_2.pdf (accessed 3 March 2010).

Feeley, M. (2002) 'Entrepreneurs of punishment: the legacy of privatisation', *Punishment and Society*, 4:3, pp. 321–344.

Feeley, M. and Simon, J. (1992) 'The new penology: notes on the emerging strategy of corrections and its implications', *Criminology*, 30:4, pp. 449–474.

Fisher, T. (2006) 'Race, neoliberalism and welfare reform', *Social Justice: Crime, Conflict and World Order*, 33:3, pp. 54–65.

Frost, G. (2002) 'Florida's innovative use of GPS for community corrections', *Journal of Offender Monitoring*, 15:2, pp. 6–7, 9–10.

G4S (Group 4 Securicor) (2010) 'Electronic monitoring'. Online. Available at: www.g4s.uk.com/en-GB/What%20we%20do/Services/Care%20and%20justice%20services/Electronic%20monitoring (accessed 15 March 2010).

Groombridge, N. (2008) 'Stars of CCTV? How the Home Office wasted millions – a radical "Treasury/Audit Commission" view', *Surveillance and Society*, 5:1, pp. 73–80.

Haverkamp, R., Lévy, R. and Mayer, M. (2004) 'Electronic monitoring in Europe', *European Journal of Crime, Criminal Law and Criminal Justice*, 12:1, pp. 36–45.

Hickley, M. (2009) 'Security firm lands MOD job three months after John Reid joins as a consultant', *Daily Mail*. Online. Available at: www.dailymail.co.uk/news/article-1161911/Security-firm-lands-MoD-job-months-John-Reid-joins-consultant.html (accessed 1 March 2010).

Hope, T. (2006) 'Things can only get better', *Criminal Justice Matters*, 62, pp. 4–39.

Hopkins, R.D.N. (1993) 'The formation of UK Detention Services', paper presented at Private gevangenissen in Nederland, Seminar, Utrecht, the Netherlands, 1 December.

House of Commons Committee of Public Accounts (2006) 'The electronic monitoring of adult offenders'. Sixty-second Report of Session 2005–2006, 12 July.

Hucklesby, A. (2008) 'Vehicles of desistance: the impact of EM curfew orders', *Criminology and Criminal Justice*, 8:1, pp. 51–71.

JHSA (John Howard Society of Alberta) (2006) 'Electronic (radio frequency) and GPS monitored community based supervision programmes'. Online. Available at: www.johnhoward.ab.ca/PUB/PDF/monitorupdate.pdf (accessed 13 March 2010).

Johnston, L. and Shearing, C. (2003) *Governing Security* (London: Routledge).

Kruusement, A. (2007) Presentation at the 5th CEP conference on electronic monitoring, Egmond aan Zee. Online. Available at: www.cep-probation.org/default.asp?page_id=65&news_item=55 (accessed 13 March 2010).

Lilly, J.R. (1990) 'Tagging reviewed', *Howard Journal of Criminal Justice*, 29:4, pp. 229–245.

Lilly, J.R. (2006) 'Issues beyond empirical EM reports', *Criminology and Public Policy*, 5:1, pp. 93–101.

Lilly, J.R. and Deflem, M. (1996) 'Profit and penality: an analysis of the corrections–commercial complex', *Crime and Delinquency*, 42:1, pp. 3–20.

Lilly, J.R. and Knepper, P. (1992) 'An international perspective on the privatisation of corrections', *The Howard Journal*, 31:3, pp. 174–191.

Loader, I. (2000) 'Plural policing and democratic governance', *Social and Legal Studies*, 9:3, pp. 323–345.

Lotke, E. (1996) 'The prison–industrial complex', *Multinational Monitor*. Online. Available at: www.multinationalmonitor.org/hyper/mm1196.06.html (accessed 17 March 2010).

Mair, G. (2005) 'Electronic monitoring in England and Wales: evidence-based or not?', *Criminology and Criminal Justice*, 5:3, pp. 257–277.

Mair, G. and Mortimer, E. (1996) *Curfew Orders with Electronic Monitoring* (London: Home Office).

Mattera, P., Khan, M. and Nathan, S. (2003) 'Corrections Corporation of America: a critical look at its first twenty years'. Online. Available at: www.grassrootsleadership.org/Articles/CCAAnniversaryReport.pdf (accessed 1 March 2010).

Meek, J. (2002) 'Robocop'. *Guardian*. Online. Available at: www.guardian.co.uk/uk/2002/jun/13/ukcrime.jamesmeek (accessed 14 March 2010).

Mortimer, E. and May, C. (1997) *Electronic Monitoring in Practice: The Second Year of the Trials of Curfew Orders* (London: HMSO).

Muller, B. (2005) 'Borders, bodies and biometrics: towards identity management', in E. Zureik and M. Salter (eds) *Global Policing and Surveillance: Borders, Security, Identity* (Cullompton: Willan), pp. 83–96.

Nathan, S. (2002) 'Prison privatisation report international'. Online. Available at: www.psiru.org/justice/ppri48.asp#UK (accessed 17 March 2010).

Nathan, S. (2003) 'Private prisons: emerging and transformative countries', in A. Coyle, A. Campbell and R. Neufeld (eds) *Capitalist Punishment: Prison Privatisation and Human Rights* (London: Zed Books), pp. 189–201.

Nellis, M. (2003) '"They don't even know we're there": the electronic monitoring of offenders in England and Wales', in F. Webster and K. Ball (eds) *The Intensification of Surveillance* (London: Pluto Press), pp. 62–89.

Nellis, M. (2008) '24/7/365: mobility, locatability and the satellite tracking of offenders', in K. Franko Aas, H.O. Gundus and H.M. Lommel (eds) *Technologies of Insecurity: The Surveillance of Everyday Life* (London: Routledge), pp 105–124.

Newburn, T. (2002) 'Atlantic crossings: 'policy transfer' and crime control in the United States and Britain', *Punishment and Society*, 4:2, pp. 165–194.

Nossal, K. and Wood, P. (2004) 'The raggedness of prison privatisation', paper presented at Prisons 2004 Conference at City University, London, June 2004.

Padgett, K., Bales, W. and Blomberg, T. (2006) 'Under surveillance: an empirical test of the effectiveness and consequences of electronic monitoring', *Criminology and Public Policy*, 5:1, pp. 61–92.

Parenti, C. (2003) 'Privatized problems: for-profit incarceration in trouble', in A. Coyle, A. Campbell and R. Neufeld (eds) *Capitalist Punishment: Prison Privatisation and Human Rights* (London: Zed Books), pp. 30–38.

Paterson, C. (2007) 'Commercial crime control and the electronic monitoring of offenders in England and Wales', *Social Justice: Crime, Conflict and World Order*, 34:3–4, pp. 98–110.

Paterson, C. (2009) *Understanding the Electronic Monitoring of Offenders in England and Wales* (Saarbrucken: VDM Verlag).

Renzema, M. and Mayo-Wilson, E. (2005) 'Can electronic monitoring reduce crime for moderate to high risk offenders?', *Journal of Experimental Criminology*, 1, pp. 215–237.

Roberts, J. (2004) *The Virtual Prison: Community Custody and the Evolution of Imprisonment* (Cambridge: Cambridge University Press).

Stenson, K. (2005) 'Sovereignty, biopolitics and the local government of crime in Britain', *Theoretical Criminology*, 9:3, pp. 265–287.

Tabarrok, A. (2003) *Changing the Guard: Private Prisons and the Control of Crime* (Oakland, CA: The Independent Institute).

Wennerberg, I. and Pinto, S. (2009) '6th European electronic monitoring conference – analysis of questionnaires', CEP Electronic Monitoring Conference. Online. Available at: www.cepprobation.org/uploaded_files/EM2009%20Questionnaire%20summary.pdf (accessed 13 March 2010).

Whitfield, D. (1997) *Tackling the Tag* (Winchester: Waterside Press).

Zedner, L. (2006) 'Liquid security: managing the market for crime control', *Criminology and Criminal Justice*, 6:3, pp. 267–288.

12 Insiders' views

Offenders' and staff's experiences of electronically monitored curfews

Anthea Hucklesby

In England and Wales in 2010, 91,000 defendants/offenders were electronically monitored (Ministry of Justice 2011b). This is some way short of the 126,000 who were received into prison during 2009 (Ministry of Justice 2010) but the continuing and rapid rise in the use of electronic monitoring (EM) is likely to mean that it numerically surpasses the use of imprisonment within the next decade or so. Comparatively little research has been undertaken on EM (and community sentences more generally – see McNeill and Robinson 2012) compared to the large literature relating to prisons. Most studies of EM in the UK have been carried out on behalf of government departments and have been evaluations of pilot projects or re-convictions studies and so have had a narrow focus (for example, see Mair and Mortimer 1996; Mair and Nee 1990; Walter 2002; Walter *et al.* 2002). Consequently, we know very little about how offenders experience EM and its impact on their behaviour. This chapter discusses the findings of an exploratory study undertaken in the north of England in the mid-2000s, which aimed to explore offenders' experiences of EM. The chapter will review the findings of the research, focusing specifically upon offenders' compliance and the potential of EM to assist in the process of desistance. It will also briefly explore the views of the monitoring officers who are responsible for the day-to-day operation of EM in the community and explore how their working practices might impact upon offenders' compliance and desistance.

EM in England and Wales

EM had a shaky beginning in England and Wales. It was first used in a pilot in the mid-1980s as a condition of bail (Mair and Nee 1990). The results of the pilot were not positive and the idea of EM lay dormant until the mid-1990s, when curfew orders were introduced on a pilot basis (Mair and Mortimer 1996; Mortimer and May 1997). Curfew orders were subsequently rolled out nationally in 1999 and have been available since, albeit in slightly different guises. Since 2003, curfews have become one of 12 requirements available to sentencers when making a community order. Under this regime, curfews can be stand-alone (single) requirements or imposed alongside other requirements such as probation supervision, drug treatment and so on. Nearly three-quarters of curfew requirements in England and Wales are stand-alone orders, demarcating its use from other European countries where it is normally integrated with probation supervision (Haverkamp *et al.* 2004; Ministry of Justice 2011b). Curfew requirements can be imposed for up to six months and up to 12 hours per day. In practice, most curfews require offenders to stay at their address overnight for periods of 10–12 hours, although courts have the ability to be much more creative about how they use it. This chapter focuses upon EM's use at the sentencing stage, but it is also worth noting that in England and Wales EM is available as a condition of bail and as a condition of early release from prison under the Home Detention Curfew Scheme (see Nellis and Mair, this volume).

EM in England and Wales uses radio-frequency identification (RFID) technology. Offenders are required to stay at a particular address during specified curfew times and wear a tag, which is linked to the monitoring company through equipment placed at the address. If offenders go out of range of the equipment, by leaving the address, the monitoring company is alerted. Monitoring companies are aware when offenders are not at their specified address and when tags have been removed or the equipment in the house is unplugged or moved. All of these incidents are breachable, but may not result in a return to court, depending on their seriousness. Being out for the whole of a curfew period or a significant part of it leads to immediate breach action as does removing a tag. Less serious breaches, such as being late for the start of a curfew period, result in verbal and written warnings (see Ministry of Justice 2011b for details). RFID technology monitors that offenders are where they are supposed to be. It does not prevent offenders leaving their address and if they do, they cannot be tracked. Currently, GPS technology, which is capable of tracking offenders constantly and away from the curfew address, which is not used, at the time of writing, by the Ministry of Justice in England and Wales following mediocre results of a pilot project and concerns about costs (Shute 2007).

EM in the UK is operated by the private sector. At the time of writing, G4S and Serco hold the contracts in England and Wales, while Reliance has the Scottish contract. All three providers have been involved in the provision of EM since it started in the UK, albeit under several different names. The private sector run the whole operation of EM. They provide and fit the equipment, monitor offenders and investigate and prosecute breaches.[1] This situation arose because of the hostility of the Probation Service to EM (Mair 2001; Nellis 2003a; Nellis and Lilly 2000). While the Probation Service's concerns about EM have lessened (see Bottomley *et al.* 2004), they have not yet fully embraced it (Rogers 2011). Consequently, EM has a distinct identity and runs in parallel to the broader provision of community sentences, resulting in limited integration and information-sharing between the two sectors (CJJI 2008).

EM in England and Wales has expanded mainly for pragmatic reasons. The inexorable rise in the prison population from around 66,000 in 2001 (Home Office 2003) to over 85,000 in 2011 (Ministry of Justice 2011a) has resulted in governments needing to find legitimate ways of reducing the prison population. EM has provided an important tool, especially as a 'back door' measure – allowing non-violent prisoners to be released early from prison under the Home Detention Curfew. It has arguably been less successful in this regard when used as a sentence. An increasing amount of evidence suggests that it is used predominantly for low-tariff offenders who are not at risk of an immediate prison sentence (CJJI 2008). EM also has a legitimacy problem both inside and outside the criminal justice system and has been widely and heavily criticized. Some of the concerns expressed arise because of unrealistic expectations of what EM is able to do. EM has been over-sold, especially by politicians who have described it using terms such as 'virtual prison', 'prison without bars' and 'electronic ball and chain'. Terminology such as this gives the impression that EM is akin to imprisonment providing total incapacitation, thus preventing offenders from re-offending or causing trouble more generally. However, EM has much more in common with community sentences than it does with prison (see Hucklesby, 2012). EM requires offenders to stay at an address during curfew hours, but they are able to leave whenever they wish, although there is a heightened likelihood of being detected, and they can continue to offend either from their homes during curfew hours or by offending outside their curfew hours. In the UK, EM simply requires offenders to stay in. It places no other restrictions on what offenders can do. Consequently, they are able to use alcohol and drugs and offend as long as they do this while abiding by their curfew. In this way, curfews can be conceived of as purely punitive, making no attempt to rehabilitate offenders. But curfews have also been criticized for not being punitive enough, mainly because they enable offenders to stay in the community, seemingly carrying on with their lives (Hucklesby 2008; Nellis 2003b). Research does not support this view, showing that offenders view curfews as punitive and that they genuinely restrict their liberty (see, for example, Hucklesby 2008; Mair and Nee 1990; Mair and Mortimer 1996; Walter 2002). Public confidence in EM has also been knocked by a small number of high-profile cases in which serious offences have been committed by offenders on EM (see, for example, Nellis 2006).

Research evidence relating to EM is limited both in the UK and elsewhere (Mair 2005). Most of the research in the UK has been undertaken or funded by the government and has focused on the attitudes of offenders, their families and the staff involved in running the EM (Mair 2005; Nellis 2003a). This research suggests that offenders and their families are generally positive about EM, particularly as a way of keeping offenders out of prison and out of trouble, and as a stabilizing influence in their lives (Mair and Mortimer 1996; Walter 2002). Evidence relating to its potential impact on offending, both while on EM and afterwards, is more limited and inconclusive (see, for example, Marie et al. 2011; Renzema and Mayo-Wilson 2005).

EM has some advantages over other forms of community sentence. EM is able to provide information on offenders' whereabouts for significant periods of time and in the UK for up to 12 hours per day (longer for bail cases). It provides almost instantaneous information that offenders have broken their curfew as well as providing concrete evidence of breach. The information can be used in court during breach proceedings or by offender managers to try and illicit greater compliance in the future. More controversially, the information gleaned from EM can be used by the police for intelligence purposes and by offenders to provide alibis.

EM would be less controversial and a more acceptable measure if it could be shown to have an impact on both short-term and long-term compliance (Bottoms 2001). Short-term compliance relates to offenders' behaviour while under EM and long-term compliance relates to compliance with the law after a sentence has been completed, i.e. desistance. Short-term compliance, i.e. sticking to the conditions or restrictions of an order, has largely been ignored by theory, policy and research (for exceptions, see Bottoms 2001; Hucklesby 2009; Nellis 2006; Robinson and McNeill 2008). Instead, attention has focused on long-term compliance relating to whether offenders re-offend or abide by the law more generally (see, for example, Chapman and Hough 1998; Farrall 2002; Harper and Chitty 2005; Maruna 2001; McGuire 1995). The relationship between the two types of compliance has not been extensively researched (see Hearnden and Millie 2003 for an exception), but it is possible to theorize that the two are linked. Commonsense would suggest that offenders who comply with the requirements of the order are more likely to be the ones who will desist in the future and there is some support for this in research. The 'What Works' literature suggests that offenders who fail to complete their programmes have higher re-conviction rates than those who complete programmes and those who do not participate in programmes (see, for example, Harper and Chitty 2005). However, how the two types of compliance are linked is not clear. There may not be a causal link and, certainly, short-term compliance is not a sufficient or a necessary condition for desistance to take place and vice versa.

This chapter draws on an empirical study of EM in England and Wales which explored offenders' views of EM. The chapter will first describe the research design of the study before moving on to discuss its findings in relation to short-term and long-term compliance. The final section of the chapter examines the views and working practices of monitoring officers with specific reference to their potential impact on offenders' likelihood of complying and desisting.

Research design

The purpose of the research was to explore the experiences and attitudes of offenders to their curfew orders and the working practices of monitoring officers. Data were collected from four sources: administrative data, interviews with offenders, observations of monitoring officers and interviews with monitoring officers. Administrative data were collated from case files on 217 offenders who were subject to stand-alone curfew orders. Some of these offenders may have had other community sentences running concurrently, but accurate data were not available (see Bottomley *et al.* 2004; CJJI 2008). Data collected included demographic characteristics, details of compliance, violations and breach proceedings and records of communications between offenders and the monitoring company (further details can be found in Hucklesby 2009). Interviews were carried out with 78 offenders. The interviews took place at the end of the curfew when the equipment was decommissioned. Data were collected on offenders' backgrounds, their experiences of their curfews, their behaviour while under curfew and the impact of the curfew orders on their lives. The data and interviews relating to offenders were supplemented by observations of monitoring officers at work. A total of 55 shifts were observed, each lasting between four and eight hours. Twenty in-depth interviews were conducted with monitoring officers employed by the EM contractor. The interviews with monitoring officers lasted between an hour-and-a-half and three hours and usually took place before shifts began. Interviewees were asked about their employment backgrounds, their reasons for applying to be monitoring officers, the training they had received, their views on supervision and management, EM and offenders, as well as how they went about their work, how they dealt with specific events and any problems or concerns they had relating to their work (for more details, see Hucklesby 2008, 2009, 2011).

Short-term compliance

This section examines the extent of non-compliance with curfew orders using data recorded on case files and self-reported data from offenders. Non-compliance with curfew orders is normal (NAO 2006), mainly because the equipment is very sensitive, enabling non-compliance events involving offenders being just over five minutes late for the start of their curfew or knocking the monitoring box to be recorded. All but two of the offenders' files showed that they had failed to abide by their curfew on at least one occasion and over half of offenders had 50 or more violations recorded against them. However, most of the non-compliance was relatively minor, comprising short time violations (being away from the curfew address for part of the curfew period). Given the chaotic lives that many offenders lead, minor lapses in timekeeping are to be expected and the breach regime allows offenders leeway in this regard (see CJJI 2008). Two-fifths of files recorded that offenders had more seriously breached their curfews either by being out for a whole curfew period or removing the tag. These types of serious breaches should result in formal breach action in which offenders are returned to court. A total of 99 offenders in the file sample had been formally breached. Just over half of these offenders had been breached for accumulated time violations.[2] Less serious breaches are dealt with by verbal and written warnings – three-fifths of offenders had received at least one verbal warning and two-fifths of offenders had received written warnings.

In terms of the 78 interviewees, their files recorded that 28 had not been formally breached or received a written or verbal warning. A total of 29 interviewees had been formally breached, mostly for accumulated time violations and a further ten interviewees were recorded as receiving written warnings. A similar number of interviewees admitted non-compliance during interviews as was recorded on files, suggesting that offenders were generally truthful about their behaviour. Most commonly, interviewees admitted not complying with their orders on only one or two occasions and over half admitted to being away from their address for short periods of time during curfew hours. Offenders reported that the majority of non-compliance was not deliberate and resulted from poor planning, chaotic lifestyles or public transport difficulties. Only a minority of interviewees reported deliberate and persistent non-compliance, which was usually a series of relatively short time violations. On returning home, offenders commonly reported contacting the company to explain their absence – why they did this and whether they believed that this mitigated the breach was not clear. Only three interviewees admitted to more serious breaches – i.e. being out for a whole curfew period or removing their tag.

Offenders have to make choices about whether or not to comply with EM. The reasons for their decisions are complex and dynamic and are related to both objective factors and subjective perceptions of offenders. The preeminent reason given by interviewees for complying with their curfews was the fear of the consequences of not doing so. They feared going to prison, not simply because of the punishment this involved but also because of its consequences for their lives. They were particularly concerned about the impact it would have upon their relationships with significant others. Most interviewees believed that going to prison as a result of breaching their curfew order was a real possibility, despite this being unlikely in reality (Hucklesby 2009).

Offenders' accounts of why they complied with curfew orders suggested that both distributive (a fair outcome) and procedural (a fair process) justice were important influences on their compliance (see, for example, Tyler 1990). Decisions about whether to comply were also linked to whether offenders felt that they had been treated fairly by the courts. Those who received either the sentence they expected or a more lenient one reported higher levels of compliance than those offenders who expected another sentence or believed that they had been treated harshly. Offenders who felt that the courts had given them a chance linked this to their compliance. Similarly, offenders suggested that the treatment they received from monitoring officers impacted upon their compliance so that positive interactions improved compliance whereas negative experiences were linked to an increased likelihood of non-compliance (see Hucklesby 2010, 2012).

The unique element of EM is that it is a surveillance-based sentence. Offenders were aware that they were under surveillance, making references to being watched and/or monitored. Most interviewees had confidence that the equipment worked and were fully aware that if they left their address during their curfew it would be detected. However, they linked the technology and its influence on their decisions to an increased likelihood of being caught. As a result, untangling the role of surveillance and the consequent increased likelihood of getting caught is not practically, or probably theoretically, possible (see Hucklesby, 2012). Believing in the reliability of the equipment was a very important determinant of compliance, but the existence of the equipment alone was not enough to bring about compliance. Interviewees reported that compliance was enhanced through contact with the monitoring company. General reminders, as well as swift and specific contact after they had not complied, bolstered interviewees' compliance.

In common with other community sentences, EM relies on offenders' motivation. Interviewees were aware that compliance was their choice and were generally pragmatic about wanting to complete their sentences. Their success was linked to a number of factors. First, whether or not they used alcohol or drugs while under curfew. Both alcohol and drug use were linked to increased non-compliance. Second, offenders' concerns about their personal safety impacted upon compliance. EM makes offenders locatable, not only by the authorities but anyone else who might be looking for them, such as drug dealers or criminal associates. Several interviewees also raised issues with opening their doors to strangers, especially late at night when many visits from the monitoring company take place. Third, the support or otherwise of significant others impacted upon compliance. Friends and family were reported to play a significant role in offenders' compliance. Some provided moral support and practical assistance with complying, including texting just before curfews were due to begin, going to pick offenders up and take them home and fetching goods from shops during curfew hours. By contrast, significant others could be a source of tension, resulting in offenders breaching their curfews because of disagreements that meant offenders felt compelled to leave their address or because of pressure being exerted to accompany partners or friends on nights out.

Desistance and EM

Preventing further offending both during sentences and afterwards is one of the primary aims of any sentence. This section examines the evidence gleaned from the interviews with offenders about their offending during their curfew orders and discusses their future intentions in this regard. The data are self-reported so they need to be treated with some caution because offenders may underestimate or exaggerate their offending.

Reductions in offending while on EM were reported by just under half ($n=35$, 46 per cent) of the interviewees. Nine of the offenders claimed that they had not offended on EM, while also suggesting that they had no intention of re-offending because they were not regular offenders and/or their current offence was a one-off. Significant reductions in offending while under curfew were reported by 14 interviewees. Three reasons for curtailing their offending were described. The first set of reasons related to incapacitation. Offenders thought that they were unable to leave their addresses during curfew hours, which was when they usually offended. Some offenders were reluctant to change their patterns of offending because of the greater risks involved in offending during the day. The second set of reasons related to deterrence. Offenders reduced their offending because they feared going to prison. They explained this either in terms of relief that they had not been sent to prison for their current offence or that they did not want to go to prison in the future. The third set of reasons related to their personal circumstances and were linked to what has been termed the 'English dream' (Bottoms *et al.* 2004) – gaining employment, settling down, children and reductions in substance use (Farrall and Calverley 2006; Sampson and Laub 1993), although EM still played a role (Hucklesby 2008).

Just over half (*n*=41, 54 per cent) of interviewees claimed that EM had not impacted upon their offending, reporting to have been offending as frequently as before their curfew was imposed. A displacement effect was evident for some interviewees. They reported changing the types of offences they committed and/ or the times they offended so that they avoid curfew periods.

When interviewees were asked about their future intentions in terms of offending once their curfew was completed they fell into two groups: 'persisters' and 'desisters', suggesting that the longer-term impact of curfew orders depends on offenders' readiness to change (Maruna 2001; Farrall and Calverley 2006). 'Desisters' are offenders who have already embarked on the process of desistance, whereas 'persisters' have no plans to cease offending. Around one-third (*n*=25, 32 per cent) of interviewees were 'persisters', suggesting that they intended to continue to offend and that curfew orders had made no difference to their plans. Their reasons were that curfew orders were not a deterrent, that they could not avoid trouble or that they intended to return to their old lifestyle, reflecting explanations provided in other studies (Rex 1999; Farrall 2002; Farrall and Calverley 2006).

'Desisters' comprised around two-thirds (*n*=53, 68 per cent) of interviewees. They claimed that curfew orders had reduced the likelihood that they would offend in the future, although it must be recognized that good intentions articulated while under sentence often dissolve in practice (see Burnett 2004). Deterrence, and particularly fear of going to prison, was a central theme in offenders' explanations for their intended desistance. Other interviewees suggested that their curfews had taught them a lesson, they had grown out of offending or changed their lifestyle so that employment and family commitments took priority. The accounts of 'desisters' suggest that curfew orders may be effective in supporting offenders who are already thinking about or actively trying to stop offending, as one interviewee described: 'Just the time in my life where I found it [the curfew order] was not a problem. I want to stay out of trouble and it helped me in that way. If they give [me] another three months [I would] gladly take it.'

Although desistance from offending is the ultimate goal of the criminal justice system, improvements in other aspects of offenders' lives are aims in themselves because they might have an impact upon their inclination to offend. In the following section the impact of curfew orders on various facets of offenders' lives is discussed.

Lifestyle changes and EM

Desistance research has linked a number of factors, including finding employment, settling down with a partner and having children, to the cessation of offending (see, for example, Bottoms *et al.* 2004; Farrall 2002; Farrall and Calverley 2006; Maruna 2001; Sampson and Laub 1993). Another body of research has suggested that there are a range of criminogenic factors which make it more likely that individuals will offend (Harper and Chitty 2005). Examples of criminogenic factors/needs include drug and alcohol use, low educational attainment and a lack of employment skills. If factors such as these are the drivers for desistance and the continuation of offending, then it is important to understand how curfew orders impact upon them, i.e. how they might reduce criminogenic needs and enhance desistance-related factors. In the section that follows interviewees' perspectives on a range of factors linked with offending/desistance are explored. Before this, the concept of social capital is examined in order to elucidate some of the findings.

Farrall (2004) has argued persuasively that accumulating social capital increases the likelihood of desistance and a lack of social capital may support offending. The concept of social capital has been numerously defined but fundamentally refers to the social connections, ties and networks of individuals (see, for example, Hagan and McCarthy 1997). Employment and family ties are particularly important elements of social capital and addressing problems in these areas will support the process of desistance. Farrall and others conceptualize social capital as intrinsically pro-social, but it can also be anti-social because it can foster offending as well as desistance (Hucklesby 2008). Reducing levels of anti-social capital may be just as important to the desistance process as building up pro-social capital and intuitively the former might be a necessary precursor of the latter in at least some cases. This poses the central question explored in this section of the chapter: whether curfew orders impact upon either anti-social or pro-social capital, or both, and if so, how.

It has been suggested that curfew orders can assist offenders to stabilize their lives, providing an opportunity for them to take a break from their usual lifestyles and their peers (Walter 2002). This was a constant theme in this research also, with interviewees' narratives reporting that curfews had given them time to reflect upon their offending and its consequences and provided them with an opportunity to break from the habits – people, places and situations – which were linked with their offending. This suggests that curfew orders have an important role to play as habit breakers, dissolving the connections that curfewees had with anti-social associates and environments. Whether the connections were permanently broken, resulting in long-term lifestyle changes, is open to debate, but it gave offenders a break, an opportunity to reflect; at least some offenders suggested that they would not be returning to their old habits.

The impact of EM on relationships with significant others has been commented upon extensively in the literature (Elliott *et al.* 2000; Lobley and Smith 2000; Smith 2001; Whitfield 1997). Attention has been drawn, *inter alia*, to the role of family and friends in consenting to EM being used in their homes; the policing role that they might perform; and the propensity for violence to occur between curfewees and family members. The literature points to widely differing effects on relationships (see, for example, Dodgson *et al.* 2001; Elliott *et al.* 2000; Mair and Mortimer 1996; Mair and Nee 1990; Mortimer and May 1997; Walter 2002; Whitfield 2001) and this research supports its findings. Most interviewees (*n*=61, 80 per cent) reported that their relationships did not change while subject to curfew orders, suggesting that concerns about the impact of EM on relationships might have been overstated. Some offenders reported that their relationships improved. They suggested that being confined at home had brought the family closer together, building and strengthening relationships mainly because they had spent more time with their partner and/or children. By contrast, some offenders reported increased levels of tension between family members and a general deterioration in their relationships. These problems were particularly prevalent when children were confined to parents' homes, even when they usually resided together. The problems arose because of the increased amount of time spent together and the fact that offenders were unable to leave if situations became difficult. Increased tensions were also reported with partners because of not being able to go out or having to return home early. In summary, curfews appeared to increase tensions in households where relationships were already strained, but assisted in improving and building up relationships if they were not. Worryingly, curfews were reported to impact adversely on visiting relatives and friends who lived some distance away from offenders and put additional obstacles in the way of caring responsibilities.

Legitimate employment is an important element in pro-social capital and desistance and a protective factor against offending (see, for example, Bottoms *et al.* 2004; Farrall 2002; Farrall and Calverley 2006). Curfew orders could therefore harm or support offenders' efforts to desist by affecting their current job or their employment prospects. Nearly half of the interviewees were working when they were sentenced. Most of this group reported that the curfew had affected their work negatively and this had financial consequences. In the majority of cases, it had impacted upon the hours that they were able to work. Some offenders reported having to alter their working hours to accommodate their curfew. Others commented that they had lost work because they were unable to stay away from home overnight. Several interviewees claimed that they could have lost their jobs because of the curfew restrictions and a few offenders stopped working during the lifetime of their curfew.

Some unemployed offenders claimed that curfews had impacted upon their ability to find work, partly because they had criminal records but also because they believed that they were unable to work shifts. By contrast, several offenders suggested that curfew orders had made them more 'job ready' – providing them with a routine and confining them to home at night, therefore assisting them to get up in the mornings. Additionally, these new routines were reported to improve offenders' engagement and compliance with other community sentences that they were serving concurrently.

Substance use – drugs and alcohol – have been identified as criminogenic needs which are linked with offending, although the nature of the link is contested (see, for example, Dingwall 2005; Hough 1996; Hucklesby and Wincup 2010). Substance use among interviewees was prolific. All but five of the interviewees reported using drugs, alcohol or both, and many of them reported problematic use directly before curfew orders were imposed (see Hucklesby 2008). The impact of curfews on drug and alcohol use was mixed, with some offenders reporting no changes in use while others reported increasing or reducing use. In terms of drugs, around half ($n=23$, 58 per cent) of offenders, predominantly can-nabis users, stated that their drug use had not changed. Only a small number of interviewees ($n=3$) reported increased use, which they blamed on being bored or depressed or having nothing better to do. The reductions in drug use reported by 14 interviewees were often linked to less use of stimulants and 'dance' drugs because they were not able to go out. Cannabis use was less affected by curfews except for a very small number of offenders who were prohibited from smoking in the house. Several offenders suggested that they had stopped using drugs entirely as a result of curfew orders.

The overall effects of curfew orders on alcohol use were similar to those on drug use, but a higher proportion of interviewees (62 per cent) had changed their drinking patterns while under curfew. Eleven interviewees reported drinking more alcohol, suggesting that this was because they had more time on their hands, that alcohol was more available at home and that they drank earlier and quicker in order to get home in time for their curfews to begin. By contrast, two-thirds of interviewees ($n=25$) reported drinking less because they were unable to go out, did not drink at home or because curfews gave them an opportunity to cut down.

So far this chapter has explored offenders' perspectives on the experience of being electronically monitored. The next section signals a change in focus, examining monitoring officers' views of EM.

Monitoring officers

While under curfew, offenders would have contact routinely with only two groups of people because it is a home-based sentence. In England and Wales, they would not have any contact with the Probation Service unless they have been sentenced to a community order with multiple requirements or they happen to be serving another community sentence concurrently. Consequently, employ-ees of the monitoring company are offenders' only contact point, and for this reason are the public face of EM (Hucklesby 2011). Even offenders serving multiple-requirement community orders are only likely to receive advice on and assistance with EM from monitoring company employees, given the Probation Service's ambivalence towards, and detachment from, EM (CJJI 2008). Offend-ers will have contact with two groups of employees from monitoring companies: control-room personnel who staff the telephones which provide offenders with 24-hour access to the monitoring company; and monitoring officers who visit offenders' homes to install, maintain and decommission equipment and to inves-tigate non-compliance events. It is the second of these groups which is discussed in this section of the chapter. It explores who these employees are, their working values and how they go about their work, with particular reference to the impact this will have on offenders' experiences of EM and the potential to influence offenders' compliance and desistance.

Distinct differences exist between monitoring officers and probation officers (Hucklesby 2011). Their backgrounds, training, promotion prospects and terms and conditions of employment differ markedly. Monitoring officers are in a structurally weaker position than probation staff and other criminal justice professionals (Hucklesby 2011). The working environment of monitoring officers also differs in that they spend most of their working lives in the community, visiting offenders' homes during the evening and night. They usually work alone but meet up with colleagues occasionally to do tasks that require more than one member of personnel. The consequence of working in such an environment was that monitoring officers had considerable concerns about their personal safety (Hucklesby 2011). They reported that they always felt vulnerable and often unsafe when working. Their concerns were well-founded because they reported frequently receiving abuse (usually verbal), mainly from 'neighbours' and other household members rather than offenders. They generally viewed the abuse they received as an occupational hazard, but it remained a source of unease.

Monitoring officers consistently mentioned that one of the main ways to ensure their safety was to demarcate themselves from the police and ensure that offenders and their families were clear that they were not police officers. They consistently spoke about not acting in an authoritarian manner to avoid being viewed as police officers, which would somehow, yet in an unexplained way, threaten their safety. Monitoring officers also used a range of other strategies to alleviate their concerns about personal safety, each of which would impact upon how offenders experienced EM and potentially their compliance (Hucklesby 2011). The first group of strategies involved not undertaking visits. Sometimes monitoring officers would inform the company that they felt too unsafe to go into a house. On other occasions they pretended they had visited an address and received no reply, which has direct consequences for offenders who should be breached in such circumstances for being out during curfew hours. The second group of strategies involved a range of behaviours, all of which were used to limit the amount of time spent in an address and talking to offenders. The potential problems arising from such approaches include equipment being fitted incorrectly and therefore giving false alerts for non-compliance, and the requirements of EM not being fully explained to offenders and other household members, making accidental non-compliance more likely. One monitoring officer explained the consequences: 'If you are nervous in someone's house, you want to get the job done as quickly as possible and get out and obviously you are not explaining things properly or fitting the equipment correctly.'

The third group of strategies used by monitoring officers to deal with safety concerns were normative strategies linked to managing offenders and any situations that might arise. They included engaging offenders in conversation, using humour, treating offenders with dignity and respect, being non-judgemental and not accusing them of non-compliance. These strategies correspond to procedural justice principles, suggesting that they should have a positive impact upon compliance (see, for example, Tyler 1990, Tyler and Huo 2002).

Generally, monitoring officers thought that the equipment was reliable and that it was difficult for offenders to deceive the equipment. They recognized that problems sometimes arose with the equipment because it was faulty, had not been installed correctly or signals from the equipment were interrupted so that offenders were shown as being out when they were not. They acknowledged that equipment problems could result in offenders being breached unfairly. They also discussed how problems with the equipment can frustrate offenders and increase their chances of non-compliance. One monitoring officer explained:

> Those time violations ... they are adamant that they have not been out ... you check their history ... [you find] all these stupid time violations that are in the very early hours of the morning, bedtime, between one and five, and they are only out for a quarter of an hour ... they get a warning and they think this isn't working. [Offenders think] I am going to end up being breached here, why should I bother. Some of them get upset and just take the kit off and throw it away. [They think] why bother with it, take me back to court and do what you want.

By contrast, they acknowledged that offenders sometimes attempted to use equipment problems as excuses for not complying and as a way of getting accumulated time violations cancelled. A monitoring officer explained:

> They are always saying that the equipment is at fault and trying to get you to change it. They are clever, they know that if you change the equipment then the time violations will get cancelled ... they could have gone out committed a crime ... you change their equipment and you are acting as an alibi.

Not realizing the contradictions in their behaviour, monitoring officers consistently stated that they used the excuse of needing to check the equipment when undertaking visits to investigate potential breaches. They did this as a safety strategy. They very clearly viewed accusing offenders of non-compliance as confrontational and potentially putting themselves at risk. But using equipment checks as excuses for visits has a detrimental impact upon compliance. First, it gives the impression to offenders that the equipment is faulty, reducing their trust in its reliability; and, second, it suggests that visits are being undertaken not because of something offenders have done but because of the incompetence of the monitoring company. Some offenders explained during interviews how constant problems with the equipment and/or continuous visits to check equipment made them suspicious of its reliability and less likely to comply.

Monitoring officers' discussion of the equipment and how offenders can use it to their advantage demonstrates the conflicting feelings that monitoring officers had towards offenders and the difficult and uncertain situations they have to work in (see Hucklesby 2011). Monitoring officers had a shared value system which assisted them in working in these circumstances. They generally had punitive attitudes towards offenders as well as being suspicious of them and the motives for, and explanations of, their behaviour. They had a shared sense of mission in that they believed strongly that offenders should be electronically monitored. This meant that most monitoring officers would ensure that offenders were tagged, whatever the risks to themselves. This mission was tempered only by the realization that their job was just that – it was not a vocation, so there were limits to what they were prepared to do (Hucklesby 2011). These views were reinforced by a shared aim of completing tasks as quickly as possible. Although monitoring officers shared some core attitudes and values, there were also some discernable differences between them which fell into three working credos corresponding roughly with those found in studies of criminal justice personnel (see Hucklesby 2011 for more discussion on this point). The three working credos were: probation workers, pragmatists and technicians. They are likely to have different impacts upon offenders' compliance for two reasons: first, because they conform to procedural justice principles to different degrees; and second, because different levels of information about how EM works are provided to offenders and their families. Compliance with procedural justice principles might also increase the potential for longer-term desistance.

Seven probation workers were interviewed. They conformed to the ideals of procedural justice, treating offenders and their families with dignity and respect (Tyler 1990). They had a heightened level of trust of offenders and a greater awareness and empathy of offenders' lives and circumstances. They ensured that offenders received all the necessary information about EM and took extra time to do this. The largest group of monitoring officers were pragmatists, who comprised half of the interviewees. Their central concern was that they completed their tasks efficiently and effectively. They held non-judgemental attitudes of offenders and their families but displayed a lack of trust of them. They stuck to their job description, providing limited information and advice about EM only. Technicians, the smallest group of the three types, prioritized fitting the equipment in the shortest possible time. They displayed no empathy with offenders or their families, and distrusted them. They kept their distance from them with as little time as possible spent interacting with them.

According to procedural justice principles, offenders' compliance should be greater when dealt with by probation workers and lower when dealt with by technicians. Offenders may have very different experiences of EM, depending on the monitoring officers they have contact with, but they are likely to see a range of monitoring officers during the time they are electronically monitored, which will dilute the impact of any one individual.

Conclusions

EM in England and Wales is viewed primarily as a punitive sanction. This is one of the reasons, alongside private sector involvement, why EM has not been universally welcomed as a measure to reduce prison populations. Added to concerns from some quarters that it is not punitive enough and fails to incapacitate offenders sufficiently, EM has struggled to gain acceptance and legitimacy. In many respects the use of EM has grown despite such concerns, primarily because it provides one potential solution to rising prison populations.

The research reported in this chapter begins to question some of the assumptions made about EM in respect of issues related to compliance and desistance. It suggests that EM has positive effects on some offenders' behaviour but that these are not universal. In common with all measures, EM influences some offenders and not others. Offenders' readiness to change was a key determinant of whether EM impacted upon offending and offenders' longer-term intentions about ceasing or continuing to offend, with offenders who have already taken steps to stop offending – 'desisters' – gaining most benefit from EM. EM contributes to desistance by giving offenders the opportunity and excuse to break away from the situations, places and individuals that are linked to their offending. In short, EM appears to be habit-breaking, allowing ties with anti-social capital to be severed. It may also assist in building up social capital by facilitating improved relationships between offenders and their families and friends and making offenders more 'job ready'. For some offenders – 'persisters' – 'old habits die hard' and they continue to offend and/or their social capital depreciates because relationships become increasingly strained and employment is disrupted.

At first sight the non-compliance rate for EM is high, but most incidents were found to be relatively minor, mostly short time violations which resulted from offenders' chaotic lifestyles and inability to plan rather than malicious intentions. High breach rates for EM are what would be expected given the precise recording and measurement of non-compliant behaviour, which is made possible by EM and is one of its stated advantages. The majority of offenders suggested that they wanted to comply with their curfew orders. Decisions to comply were complex and based on a range of factors. It was clear that EM acted as a deterrent because offenders consistently commented on their fear of going to prison as a motivating fact for their compliance and desistance. Distributive and procedural justice, the fact that surveillance enables offenders to be watched and increases the likelihood of getting caught, offenders' motivation and support from significant others were all described as influencing offenders' compliance decisions.

Distinguishing between short-term compliance with the requirements of an order and longer-term desistance is useful conceptually and analytically because it clearly delineates between two outcomes and demonstrates that compliance with orders has been neglected by theory and in practice. The overlapping explanations of compliance and desistance provided by offenders in this study suggest that many of the influences on decisions are common to both processes. Consequently, distinguishing between the two may overly complicate matters because any improvements (or deterioration) in a range of factors is likely to pay dividends in terms of both compliance and desistance.

Offenders' experiences of EM are inextricably linked to the individuals operating it because the technology is only as effective as the people working with it (Hucklesby 2008). England and Wales differ from many other jurisdictions in this regard because EM is solely operated by the private sector. Their employees, the monitoring officers, were primarily concerned about their personal which influenced how they went about their work and how they interacted with offenders. Reassuringly, monitoring officers had a set of shared values which meant that they were committed to ensuring that offenders were monitored when they should be. There was no sense that they were on the side of the offenders; they were generally suspicious of them, consistently questioning the motives for their behaviour and the explanations provided by them. This might allay some of the fears associated with other community sentences about the commitment of staff to the punitive and enforcement elements of EM. Monitoring officers had distinct working credos, each of which resulted in different working practices and different ways of interacting with offenders. According to procedural justice principles, probation workers' practices were the most likely to have positive impacts upon offenders' compliance and desistance.

There are many reasons to surmise why the experience of being electronically monitored in the UK might be different from elsewhere, most notably because EM is operated wholly by the private sector and is not integrated with probation supervision. The UK context will have influenced the findings of the research and it will be interesting and important to conduct similar research in other jurisdictions to find out how offenders experience EM and how different models of operation impact upon their experiences, compliance and long-term desistance.

Notes

1 Breaches of community orders where EM is one of a number of requirements are dealt with by the Probation Service after initial investigations by the monitoring companies.
2 This is the process whereby time absent from the curfew address is accumulated until it reaches a certain level, at which point formal breach action is instigated (see CJJI 2008 for more details).

References

Bottomley, A.K., Hucklesby, A. and Mair, G. (2004) 'The new uses of electronic monitoring: findings for the implementation phase in three pilot areas', in *Issues in Community and Criminal Justice Monograph 5* (London: NAPO), pp. 13–51.

Bottoms, A. (2001) 'Compliance and community penalties', in A. Bottoms, L. Gelsthorpe and S. Rex (eds) *Community Penalties: Change or Challenges* (Cullompton: Willan), pp. 87–116.

Bottoms, A., Shapland, J., Costello, A., Holmes, D. and Muir, G. (2004) 'Towards desistance: theoretical underpinnings for an empirical study', *Howard Journal*, 43:4, pp. 368–389.

Burnett, R. (2004) 'To reoffend or not to reoffend? The ambivalence of convicted property offenders', in S. Maruna and R. Immarigeon (eds) *After Crime and Punishment: Ex-offender Reintegration and Desistance from Crime* (Cullompton: Willan), pp. 152–180.

Chapman, T. and Hough, M. (1998) *Evidence-based Practice* (London: Home Office).

CJJI (Criminal Justice Joint Inspection) (2008) *A Complicated Business: A Joint Inspection of Electronically Monitored Curfew Requirements, Orders and Licences* (London: Ministry of Justice).

Dingwall, G. (2005) *Alcohol and Crime* (Cullompton: Willan).

Dodgson, K., Goodwin, P., Howard, P. Llewellyn-thomas, S., Mortimer, E., Russell, N. and Weiner, M. (2001) *Electronic Monitoring of Released Prisoners: An Evaluation of the Home Detention Curfew Scheme* (London: Home Office).

Elliot, R., Airs, J., Easton, C. and Lewis, R. (2000) *Electronically Monitored Curfew for 10–15 Year Olds: Report of the Pilot* (London: Home Office).

Farrall, S. (2002) *Rethinking What Works with Offenders* (Cullompton: Willan).

Farrall, S. (2004) 'Social capital and offender re-integration: making probation desistance focussed', in S. Maruna and R. Immarigeon (eds) *After Crime and Punishment: Ex-offender Reintegration and Desistance from Crime* (Cullompton: Willan), pp. 57–84.

Farrall, S. and Calverley, A. (2006) *Understanding Desistance from Crime* (Maidenhead: Open University Press).

Hagan, J. and McCarthy, B. (1997) *Mean Streets: Youth Crime and Homelessness* (Cambridge: Cambridge University Press).

Harper, G. and Chitty, C. (2005) *The Impact of Corrections on Re-Offending: A Review of 'What Works'* (London: Home Office).

Haverkamp, R., Mayer, M. and Lévy, R. (2004) 'Electronic monitoring in Europe', *European Journal of Crime, Criminal Law and Criminal Justice*, 12:1: pp. 36–45.

Hearnden, I. and Millie, A. (2003) *Investigating Links between Probation Enforcement and Reconviction* (London: Home Office).

Home Office (2003) *Prison Statistics England and Wales*. (London: HMSO).

Hough, M. (1996) 'Problem Drug use and criminal justice: a review of the literature', Drug Prevention Initiative Paper no. 15, Home Office.

Hucklesby, A. (2008) 'Vehicles of desistance: the impact of electronically monitored curfew orders', *Criminology and Criminal Justice*, 8:1, pp. 51–71.

Hucklesby, A. (2009) 'Understanding offenders' compliance: a case study of electronically monitored curfew orders', *Journal of Law and Society*, 36:2, pp. 248–271.

Hucklesby, A. (2010) 'Drug interventions in the remand process', in A. Hucklesby and E. Wincup (eds) *Drug Interventions in Criminal Justice* (Maidenhead: Open University Press), pp 110–134.

Hucklesby, A. (2011) 'The working life of electronic monitoring officers', *Criminology and Criminal Justice*, 11:1, pp. 1–18.

Hucklesby, A. (2012) 'Compliance with electronically monitored curfew orders: some empirical findings', in A. Crawford and A. Hucklesby (eds) *Legitimacy and Compliance in Criminal Justice* (London: Routledge), pp. 138–158.

Hucklesby, A. and Wincup, E. (eds) (2010) *Drug Interventions in Criminal Justice* (Maidenhead: Open University Press).

Lobley, D. and Smith, D. (2000) *Evaluation of Electronically Monitored Restriction of Liberty Orders* (Edinburgh: Scottish Executive Research Unit).

McGuire, J. (1995) *What Works: Reducing Reoffending* (Chichester: Wiley).

McNeill, F. and Robinson, G. (2012) 'Liquid legitimacy and community sanctions', in A. Crawford and A. Hucklesby (eds) *Legitimacy and Compliance in Criminal Justice* (London: Routledge).

Mair, G. (2001) 'Technology and the future of probation', in A.E. Bottoms, L. Gelsthorpe and S. Rex (eds) *Community Penalties: Change and Challenges*, (Cullompton: Willan), pp. 168–182

Mair, G. (2005) 'Electronic monitoring in England and Wales: evidence-based or not?', *Criminal Justice*, 5:3, pp. 257–278.

Mair, G. and Mortimer, E. (1996) *Curfew Orders and Electronic Monitoring* (London: Home Office).

Mair, G. and Nee, C. (1990) *Electronic Monitoring: The Trials and Their Results* (London: Home Office).

Marie, O., Moreton, K. and Goncalines, M. (2011) *The Effect of Early Release of Prisoners on Home Detention Curfew (HDC) on Recidivism* (London: Ministry of Justice).

Maruna, S. (2001) *Making Good: How Ex-convicts Reform and Rebuild Their Lives* (Washington, DC: American Psychological Association Books).

Ministry of Justice (2010) *Offender Management Caseload Statistics 2009 England and Wales* (London: Ministry of Justice).

Ministry of Justice (2011a) 'Offender management statistics quarterly bulletin October to December 2010'. Online. Available at: www.justice.gov.uk/downloads/publications/statistics-and-data/mojstats/omsq-oct-dec10.pdf (accessed 10 June 2011).

Ministry of Justice (2011b) 'Service specification for deliver curfew requirement'. Online. Available at: www.justice.gov.uk/downloads/about/noms/directory-of-services/2011–04–26%20Curfew%20Requirement%20Specification%20P1%200.pdf (accessed 10 June 2011).

Mortimer, E. and May, C. (1997) *Electronic Monitoring in Practice: The Second Year of the Trials of Curfew Orders* (London: Home Office).

NAO (National Audit Office) (2006) *The Electronic Monitoring of Adult Offenders* (London: National Audit Office).

Nellis, M. (2003a) 'Electronic monitoring and the future of probation', in W.H. Chui and M. Nellis, *Moving Probation Forward* (Harlow: Pearson Education), pp. 245–260.

Nellis, M. (2003b) 'They don't even know we're there: the electronic monitoring of offenders in England and Wales', in K. Ball and F. Webster (eds) *The Intensification of Surveillance: Crime, Terrorism and Warfare in the Information Age* (London: Pluto Press), pp. 62–89.

Nellis, M. (2006) 'The limitations of electronic monitoring: reflections on the tagging of Peter Williams', *Prison Service Journal*. Online. Available at: www.hmprisonservice.gov.uk/resourcecentre/prisonservicejournal/index.asp?id=5017,3124,11,3148,0,0 (accessed 10 June 2011).

Nellis, M. and Lilly, J.R. (2000) 'Accepting the tag: probation officers and home detention curfew', *VISTA*, 6, pp. 68–80.

Renzema, M. and Mayo-Wilson, E. (2005) 'Can electronic monitoring reduce crime for moderate to high risk offenders?', *Journal of Experimental Criminology*, 1, pp. 215–237.

Rex, S. (1999) 'Desistance from offending: experiences of probation', *Howard Journal*, 38:4, pp. 366–383.

Robinson, G. and McNeill, F. (2008) 'Exploring the dynamics of compliance with community penalties', *Theoretical Criminology*, 12:4, pp. 431–450.

Rogers, P. (2011) 'Specification, benchmarking and costing of EM', paper presented at the 7th CEP Conference on Electronic Monitoring, Evora, Portugal, 5–7 May. Online. Available at: www.cep-probation.org/default.asp?page_id=157&map_id=85 (accessed 10 June 2011).

Sampson, R.J. and Laub, J.H. (1993) *Crime in the Making: Pathways and Turning Points Through Life* (Cambridge, MA: Harvard University Press).

Shute, S. (2007) *Satellite Tracking of Offenders: A Study of the Pilots in England and Wales* (London: Ministry of Justice).

Smith, D. (2001) 'Electronic monitoring of offenders: the Scottish experience', *Criminal Justice*, 1:2, pp. 201–214.

Tyler, T. (1990) *Why People Obey the Law* (New Haven, CT: Yale University Press).

Tyler, T. and Huo, Y.J. (2002) *Trust in the Law: Encouraging Public Cooperation with the Police and the Courts* (New York: Russell Sage).

Walter, I. (2002) *Evaluation of the National roll-out of Curfew Orders* (London: Home Office).

Walter, I., Sugg, D. and Moore, L. (2001) *A Year on the Tag: Interviews with Criminal Justice Practitioners and Electronic Monitoring Staff about Curfew Orders* (London: Home Office).

Whitfield, D. (1997) *Tackling the Tag* (Winchester: Waterside Press).

Whitfield, D. (2001) *The Magic Bracelet* (Winchester: Waterside Press).

13 Evaluative research on electronic monitoring

Marc Renzema

If one looks at the history of corrections, one sees that most – if not all – innovations in corrections have been greeted with enthusiasm and great expectations. The 'crime problem' was going to yield to the penitentiary, the reformatory, indeterminate sentences, probation, intensive probation supervision and boot camps – to cite only a few of the best-known examples of major changes. So far, crime has proven quite resilient and the innovations, although they never lived up to the expectations of their creators, have become part of the criminal justice system despite their disappointing impacts on the 'crime problem'.

Almost four decades ago Ralph Schwitzgebel (1968: 99) wrote:

> Recent developments in electronic technology greatly increase the possibility of deterring the commission of certain types of offenses in the community. When specific, offending behaviors can be prevented, it will no longer be necessary to imprison an offender in order to protect the community. The offender may be safely released on parole, thus increasing his or her freedom, while at the same time the community will be exposed to less risk than under present release procedures.

Was Dr Schwitzgebel correct? Certainly the potential existed, but after more than two decades of large-scale use of electronic monitoring (EM), do we yet know whether there has been a significant impact on offender behaviour? The short answer is that we know a little and that by and large the potential implicit in the technology remains unfulfilled. But, as always in matters of criminal justice policy, the realities are complex and sometimes elusive.

First off, to gauge whether Dr Schwitzgebel's[1] optimism was warranted, one needs to break down the overall issue of impact into several researchable questions.

Key questions for empirical research

1 *Does EM affect recidivism after the EM period has concluded?* In the early days of EM, there was folklore among agencies using the technology about what might be called the rustification of offenders.[2] To exaggerate only a

little, the idea was that if one put enough structure in an offender's life and restricted access to criminal associates and a criminogenic environment, after a time the offender would come to enjoy the satisfactions of a cottage with a white picket fence, working for a living and playing with his or her children – thereby desisting from crime. In essence, EM could be rehabilitative per se. Also possible was that EM would be so unpleasant that offenders would be deterred from future misdeeds even after it ended. A third rationale is that EM could increase participation in and compliance with other kinds of programmes that would carry most of the burden of rehabilitation – for example, vocational training or substance abuse treatment.

In terms of published research, this means that one needs to look at who receives EM, for how long, what the alternatives are[3] and what other programme elements are delivered to both the EM recipients and to those with whom their recidivism is compared. Sadly, even when groups are reasonably equated, many of the needed descriptive elements have not been reported. Especially defective are reports of what adjunctive treatments or services are received, particularly for comparison groups. Attempting to sort out why one study reports favourable results while another is slightly negative is often fruitless.

2   *Does EM affect offender criminal behaviour during the monitored period?*
Whether one wants to call on classical criminological theory, routine activity theory or other theories that consider the social and/or psychological dynamics of criminal behaviour, there is good reason to think that, at least for its duration, at least some offenders would be more likely to desist from crime than if they were not under monitoring. On the other hand, although empirical evidence is largely missing, is the idea that resentment, stigmatization, family conflict and labelling could actually worsen the probabilities that those under EM will commit crime. Also arguable is that EM might not affect criminal behaviour at all, but that those under EM are more easily caught for new crimes and would thus manifest higher official recidivism than those not monitored. It is easy to conceive why EM might reduce recidivism while in operation, but not afterward, and one can also conceive a positive post-EM effect but a negative impact during monitoring. Thus, the questions of impact during and afterward both need to be asked separately.

3   *Does EM have positive or negative impacts other than those on offender criminal behaviour?* Do, for example, offenders become depressed or commit more domestic assaults while on EM? Are family members positive or negative about their offender's EM? The evidence here is often anecdotal or from poorly crafted exit surveys, but some information is known and will be discussed briefly later in this chapter. This chapter is a secondary product of an ongoing and unfinished meta-analysis commissioned by the Campbell Collaboration on the impact of EM on offender behaviour. Because of this primary mission, I am less prepared to address two other critical research questions, but an agency using or considering EM absolutely needs to marshal the evidence on them. If one is able to conclude that EM reduces

recidivism, or *at least does not worsen it,* and EM does not worsen the psychological situation of the offender or the offender's family, one also needs to ask two additional questions.

4 *Aside from recidivism impacts, what is the financial impact of operating EM?* On one hand, EM could potentially avert prison construction or inhuman conditions. On the other, it could divert funds from programmes that might have a higher payoff in terms of public safety.[4]

5 *Does EM allow more people to be dealt with more severely than they would have been had it not been used?* These are the issues usually called net-widening and net-strengthening. Most criminologists decry 'net-widening' while others (often politicians and talk-show hosts) conclude that more people need to be more highly controlled. Wherever one stands on the issue, it is clear that EM and other intermediate sanctions have the potential to expand and increase the control of the criminal justice system and that the degree to which this occurs needs to be understood so that unintended consequences do not occur.

Unlike the general issues of recidivism and unintended side-effects, these last two questions are likely very much jurisdiction specific and not as susceptible to a systematic review. They should, however, be very important to the planners and operators of offender monitoring systems.

Having set out some general questions, it is necessary to deal with some obstacles immediately apparent when one attempts to answer them.

The slippery nature of EM

Does surgery work? Anyone with half a brain instantly grasps that this is a stupid and impossible-to-answer question. Before starting to answer, one would need to know the diagnosis, how far the disease has progressed, the general condition of the patient, co-existing conditions, concurrent treatments, the specific procedure being used and probably something about the surgeon's training, prior experience and instrumentation. Yet I am frequently asked whether EM 'works'. In most cases, what the questioner wants to know is whether it affects recidivism, but not always.

As suggested by the research questions above, there are different goals for EM use, but there are also different means by which it might achieve those and other goals. For example:

• EM might reduce recidivism by aiding the shaping of behaviour through positive reinforcements of the sort envisioned by the Schwitzgebel brothers.
• EM might reduce recidivism by increasing offender accountability during the period of monitoring, as suggested in research question 2 above.
• EM might not have an independent impact on behaviour, but the accountability it brings to treatment attendance might increase the impact of treatment, thereby reducing recidivism.

- EM might have no direct impact on recidivism, but could contribute to slowing down rises of correctional expenditure and reduced taxpayer burdens by helping to avoid the construction and operational costs of jails and prisons.
- EM might increase the frequency of official recidivism while simultaneously reducing the amount of overall harm done by recidivists through more efficient detection of criminal behaviour and removal of the offender from the community before much harm is done.[5]
- EM could increase general deterrence by making community sanctions more onerous, or it could reduce it if potential offenders perceive that the consequence of a given act is not jail, but 'only EM'.

Not only are the real and potential programme goals diverse, and possible indicators of success and failure sometimes conflicting (i.e. recidivism could be a success in one programme but a failure in another), but the populations subjected to EM are diverse. My colleague in the Campbell project, Evan Mayo-Wilson, argues that the psychological impact of being placed on EM might be quite different depending on whether the offender perceives it as a 'gift' (e.g. early release) or 'intensified punishment' (e.g. as an alternative to minimally supervised probation).

Diverse populations

It seems unreasonable to expect EM to have similar impacts on juvenile delinquents awaiting disposition (who would otherwise be detained) and adjudicated delinquents for whom it is an enhancement to regular probation. EM has been used for pre-trial release for those accused of everything from shoplifting to non-capital murder. Ages of those monitored have ranged from 10 years to at least into the eighties and, of course, contingencies change during the lifespan.[6] Some using agencies have excluded alcoholics and other addicts, others have accepted them. At least one agency has used Global Positioning System (GPS) monitoring with developmentally disabled paedophiles. Although the conventional wisdom is that to succeed on monitoring an offender should not be psychotic (or in the throes of addiction), EM is routinely used on stalkers and domestic violence offenders. Criminal histories range from fairly minor first offenders to people who have had multiple felony convictions. I have encountered offenders who were very embarrassed or felt humiliated by wearing monitoring bracelets, but have heard of others, particularly adolescents, who are said to enjoy the status of being 'bad' signified by their monitoring bracelet. For them, EM may be akin to getting a jailhouse tattoo, a sign of manliness and potency.

Application at diverse stages in the criminal justice process

EM has been used in the criminal justice process at both the 'front end' and the 'back end'. The 'front end' uses of EM include pre-trial (or pre-adjudication) as a condition of bail or in lieu of bail, as an alternative to the criminal process (pre-trial diversion), probation and intermediate sanctions such as work-release centres and day-reporting programmes, where the legal status of the monitoree is closer to that of an inmate than to a probationer. It has also been used as an alternative to the incarceration of rule-violating probationers. On the 'back end', that is after incarceration, EM has been used in an attempt to gradually increase the responsibilities of reintegrating parolees (a 'step down' in structure and control). Other uses have included increasing surveillance of inmates in work-release centres and sanctioning rule violations that fall short of those mandating reincarceration. In some cases EM appears to be used solely to punish or for the appearance of toughness. An example is rich American entrepreneur and celebrity Martha Stewart, who served five months on EM following a short prison sentence for obstructing a federal investigation of insider stock trading (Masters 2004). I recall one particular case, a California parolee who had mutilated a 15-year-old girl, where two monitors of different types were placed on him because of both genuine risk and need to pacify a public that was horrified by his release.[7]

Diverse and changing technology

Evaluation of impact is difficult given that the diversity of programmes, offenders and the several families of technologies are all subsumed under the term 'electronic monitoring'. With the exception of the works by Padgett *et al.* (2006) and Bales *et al.* (2010) that included GPS monitoring and a couple of early pieces that used 'token verifiers' or a mix of 'token verifiers' and 'continuous signalling' equipment, all of the published research to date has focused on 'continuously signalling equipment', which is a small blessing that is unlikely to endure for long as technology continues to evolve. In the early days of EM there were only two basic approaches available. One involved a machine placing random calls to the offender's residence. The offender would answer the phone and verify his or her identity by inserting a wrist- or ankle-worn keystone-shaped magnet into a wand attached to a telephone, i.e. a 'token verifier'. Other approaches to identity verification involved electronic analysis of speech (so-called 'voiceprints'), an officer later listening to the telephone robot's tape recording, the offender punching in a code on the telephone keypad with the code being generated by a watch-like device securely attached to the offender, or even slow-scan television images transmitted over the telephone line and compared to reference images by a human operator.

The second core approach, usually called 'continuous signalling', involved a radio transmitter secured to the offender's ankle or wrist and a receiver attached to the offender's home telephone. The receiver was programmed to 'listen' for the transmitter's signal and to store and report when the offender was and was not in the vicinity of the receiver. It is difficult to compare more recent research done using continuous signalling equipment with some of the early research; early equipment did not work very well, generated abundant false alarms and its limitations were often not well understood by either justice system agencies or contractors doing monitoring for those agencies.

Both the random calling (RC) and continuous signalling (CS) approaches are still in use, but additional features have been added. Early in EM's lifetime (late 1980s), RC was offered with breath alcohol testing. In the United States the proportion of people who admit driving while under licence-suspension ranges from 52 per cent (older men) to 94 per cent (first offenders) (Scopatz *et al.* 2003, citing other sources). Using California survey data, a speech by National Transportation Safety Board official Danielle Roeber (2005) offers a 65 per cent continued driving rate for suspended drivers and a 71 per cent rate for revoked drivers. Strangely, while there is solid research showing significant impact of alcohol-sensing ignition interlocks on recidivism, I have found only one study that included a remote alcohol testing programme as a treatment component (Lapham *et al.* 2007).[8]

CS technology has also evolved. An early addition was the equipping of probation and parole officers with portable receivers that could detect signals from the body-worn transmitters, so-called 'drive by' receivers. These could be used to unobtrusively and efficiently determine whether offenders away from their home phones were where they were scheduled to be (e.g. at work or Alcoholics Anonymous meetings) or where they were not supposed to be (e.g. pubs). Since 2003 an ankle-worn transmitter that transdermally tests for alcohol has been available. In typical application it monitors both the presence/absence of the offender and uploads alcohol-testing information to the supervising officer through the same phoneline-attached receiver used for the basic CS monitoring. To date, no evaluative research on this application has been found.

Another variant of CS equipment has been used in domestic violence cases where the offender has been restricted from having contact with the victim. In this application the victim is given a receiver that generates an audible alarm and telephones the police if the offender's transmitter approaches the victim's residence. No creditable evaluations of this application have been found, although there are both lawsuits from its failures and glowing anecdotal reports of its success.

Real-time tracking of offenders using GPS began in 1997 and grew slowly for the first few years. As with CS equipment more than a decade earlier, the initial applications were plagued by equipment problems and incomplete understanding by agencies of equipment limitations. Recently the equipment has become cheaper and more reliable, and has begun to partially displace CS equipment in the marketplace. There are three primary variants: near-real-time tracking with exclusion zones, near-real-time tracking without exclusion zones and track logging with infrequent (e.g. daily to weekly) data uploads. In the tracking with exclusion zones application, the offender-worn (or offender-carried) device radios its location on a schedule that can range from every few seconds to perhaps hourly intervals; the tradeoff is battery life – more reporting yields more frequent battery recharges. The offender can be restricted to a certain area (e.g. home, work and the shortest route between home and work); leaving the permitted area results in a violation alert being sent. The devices can also permit a large area of travel (e.g. a county) but exclude certain areas such as school-yards, 'drug corners' or the homes of victims or witnesses. Another approach is to simply track the offender; the assumption here is that knowing he or she will be held accountable will affect the offender's behaviour. In the last couple of years, agencies and vendors have realized that tracking does not always have to be in real time and that a device which simply records where an offender has been and uploads the information by modem at intervals may be sufficient for their goals.[9] Another variant of GPS integrates offender tracking, whether real-time or delayed, with police crime report databases. This has been shown to be technically feasible and pilot studies have yielded a few cases of solved crimes as well as electronically alibied suspects, but no research has yet been done on the impact of this technology on either specific deterrence or police investigative costs. Just as RC and CS technologies improved and became more flexible, even now GPS continues to evolve. About ten years ago a psychologist acquaintance of mine approached GPS manufacturers about integrating a penile plethysmo-graph into their tracking equipment and found no current interest, but that was before the Jessica Lunsford tragedy that provoked a wave of harsh new laws in the United States, some of which authorize lifetime monitoring of some sex offenders.[10] Because GPS monitoring cannot be used in some locations, vendors are experimenting with various radio systems to supplement GPS information so that almost no place will be excluded from coverage. When this succeeds, the use of geotracking will become more attractive and programme protocols are likely to be greatly altered. Even more technology options than described above are now newly in the market or in various stages of pre-production testing. A system now on the market records body movements during sleep through a wrist-worn device. These movements are uploaded every morning to a remote computer that analyses patterns for indications of alcohol (and other substance) abuse. I have seen demonstrations of devices that measure pupillary responsive-ness, eye muscle movements, speech patterns and tremors during writing that correlate with substance abuse. Sweat-patch testing for substance abuse is now fairly routine, but experiments are being done with microelectronic capsules implanted in patches that use telemetry to detect the levels of abused substances.

Diverse programme components and protocols

As if being confronted by diverse populations, differing points of use in the criminal justice system and a proliferating variety of technologies were not enough to make evaluation of EM's impact extremely difficult, the would-be evaluator must admit the fact that programmes dealing with similar offenders (e.g. addicted young burglars) at the same point in the system (e.g. probation) with similar technologies (e.g. CS monitoring) may operate very differently and produce a very different experience for the offender. Some programmes see the offender daily; others bring him in for a monthly equipment check. Some divorce the human supervision and equipment installation and maintenance aspects of EM. In some agencies one employee supervises the offender and does all of the installation and maintenance tasks; in others, parts of the technical aspects of EM are sub-contracted. One of the complaints in the early days of EM was that it was turning social workers into technicians, that the demands of EM were interfering with the relationship that the officer was supposed to be using to induce offender change. I have not heard this complaint lately, but I am not aware of anyone having done a time study analysis of how officers involved in EM actually use their contact time with offenders versus those not using EM. It is becoming increasingly difficult to identify the EM component of correctional treatment. In the early days one found evaluations of 'EM programmes' where EM was seen as the primary component. Currently, it appears, at least in the United States, to be used more prescriptively (or perhaps capriciously). Rather than everyone in a certain classification receiving a standard duration of EM, John Probationer will receive EM 'because he needs it'. Unfortunately, the factors that precipitated the need are not consistently described and one is often left wondering why John was sent home with EM while Harry stayed at the work-release facility when John and Harry look identical in terms of demographic and criminal history. After eight years of reviewing EM evaluations, I have become extremely distrustful of studies with matched comparison groups where some human decision-maker decided which offenders would receive EM as opposed to the other dispositions available at the same time. Although the literature on clinical versus statistical prediction routinely favours statistical prediction, I think it is dangerous to assume that all judges and classification officers are deaf and blind. I found only seven studies that attempted random assignment and only four succeeded. The best of the rest involved historical comparison groups. Most studies involve mining files (or databases) for similar-appearing offenders.

Even when EM is standardized, offenders in evaluated programmes often receive a witch's brew of adjunctive treatments of uncertain appropriateness, quality and duration. Evaluation reports typically report statistics such as '37 per cent of the EM group were receiving drug counseling and 15 per cent were attending Alcoholics Anonymous' without bothering to delineate the frequency or duration of attendance at either programme, what precipitated attendance (i.e. judicial assignment, classification instrument score or volunteering), or whether the drug counsellor had any qualifications whatsoever. A competent study of violent male parolees in Georgia (Finn and Muirhead-Steves 2002) seemed to indicate no suppression effects on recidivism in the whole sample, but noted in the text differentially more positive effects on sex offenders. My contact with the Georgia Department of Corrections revealed that during the EM test period, as opposed to the comparison group released earlier, Georgia was implementing the containment model but that not everyone eligible during the EM period had received either polygraph exams or sex offender therapy and there had also been quality control issues with some of the contracted polygraphers and therapists. Thus, something may have 'worked', but the state department of corrections, the evaluators and the meta-analysts cannot decipher what it was. Although much better than most of what came before, even the most recent and most positive studies I have seen (Padgett *et al.* 2006; Lapham *et al.* 2007; Marklund and Holmberg 2009; Di Tella and Schargrodsky 2009) do not shed enough light in this respect. Something in the 'black box' worked but more research will be needed to clarify the results sufficiently so that replication can be attempted elsewhere.

The situation with respect to comparison groups is even worse than for those receiving EM. Life goes on, things happen, even if one is not on EM. Details on the treatment, supervision and surveillance received by members of comparison groups are usually either absent or sketchily reported.

Although everyone who does research on EM's impact faces abundant challenges and most make missteps, at least finding the research should be easy – or so I thought when I signed on to the Campbell project. I was wrong.

Finding EM research

Every meta-analysis attempts a comprehensive collection of evaluation studies. The Campbell project is particularly rigorous in its insistence that attempts be made to capture the 'fugitive' (unpublished, unindexed) literature. Past meta-analytic studies have delineated publication bias, i.e. studies which have positive findings are more likely to be published than 'no significant difference' studies, and studies done by scholars at prestigious universities are more likely to be published than those done by backwater governmental agencies, even if both are competently done.

To uncover this fugitive literature I wrote to all of the manufacturers of EM equipment (24 at the time) and asked for help locating research done by users of their equipment. Two responded with studies, but neither passed my methodology filter. I wrote to all of the research directors or administrators of state departments of correction in the United States and received a few responses but no usable studies. All major abstracts were mined, including Academic Search Premier, C2-SPECTR, Criminal Justice Abstracts, Criminal Justice Periodical Index, ERIC, CINCH, Healthsource Nursing/Academic Edition, Ingenta, MEDLINE, NCJRS, ProQuest Digital Dissertations, PsycINFO, Social Science Citation Index, Social Work Abstracts and Sociological Abstracts. In addition, Copernic Agent Professional, a web metasearch and filtering program, was used to search the internet; more recently I have used Google as well. For several years, the University of Toronto maintained a web-accessible bibliography on EM that was occasionally updated and which provided access to a few studies not otherwise found. My position as ex-editor of the *Journal of Offender Monitoring* produced a number of queries from people who were conducting research that I was able to obtain when it was completed as well as opportunities to review manuscripts.

After all was said and done, although many studies were found in multiple sources, two resources stood out: NCJRS (National Criminal Justice Reference Service) and Criminal Justice Abstracts had indexed at least 95 per cent of all studies found. The biennial EM conference at Egmond aan Zee, the Netherlands, sponsored by the Conferénce Permanente Europénne de la Probation, provided access to many studies conducted by European, Australian and New Zealand governments and to European administrators and scholars who have been very cooperative in supplying European research as it has been completed. Currently I have almost 900 EM articles in my bibliography, of which 152 are serious attempts at evaluation. Fewer than 20 have sufficient methodological rigour to be mentioned in the Campbell review now being prepared; probably only half a dozen will be included in the formal meta-analysis. I update my own website (http://renzema.net) bibliographies twice a year and will do so for at least through 2011.

So, what can be said about EM research after reviewing more than 20 years of it?

Overview of trends in EM research

The early research in the United States was quite diverse in terms of objectives and methods. Between 1987 and 1995, five experiments were attempted using random assignment, but only two resulted in interpretable studies, and those showed no significant differences. Curtis and Pennel (1987) was funded to do a randomized evaluation of a San Diego work furlough programme, but operational difficulties halted the research. Petersilia and Turner (1990) used random assignment in a study of California probationers, but only a minority of those supposed to be on EM actually received it. Baumer *et al.* (1990) did a small but clean study of Indianapolis probationers, but results are less than clear because of programme integrity issues. Austin and Hardyman (1991) attempted random assignment in a study of Oklahoma parolees, but the treatment and control groups were not prequalified on the availability of telephones (so some of the experimental group were denied EM) and follow-up periods for the two groups were different. Of the five early attempts at random assignment, only Baumer *et al.* (1990) and a small study done in Georgia by Erwin (1987) as part of the larger Rand Corporation study of intensive supervision programmes are likely to be reported in the Campbell meta-analysis. Not until a Swiss study done in 2005 (Villetaz and Killias) did another randomized study appear; it was followed in 2007 by Lapham *et al.*'s study of recidivism of drink drivers who received a variety of dispositions, including EM. Although not randomly assigned by the researcher, the procedures by which Di Tella and Schargrodsky's (2009) Argentinean offenders were assigned appear to have achieved randomization as well.

The bulk of evaluation studies did not involve comparison groups, and those that did match were often clearly inadequate in the quality of the matches. Evaluation objectives of studies have varied widely. Early studies in the United States often did exit interviews of monitorees to try to gain a qualitative understanding of the experience of being on EM. The same thing happened in Europe, Australia and New Zealand about a decade later as EM began to gain support as a sentencing alternative. Some studies focused on survival without revocation to the end of the monitored period, while others looked at recidivism after release from monitoring, but usually only for a short period. Very few looked at both, but they should have if one is to understand the overall impact of EM. Notable exceptions to the typical six-month to two-year post-EM follow-ups are the four-year follow-up reported by Finn and Muirhead-Steves (2002) and the three years of Jones and Ross (1997); however, the latter study had both programme-definition and matching problems. Gainey *et al.* (2000) did a study of a mixed group of traffic, misdemeanour, and felony offenders with mixed amounts of jail and EM that were followed for 5–12 years, but there was no comparison group. In many studies there is an issue of dosage; just as one would not look at the five-year survival rates of lung cancer patients who had been given a single aspirin, it seems unreasonable to examine long-term success rates of monitorees who have experienced EM for a few days or for whom durations were not reported. Many studies report average durations, but when one looks closely one finds that some offenders experienced only a few days (and not because of violations) while others experienced multiples of the average. Juvenile populations are particularly treacherous in terms of variability of duration.

While the volume of EM evaluation in the United States slowly declined until a recent upturn, studies seem to be improving in quality. Table 13.1 shows the volume of studies by five-year periods since the first article tagged in my bibliography as a programme evaluation appeared in 1986. Purely descriptive articles and review articles were not included.

Over the last ten years, in the UK, the Home Office Research Unit has carried out a number of competent studies that have shown no significant impact on recidivism. A general issue with the Home Office studies is the relatively brief duration of monitoring and, in most cases, lack of adjunctive services.

The more recent studies often attempt to deal with the problem of equating comparison groups through multivariate techniques. This is not always an advantage: although statistical risk of recidivism may indeed be the same, there may be qualitative differences in groups that make the EM group more or less responsive to EM than the compared group would have been. Given all that has been said above concerning difficulties of EM research, it is time to take a look at the first three of the empirical questions listed at the beginning of this chapter.

Table 13.1 Number of EM evaluation studies collected per five-year period

Period	Number of articles
1986–1990	37
1991–1995	36
1996–2000	34
2001–2005	23
2006–2010 (May)	30

Where we are now on the empirical questions?

Does EM affect recidivism after it has concluded?

If one looks at only reasonably clean studies that had comparison groups, i.e. the core of the Campbell Collaboration protocol standard, the answer has to be 'if at all, probably not much'. Evan Mayo-Wilson and I excluded low-risk offenders and juveniles and analysed part of the Campbell EM studies on the premise that if EM 'worked' it was likely to work best with higher-risk offenders (Renzema and Mayo-Wilson 2005). We considered 12 studies but included only the three cleanest (Bonta *et al.* 2000; Finn and Muirhead-Steves 2002; Sugg *et al.* 2001) in calculation of an odds ratio that turned out to be 0.96 ($p=0.82$), just slightly favouring the EM groups but nowhere near significance or practical importance. Not included in the article were other analyses that included all of the studies, clean and dirty, all risk levels, as well as juveniles; those results were about the same. Our reported findings were clearly not simply the result of obsessive rigour in study selection.

Over the decade from 1991 to 2001, using other criteria for study selection none of the systematic reviewers or meta-analysts found different results (Corbett and Marx 1991; Mainprize 1996; MacKenzie 1997; Schmidt 1998; Gendreau *et al.* 2000; Whitfield 2001). Despite the overall lack of impact, in some studies there were hints that EM combined with other elements might make a difference. Bonta *et al.* (2000: 324) found that compared to imprisoned offenders of the same risk levels, high-risk offenders receiving a combination of EM and cognitive behavioural treatment recidivated less; in contrast, lower-risk prisoners did better than those receiving the same combination of treatments. As noted above, Finn and Muirhead-Steves (2002) found better results for sex offender parolees. Their whole group found that 23.4 per cent of both violent male parolees and the historical comparison group returned to custody within three years. For sex offenders released in the control period, 29.6 per cent of the 44 studied returned; during the EM period only 5.7 per cent of 35 returned. In neither case can it be claimed on the basis of published results that EM made a critical difference, but the results are suggestive in themselves and also suggest that future evaluations of EM should be much more focused. If positive results are to be found, they will be found by studying carefully defined homogeneous populations receiving carefully defined treatments directed at reducing specific risk factors. In other words, we should be using rifles, not shotguns, as we try to target EM's effects.

Just in the past year, two studies have appeared that suggest long-term recidivism reduction. Di Tella and Schargrodsky's 2009 manuscript described the impact of EM in Argentina's province of Buenos Aires. They compared the eventual recidivism of 386 people who had experienced EM with 1,152 matched offenders released at the same time (±6 months) over a ten-year period. Most of the EM people were pre-trial, but so were the bulk of those imprisoned. Unlike most EM programmes, there were no restrictions on the crimes of which the EM candidates were accused. In both the EM and matched prison samples, for example, 7 per cent were accused of homicide. There were many unusual circumstances – at least to a North American reader – about Argentina's criminal justice system, from the assignment of cases to judges, to lengthy pre-trial detention, to the nature of the prison experience. In the end, 22 per cent of the former prisoners recidivated, while only 13 per cent of those who had experienced EM did. The at-risk period was very variable, but at least the EM participants were exposed for the same length of time as the prison releasees. For reference, first-year recidivism was 7.1 per cent for the EM group and 10.5 per cent for the prison group.

Another recent study is exempt from the 'shotgun approach' criticism. Marklund and Holmberg (2009) followed for three years after release the reconvictions of matched groups of Swedish EM early prison releasees and convicts released at the end of their regular terms. Although it was essentially a 'salvage evaluation' in that there were some non-EM offenders released during the EM operation period, they took great care in their analysis to show that selection was not impacting validity. Unlike most studies, they tried to ascertain not only that EM had 'worked', but upon whom it had impact. Table 13.2 summarizes their results. It is noteworthy that EM appeared to have its greatest impact on mid-range offenders, whether indicated by the agency's risk score or by number of prior convictions. Older offenders responded better than younger offenders.

Although the results are impressive, I suspect that the generalizability is somewhat limited given the umbrella of Sweden's employment, housing, social and medical services available to both the EM and control groups.

Table 13.2 Three-year re-conviction outcomes by three measures of risk in Marklund and Holmberg's study

Trichotimized risk	*Early releases on EM*[†] *(N = 260) (%)*	*Control (normal term) (N = 260) (%)*
Low	10	24*
Medium	27	42*
High	44	49
Prior convictions		
0	12	21
1–2	24	43**
≥2	60	66
Age		
≤37	36	44
>37	17	32**

Source: Renzema 2010.

Notes
† Rounded to the nearest per cent.
* $p < 0.05$; ** $p < 0.01$.

The flaws in the reviewed research suggest that much greater attention to both programme delineation and programme integrity must be paid than has been done up to now. Users of EM have known for at least 20 years that it is not a panacea, yet when research is done it still typically uses a shotgun approach (a great diversity of offenders and a mélange of ill-defined treatments) as opposed to the more appropriate sniper rifle (single population, defined treatment, careful programme delineation).

Does EM affect offender criminal behaviour during the monitored period?

For some years the Florida Department of Corrections has been publishing statistics in its annual reports and occasional special reports showing that offenders on EM are returned to prison less often than other offenders under Community Control. Given incomplete information on group comparability, it was impossible to be sure whether this was due to the impact of EM, EM plus other programmes or simply the assignment of lower-risk offenders to EM. A study by Padgett et al., published in February 2006, clearly disposed of the idea that lower-seriousness offenders were receiving EM; in fact, offenders receiving EM were significantly more serious. The study was much larger than most, with a total of 74,276 subjects. In a statistically sophisticated analysis based on the records of offenders under home confinement without EM, those with CS monitoring and those with GPS monitoring, Padgett et al. (2006: 79) concluded that 'offenders on [CS] monitoring are 95.7% less likely and offenders on GPS monitoring are 90.2% less likely than offenders on home confinement without EM to be revoked for technical violations'. For new offences, the reduction was 94.7 per cent for both types of monitoring. Although fairly long and complicated, the article is destined to become a classic and deserves study by anyone involved with monitoring. Among other points made are that CS is not necessarily superior to GPS, as the two technologies have been applied to somewhat different kinds of offenders. The article also makes the point that net-widening appears to have occurred for drug offenders but not property or violent offenders. The article is not perfect; it is essentially a 'black box' evaluation that does little to delineate process. It is not clear whether some of the failures in the non-EM group are people who were removed from EM, i.e. group cross-over may or may not have occurred.

In their 2010 report, Bales et al. took a second dip into the Florida data with sophisticated analytical techniques as part of a National Institute of Justice-funded study (*A Quantitative and Qualitative Assessment of Electronic Monitoring*) and formulated five primary conclusions for the quantitative section of their report.

1   EM reduces the likelihood of failure under community supervision. The reduction in the risk of failure is about 31 per cent, relative to offenders placed on other forms of community supervision.

2   GPS typically has more of an effect on reducing failure than RF (*same as CS*) technology. There is a 6 per cent improvement rate in the reduction of supervision failures for offenders placed on GPS supervision relative to offenders placed on RF supervision.

3   EM supervision has less of an impact on violent offenders than on sex, drug, property and other types of offenders, although there are significant reductions in the hazard rate for all of these offence types.

4   There are no major differences in the effects of EM supervision across different age groups.

5   There were no major differences in the effects of EM for different types of supervision (Bales *et al.* 2009: x)

That these conclusions are a little different from the earlier report probably reflects the evolution of Florida's monitoring programme, improvement in GPS technology and differences in the samples used. In the second report a majority of the offenders were on Community Control, which is generally seen as a prison diversion programme for offenders not manageable on probation. Other significant groups were felony probationers, conditional releasees from prison and sex offender probation: in short, a very risky and high crime-severity group when compared with how EM is used in most US jurisdictions.

A much more homogeneous group was studied by Lapham *et al.* (2007): recidivist drink drivers in the northwest of the United States (specifically, Oregon). They randomly assigned 477 treated recidivist drink drivers to four different treatment conditions. All groups received intensive supervision that included alcoholism treatment and polygraph testing (hereafter, ISP). The base group received nothing else. The EM group received a relatively short period of EM that included both CS curfew monitoring and in-home remote alcohol testing. A third group received forced sale of their car(s). A fourth group received both EM and forced vehicle sales. They tabulated hazard ratios for risk of arrest at three months, one year and three years after intake. The results are fairly clear at the three-month point but quickly dissipated: at the end of three years the group that had received only ISP was doing better (fewer arrests) than the others. But what is interesting here is the three-month result. For the fourth group (all possible treatments) the risk was lowest. For the EM group the risk was twice as high as the 'everything' group. For the 'forced sale group' the risk was four times higher. For the ISP-only group the risk was three times higher. In other words, at the three-month point EM was the most potent single addition to the basic ISP protocol.

For the moment this is the best evidence of a surveillance effect depressing both technical violations (rule breaking and absconding) and new offences for the duration of monitoring. Prior work on suppression effects has been largely ambiguous because of group equivalency issues. As survival analysis becomes more commonly used it should become clearer whether the Florida findings replicate or are anomalous.

Does EM have positive or negative impacts other than those on offender criminal behaviour?

In other words, does it help or hurt the employment, psychological health or social relationships of the offender or those around the offender? Some systematic work has been done on these issues and I will highlight a few of the findings of the better studies. The earliest I found that dealt with this issue was a monograph from North Texas State University (1987). Its sample of 18 received the Beck Depression Inventory (BDI) and the Family Environment Scale (FES) before being placed on EM. Although the BDI scores for those who became absconders indicated slight depression as opposed to normal values for those who did not, the differences were not significant. Most of the ten subscale scores on the FES were close to normal both before and after EM. One scale statistically distinguished programme completers from absconders: cohesion. The authors suggest screening before placement on family cohesion as

> potential ... clients whose family environment is perceived by them as providing a low degree of help and support are much more likely to abscond from the program prior to completing it than are those potential clients with normal or above scores.

Family cohesion during EM declined somewhat from above normal levels to normal levels.

The North Texas study authors expanded their work with data collected in 1988 and 1989 at three locations in Texas from both probationers and parolees (total $n=261$). Each status had an EM and a non-EM group; all information was obtained from volunteers. All groups were given pre-tests and post-tests on both the BDI and the FES. In brief, the parolees were less dysphoric than the probationers and the EM-parolees were the least dysphoric of all (Enos *et al.* 1999: 188–189). In all groups, family conflict and dysphoria were correlated; probationers registered higher levels of dysphoria and conflict than parolees. Comparing pre-test to post-test measures, family control declined in all groups, but significantly more in the EM groups than the non-EM groups. The authors explain:

> These results imply that EM may serve to relieve the family of some of its control responsibilities. This may explain the decline in dysphoria since the replacement of controls associated with the family by correctional authorities (i.e. EM) provides the offender with a highly structured lifestyle but keeps the responsibility for its imposition outside the family unit. Thus, the effects of EM may well be beneficial for the offender as well as for the family with which he/she lives.

Sandhu *et al.* (1990) administered an open-ended questionnaire to 156 southwest United States parolees on EM house arrest and compared the results with the responses of 63 residents of a Community Treatment Center (CTC). They found that those on EM reported fewer adjustment problems than those in the CTC and that they resolved problems more rapidly than those living at the CTC. Perceived sources of support were somewhat different. Noteworthy is that when asked about leisure time activities, 'one-fourth of house arrestees said they were simply doing time' (p. 153), which implies boredom and resentment. One is left asking whether it was that particular programme or the nature of EM in general that led to this perception. Reports of family problems were rare in both groups. Twice the percentage of those on EM reported 'good things' happening involving family as those at the CTC.

Mainprize (1995) conducted open-ended interviews with 60 people on EM in British Columbia during an EM pilot project, apparently in 1988. He interviewed volunteers who understood that if it had not been for EM they would have been jailed. Time spent on EM was short, with an average of 22.7 days, and most were interviewed while still on EM. Mainprize calls attention to a number of situational factors that could have distorted responses; most can be characterized as incentives to make the experience appear more positive to the offender than it might have been. It is impossible to concisely summarize a long and detailed article that comprehensively dealt with the impact of EM on the offender and the offender's relationships; however, I will note a few of the more positive and negative findings. To the question of whether EM 'had in any way affected, changed, improved or worsened relationships with the person with whom you live', of those residing with others 52 per cent saw no effect while 20.8 per cent saw improvement and 6.2 per cent saw worsening. EM was seen as interfering with family activities to some extent. Although 35 per cent saw no effects on social relationships, 50 per cent reported a general reduction. Feelings of social isolation were reported by 16.6 per cent. Physical activities were most affected (75 per cent) but 'social activities with friends and co-workers' were a close second at 73.3 per cent. Multiple coping styles were observed; some became sedentary, others used the new-found time productively. One-sixth of the offenders used social isolation as a way of concealing their EM status from others, a strategy that may have been viable given the short durations of EM. 'Minor effects' at work were experienced by 49 per cent of the employed offenders, while 9.8 per cent reported significant effects. The inflexible schedules mandated by EM seemed to be most disruptive, but limiting of socialization and feeling that the EM status needed to be concealed were also reported. Most offenders (80 per cent) attempted to conceal EM status to at least some people, with co-workers being the people from whom the offenders most wanted to hide their status. Probably the clearest endorsement of EM was the preference of most for accepting EM again if it were offered after another offence. No one said 'no' and only a few were unsure; most saw it as a bargain. In terms of how they felt about themselves, 60 per cent were coded as 'better', 35 per cent as 'no change' and only 5 per cent 'worse'.

Mainprize summarizes the effects on others in the workplace: 'The indirect evidence suggests that EMS [electronic monitoring] program status has largely minor (and mostly manageable) effects on the work settings of offenders' (Main-prize 1995: 171). In terms of spousal and family roles, 10 per cent reported being negatively affected, 'mainly from reports of not being able to participate with the spouse in social activities beyond the home' or being able to supervise children to the extent needed. In total, despite being on a very early group of monitorees who were monitored for a very short period and who agreed to interviews, Mainprize's work is significant because it found significantly different individual reactions to the EM experience but nothing that suggested general harm from the experience to either offender or the offender's relationships. Many of the negative impacts could have been reduced by better programme management.

As part of an evaluation of the New South Wales Home Detention Scheme, Heggie (1999) mailed an exit survey to 140 people leaving EM; only 65 were returned. The most disruptive aspect of EM was reported to be the monitoring calls, which ranged from 5 to 18 calls per day, obviously not a feature of all monitoring protocols. Only 8.1 per cent of the respondents reported 'no disruption' to their normal routine/lifestyles, while 22.6 per cent found the calls 'very disruptive' (Heggie 1999: 89). On a question about positive aspects of the experience, 90 per cent of those responding checked 'interaction with family' (Heggie 1999: 91).

Gainey and Paine (2000) administered a 24-item survey to 49 offenders on EM in Virginia. Some were given in face-to-face interviews, others by phone, on-site written administration or mail. Response choices were: '1 = no problem'; '2 = a little problem'; '3 = a moderate problem'; and '4 = a very big problem' (Gainey and Paine 2000: 87). Questions were drawn from the literature, qualitative interviews with other offenders and 'insights from administrative staff' (p. 87). Responses were grouped into the dimensions of privacy issues, shaming issues, disruptiveness, social restrictions and (restrictions on) drug use (p. 89). The most onerous aspect (M=2.51/4) was 'social restrictions', i.e. not being able to exercise, run errands, meet friends and eat out. Also high were 'shaming issues' at M=2.12/4, i.e. 'having to tell friends you can't go out', having to explain to friends or family, 'having to wear a visible monitor'. Close behind were work problems (M=2.02/4) centring on not being able to do overtime and having to receive law enforcement phone calls at work. Although the authors were looking for the negative and/or punitive aspects of EM, they also asked open-ended questions and found that the perception of the majority was that EM 'was positive, at least in comparison to jail' (Gainey and Paine 2000: 88). Associations were tested between demographic characteristics and dimension scores; the only significant association was that women and married men tended to view shame as more of a problem than others.

Maidment (2002) interviewed all of the 16 available women who completed a Newfoundland EM programme and compared their responses to those from a random sample of 16 men who had been on EM. This qualitative study made clear that the women, mostly single mothers with young children, were having a much more difficult time coping with the demands of EM than the males were. Everything from having other people available to run errands and do shopping seemed less complex for the men, most of whom lived with other people, than for the more isolated women. Even when there was a male in the house, women on EM found themselves disproportionately burdened with housework and child-care by virtue of the EM status. Maidment remarks:

> A rather surprising response from a number of women on EM was that, in hindsight of program completion, they felt that, compared to prison, 'serving their time at home' was more difficult as they experienced increased stress while being responsible for more tasks with little support. Clearly, these women felt that had it not been for the presence of their children in the home, they might have preferred to serve their sentences in prison as opposed to home confinement. This was due, in large part, to the dependencies EM created for women on their families, spouse, social service agencies, friends, and correctional personnel.
>
> (Maidment 2000: 60)

A small New Zealand study by King and Gibbs (2003) echoes Maidment's conclusion. Although the study interviewed 14 male and seven female offenders on EM, it also interviewed 21 sponsors of people on EM (often female partners of men on EM), probation officers, security managers and prison board members. Whether as detainees themselves or as sponsors of males on EM, women appeared to be more burdened by EM than men. The female monitorees were more subject to the shame of the anklet. They tended to ask for more support from the correctional agency. Those that undertook the sponsor role often did it for the sake of their children. Many experienced tension in their relationships, which they attributed to being on EM or having an EM offender in the house; they reported more arguments than males on EM.

Two recent studies from the UK (Hucklesby 2008, 2009) are largely congruent with those cited above.

The 2010 Bales *et al.* study breaks some new ground, particularly on the issues of stigmatization and employment problems with GPS tracking. Given the widespread publicity in the United States about paedophile abduction/murders and harsh new laws that authorize lifetime GPS tracking in some states, the meaning of 'being on GPS monitoring' seems to be changing in the public perception. If formerly it meant that someone had gotten into a bit of trouble, it now seems common – as one interprets the Florida interviewees comments – for people to assume that the offender is dangerous and quite possibly a sex offender. The Bales *et al.* study interviewed 105 offenders and found substantial problems related to relationships and finding and keeping employment. Roughly half of the offenders experienced at least some negative impact in each of three areas of relationships: spouses/significant others, their children and friends (Bales *et al.* 2010: 92). Sixty-one per cent of the interviewees 'stated that EM did affect their ability to obtain employment' (p. 94). Twenty-two per cent reported being fired or being asked to leave a job because of EM (p. 95). Part of the problem seems to have been that the devices in use were two-piece units that could not be easily concealed, but operational requirements (e.g. having to go outside to expose the GPS unit to the sky when tracking was lost) also interfered with both employment and social relationships. I expect that technical improvement, increasing miniaturization of GPS equipment and integrating GPS with ground-based location technologies will eventually reduce the social and employment problems, but for the moment they are quite significant. Offenders wearing future generations of GPS equipment may react differently to the experience, necessitating continuing research.

What can be concluded about the impact of EM on offenders and those around them? For most offenders, but particularly for those for whom it is a clear alternative to prison, it is seen as either beneficial or innocuous. There are problems for both offenders and those in their households; for the most part they are minor. Many of the small problems could be reduced by using more appropriate technologies and by more flexible programme management. My view is that society does not owe offenders stress-free lives, but that any stresses society imposes need to be manageable. For some, particularly single mothers and those who are depressed at the outset, there is reason to be wary of using EM without assessing the whole situation of the offender and his or her family.

Conclusions

I have not dealt with the financial impact of EM on correctional systems or with net-widening, which are, of course, interrelated. There is some research on these subjects, but much more needs to be done. I have also not dealt with the consequences of extremely long-duration EM for sex offenders, now authorized in several jurisdictions: no one knows how offenders will react to monitoring that extends into decades. Despite the good intentions of many of those who founded and who were early adopters, EM is now mainly about punishment on the cheap, not rehabilitation. Yet, in the attempt to deter and punish humanely and inexpensively, most users of EM are not even trying to use it as a tool for rehabilitation. Better planning and record keeping would add little to the expense of using EM, but might have great benefits in terms of producing better payoffs. In particular, users need to target:

- offender characteristics beyond simply including and excluding certain classes of crimes – both psychological characteristics and characteristics of the offender's environment are relevant;
- transparency of the selection process for EM in order that usable comparison groups may be found or created;
- support and treatment services that would be needed for those on EM so that the demands of EM can be managed;
- programme monitoring – for example, rather than 'drug counselling' evaluators need to know how much and by whom;
- careful recording of violations and new offences both during and after EM, preferably for at least three years;

- equivalent record keeping for offenders receiving whatever disposition is the alternate (or predecessor) to EM.[11]

We should know more about the impacts of EM than we know now and, if we are responsible and humane, we will focus on doing quality research on the issues outlined above.

Notes

1 Ralph Kirkland Schwitzgebel and his brother Robert are widely credited as being the first people to experiment with EM devices on offenders. They both continue to write seminal articles under the changed family name of Gable.

2 Rustification appears to be a 'made-up' word derived from the word rustic and seems to mean moving the offender from a fast-paced, frenetic existence to a slower, simpler, more countryside-like life. Such anecdotes were common at practitioner professional meetings in the late 1980s.

3 In terms of deterrence, whether EM is seen by the offender as a gift (the alternative being jail) or as an enhanced sanction (the alternative being community status without EM) could be relevant.

4 For example, in a seminar at the US National Justice in Washington, DC on 21 April 2010, entitled 'Less prison, more police, less crime: how criminology can save the States from bankruptcy', Professor Lawrence Sherman argued that, in general, the crime-reduction impacts of certain police innovations have been well-proven, while most correctional interventions have not been; society would be safer and crime control would cost less if money currently being spent on prisons and other correctional programmes were instead spent on police.

5 Although few EM programme administrators are willing to formally declare precipitating incarceration as a programme goal, it is clear from my informal conversations with both line staff and programme administrators that EM is sometimes used to expedite collection of evidence of rule violations on the theory that once an offender gets on the 'slippery slope', then rule violations and criminal behaviour will become more frequent and severe.

6 A 10-year-old was reported in a personal communication from Dennis Doffing; a table in a California evaluation report showed one sex offender on GPS parole was 81.

7 I am referring to Lawrence Singleton, who cut off the forearms of his victim and left her to die, although she did survive. He succeeded on parole but a decade later killed a woman in another state.

8 The Campbell protocol excluded ignition interlocks from the protocol on EM. Certainly this is EM, but it does not involve daily or more frequent reporting to a supervising agency. I also discovered early that there was a reasonable amount of quality research being done on interlocks and that good systematic reviews had been done; it seemed unnecessary to include interlocks in the Campbell project.

9 According to Peggy Conway, editor of the *Journal of Offender Monitoring*, the distinctions among active (real-time), passive (delayed upload) and hybrid GPS devices are becoming blurred. The current trend is for devices to contain substantial on-board processing power and to be able to upload data at almost any interval desired, as well as by exceptions to programmed inclusion and inclusion zones (personal communication, 30 May 2010). Future evaluation research will need to consider not only which device was used, but also to consider the details of the reporting protocols.

10 Jessica Lunsford was a 9-year-old Florida girl who was murdered in February 2005 by a convicted sex offender who was on probation for a non-sexual offence.

11 Readers may examine the Campbell EM code sheets available at http://renzema.net for more guidance and operationalization of some of the key pieces of information that are needed to assure comparability among research studies.

References

Austin, J. and Hardyman, P. (1991) 'The use of early parole with electronic monitoring to control prison crowding: evaluation of the Oklahoma Department of Corrections pre-parole supervised release with electronic monitoring', National Institute of Justice, unpublished report.

Bales, W., Mann, K., Blomberg, T., Gaes, G., Barrick, K., Dhungana, K. and McManus, B. (2010) *A Quantitative and Qualitative Assessment of Electronic Monitoring* (Tallahassee, FL: Florida State University, College of Criminology and Criminal Justice).

Baumer, T.L., Mendelsohn, R.I. and Rhine, C. (1990) *Executive Summary: The Electronic Monitoring of Non-Violent Convicted Felons – An Experiment in Home Detention* (Indianapolis, IN: School of Public and Environmental Affairs).

Bonta, J., Wallace-Capretta, S. and Rooney, J. (2000) 'A quasi-experimental evaluation of an intensive rehabilitation supervision program', *Criminal Justice and Behavior*, 27:3, pp. 312–329.

Corbett, R. and Marx, G.T. (1991) 'Critique: no soul in the new machine – technofallacies in the electronic monitoring movement', *Justice Quarterly*, 8:3, pp. 399–414.

Curtis, C. and Pennell, S. (1987) *Research on Electronic Surveillance of Work Furlough Inmates: Methodological Considerations* (San Diego, CA: San Diego Association of Governments, Criminal Justice Research Unit).

Di Tella, R. and Schargrodsky, E. (2009) 'Criminal recidivism after prison and electronic monitoring', unpublished.

Enos, R., Homan, J.E. and Carroll, M. (1999) *Alternative Sentencing: Electronically Monitored Correctional Supervision*, 2nd edn (Bristol, IN: Wyndham Hall).

Erwin, B.S. (1987) *Evaluation of Intensive Probation Supervision in Georgia: Final Report* (Atlanta, GA: Department of Corrections).

Finn, M.A. and Muirhead-Steves, S. (2002) 'The effectiveness of electronic monitoring with violent male parolees', *Justice Quarterly*, 19:2, pp. 293–312.

Gainey, R.R. and Payne, B.K. (2000) 'Understanding the experience of house arrest with electronic monitoring: an analysis of quantitative and qualitative data', *International Journal of Offender Therapy and Comparative Criminology*, 44:1, pp. 84–96.

Gainey, R.R., Payne, B.K. and O'Toole, M. (2000) 'The relationships between time in jail, time on electronic monitoring, and recidivism: an event history analysis of a jail based program', *Justice Quarterly*, 17:4, pp. 733–752.

Gendreau, P.L., Goggin, C., Cullen, F. and Andrews, D. (2000) 'The effects of community sanctions and incarceration on recidivism', *Forum on Corrections Research*, 12:2, pp. 10–13.

Heggie, K. (1999) *Review of the NSW Home Detention Scheme: Sydney NSW, Research and Statistics Unit* (NSW: Department of Corrective Services).

Hucklesby, A. (2008) 'Vehicles of desistance? The impact of electronically monitored curfew orders', *Criminology & Criminal Justice*, 8:1, pp. 51–71.

Hucklesby, A. (2009) 'Understanding offenders' compliance: a case study of electronically monitored curfew orders', *Journal of Law and Society*, 36:2, pp. 248–271.

Jones, M. and Ross, D.L. (1997) 'Electronic house arrest and boot camp in North Carolina: comparing recidivism', *Criminal Justice Policy Review*, 8:4, pp. 383–404.

King, D. and Gibbs, A. (2003) 'Is home detention in New Zealand disadvantaging women and children?', *Probation Journal*, 50:2, pp. 115–126.

Lapham, S.C., de Baca, J.C., Lapidus, J., McMillan, G.P. (2007) 'Randomized sanctions to reduce re-offense among repeat impaired-driving offenders', *Addiction*, 102, pp. 1618–1625.

MacKenzie, D.L. (1997) 'Criminal justice and crime prevention', in L.W. Sherman, D. Gottfredson, D. MacKenzie, J. Eck, P. Reuter and S. Bushway (eds) *Preventing Crime: What Works, What Doesn't, What's Promising: A Report To The United States Congress* (Washington, DC: US Department of Justice, National Institute of Justice), pp. 9-1–9-83.

Maidment, M.R. (2002) 'Toward a "woman-centered" approach to community-based corrections: a gendered analysis of electronic monitoring (EM) in Eastern Canada', *Women & Criminal Justice*, 13:4, pp. 47–68.

Mainprize, S. (1995) 'Social, psychological, and familial impacts of home confinement and electronic monitoring: exploratory research findings from B.C.'s pilot project', in K. Schulz (ed.) *Electronic Monitoring and Corrections: The Policy, the Operation, the Research* (Burnaby, BC: Simon Fraser University), pp. 141–187.

Mainprize, S. (1996) 'Elective affinities in the engineering of social control: the evolution of electronic monitoring', *Electronic Journal of Sociology*. Online. Available at: www. sociology.org/content/vol. 002.002/mainprize.html?PHPSESSID=8e29eb0920aff4a54e 82d134272830f3.

Marklund, F. and Holmberg, S. (2009) 'Effects of early release from prison using electronic tagging in Sweden', *Journal of Experimental Criminology*, 5:1, pp. 41–61.

Masters, B.A. (2004) 'Martha Stewart sentenced to prison: punishment postponed as she appeals', *Washington Post*.

North Texas State University Institute of Criminal Justice (1987) *Evaluation and Research Report on the National Center on Institutions and Alternatives Community Incapacitation (Electronic House Arrest) Program* (North Texas: North Texas State University).

Padgett, K.G., Bales, W.D. and Blomberg, T. (2006) 'Under surveillance: an empirical test of the effectiveness and consequences of electronic monitoring', *Criminology and Public Policy*, 5:1, pp. 201–232.

Petersilia, J. and Turner, S. (1990) *Intensive Supervision for High-risk Probationers: Findings from Three California Experiments* (Santa Monica, CA: Rand Corporation).

Renzema, M. (2010) 'Rationalizing the use of electronic monitoring', *Journal of Offender Monitoring*, 22:1, pp. 5–11.

Renzema, M. and Mayo-Wilson, E. (2005) 'Can electronic monitoring reduce crime for moderate to high-risk offenders?', *Journal of Experimental Criminology*, 1:2, pp. 215–237.

Roeber, D. (2005) 'Testimony before the Joint Committee on the Judiciary Massachusetts General Court, regarding impaired driving legislation', 13 September 2005.

Sandhu, H.S., Dodder, R.A. and Davis, S.P. (1990) 'Community adjustment of offenders supervised under residential vs. non-residential programs', *Journal of Offender Rehabilitation*, 16:1–2, pp. 139–162.

Schmidt, A.K. (1998) 'Electronic monitoring: what does the literature tell us?', *Federal Probation*, 62:2, pp. 10–15.

Schwitzgebel, R.K. (1968) 'Electronic alternatives to imprisonment', *Lex & Scienta*, 5:3, pp. 99–104.

Scopatz, R.A., Hatch, C.E., Hilger DeLucia, B. and Tays, K.A. (2003) 'Unlicensed to kill: the sequel', AAA Foundation for Traffic Safety.

Sugg, D., Moore, L., and Howard, P. (2001) *Electronic Monitoring and Offending Behavior-Reconviction: Results for the Second Year of Trials of Curfew Orders* (London: Home Office Research, Development and Statistics Directorate).

Villettaz, P. and Killias, M. (2005) *Les arrêts domiciliaires sous surveillance électronique: une sanction 'expérimentale'* (Lausanne: Université de Lausanne Institut de Criminologie et de Droit Pénal).

Whitfield, D. (2001) *The Magic Bracelet* (Winchester: Waterside Press).

Index

Page numbers in *italics* denote tables, those in **bold** denote figures.

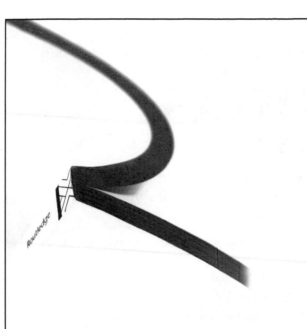